10453388

D0491558

ACCA

P
R
A
C
T
I
C
E

&

R
E
V
I
S
I
O
N

K
I
T

TAXATION

(TX – UK)

FA 2017

WITHDRAWN

BPP Learning Media is an **ACCA Approved Content Provider** for the ACCA qualification. This means we work closely with ACCA to ensure our products fully prepare you for your ACCA exams.

In this Practice and Revision Kit, which has been reviewed by the **ACCA examining team,** we:

- Discuss the **best strategies** for revising and taking your ACCA exams

- Ensure you are well **prepared** for your exam

- Provide you with **lots of great guidance** on tackling questions

- Provide you with **three** mock exams

Our **Passcards** also support the Taxation (TX – UK) syllabus.

FOR EXAMS IN JUNE 2018, SEPTEMBER 2018, DECEMBER 2018 AND MARCH 2019

BPP
LEARNING MEDIA

First edition 2008
Twelfth edition October 2017

ISBN 9781 5097 1538 1
(previous ISBN 9781 5097 0838 3)

e-ISBN 9781 5097 1542 8

British Library Cataloguing-in-Publication Data
A catalogue record for this book
is available from the British Library

Published by

BPP Learning Media Ltd
BPP House, Aldine Place
London W12 8AA

www.bpp.com/learningmedia

Printed in the United Kingdom

Your learning materials, published by BPP Learning
Media Ltd, are printed on paper obtained from traceable
sustainable sources.

We are grateful to the Association of Chartered Certified
Accountants for permission to reproduce past examination
questions. The suggested solutions in the Practice &
Revision Kit have been prepared by BPP Learning Media
Ltd, except where otherwise stated.

BPP
LEARNING MEDIA

About this Practice & Revision Kit

ACCA have commenced the transition of this paper to computer-based examination (CBE), beginning with a pilot in limited markets in September 2016. Students will initially have the choice of CBE or paper exams and as a result, changes will be made to BPP's learning materials to ensure that we fully support students through this transition.

This Practice & Revision Kit is valid for exams from the June 2018 sitting through to the March 2019 sitting and in this Practice & Revision Kit you will find questions in both multiple choice question (MCQ) and objective testing question (OTQ) format. OTQs include a wider variety of questions types including MCQ as well as number entry, multiple response and drag and drop. More information on these question types will be available on the ACCA website.

OTQs will only appear in computer-based exams but these questions will still provide valuable practice for all students whichever version of the exam is taken. These are clearly marked on the contents page as either CBE style OTQ bank or CBE style OTQ case.

More information on the exam formats can be found on page xvii.

All timings given throughout this Practice & Revision Kit are based on the computer-based exam which is 3 hours and 20 minutes long. Within session CBEs there will be additional questions used for quality assurance purposes, to ensure that all students now and in the future receive fair and equal exams. These extra questions are referred to by the technical term 'seeded questions' and do not contribute to a student's result. Seeded questions will either be five randomly distributed Section A questions or five questions relating to one Section B scenario and will not be indicated as such, so you will not be able to determine whether or not a question is seeded content. As a result of the inclusion of seeded questions, session CBEs will contain 110 marks of exam content, 100 marks contributing to the student result. Exam timings are allocated on the basis of 110 marks across the 3 hours and 20 minutes. Time management is a key skill for success in this exam and so we recommend you use these indicative timings when attempting questions to time on paper.

ACCA are recommending that all students consult the ACCA website on a regular basis for updates on the launch of the new CBEs.

Contents

BPP
LEARNING MEDIA

Question index

The headings in this checklist/index indicate the main topics of questions, but questions may cover several different topics.

Questions set under the old F6 Taxation (UK) exam format are included in this Kit because their style and content are similar to those that may appear in the Taxation (TX – UK) exams from 1 September 2016. Some of these questions have been amended to reflect new exam format and this is shown by (amended) in the title of the question.

	Marks	Time allocation Mins	Page number Question	Answer
Part A: The UK tax system and its administration				
Section A Questions				
1 – 10 MCQ bank – The UK tax system and its administration 1	20	36	3	123
11 – 20 CBE style OTQ bank – The UK tax system and its administration 2	20	36	5	124
Section B Questions				
21 – 25 Domingo and Fargo (06/09) (amended)	10	18	8	125
26 – 30 CBE style OT case – Joe (A) (12/10) (amended)	10	18	9	126
31 – 35 CBE style OT case – Ernest (06/10) (amended)	10	18	10	126
36 – 40 CBE style OT case – Thai Curry Ltd	10	18	12	127
Section C Questions				
41 John	10	18	13	128
42 Sugar plc	10	18	14	129
Part B: Income tax and NIC liabilities				
Section A Questions				
43 – 52 MCQ bank – Income tax and NIC liabilities 1	20	36	15	131
53 – 62 CBE style OTQ bank – Income tax and NIC liabilities 2	20	36	17	133
63 – 72 CBE style OTQ bank – Income tax and NIC liabilities 3	20	36	20	135
Section B Questions				
73 – 77 CBE style OT case – Ann, Basil and Chloe (12/08) (amended)	10	18	22	137
78 – 82 Ae, Bee, Cae, and Eu (12/08) (amended)	10	18	24	138
83 – 87 CBE style OT case – Rosie and Sam (12/12) (amended)	10	18	25	139
88 – 92 CBE style OT case – Fang and Hong (12/13) (amended)	10	18	26	140
93 – 97 CBE style OT case – Chi (06/14) (amended)	10	18	28	141

BPP LEARNING MEDIA

BPP
LEARNING MEDIA

Topic index

Listed below are the key Taxation (TX – UK) syllabus topics and the numbers of the questions of this Kit (excluding the Mock exams) covering those topics.

If you need to concentrate your practice and revision on certain topics or if you want to attempt all available questions that refer to a particular subject, you will find this index useful.

Syllabus topic	Question numbers
UK tax system	1, 2, 3, 8, 16, 31, 32, 39, 40, 41, 296
Computing taxable income and the income tax liability	43, 44, 46, 48, 49, 53, 56, 75, 86, 67, 93, 102, 104, 108, 109, 110, 111, 114, 116, 117, 118, 299
Employment income	26, 27, 28, 29, 30, 47, 50, 51, 52, 54, 102, 103, 104, 105, 106, 110, 111, 113, 115, 116, 117, 118, 299
Pensions	55, 73, 74, 76, 77, 83, 84, 85, 113, 114, 117, 118
Property income for individuals	45, 57, 110, 113, 114, 117, 118
Computing trading income for individuals	58, 59, 60, 90, 95, 96, 97, 107, 108, 109, 112, 117
Capital allowances for individuals	61, 62, 63, 82, 90, 110, 112, 114, 117
Assessable trading income for individuals	64, 65, 66, 78, 79, 80, 88, 89, 101, 102, 108, 109, 111, 114, 117
Trading losses for individuals	67, 68, 81, 91, 92, 99, 100, 103
Partnerships	69, 70, 98, 103, 110
National insurance contributions	71, 72, 94, 98, 102, 104, 106, 107, 112, 299
Computing chargeable gains for individuals	87, 100, 107, 117, 119, 120, 121, 122, 129, 130, 131, 136, 138, 143, 145, 148, 149, 153, 155, 156, 157, 197
Chargeable gains for individuals: chattels and PPR exemption	123, 124, 125, 137, 152, 154
Chargeable gains for individuals: business reliefs	126, 127, 132, 133, 139, 140, 142, 146, 147, 150, 151, 155, 156, 299
Chargeable gains for individuals: shares and securities	128, 134, 135, 144, 157
Self assessment and payment of tax by individuals	4, 5, 10, 11, 12, 17, 18, 19, 20, 21, 22, 23, 24, 25, 33, 34, 35, 41, 141, 299
Inheritance tax	157, 158, 159, 160, 161, 162, 163, 164, 165, 166, 167, 168, 169, 170, 171, 172, 173, 174, 175, 176, 177, 178, 179, 180, 181, 182, 183, 184, 185, 186, 187, 188, 189, 190, 191, 192, 193, 194, 195, 196, 197
Computing taxable total profits (including property income and capital allowances for companies) and the corporation tax liability	106, 198, 199, 200, 201, 223, 228, 229, 230, 231, 232, 233, 235, 236, 237, 238
Chargeable gains for companies	202, 208, 209, 210, 211, 212, 213, 214, 215, 216, 222, 224, 226, 233, 234, 238
Losses for companies	203, 209, 217, 225, 228, 229, 231, 235, 237
Groups of companies	205, 206, 207, 218, 219, 220, 221, 227, 232, 234

BPP
LEARNING MEDIA

Helping you with your revision

BPP Learning Media – Approved Content Provider

As an ACCA **Approved Content Provider**, BPP Learning Media gives you the **opportunity** to use revision materials reviewed by the ACCA examining team. By incorporating the ACCA examining team's comments and suggestions regarding the depth and breadth of syllabus coverage, the BPP Learning Media Practice & Revision Kit provides excellent **ACCA approved** support for your revision.

Tackling revision and the exam

Using feedback obtained from the ACCA examining team review:

- We look at the dos and don'ts of revising for, and taking, ACCA exams

- We focus on Taxation (TX – UK); we discuss revising the syllabus, what to do (and what not to do) in the exam, how to approach different types of question and ways of obtaining easy marks

Selecting questions

We provide signposts to help you plan your revision.

- A full **question index**

- A **topic index** listing all the questions that cover key topics, so that you can locate the questions that provide practice on these topics, and see the different ways in which they might be examined

Making the most of question practice

At BPP Learning Media we realise that you need more than just questions and model answers to get the most from your question practice.

- Our **Top tips** included for certain questions provide essential advice on tackling questions, presenting answers and the key points that answers need to include.

- We show you how you can pick up **easy marks** on some questions, as we know that picking up all readily available marks often can make the difference between passing and failing.

- We include **marking guides** to show you what the examining team rewards.

- We include **comments from the examining team** to show you where students struggled or performed well in the actual exam.

- We refer to the **FA 2017 Study Text** (for exams in June 2018, September 2018, December 2018 and March 2019) for detailed coverage of the topics covered in questions.

Attempting mock exams

There are three mock exams that provide practice at coping with the pressures of the exam day. We strongly recommend that you attempt them under exam conditions.

Mock exam 1 is the September 2016 exam in a computer-based exam style, **Mock exam 2** is the Specimen exam paper in a computer-based exam style, **Mock exam 3** is the December 2016 exam in a paper-based exam style.

Revising Taxation (TX – UK)

All questions are compulsory so you must revise the **whole** syllabus. Since the exam includes 15 objective test questions in Section A and 15 objective test questions in Section B, you should expect questions to cover a large part of the syllabus. Selective revision **will limit** the number of questions you can answer and hence reduce your chances of passing. It is better to go into the exam knowing a reasonable amount about most of the syllabus rather than concentrating on a few topics to the exclusion of the rest.

Question practice

Practising as many exam-style questions as possible will be the key to passing this exam. You must do questions under **timed conditions** and ensure you write full answers to the discussion parts as well as doing the calculations.

Also ensure that you attempt all three mock exams under exam conditions.

Passing the Taxation (TX – UK) exam

Displaying the right qualities

- You will be required to identify the requirements of objective test questions quickly, so that you can make your answers confidently within the available time.

- In constructed response questions you will be required to carry out calculations, with clear workings and a logical structure. If your numbers are not perfect you will not necessarily lose too many marks so long as your method is correct and you have stated any assumptions you have made.

- You will also be expected to apply your tax knowledge to the facts of each particular question and also to identify the compliance issues for your client.

- You may also be required to describe rules and conditions, so take care to practise the descriptive elements of the answers.

Avoiding weaknesses

- There is no choice in this exam, all questions have to be answered. You must therefore study the entire syllabus, there are no short-cuts.

- Ability to answer objective test questions and cases improves with practice. Try to get as much practice with these questions as you can.

- The constructed response questions will be based on simple scenarios and answers must be focused and specific to the requirement of the question.

- Answer all parts of the constructed response questions. Even if you cannot do all the calculation elements, you will still be able to gain marks in the descriptive parts.

Gaining the easy marks

Easy marks in this exam tend to fall into three categories.

Objective test questions (OTQs)

Some OTQs are easier than others. Answer those that you feel fairly confident about as quickly as you can. Come back later to those you find more difficult. This could be a way of making use of the time in the examination most efficiently and effectively. Some OTQs will not involve calculations. Make sure that you understand the wording of 'written' OTQs before selecting your answer.

Calculations in Section C questions

There will always be basic marks available for straightforward tasks such as putting easy figures into proformas, for example putting the cost figure for an addition into a capital allowances proforma. Do not miss out on these easy marks by not learning your proformas properly.

Discussions in Section C questions

A constructed response question may separate descriptive requirements from calculations, so that you do not need to do the calculations first in order to answer the descriptive parts. This means that you should be able to gain marks from the descriptive parts without having to complete the calculations.

Descriptive requirements may focus on administrative, or compliance, details such as filing deadlines and tax payment dates. Make your points concisely, bearing in mind that one mark usually equates to one point to be made.

Read the question carefully and more than once, to ensure you are actually answering the specific requirements. Don't write about matters which are not specifically required – even if these are technically correct, you will not gain any marks and will waste valuable time.

Tackling Objective Test Case Questions

First, read the whole case scenario. Make a note of any specific instructions or assumptions, such as 'Ignore the annual exempt amount' in a capital gains tax question. Then skim through the requirements of the five questions. The questions are independent of each other and can be answered in any order.

Some of the OTQs will be easier than others. For example, you may be asked to identify the filing date for a tax return and the penalty for late filing. Answer these OTQs quickly.

Other OTQs will be more difficult and/or complex. There are two types of OTQ that may take you longer to answer.

The first more time-consuming OTQ will involve doing a computation. For example, you may be asked to calculate the personal allowance available to a taxpayer whose adjusted net income exceeds £100,000. You will probably need to jot down a quick pro-forma to answer a computational question like this.

If the OTQ is a multiple choice question, remember that the wrong answers will usually involve common errors, so don't assume that because you have the same answer as one of the options that your answer is necessarily correct! Double check to make sure you haven't made any silly mistakes, such as deducting the whole of excess of adjusted net income over the £100,000 threshold (instead of half of it) when working out the restriction for the personal allowance. If you haven't got the same answer as any of the options, rework your computation, thinking carefully about what errors you could have made. If you still haven't got one of the options, choose the one which is nearest to your answer.

The second more time-consuming OTQ is one where you are asked to consider a number of statements and identify which one (or more) of them is correct. Make sure that you read each statement at least twice before making your selection. Be careful to follow the requirements of the OTQ exactly, for example if you are asked to identify **TWO** correct statements.

Exam information

Computer-based exams

ACCA have commenced the launch of computer-based exams (CBEs) for this paper. They have been piloting CBEs in limited markets since September 2016 with the aim of rolling out into all markets internationally over a five-year period. Paper-based examinations will be run in parallel while the CBEs are phased in and BPP materials have been designed to support you, whichever exam option you choose.

Format of the exam

The exam format is the same irrespective of the mode of delivery and will comprise 3 exam sections.

Section	Style of question type	Description	Proportion of exam, %
A	Objective test (OT)	15 questions × 2 marks	30
B	Objective test (OT) case	3 questions × 10 marks Each question will contain 5 subparts each worth 2 marks	30
C	Constructed Response (Long questions)	1 question × 10 marks 2 questions × 15 marks	40
Total			100

Section A and B questions will be selected from the entire syllabus. The paper version of these objective test questions contains multiple choice only and the computer-based version will contain a variety. The responses to each question or subpart in the case of OT cases are marked automatically as either correct or incorrect by computer.

The 10-mark Section C question can come from any part of the syllabus. The 15-mark Section C questions will mainly focus on the following syllabus areas but a minority of marks can be drawn from any other area of the syllabus:

*   Income tax (syllabus area B)
*   Corporation tax (syllabus area E)

The responses to these questions are human marked.

Additional information

The study guide provides more detailed guidance on the syllabus and can be found by visiting the exam resource finder on the ACCA website: www.accaglobal.com/uk/en/student/exam-support-resources.html

Useful websites

The websites below provide additional sources of information of relevance to your studies for *Taxation (TX – UK)*.

- www.accaglobal.com

  ACCA's website. The students' section of the website is invaluable for detailed information about the qualification, past issues of *Student Accountant* (including technical articles) and a free downloadable Student Planner App.

- www.bpp.com

  Our website provides information about BPP products and services, with a link to the ACCA website.

Note on exam name (F6 UK)

This text is valid for exams from June 2018 to March 2019. From the September 2018 session, a new naming convention is being introduced for all of the exams in the ACCA Qualification, so from that session, the name of the exam will be Taxation (TX – UK). June 2018 is the first session of a new exam year for tax, and the exam name continues to be F6 Taxation (UK). Since this name change takes place during the validity of this text, both the old and new names have been used.

Questions

Questions 1 to 42 cover the UK tax system and its administration, the subject of Chapters 1, 17 and 23 of the BPP Study Text for Taxation (TX – UK).

MCQ bank – The UK tax system and its administration 1

36 mins

1   Which **TWO** of the following statements are true about inheritance tax?

   (1)   It is an indirect tax.
   (2)   It is a progressive tax.
   (3)   It is an environmental tax.
   (4)   It is a redistributive tax.

   ○   1 and 3
   ○   1 and 4
   ○   2 and 3
   ○   2 and 4   **(2 marks)**

2   Which **TWO** of the following have legal force?

   (1)   Revenue and Customs Brief
   (2)   A Statutory Instrument
   (3)   An Act of Parliament
   (4)   An Extra Statutory Concession

   ○   1 and 2
   ○   2 and 3
   ○   1 and 3
   ○   2 and 4   **(2 marks)**

3   Fare plc wishes to appeal against the assessment of £10,000,000 of corporation tax by HM Revenue & Customs (HMRC).

   By whom is Fare plc's appeal most likely to be heard?

   ○   By the First Tier Tribunal
   ○   By the Upper Tribunal
   ○   By the Supreme Court
   ○   By the Court of Appeal   **(2 marks)**

4   Daren made a chargeable gain of £50,000 on 30 June 2017. This was Daren's only disposal in the tax year 2017/18. He had previously paid his income tax through deduction at source so has not had to submit a self-assessment tax return.

   By what date must Daren notify HM Revenue & Customs (HMRC) of his chargeability to capital gains tax in relation to the gain made on 30 June 2017 and by what date must he pay the capital gains tax liability?

	Notification	*Payment*
○	31 January 2019	31 January 2019
○	5 October 2018	31 January 2019
○	5 October 2018	31 July 2019
○	31 January 2019	31 July 2019

                                                             (2 marks)

5   Sarah received NS&I investment account interest of £5,300 in the tax year 2017/18 which she deliberately omitted from her self-assessment tax return for that tax year. She did not attempt to conceal the omission. HM Revenue & Customs (HMRC) discovered the error from records collected from NS&I and Sarah then made a prompted disclosure of the error. Sarah is a higher rate taxpayer and she had already used her savings income nil rate band on other income.

What is the minimum penalty that HMRC may impose on Sarah in respect of this error?

○   £742
○   £1,484
○   £424
○   £1,855   (2 marks)

---

6   For the year ended 30 June 2017, Forgetful Ltd had a corporation tax liability of £166,250, which it did not pay until 31 July 2018. Forgetful Ltd is not a large company.

How much interest will Forgetful Ltd be charged by HM Revenue & Customs (HMRC) in respect of the late payment of its corporation tax liability for the year ended 30 June 2017?

○   £381
○   £2,286
○   £4,953
○   £1,524   (2 marks)

---

7   Mammoth Ltd commenced trading on 1 January 2018. The company's profits have been as follows:

Period	£
Year ended 31 December 2018	524,000
Year ended 31 December 2019	867,000
Year ended 31 December 2020	912,000

Throughout all of these periods, Mammoth Ltd had one related 51% group company.

What is the first year for which Mammoth Ltd will be required to pay its corporation tax liability by quarterly instalments?

○   Year ended 31 December 2019
○   None of the years ended 31 December 2018, 2019 or 2020
○   Year ended 31 December 2020
○   Year ended 31 December 2018   (2 marks)

---

8   Taxes can be either capital taxes or revenue taxes, although some taxes are neither type of tax.

Which is the correct classification for the following three taxes?

	Value added tax	Inheritance tax	National insurance contributions
○	Neither type	Revenue tax	Capital tax
○	Revenue tax	Capital tax	Neither type
○	Capital tax	Neither type	Revenue tax
○	Neither type	Capital tax	Revenue tax

(2 marks)

9   In the year ended 31 March 2018, Luck Ltd had taxable total profits of £400,000 and received the following dividends:

	£
From unconnected companies	5,200
From a company in which Luck Ltd has an 80% shareholding	4,300
From a company in which Luck Ltd has a 45% shareholding	1,400

What is the value of Luck Ltd's profits for the year ended 31 March 2018 for the purposes of determining whether it should pay corporation tax in instalments?

○   £406,600
○   £410,900
○   £405,700
○   £405,200   **(2 marks)**

10   For the tax year 2017/18, what are the latest dates by which a taxpayer, who is an individual and who does not wish to incur a penalty, should file a self-assessment tax return on paper or online?

	Paper tax return	Online tax return
○	31 October 2018	31 January 2020
○	31 October 2018	31 January 2019
○	31 October 2019	31 January 2019
○	31 October 2019	31 January 2019

                                                            (2 marks)

(Total = 20 marks)

CBE style OTQ bank – The UK tax system and its administration 2   36 mins

11   HM Revenue & Customs (HMRC) issued Lenny with a notice to file his tax return for the tax year 2017/18 on 30 April 2018. Lenny submitted the return online on 15 March 2019.

Match the due date for submission of the online return and the date by which HMRC will have to notify Lenny of a compliance check into this return.

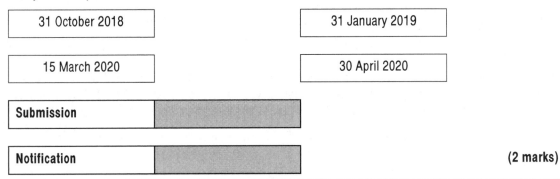

31 October 2018	31 January 2019

15 March 2020	30 April 2020

Submission	

| **Notification** | | **(2 marks)** |

12   Gareth's tax payable for 2016/17 and 2017/18 is as follows:

	2016/17	2017/18
	£	£
Income tax	10,000	12,500
Class 2 NIC	146	148
Class 4 NIC	2,000	2,500
Capital gains tax	1,000	2,000

Gareth always pays the correct amount of tax on each due date.

What is the amount payable by Gareth to HM Revenue & Customs (HMRC) on 31 January 2019 in respect of the tax year 2017/18?

Select...   ▼
£5,000
£5,148
£4,500
£4,148

(2 marks)

---

13   For the year to 31 March 2018 Key Ltd, which is not a large company, had a corporation tax liability of £22,400. It paid £10,000 of this liability on 1 December 2018 and the remaining £12,400 on 1 February 2019.

What is the interest payable by Key Ltd on late paid tax?

£ [   ]

(2 marks)

---

14   Jess plc is required to pay corporation tax by instalments. It had prepared accounts to 31 March each year but decided to prepare accounts for the 10-month period to 31 January 2018. Jess plc's corporation tax liability for the period to 31 January 2018 was £500,000.

What is the amount of the final instalment of corporation tax for the period ended 31 January 2018 and when is it due?

○   £125,000 due on 1 November 2018
○   £166,667 due on 14 January 2018
○   £50,000 due on 14 May 2018
○   £150,000 due on 14 May 2018

(2 marks)

---

15   More Ltd prepares accounts to 30 September each year. It was given notice by HM Revenue & Customs (HMRC) to submit its corporation tax return for the year to 30 September 2017 on 30 November 2017. The return was submitted on 1 December 2018. This was the first late return for the company.

What is the maximum penalty payable by More Ltd as a result of its late submission?

£ [   ]

(2 marks)

16   Which of the following statements correctly explains the difference between tax evasion and tax avoidance?

    ○   Both tax evasion and tax avoidance are illegal, but tax evasion involves providing HM Revenue and Customs with deliberately false information.

    ○   Tax evasion is illegal, whereas tax avoidance involves the minimisation of tax liabilities by the use of any lawful means.

    ○   Both tax evasion and tax avoidance are illegal, but tax avoidance involves providing HM Revenue and Customs with deliberately false information.

    ○   Tax avoidance is illegal, whereas tax evasion involves the minimisation of tax liabilities by the use of any lawful means.   **(2 marks)**

17   Quinn will not make the balancing payment in respect of her tax liability for the tax year 2016/17 until 17 October 2018.

What is the total percentage penalty which Quinn will be charged by HM Revenue & Customs (HMRC) in respect of the late balancing payment for the tax year 2016/17?

Select... ▼
15%
10%
5%
30%

(2 marks)

18   For the tax year 2016/17, Willard filed a paper self-assessment tax return on 10 August 2017.
What is the deadline for Willard to make an amendment to his tax return for the tax year 2016/17, and by what date will HM Revenue & Customs (HMRC) have to notify Willard if it intends to carry out a compliance check into this return?

	Amendment	*Compliance check*
○	10 August 2018	31 January 2019
○	10 August 2018	10 August 2018
○	31 January 2019	10 August 2018
○	31 January 2019	31 January 2019

(2 marks)

19   Daljit received a notice from HM Revenue & Customs (HMRC) to submit his self-assessment tax return for the tax year 2017/18. He did not submit the return by the due date.

What can HMRC do to collect any tax owing in respect of Daljit's unfiled return?

Select... ▼
Start a compliance check enquiry into the return
Make a determination
Raise a discovery assessment
Offer an internal review

(2 marks)

20   Based on her income tax liability of £15,600 for the tax year 2016/17, Sarah was liable to make two payments on account for the tax year 2017/18 of £7,800 each.

In May 2018, Sarah made a claim to reduce her second payment on account to £6,000. This reduced payment was made on 30 September 2018.

Sarah's actual income tax liability for the tax year 2017/18 was £16,000, and she paid the full balance outstanding on 31 January 2018.

How much interest is payable by Sarah to HM Revenue and Customs (HMRC) in respect of her second payment on account for the tax year 2017/18?

      O   £52
      O   £36
      O   £25
      O   £27   **(2 marks)**

(Total = 20 marks)

Domingo and Fargo (06/09) (amended)   18 mins

The following scenario relates to Questions 21 to 25.

Domingo and Fargo are brothers. In the tax year 2017/18 Domingo is employed and Fargo is self-employed. Fargo is required to make a balancing payment of £1,800 in respect of his income tax liability for the tax year 2017/18 and payments on account for the tax year 2018/19.

For the tax year 2017/18 Domingo wants to file a.paper self-assessment tax return. Fargo wants to file his tax return online. Both notices to file returns were issued by HM Revenue & Customs (HMRC) to Domingo and Fargo on 1 July 2018.

21   What are the latest dates for Domingo and Fargo to submit their respective self-assessment tax returns for the tax year 2016/17 given their stated filing preferences?

	Domingo	Fargo
O	31 October 2018	31 October 2018
O	31 October 2018	31 January 2019
O	31 January 2019	31 October 2018
O	31 January 2019	31 January 2019

                                                 (2 marks)

22   How long must Domingo and Fargo retain the records used in preparing their respective tax returns for the tax year 2017/18?

	Domingo	Fargo
O	31 January 2024	31 January 2020
O	31 January 2024	31 January 2024
O	31 January 2020	31 January 2020
O	31 January 2020	31 January 2024

                                                 (2 marks)

23   What is the maximum penalty that may be imposed on Domingo and Fargo for not retaining their records for the required period?

      O   £100
      O   £500
      O   £1,500
      O   £3,000   **(2 marks)**

24 What are the dates by which Fargo should make the balancing payment for the tax year 2017/18 and the first payment on account for the tax year 2018/19, and the second payment on account for the tax year 2018/19?

Balancing payment 2017/18 and first POA 2018/19   *Second POA 2018/19*

- ○ 31 July 2018   31 July 2019
- ○ 31 July 2018   31 January 2020
- ○ 31 January 2019   31 July 2019
- ○ 31 January 2019   31 January 2020   **(2 marks)**

25 What are the interest payable and maximum penalty payable if Fargo makes the balancing payment for the tax year 2017/18 exactly four months late?

- ○ Interest £16, penalty £90
- ○ Interest £49 penalty £90
- ○ Interest £16, penalty £180
- ○ Interest £49, penalty £180   **(2 marks)**

(Total = 10 marks)

CBE style OT case – Joe (A)(12/10) (amended)   18 mins

This objective test question contains question types which will only appear in a computer-based exam, but this question provides valuable practice for all students whichever version of the exam they are taking.

The following scenario relates to Questions 26 to 30.

On 31 December 2017 Joe resigned as an employee of Firstly plc, and on 1 January 2018 commenced employment with Secondly plc. He received a salary and taxable benefits from both Firstly plc and Secondly plc. He is paid monthly by both Firstly plc and Secondly plc.

Secondly plc has 700 employees. It filed its PAYE return due on 31 January 2018 on 4 April 2018. This was the second return that it had submitted late in the tax year 2017/18.

26 Which **TWO** of the following statements about Joe's PAYE tax code are correct?

- ☐ The code number for Joe, if he was only entitled to a personal allowance, would be 1150L.
- ☐ Joe's tax code cannot be adjusted for unpaid tax on income from earlier years.
- ☐ Joe's tax code will be applied to his salary when calculating the amount of income tax that has to be paid each month under the PAYE system.
- ☐ Joe's employer will be issued with the tax code at the start of the tax year and must use the same code throughout the tax year.   **(2 marks)**

27 Match the date for provision of the PAYE form P45 to Joe and the employer who must provide it.

| 31 May 2018 | | Firstly plc |

| 31 December 2017 | | Secondly plc |

| **Date** | |

| **Employer** | | **(2 marks)** |

28   By what date and by whom must Joe be provided with PAYE form P60?

	Date	By whom
O	31 May 2018	Firstly plc
O	31 May 2018	Secondly plc
O	6 July 2018	Firstly plc
O	6 July 2018	Secondly plc

(2 marks)

29   Match the date by which Joe must be provided with PAYE form P11D and the information it will it contain.

31 May 2018		Cash equivalents of the benefits

6 July 2018		Total taxable earnings

Date	

Information	

(2 marks)

30   What is the penalty that may be imposed by HM Revenue & Customs (HMRC) on Secondly plc for the late filing of its PAYE return due on 31 January 2018?

£ [   ]

(2 marks)

(Total = 10 marks)

CBE style OT case – Ernest (06/10) (amended)   18 mins

This objective test question contains question types which will only appear in a computer-based exam, but this question provides valuable practice for all students whichever version of the exam they are taking.

The following scenario relates to Questions 31 to 35.

You should assume that today's date is 30 June 2018.

You are a trainee Chartered Certified Accountant and your firm is dealing with the tax affairs of Ernest.

Ernest's self-assessment tax return for the tax year 2016/17 was submitted to HM Revenue & Customs (HMRC) on 15 May 2017 and Ernest paid the resulting income tax liability by the due date. However, you have just discovered that during the tax year 2016/17 Ernest disposed of a freehold property, the details of which were omitted from his self-assessment tax return. The capital gains tax liability in respect of this disposal is £18,000 and this amount has not been paid.

Ernest has suggested that since HMRC's right to make a compliance check enquiry into his self-assessment tax return for the tax year 2016/17 expired on 15 May 2018, no disclosure should be made to HMRC of the capital gain.

31 Identify, by clicking on the relevant boxes in the table below, whether each of the following statements concerning tax evasion and tax avoidance is true or false.

Tax evasion is illegal.	**TRUE**	**FALSE**
Both tax evasion and tax avoidance are illegal.	**TRUE**	**FALSE**
Tax avoidance involves any legal method of reducing the taxpayer's tax burden.	**TRUE**	**FALSE**
Tax evasion always involves providing HM Revenue & Customs with false information.	**TRUE**	**FALSE**

(2 marks)

32 Which **TWO** of the following statements are correct about how your firm should deal with the suggestion from Ernest that no disclosure is made to HMRC of his capital gain?

☐ Ernest should be advised to disclose details of the capital gain to HMRC.

☐ If Ernest does not disclose the gain to HMRC, your firm can definitely still continue to act for him.

☐ If your firm ceases to act for Ernest, it must disclose this to HMRC and provide detailed reasons why it has ceased to act.

☐ If Ernest does not disclose the gain to HMRC, your firm would be obliged to report under the money laundering regulations.

(2 marks)

33 What is the maximum penalty that could be imposed on Ernest for the error by omission in his tax return in relation to the capital gain, assuming that it is considered to be deliberate but not concealed?

○ £18,000
○ £12,600
○ £9,000
○ £5,400

(2 marks)

34 Assuming that HMRC discovers the capital gain and Ernest then makes a disclosure of it, what is the minimum penalty that could be imposed on Ernest for the error if it is considered to be deliberate but not concealed?

Select... ▼
£0
£2,700
£6,300
£9,000

(2 marks)

35 If Ernest pays the capital gains tax liability on 31 July 2018, what is the interest that will be charged on this late payment?

○ £495
○ £371
○ £247
○ £124

(2 marks)

(Total = 10 marks)

CBE style OT case – Thai Curry Ltd

18 mins

This objective test question contains question types which will only appear in a computer-based exam, but this question provides valuable practice for all students whichever version of the exam they are taking.

The following scenario relates to Questions 36 to 40.

Thai Curry Ltd prepares accounts for the year ended 31 March 2018 and has taxable total profits of £171,705, resulting in a corporation tax liability of £32,624.

Thai Curry Ltd has previously always submitted its corporation tax returns on time and had a corporation tax liability for the year to 31 March 2017 of £22,000.

The company is in dispute with HM Revenue & Customs (HMRC) in relation to its corporation tax return for the year ended 31 March 2017 and has been offered an internal review of the case. The case is likely to be allocated to either the complex track or the standard track if it instead chooses to go to a formal appeal.

36   What is the date by which Thai Curry Ltd's self-assessment corporation tax return for the year ended 31 March 2018 should be submitted?

- ○   31 December 2018
- ○   31 January 2019
- ○   31 March 2019
- ○   31 July 2019   **(2 marks)**

37   What is the total amount of late filing penalties that will be charged on Thai Curry Ltd if it submits its return for the year ended 31 March 2018 and pays the corporation tax due eight months late?

Select...   ▼
£3,262
£6,525
£6,725
£3,462

(2 marks)

38   How should Thai Curry Ltd's corporation tax liability for the year ended 31 March 2018 be paid?

- ○   £32,624 on 1 January 2019
- ○   £11,000 on 31 January 2018 and 31 July 2018, £10,624 on 31 January 2019
- ○   £8,156 on 14 October 2017, 14 January 2018, 14 April 2018 and 14 July 2018
- ○   £5,500 on 14 October 2017, 14 January 2018 and 14 April 2018, £16,124 on 14 July 2018

(2 marks)

39   Which **TWO** of the following statements are correct about the internal review procedure?

☐   An internal review is a less costly and more effective way to resolve disputes informally than a formal appeal.

☐   The review is carried out by the HMRC officer who has previously dealt with the case.

☐   HMRC must usually carry out the review within 45 days.

☐   After the review conclusion is notified, the company cannot make a further appeal.   **(2 marks)**

40   Match what body is initially likely to hear Thai Curry Ltd's appeal if it does not take up the offer of an internal review.

┌─────────────────────────┐
│   First tier   │
└─────────────────────────┘

┌─────────────────────────┐
│   Upper tier   │
└─────────────────────────┘

┌─────────────────────────┬───────────────────────┐
│ **Complex track**   │   │
└─────────────────────────┴───────────────────────┘

┌─────────────────────────┬───────────────────────┐
│ **Standard track**   │   │
└─────────────────────────┴───────────────────────┘

(Total = 10 marks)

41 John   **18 mins**

(a)   **You should assume today's date is 30 November 2017.**

John is a new client whom you met today. On 6 April 2016, he commenced in self-employment and prepared his first set of accounts to 5 April 2017. John had not previously filed a self-assessment tax return and has not received any communication from HM Revenue & Customs (HMRC) about his tax affairs.

As this will be his first self-assessment tax return, John is also concerned that HMRC might carry out a compliance check.

Required

(i)   Advise John of the latest date by which he should have notified HMRC of his chargeability to income tax for the tax year 2016/17 and the maximum and minimum penalties for late notification if he immediately notifies HMRC of his chargeability and is deemed to have been careless.   **(3 marks)**

(ii)   State the period during which HMRC will have to notify John if it intends to carry out a compliance check in respect of his self-assessment tax return for the tax year 2016/17, and the possible reasons why such a check would be made.

       Note. You should assume for part (ii) that John will file his tax return by the due filing date.   **(3 marks)**

(b)   The UK Government uses tax policies to encourage certain types of activity.

Required

Briefly explain how the UK Government's tax policies encourage:

(i)   Individuals to save   **(1 mark)**
(ii)   Individuals to support charities   **(1 mark)**
(iii)   Entrepreneurs to build their own businesses and to invest in plant and machinery   **(2 marks)**

(Total = 10 marks)

42 Sugar plc

Sugar plc has been in business for many years. It owns 45% of the ordinary shares of Honey plc and 75% of the ordinary shares of Molasses plc. Molasses plc owns 70% of the ordinary shares of Treacle plc. This structure has existed for many years.

In the year to 31 March 2018, Sugar plc had taxable total profits of £470,000. It also received dividends of £50,000 from Honey plc. In the year to 31 March 2019, Sugar plc will have taxable total profits of £600,000. It will not receive any dividends in that year.

Required

(a) Define what is meant by a related 51% group company and explain which companies are related 51% group companies of Sugar plc. **(3 marks)**

(b) Explain whether or not Sugar plc is a large company for the purposes of payment of corporation tax for the years ended 31 March 2018 and 31 March 2019. **(3 marks)**

(c) Assuming that Sugar plc is a large company in both years but was not a large company for any previous year, calculate Sugar plc's corporation tax liabilities for the years ended 31 March 2018 and 31 March 2019 and explain when these will be paid. Assume the rate of corporation tax in financial year 2018 is the same as in financial year 2017. **(4 marks)**

(Total = 10 marks)

Questions 43 to 118 cover income tax and NIC liabilities, the subject of Chapters 2 to 12 of the BPP Study Text for Taxation (TX – UK).

MCQ bank – Income tax and NIC liabilities 1   36 mins

43   Hamza and Sofia arrived in the United Kingdom (UK) during the tax year 2017/18. Neither of them had previously been resident in the UK and they did not work in the UK during the tax year 2017/18. During the tax year 2017/18, they both acquired homes in the UK, and neither of them has any other home. During the tax year 2017/18, Hamza spent 42 days in the UK and Sofia spent 67 days in the UK.

Which of Hamza and Sofia is/are resident in the UK for the tax year 2017/18?

    O   Both Hamza and Sofia
    O   Hamza only
    O   Sofia only
    O   Neither Hamza nor Sofia   **(2 marks)**

44   In the tax year 2017/18 Claudio has taxable income (after deduction of his personal allowance) consisting of £3,000 of non-savings income and £12,500 of savings income.

What is Claudio's income tax liability for the tax year 2017/18?

    O   £2,500
    O   £2,900
    O   £2,700
    O   £3,100   **(2 marks)**

45   Luke rents out a room in his own residence throughout 2017/18. The rent is £150 a week. Luke's expenses of the letting are £20 per week, none of which is loan interest on the property.

What is the amount of property business income taxable on Luke for 2017/18 if he makes any relevant election?

    O   £6,760
    O   £0
    O   £7,800
    O   £300   **(2 marks)**

46   Mike and Delia are a married couple. In the tax year 2017/18, Mike has taxable non-savings income (after deducting his personal allowance) of £12,400. Delia has no income in the tax year 2017/18. Delia has made an election in relation to her personal allowance for the tax year 2017/18.

What is Mike's income tax liability for the tax year 2017/18?

    O   £180
    O   £2,250
    O   £1,330
    O   £2,480   **(2 marks)**

47 John is employed by Zebra plc. He was provided with a computer for private use on 6 November 2016. The market value of the computer when first provided to an employee for private use was £3,600 and the computer had a market value of £2,000 when first provided to John for private use. Z plc gave the computer to John on 5 April 2018 when it had a market value of £1,000.

What are the total taxable benefits for John in respect of the computer for the tax year 2017/18?

- ○ £2,880
- ○ £3,300
- ○ £1,720
- ○ £1,833   **(2 marks)**

48 In the tax year 2017/18 Susie receives employment income of £170,000. She made a gross gift aid donation of £10,000 in January 2018.

What is Susie's income tax liability for the tax year 2017/18?

- ○ £60,300
- ○ £62,300
- ○ £59,800
- ○ £54,700   **(2 marks)**

49 Petunia is a single parent with a 2 year old son. She receives child benefit of £1,076 in the tax year 2017/18. Petunia has net income of £57,000 in 2017/18 and she made gross personal pension contributions of £2,000 during 2017/18.

What is Petunia's child benefit income tax charge for the tax year 2017/18?

- ○ £1,076
- ○ £430
- ○ £538
- ○ £753   **(2 marks)**

50 Judith works for Sabre Ltd for an annual salary of £18,000. On 30 September 2017, she received a bonus of £4,000 in respect of Sabre Ltd's trading results for the year ended 31 March 2017. She expects to receive a bonus of £4,800 on 30 September 2018 in respect of Sabre Ltd's results for the year ended 31 March 2018. Judith also received £500 from a customer on 1 December 2017 as a gratuity for good service.

What is Judith's employment income for the tax year 2017/18?

- ○ £22,000
- ○ £22,800
- ○ £22,500
- ○ £23,300   **(2 marks)**

51 Trevor is employed by Cress plc at a salary of £25,000 a year. He is provided with a car available for private use for the tax year 2017/18. The car has CO_2 emissions of 108 g/km and a list price of £20,000 although Cress plc actually paid £18,000 for the car as the result of a dealer discount. The car has a diesel engine. No private fuel is provided.

What is Trevor's taxable car benefit for the tax year 2017/18?

- ○ £3,600
- ○ £4,140
- ○ £4,000
- ○ £4,600   **(2 marks)**

52   Jonas is an employee of the LP partnership. His employer provided him with the use of free accommodation from 6 April 2017 to 5 April 2018. It was not deemed to be job related. The accommodation cost the LP partnership £93,000 in February 2015 and has an annual value of £8,000. The accommodation was valued at £109,000 on 6 April 2017.

What are the total taxable benefits for Jonas in respect of the accommodation for the tax year 2017/18?

○   £8,850
○   £10,325
○   £8,450
○   £8,000   (2 marks)

(Total = 20 marks)

CBE style OTQ bank – Income tax and NIC liabilities 2 36 mins

53   Marion bought £20,000 (nominal value) 5% UK Government Loan Stock on 1 July 2017. Interest is payable on 30 June and 31 December each year. Marion sold the loan stock to Gerald on 31 October 2017 including interest.

Match the amounts amount of savings income taxable on Marion and Gerald in respect of the loan stock for the tax year 2017/18.

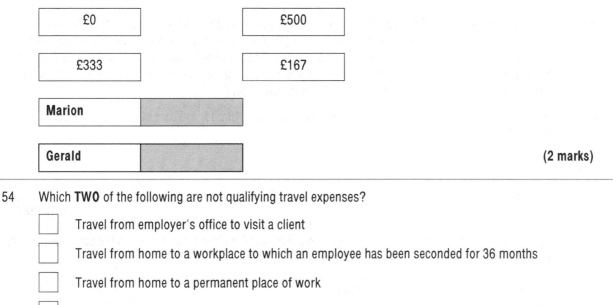

| £0 | £500 |
| £333 | £167 |

Marion

Gerald   (2 marks)

54   Which **TWO** of the following are not qualifying travel expenses?

☐   Travel from employer's office to visit a client

☐   Travel from home to a workplace to which an employee has been seconded for 36 months

☐   Travel from home to a permanent place of work

☐   Travel from home to visit a trade fair relevant to the employer's business 100 miles away from permanent place of work   (2 marks)

55 Troy is a sole trader who had trading income of £60,000 in the tax year 2016/17 and £80,000 in the tax year 2017/18. He has no other income. He joined a personal pension scheme on 6 April 2016 and made gross contributions of £25,000 in 2016/17. This was the first pension provision that Troy had made.

What gross amount can Troy contribute to his personal pension scheme in March 2018 without incurring an annual allowance charge?

Select...   ▼
£55,000
£40,000
£135,000
£25,000

(2 marks)

56 Which **TWO** of the following types of income are exempt from income tax?

☐ Interest on an NS&I Investment account

☐ Premium bond prizes

☐ Interest on UK government stocks ('gilts')

☐ Dividends on shares held in an Individual Savings Account

(2 marks)

57 Susie rents out a furnished house. The house does not qualify as a furnished holiday letting. The furnishings include a new sofa which was bought in the tax year 2017/18 to replace an old one which was disposed of at the same time. The old sofa cost £3,000 in 2007 and was disposed of in January 2018 for proceeds of £200. The new sofa was bought in January 2018 for £5,500 and was larger than the old one. If Susie had bought a newer sofa of the same model as the old one it would have cost £4,000.

What deduction against property business income can Susie claim for the cost of the sofa bought in 2017/18?

○ £5,500
○ £3,800
○ £5,300
○ £4,000

(2 marks)

58 Greg is a sole trader. His accounts for the year to 5 April 2018 included a deduction in the statement of profit or loss for legal expenses of £7,240. These comprised:

	£
Grant of a new short lease on retail premises	2,400
Preparation of employment contract	720
Purchase of freehold retail premises	3,200
Debt collection for trade debts	920
	7,240

What are the legal fees deductible for the year to 5 April 2018?

Select...   ▼
£4,040
£1,640
£920
£7,240

(2 marks)

59 Harry is a sole trader. He prepares accounts for the year ended 5 April 2018 and has deducted the following items of expenditure in the statement of profit or loss:

	£
Depreciation	3,000
Accountancy fees for preparing accounts	1,000
Entertainment of: staff (party at £300 per person for 6 employees)	1,800
customers	2,400

How much should be added back to Harry's net profit to arrive at his adjusted taxable profit?

£ [   ]   (2 marks)

60 Rose is a sole trader who prepares accounts to 5 April each year using the cash basis of accounting. Her results for the period of account to 5 April 2018 show the following:

	£
Cash sales	41,000
Invoice sales	4,000
Cash expenses	20,200

The figure for invoice sales includes an invoice for £1,500 which was paid on 10 April 2018. In addition to the cash expenses of £20,200, Rose incurred motoring expenses of £2,800 for driving 8,000 miles of which 6,500 miles were for business purposes. Rose wishes to use the flat rate allowance for motoring.

What is Rose's taxable trading income for the tax year 2017/18?

£ [   ]   (2 marks)

61 Philip is a sole trader who prepares accounts to 5 April each year. He purchased a motor car for both business and private purposes on 6 April 2017. The motor car has CO_2 emissions of 160 grams per kilometre and cost £22,000. In the year to 5 April 2018, Philip drove a total of 9,000 miles of which 4,950 miles were for business journeys.

What is the maximum capital allowance that Philip can claim in respect of the motor car for the period of account to 5 April 2018?

O   £968
O   £2,178
O   £1,760
O   £792   (2 marks)

62 Ella started in business as a sole trader on 6 November 2017 and prepared her first set of accounts to 5 April 2018. On 6 December 2017 she acquired plant at a cost of £95,000.

What are the maximum capital allowances that Ella can claim for the period of account to 5 April 2018?

Select...   ▼
£68,367
£85,433
£84,208
£95,000

(2 marks)

(Total = 20 marks)

CBE style OTQ bank – Income tax and NIC liabilities 3 36 mins

63   Joe has been in business for many years preparing accounts to 5 April each year. The tax written down value of his main pool at 6 April 2017 was £12,000. Joe sold machinery on 10 June 2017 for £11,900 which had originally cost £11,600. He made no acquisitions during the year ended 5 April 2018.

What is the maximum capital allowance that Joe can claim for the period of account to 5 April 2018?

- ○   £1,000
- ○   £400
- ○   £100
- ○   £72   (2 marks)

64   Alexandra started in business as a sole trader on 1 August 2016 and prepared her first set of accounts to 30 April 2018.

Match the start date and the end date of Alexandra's basis period for the tax year 2017/18, her second tax year of trading.

1 August 2016	6 April 2017	1 May 2017

31 July 2017	5 April 2018	30 April 2018

Start date [   ]

End date [   ]   (2 marks)

65   Timothy started in business as a sole trader on 1 February 2016. He prepared his first set of accounts to 30 November 2016 and his second set of accounts to 30 November 2017. His taxable trading profits were as follows:

p/e 30 November 2016   £30,000
y/e 30 November 2017   £42,000

What are Timothy's overlap profits?

£ [   ]   (2 marks)

66   Walter had been in business as a sole trader for many years preparing accounts to 31 December each year. He ceased trading on 31 March 2018. Walter had overlap profits of £2,000 on commencement. His taxable trading profits were as follows:

y/e 31 December 2017   £18,000
p/e 31 March 2018   £3,000

What is Walter's taxable trading income for the final year of trading?

£ [   ]   (2 marks)

67 Joyce started in business as a sole trader on 1 January 2017 and prepared her first set of accounts to 30 September 2017 and her second set of accounts to 30 September 2018. She made the following losses in her first two periods of trading:

	£
p/e 30 September 2017	(9,000)
y/e 30 September 2018	(14,400)

Match the amounts of the trading losses with the tax years.

£3,000	£9,000	£9,600

£11,400	£12,600	£14,400

2016/17	

2017/18		(2 marks)

---

68 Francis is a sole trader who has been in business for many years preparing accounts to 5 April each year. His recent results have been as follows:

	£
y/e 5 April 2017 Profit	16,000
y/e 5 April 2018 Loss	(25,000)

Francis has gross investment income of £3,000 each year. He is expected to make trading profits of around £12,000 per annum over the next few years.

What is the trading loss to carry forward to the tax year 2018/19 if Francis makes the most advantageous claim for loss relief?

£ [   ]   (2 marks)

---

69 Peter and Jane have been in partnership for many years preparing accounts to 31 July each year and sharing profits equally. On 1 September 2016, they changed their profit sharing agreement so that Peter was entitled to a salary of £9,000 each year and the remaining profits were then split two parts to Peter and three parts to Jane. The partnership made a trading profit of £96,000 in the year to 31 July 2017.

What is Peter's taxable trading profit for the tax year 2017/18?

£ [   ]   (2 marks)

---

70 Robin and Stuart had been in partnership for many years preparing accounts to 31 December each year and sharing profits equally. On 1 January 2018, Tania joined the partnership and profits were then split 2:2:1. The partnership made a profit of £96,000 in the year to 31 December 2017 and £112,000 in the year to 31 December 2018.

Match the taxable trading profits of the partners for 2017/18.

£5,600	£11,200	£22,400

£47,200	£48,000

Robin and Stuart each	

Tania		(2 marks)

71 Shona started in business on 1 January 2018 as a sole trader and prepared her first set of accounts for the 14 weeks to 5 April 2018. Her taxable trading profit for that period was £9,400.

What are Shona's total national insurance contributions for the tax year 2017/18?

£ [   ]   (2 marks)

72 Mark has been in business as a sole trader for many years preparing accounts to 5 April. He made a trading loss of £(2,000) in the year to 5 April 2017 and has not made any claim in respect of this loss. In the year to 5 April 2018, he made a trading profit of £13,500.

What are Mark's Class 4 national insurance contributions for the tax year 2017/18?

£ [   ]   (2 marks)

(Total = 20 marks)

CBE style OT case – Ann, Basil and Chloe (12/08) (amended)
18 mins

This objective test question contains question types which will only appear in a computer-based exam, but this question provides valuable practice for all students whichever version of the exam they are taking.

The following scenario relates to Questions 73 to 77.

Ann

Ann is self-employed. Her taxable income for the tax year 2017/18 was £76,000 which was all trading income. Ann made contributions of £49,000 (gross) into a personal pension scheme between September 2017 and March 2018. This was the second year that she had been a member of a pension scheme and she had an unused annual allowance of £20,000 brought forward from 2016/17.

Basil

Basil is employed. During the tax year 2017/18 Basil had taxable income of £160,000 which was all employment income. Basil made contributions of £50,000 (gross) into a personal pension scheme during the tax year 2017/18. This was the first year that he had been a member of a pension scheme. In future, his employer may contribute to Basil's personal pension scheme.

Chloe

Chloe lets out an unfurnished property. For the tax year 2017/18 her taxable income was £16,630 which was all property business income. Chloe made contributions of £8,200 (gross) into a personal pension scheme during the tax year 2017/18. This was the first year that she had been a member of a pension scheme. Chloe does not have any interest payable on her buy-to-let property.

73 Which **TWO** of the following statements about relevant earnings are correct?

☐ Individuals can always make gross pension contributions of £3,600 in 2017/18 even if they do not have any relevant earnings in that tax year.

☐ Relevant earnings relate both to contributions to personal pension schemes and to occupational pension schemes.

☐ If an individual makes pension contributions less than relevant earnings in a tax year, the excess can be carried forward for three years and used to cover pension contributions.

☐ Relevant earnings do not include income from furnished holiday lettings.   (2 marks)

74   Identify, by clicking on the relevant boxes in the table below, whether each of the following statements about the annual allowance is true or false.

Employer contributions do not count towards the annual allowance.	TRUE	FALSE
The annual allowance can be carried forward for three years to the extent that it is unused in the tax year.	TRUE	FALSE
The annual allowance is available even if the individual is not a member of a pension scheme in a tax year and so can be carried forward.	TRUE	FALSE
If tax-relievable pension contributions exceed the annual allowance, there is a charge to income tax.	TRUE	FALSE

(2 marks)

75   What is Ann's income tax liability for the tax year 2017/18?

£ [   ]

(2 marks)

76   What is Basil's annual allowance charge for the tax year 2017/18?

£ [   ]

(2 marks)

77   What is Chloe's tax relief on her pension contribution for the tax year 2017/18?

○   £0
○   £1,640
○   £900
○   £720

(2 marks)

(Total = 10 marks)

Ae, Bee, Cae, and Eu (12/08) (amended)

18 mins

The following scenario relates to Questions 78 to 82.

Ae, Bee and Cae

Ae and Bee commenced in partnership on 1 July 2015 preparing accounts to 30 April. Cae joined as a partner on 1 July 2017. Profits were always shared equally. The partnership's trading profits since the commencement of trading have been as follows:

	£
Period ended 30 April 2016	54,000
Year ended 30 April 2017	66,000
Year ended 30 April 2018	87,000

Eu

Eu ceased trading on 30 September 2019, having been self-employed since 1 July 2009.

(1)   Eu's trading profits for the final three periods of trading were as follows:

	£
Year ended 30 June 2018	62,775
Year ended 30 June 2019	57,600
Three-month period ended 30 September 2019	14,400

These figures are before taking account of capital allowances.

(2)   Eu's capital allowances in the year to 30 June 2018 were £1,575 and in the year to 30 June 2019 were £1,292.

(3)   The tax written down value of the capital allowances main pool at 1 July 2019 was £5,883. On 15 September 2019 Eu purchased office furniture for £2,400. All of the items included in the main pool were sold for £5,175 (all for less than cost) on 30 September 2019.

(4)   Until the final period of trading Eu had always prepared accounts to 30 June. Her overlap profits for the period 1 July 2009 to 5 April 2010 were £9,800.

78   What is Ae's trading income assessment for the tax year 2016/17?

- ○   £27,000
- ○   £24,300
- ○   £32,500
- ○   £33,000

(2 marks)

79   What is Cae's trading income assessment for the tax year 2017/18?

- ○   £26,583
- ○   £24,167
- ○   £29,000
- ○   £21,750

(2 marks)

80   What is Eu's trading income assessment for the tax year 2018/19?

- ○   £56,025
- ○   £62,775
- ○   £57,600
- ○   £61,200

(2 marks)

81   What are Eu's capital allowances for the three-month period ended 30 September 2019?

- ○   £3,108
- ○   £1,491
- ○   £2,775
- ○   £559

(2 marks)

82   Assuming that the capital allowances for the three-month period ended 30 September 2019 were £3,000, what is Eu's trading income assessment for the tax year 2019/20?

    ○   £1,600
    ○   £57,908
    ○   £62,200
    ○   £67,708   **(2 marks)**

(Total = 10 marks)

CBE style OT case – Rosie and Sam (12/12) (amended) 18 mins

This objective test question contains question types which will only appear in a computer-based exam, but this question provides valuable practice for all students whichever version of the exam they are taking.

The following scenario relates to Questions 83 to 87.

You should assume that today's date is 15 February 2018.

Rosie

Rosie is the managing director of Hornburg plc. During the tax year 2017/18 Rosie was paid gross director's remuneration of £220,000 and she received dividend income of £500,000. She had the same income in 2016/17. She has made the following gross personal pension contributions:

Tax year	Pension contribution £
2014/15	Nil
2015/16	26,000
2016/17	Nil

Rosie was a member of a pension scheme for the tax year 2016/17 but not in the tax year 2014/15.

Sam

In September 2016 Sam invested £7,000 in a cash ISA. In May 2017 he invested a further £6,000 in that cash ISA. He withdrew £5,000 from the cash ISA in October 2017. Sam is now considering investing more cash into the cash ISA before 5 April 2018. He also invested £4,000 in premium bonds and government securities ('gilts') in the tax year 2017/18.

83   What is the total amount of pension scheme annual allowances that Rosie has available for the tax year 2017/18?

    ○   £74,000
    ○   £34,000
    ○   £94,000
    ○   £64,000   **(2 marks)**

84   Use **ONE** of the following to complete the sentence below:

20	25
45	55

If Rosie makes pension contributions in excess of her available annual allowances there will be a charge to income tax at

[　　　　] %

on the excess contributions.   **(2 marks)**

85   What are the tax consequences for Rosie if she takes pension benefits under flexible access drawdown?

	Lump sum	*Rest of pension fund*
○	Up to 10% of fund can be taken tax free	Taxable as pension income when received
○	Up to 10% of fund can be taken as tax-free lump sum	5% of fund taxable as pension income each year whether or not received
○	Up to 25% of fund can be taken as tax-free lump sum	Taxable as pension income when received
○	Up to 25% of fund can be taken as tax-free lump sum	5% of fund taxable as pension income each year whether or not received

(2 marks)

86   What is the maximum amount that Sam can invest into the cash ISA for the tax year 2017/18 in addition to his investments already made?

Select...   ▼
£14,000
£19,000
£12,000
£15,000

(2 marks)

87   Match the income tax and capital gains tax treatments of Sam's investments in premium bonds and government securities.

Exempt from income tax, chargeable to capital gains tax		Chargeable to income tax and capital gains tax
Exempt from both income tax and capital gains tax		**Chargeable to income tax, exempt from capital gains tax**

Premium bonds	

Government securities	

(2 marks)

(Total = 10 marks)

CBE style OT case – Fang and Hong (12/13) (amended) 18 mins

This objective test question contains question types which will only appear in a computer-based exam, but this question provides valuable practice for all students whichever version of the exam they are taking.

The following scenario relates to Questions 88 to 92.

Fang

Fang commenced self-employment on 1 August 2015. She has a trading profit of £45,960 for the year ended 31 July 2016, and a trading profit of £39,360 for the year ended 31 July 2017. Fang has overlap profits on commencement.

Hong

Hong has been in self-employment since 2005, preparing accounts to 5 April. For the year ended 5 April 2018 she made a trading loss of £45,800, and has claimed this against her total income for the tax year 2016/17.

For the year ended 5 April 2017 Hong made a trading profit of £29,700. She also has a property business profit of £3,900 for the tax year 2016/17. Hong has an unused trading loss of £2,600 brought forward from the tax year 2015/16.

During the tax year 2016/17 Hong disposed of an investment property and this resulted in a chargeable gain. As Hong has claimed relief against total income of this tax year, she may include a further claim to set the trading loss against her chargeable gain for the year.

88 Match the amount of trading profit which will have been assessed on Fang for each of the tax years 2015/16 and 2016/17.

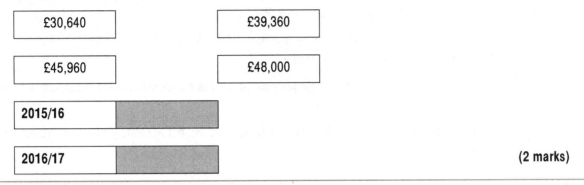

| £30,640 | £39,360 |
| £45,960 | £48,000 |

| 2015/16 | |
| 2016/17 | | **(2 marks)**

---

89 In which **ONE** of the following ways can overlap profits be relieved?

- ○ Against first available current year basis profits
- ○ Against trading income on cessation
- ○ Against general income of the tax year of commencement and/or the preceding tax year
- ○ Against general income in the three tax years preceding the year of commencement   **(2 marks)**

---

90 How could Fang have obtained relief for trading expenditure incurred prior to 1 August 2015 and for computer equipment which Fang already owned which was brought into business use on 1 August 2015?

	Trading expenditure	*Computer equipment*
○	Added to overlap profit and relieved on cessation	Addition for capital allowances purposes based on its original cost
○	Treated as incurred on 1 August 2015	Addition for capital allowances purposes based on its original cost
○	Added to overlap profit and relieved on cessation	Addition for capital allowances purposes based on its market value at 1 August 2015
○	Treated as incurred on 1 August 2015	Addition for capital allowances purposes based on its market value at 1 August 2015 **(2 marks)**

91   What was the amount of loss for the year ended 5 April 2018 which was relieved against Hong's income for the tax year 2016/17?

Select...   ▼
£2,600
£31,000
£33,600
£19,500

(2 marks)

92   Which **TWO** of the following statements about the further claim to set Hong's trading loss against her chargeable gain for the tax year 2016/17 are correct?

☐   The trading loss is first set against general income of the tax year 2016/17 and only any excess loss is set against chargeable gains of that year.

☐   The amount of chargeable gains for the tax year 2016/17 is computed ignoring the annual exempt amount for the purposes of this relief.

☐   Capital losses of the tax year 2016/17 are taken into account, but not brought forward losses, for the purposes of this relief.

☐   Hong can specify the amount to be set against chargeable gains, so her annual exempt amount for the tax year 2016/17 is not wasted.

(2 marks)

(Total = 10 marks)

CBE style OT case – Chi (06/14) (amended)   18 mins

This objective test question contains question types which will only appear in a computer-based exam, but this question provides valuable practice for all students whichever version of the exam they are taking.

The following scenario relates to Questions 93 to 97.

Chi commenced self-employment on 6 April 2017, and for the year ended 5 April 2018 her trading profit using the normal accruals basis was £53,000, calculated as follows:

	Note	£	£
Revenue	1		72,500
Expenses			
Motor expenses	2	4,400	
Other expenses	3	8,200	
Capital allowances	4	6,900	
			(19,500)
Trading profit			53,000

Notes

1   *Revenue*

The revenue figure of £72,500 includes receivables of £1,600 which were owed as at 5 April 2018.

2   *Motor expenses*

The total motor expenses for the year ended 5 April 2018 were £5,500, of which 20% was for private journeys. This proportion has been disallowed in calculating the trading profit. During the year ended 5 April 2018, Chi drove 13,200 business miles.

3   *Other expenses*

The other expenses figure of £8,200 includes payables of £900 which were owed as at 5 April 2018.

4   *Capital allowances*

Capital allowances consist of an annual investment allowance claim of £4,020 in respect of office equipment purchased on 6 April 2017, and a writing down allowance of £2,880 claimed in respect of Chi's motor car. The motor car had cost £20,000 on 6 April 2017.

93   Based on the trading profit of £53,000 for the year ended 5 April 2018, what is Chi's income tax liability for the tax year 2017/18?

£ [   ]   **(2 marks)**

94   Based on the trading profit of £53,000 for the year ended 5 April 2018, what are the Class 4 national insurance contributions payable by Chi for the tax year 2017/18?

£ [   ]   **(2 marks)**

95   Which **TWO** of the following statements about the cash basis of assessment are correct?

☐   The trader must prepare accounts to 5 April each year.

☐   The trader can deduct capital expenditure on plant and machinery (other than motor cars) as business expenses rather than using capital allowances.

☐   A trader can start to use the cash basis if his receipts for the tax year do not exceed £150,000.

☐   Under the cash basis, a trader can offset losses against other income or gains.   **(2 marks)**

96   If Chi uses the cash basis and claims fixed profit motor expenses, what is the amount of motor expenses (note 2) which are allowable?

○   £4,400
○   £5,300
○   £5,940
○   £8,180   **(2 marks)**

97   If Chi uses the cash basis, what is the amount of revenue which is chargeable (note 1) and the other expenses (note 3) which are allowable for the year ended 5 April 2018?

○   Revenue £72,500, other expenses £8,200
○   Revenue £70,900, other expenses £8,200
○   Revenue £72,500, other expenses £7,300
○   Revenue £70,900, other expenses £7,300   **(2 marks)**

98 Bayle (A) (06/11) (amended)   18 mins

Bayle is self-employed as a lawyer who prepares accounts to 30 September each year. On 1 December 2017 Bayle is planning to bring a newly qualified lawyer, Fyle, into her business. Fyle will either be taken on as an employee, being paid a gross monthly salary of £3,300, or join Bayle as a partner, receiving a 20% share of the new partnership's profits.

Bayle has forecast that her tax adjusted trading profit will be £216,000 for the year ended 30 September 2018, and £240,000 for the year ended 30 September 2019.

Fyle does not have any other income for the tax year 2017/18. He will be the sole employee of Bayle.

Required

(a) Assuming that Fyle is employed from 1 December 2017, calculate the total amount of national insurance contributions (if any) that will be paid by Bayle and Fyle in respect of his earnings for the tax year 2017/18.

Note. You are not expected to calculate the national insurance contributions that will be paid in respect of Bayle's earnings. **(4 marks)**

(b) Assuming that Fyle becomes a partner from 1 December 2017:

(i) Calculate his trading income assessments for the tax years 2017/18 and 2018/19.

Note. You are not expected to calculate any overlap profits. **(4 marks)**

(ii) Calculate the total amount of national insurance contributions that will be paid by Bayle and Fyle, if any, in respect of Fyle's trading income assessment for the tax year 2017/18.

Note. You are not expected to calculate the national insurance contributions that will be paid in respect of Bayle's trading income assessment. **(2 marks)**

(Total = 10 marks)

99 Michael and Sean (06/12) (amended)   18 mins

You are a trainee Chartered Certified Accountant and your manager has asked for your help regarding two taxpayers who have both made trading losses.

Michael

Michael commenced in self-employment on 1 July 2016, preparing accounts to 5 April. His results for the first two periods of trading were as follows:

		£
Nine-month period ended 5 April 2017	– Trading loss	(25,230)
Year ended 5 April 2018	– Trading profit	9,665

For the tax years 2012/13 to 2014/15 Michael had the following income from employment:

	£
2012/13	45,100
2013/14	19,365
2014/15	52,095

Michael did not have any income during the period 6 April 2015 to 30 June 2016.

Sean

Sean has been in self-employment since 2007, but ceased trading on 31 December 2017. He has always prepared accounts to 31 December. His results for the final five years of trading were as follows:

		£
Year ended 31 December 2013	– Trading profit	21,300
Year ended 31 December 2014	– Trading profit	14,400
Year ended 31 December 2015	– Trading profit	18,900
Year ended 31 December 2016	– Trading profit	3,700
Year ended 31 December 2017	– Trading loss	(23,100)

For each of the tax years 2013/14 to 2017/18 Sean has property business profits of £11,700.

Sean has unused overlap profits brought forward of £3,600.

Required

For each of the two taxpayers, Michael and Sean, identify the loss relief claims that are available to them, and explain which of the available claims would be the most beneficial.

Notes

1   You should clearly state the amount of any reliefs claimed and the rates of income tax saved. However, you are not expected to calculate any income tax liabilities.

2   You should assume that the tax rates and allowances for the tax year 2017/18 apply throughout.

3   The following mark allocation is provided as guidance for this requirement:

Michael, 4½ marks
Sean, 5½ marks   **(10 marks)**

(Total = 10 marks)

100 Samantha (12/07)   18 mins

Samantha has been self-employed since 2003. She has the following income and chargeable gains for the tax years 2015/16 to 2018/19:

	2015/16 £	2016/17 £	2017/18 £	2018/19 £
Trading profit/(loss)	7,290	42,600	(79,000)	18,285
Building society interest	–	6,100	3,800	2,130
Chargeable gains/(loss)	21,100	23,300	(3,400)	14,100

The chargeable gains are stated **before** taking account of loss relief and the annual exempt amount.

Required

(a)   State the factors that will influence an individual's choice of loss relief claims.   **(3 marks)**

(b)   Calculate Samantha's taxable income and taxable gains for each of the tax years 2015/16, 2016/17, 2017/18 and 2018/19 on the assumption that she relieves the trading loss of £79,000 for the tax year 2017/18 on the most favourable basis.

You should assume that the tax rates and allowances for the tax year 2017/18 apply throughout.   **(7 marks)**

(Total = 10 marks)

101 Martin   18 mins

Assume that it is 1 July 2017.

Martin started trading on 1 January 2017. His profits for the first 6 months of trading to 30 June 2017 were £3,000 each month. Martin estimates that his profits will be £4,000 each month for the next 6 months of trading to 31 December 2017 and then £5,000 each month thereafter for the foreseeable future.

Martin has decided to prepare accounts either to 5 April each year (starting with the period ending 5 April 2017) or to 30 April each year (starting with the period ending 30 April 2017).

You have advised Martin that if he chooses 30 April as his accounting date rather than 5 April this will delay the taxation of his trading profits.

Required

(a)   Assuming that Martin chooses 5 April as his accounting date, compute Martin's taxable profits for the periods of account ending 5 April 2017, 5 April 2018 and 5 April 2019.   **(2 marks)**

(b)   Using your answer to part (a), compute Martin's trading income for the tax years 2016/17, 2017/18 and 2018/19 if he chooses 5 April as his accounting date.   **(2 marks)**

(c)   Assuming that Martin chooses 30 April as his accounting date, compute Martin's taxable profits for the periods of account ending 30 April 2017 and 30 April 2018.   **(2 marks)**

(d) Using your answer to part (c), compute Martin's trading income for the tax years 2016/17, 2017/18 and 2018/19 if he chooses 30 April as his accounting date. **(3 marks)**

(e) Using your answers to parts (b) and (d), show why you have advised Martin that if he chooses 30 April as his accounting date rather than 5 April this will delay the taxation of his trading profits. **(1 mark)**

(Total = 10 marks)

102 Lucy   18 mins

Assume that it is 1 March 2017.

Lucy is considering two work arrangements. She will start her chosen arrangement on 6 April 2017 and will continue with that arrangement for the whole of the tax year 2017/18.

Employment with Red plc

Lucy has been offered employment with Red plc. She would be paid a salary of £35,000 and would be required to work at Red plc's offices.

Lucy would travel from home to Red plc's offices by train and would buy an annual season ticket costing £1,500.

Self-employment

Lucy would work for a number of clients at their offices. She would receive fees of £35,000 from her clients in the year to 5 April 2018.

Lucy would travel from home to client offices in her own car. Her business mileage would be 4,600 miles during the year and she estimates this would actually cost 40p per mile.

Lucy would prepare accounts to 5 April 2018 and elect to use the cash basis and fixed rate expenses.

Required

Determine which of the work arrangements would result in Lucy having a higher amount of disposable income after deducting income tax, national insurance contributions and travel costs. **(10 marks)**

Note. You are expected to calculate the income tax and NIC liability for Lucy for each arrangement and then calculate her disposable income in each case, taking into account her travel costs.

(Total = 10 marks)

103 Daniel, Francine and Gregor (Sep/Dec 15)   18 mins

(a) Amanda, Beatrice and Claude have been in partnership since 1 November 2011, preparing accounts to 31 October annually. Daniel joined as a partner on 1 May 2017. Profits have always been shared equally. The partnership's recent tax adjusted trading profits are as follows:

	£
Year ended 31 October 2016	147,000
Year ended 31 October 2017	96,000
Year ended 31 October 2018 (forecast)	180,000

Required

Calculate Daniel's trading income assessment for the tax year 2017/18. **(3 marks)**

(b) Francine is employed by Fringe plc. On 1 August 2017, Fringe plc provided Francine with a loan of £96,000 to help her purchase a holiday cottage. On 1 October 2017, the loan was increased by a further £14,000 so that Francine could renovate the cottage. Francine pays interest at an annual rate of 1.5% on this loan.

The taxable benefit in respect of this loan is calculated using the average method.

Required

Calculate Francine's taxable benefit for the tax year 2017/18 in respect of the loan from Fringe plc.

(3 marks)

(c) Gregor has been self-employed since 6 April 2003. He has the following income and chargeable gains for the tax years 2016/17 and 2017/18:

	2016/17 £	2017/18 £
Trading profit/(loss)	14,700	(68,800)
Business property profit/(loss)	4,600	(2,300)
Building society interest (gross)	1,300	900
Chargeable gain/(loss)	(2,900)	17,400

Required

On the assumption that Gregor relieves his trading loss of £68,800 as early as possible, calculate the amount of trading loss carried forward to the tax year 2018/19.

Note. You should assume that the tax allowances for the tax year 2017/18 apply throughout. **(4 marks)**

(Total = 10 marks)

104 George (Mar/Jun 16) 18 mins

You should assume that today's date is 1 March 2017.

George is a software developer. He has accepted a one-year contract to update software for Xpee plc.

(1) The contract will run from 6 April 2017 to 5 April 2018, with a fee of £40,000 payable for the entire year of the contract. A condition of the contract is that George will have to do the work personally and not be permitted to sub-contract the work to anyone else.

(2) George will work from home, but will have to attend weekly meetings at Xpee plc's offices to receive instructions regarding the work to be performed during the following week.

(3) George will not incur any significant expenses in respect of the contract apart from the purchase of a new laptop computer for £3,600 on 6 April 2017. This laptop will be used 100% for business purposes.

(4) During the term of the contract, George will not be permitted to work for any other clients. He will therefore not have any other income during the tax year 2017/18.

(5) George's tax liability for the tax year 2016/17 was collected through PAYE, so he will not be required to make any payments on account in respect of the tax year 2017/18.

George has several friends who are also software developers. He understands that his employment status is not clear cut but that his income tax liability for the tax year 2017/18 will be the same regardless of whether he is treated as employed or as self-employed. However, George appreciates that there are advantages to being classed as self-employed.

Required

(a) List **FOUR** factors which are indicators of George being treated as an employee in relation to his contract with Xpee plc rather than as self-employed.

Note. You should confine your answer to the information given in the question. **(2 marks)**

(b) Calculate George's income tax liability and national insurance contributions for the tax year 2017/18 if he is treated as self-employed in respect of his contract with Xpee plc. **(4 marks)**

(c) If George is treated as being an employee of Xpee plc instead of self-employed:

    (i) Explain why his income tax liability will be payable earlier **(2 marks)**

    (ii) Calculate the additional amount of national insurance contributions which he personally will suffer for the tax year 2017/18 **(2 marks)**

(Total = 10 marks)

105 Joe (B) (12/10) (amended)   27 mins

On 31 December 2017 Joe resigned as an employee of Firstly plc, and on 1 January 2018 commenced employment with Secondly plc. The following information is available for the tax year 2017/18:

Employment with Firstly plc

(1)   From 6 April 2017 to 31 December 2017 Joe was paid a salary of £6,360 per month. In addition to his salary, Joe was paid a bonus of £12,000 on 12 May 2017. He had become entitled to this bonus on 22 March 2017.

(2)   Joe contributed 6% of his monthly gross salary of £6,360 into Firstly plc's HM Revenue & Customs' registered occupational pension scheme.

(3)   On 1 May 2017 Firstly plc provided Joe with an interest-free loan of £120,000 so that he could purchase a holiday cottage. Joe repaid £50,000 of the loan on 31 July 2017, and repaid the balance of the loan of £70,000 when he ceased employment with Firstly plc on 31 December 2017.

(4)   During the period from 6 April 2017 to 31 December 2017 Joe's three year old daughter was provided with a place at Firstly plc's workplace nursery. The total cost to the company of providing this nursery place was £11,400 (190 days at £60 per day).

(5)   Firstly plc provided Joe with a home entertainment system for his personal use costing £4,400 on 6 April 2017. The company gave the home entertainment system to Joe for free when he left the company on 31 December 2017, although its market value at that time was £3,860.

Employment with Secondly plc

(1)   From 1 January 2018 to 5 April 2018 Joe was paid a salary of £6,565 per month.

(2)   During the period 1 January 2018 to 5 April 2018 Joe contributed a total of £3,000 (gross) into a personal pension scheme.

(3)   From 1 January 2018 to 5 April 2018 Secondly plc provided Joe with living accommodation. The property has an annual value of £10,400 and is rented by Secondly plc at a cost of £2,250 per month. On 1 January 2018 Secondly plc purchased furniture for the property at a cost of £16,320. The company pays for all of the running costs relating to the property, and for the period 1 January 2018 to 5 April 2018 these amounted to £1,900.

(4)   During the period 1 January 2018 to 5 April 2018 Secondly plc provided Joe with 13 weeks of childcare vouchers costing £100 per week. Joe used the vouchers to provide childcare for his three year old daughter at a registered nursery near to his workplace.

Required

Calculate Joe's employment income for the tax year 2017/18.   **(15 marks)**

(Total = 15 marks)

106 Sammi (12/10)   27 mins

You should assume that today's date is 20 March 2017.

Sammi is a director of Smark Ltd, a profitable company. The company has given her the choice of being provided with a leased company motor car or alternatively being paid additional director's remuneration and then privately leasing the same motor car herself.

Company motor car

The motor car will be provided throughout the tax year 2017/18, and will be leased by Smark Ltd at an annual cost of £27,630. The motor car will be petrol powered, will have a list price of £80,000, and will have an official CO_2 emission rate of 300 grams per kilometre.

The lease payments will cover all the costs of running the motor car except for fuel. Smark Ltd will not provide Sammi with any fuel for private journeys.

Additional director's remuneration

As an alternative to having a company motor car, Sammi will be paid additional gross director's remuneration of £27,000 during the tax year 2017/18. She will then privately lease the motor car at an annual cost of £27,630.

Other information

The amount of business journeys that will be driven by Sammi will be immaterial and can therefore be ignored.

Sammi's current level of director's remuneration is over £150,000 which means that she will pay income tax at the additional rate of 45% in 2017/18. Smark Ltd prepares its accounts to 5 April. The lease of the motor car will commence on 6 April 2017.

Required

(a) Advise Sammi of the income tax and national insurance contribution implications for the tax year 2017/18 if she (1) is provided with the company motor car, and (2) receives additional director's remuneration of £27,000. **(5 marks)**

(b) Advise Smark Ltd of the corporation tax and national insurance contribution implications for the year ended 5 April 2018 if the company (1) provides Sammi with the company motor car, and (2) pays Sammi additional director's remuneration of £27,000.

Note. You should ignore value added tax (VAT). **(5 marks)**

(c) Determine which of the two alternatives is the more beneficial from each of the respective points of view of Sammi and Smark Ltd. **(5 marks)**

(Total = 15 marks)

107 Simon (12/09)   27 mins

On 21 April 2017 Simon purchased a derelict freehold house for £127,000. Legal fees of £1,800 were paid in respect of the purchase.

Simon then renovated the house at a cost of £50,000, with the renovation being completed on 8 August 2017. He immediately put the house up for sale, and it was sold on 29 August 2017 for £260,000. Legal fees of £2,600 were paid in respect of the sale.

Simon financed the transaction by a bank loan of £150,000 that was taken out on 21 April 2017 at an annual interest rate of 6%. The bank loan was repaid on 29 August 2017.

Simon had no other income or capital gains for the tax year 2017/18 except as indicated above.

Simon has been advised that whether or not he is treated as carrying on a trade will be determined according to the six following 'badges of trade':

(1) Subject matter of the transaction
(2) Length of ownership
(3) Frequency of similar transactions
(4) Work done on the property
(5) Circumstances responsible for the realisation
(6) Motive

Required

(a) Briefly explain the meaning of each of the six 'badges of trade' listed in the question.

Note. You are not expected to quote from decided cases. **(3 marks)**

(b) Calculate Simon's income tax liability and his Class 2 and Class 4 national insurance contributions for the tax year 2017/18, if he is treated as carrying on a trade in respect of the disposal of the freehold house. **(8 marks)**

(c) Calculate Simon's capital gains tax liability for the tax year 2017/18, if he is not treated as carrying on a trade in respect of the disposal of the freehold house. **(4 marks)**

(Total = 15 marks)

108 Na (12/09) (amended)
27 mins

Na commenced self-employment as a hairdresser on 1 January 2015. She had tax adjusted trading profits of £25,200 for the 6-month period ended 30 June 2015 and £21,600 for the year ended 30 June 2016.

The following information is available for the tax year 2017/18:

Trading profit for the year ended 30 June 2017

(1) Na's statement of profit or loss for the year ended 30 June 2017 is as follows:

	Note	£	£
Income			63,635
Expenses			
Depreciation		2,635	
Motor expenses	2	2,200	
Professional fees	3	1,650	
Property expenses	4	12,900	
Purchases	5	4,700	
Other expenses	6	16,550	
			(40,635)
Net profit			23,000

(2) Na charges all the running expenses for her motor car to the business. During the year ended 30 June 2017 Na drove a total of 8,000 miles, of which 7,000 were for private journeys.

(3) The figure for professional fees includes £1,260 for legal fees in connection with the grant of a new five-year lease of parking spaces for customers' motor cars.

(4) Na lives in a flat that is situated above her hairdressing studio, and one-third of the total property expenses of £12,900 relate to this flat.

(5) During the year ended 30 June 2017 Na took goods out of the hairdressing business for her personal use without paying for them, and no entry has been made in the accounts to record this. The goods cost £250 (an amount that has been deducted under 'purchases') and had a selling price of £450.

(6) The figure for other expenses of £16,550 includes £480 for a fine in respect of health and safety regulations and £160 for a trade subscription to the Guild of Small Hairdressers.

(7) Na uses her private telephone to make business telephone calls. The total cost of the private telephone for the year ended 30 June 2017 was £1,200, and 20% of this related to business telephone calls. The cost of the private telephone is not included in the statement of profit or loss expenses of £40,635.

(8) Capital allowances for the year ended 30 June 2017 are £810.

Other information

(9) During the tax year 2017/18 Na received interest of £310 from an individual savings account (ISA) and dividends of £1,200 from quoted company shareholdings.

Required

(a) Calculate the amount of trading profits that will have been assessed on Na for the tax years 2014/15, 2015/16 and 2016/17 respectively, clearly identifying the amount of any overlap profits.   **(5 marks)**

(b) Calculate Na's tax adjusted trading profit for the year ended 30 June 2017.

   Note. Your computation should commence with the net profit figure of £23,000, and should list all of the items referred to in notes (1) to (8) indicating by the use of zero (0) any items that do not require adjustment.   **(7 marks)**

(c) Calculate Na's income tax liability for the tax year 2017/18.   **(3 marks)**

(Total = 15 marks)

109 Bayle (B) (06/11) (amended)   27 mins

Bayle is self-employed as a lawyer. She is also a director of Acquit & Appeal Ltd. The following information is available for the tax year 2017/18:

Self-employment

(1) Bayle's statement of profit or loss for the year ended 30 September 2017 is as follows:

	Note	£	£
Revenue	2		318,987
Expenses			
Gifts and donations	3	8,680	
Lease of motor car	4	4,345	
Professional fees	5	3,240	
Property expenses	6	46,240	
Travel expenses	7	16,770	
Other expenses	8	66,410	
			(145,685)
Net profit			173,302

(2) Revenue includes £2,800 received during May 2017 in respect of an impairment loss that Bayle had written off when calculating her trading profit for the year ended 30 September 2015.

(3) Gifts and donations are as follows:

	£
Gifts to customers (clocks costing £110 each and displaying Bayle's name)	3,300
Gifts to customers (bottles of champagne costing £40 each and displaying Bayle's name)	2,480
Donations to political parties	2,900
	8,680

(4) The lease commenced on 1 May 2017, and is in respect of a motor car with CO_2 emissions of 244 grams per kilometre. There is no private use of the motor car.

(5) The figure of £3,240 for professional fees is in respect of accountancy services, of which £600 is for inheritance tax planning advice.

(6) Bayle lives in an apartment that is situated above her office, and two-fifths of the total property expenses of £46,240 relate to this apartment.

(7) The figure of £16,770 for travel expenses includes £520 for parking fines incurred by Bayle.

(8) The figure for other expenses of £66,410 includes £670 for Bayle's professional subscription to the Law Society, and £960 for her golf club membership fee.

Director's remuneration

(9)   Bayle will be paid gross director's remuneration of £42,000 by Acquit & Appeal Ltd during the tax year 2017/18.

(10)   In addition to her director's remuneration, Bayle received two bonus payments of £6,000 from Acquit & Appeal Ltd during June 2017, both of which were in respect of the year ended 31 December 2016. Bayle became entitled to the first bonus payment of £6,000 on 10 March 2017, and to the second bonus payment of £6,000 on 20 April 2017.

(11)   Acquit & Appeal Ltd deducts PAYE at a flat rate of 45% from all of Bayle's earnings.

Other information

(12)   During the tax year 2017/18 Bayle will receive dividends of £11,000 and interest of £5,240 on the maturity of a savings certificate issued by National Savings & Investments (NS&I).

(13)   Bayle owned £160,000 3% Treasury Stock (gilts) which pay interest on 30 June and 31 December each year. She sold the Treasury Stock on 30 September 2017 including interest.

(14)   On 1 November 2017 Bayle made a gross gift aid donation of £5,000.

Required

(a)   Calculate Bayle's tax adjusted trading profit for the year ended 30 September 2017.

       Note. Your computation should commence with the net profit figure of £173,302, and you should also list all of the items referred to in notes (2) to (8) indicating by the use of zero (0) any items that do not require adjustment.   **(6 marks)**

(b)   Calculate the income tax payable by Bayle for the tax year 2017/18.   **(9 marks)**

                                                                                    (Total = 15 marks)

110 Flick (A) (06/12) (amended)   27 mins

On 6 April 2017 Flick commenced employment with 3D Ltd. On 1 January 2018 she commenced in partnership with Art Reel running a small cinema, preparing accounts to 30 April. The following information is available for the tax year 2017/18:

Employment

(1)   During the tax year 2017/18 Flick was paid a gross annual salary of £28,030.

(2)   Throughout the tax year 2017/18 3D Ltd provided Flick with living accommodation. The company had purchased the property in 2008 for £89,000, and it was valued at £145,000 on 6 April 2017. The annual value of the property is £4,600.

Partnership

(1)   The partnership's tax adjusted trading profit for the four-month period ended 30 April 2018 is £29,700. This figure is before taking account of capital allowances.

(2)   The only item of plant and machinery owned by the partnership is a motor car that cost £18,750 on 1 February 2018. The motor car has a CO_2 emission rate of 190 grams per kilometre. It is used by Art, and 40% of the mileage is for private journeys.

(3)   Profits are shared 40% to Flick and 60% to Art. This is after paying an annual salary of £6,000 to Art.

Property income

(1)   Flick owns a freehold house which is let out furnished. The property was let throughout the tax year 2017/18 at a monthly rent of £660.

(2)   During the tax year 2017/18 Flick paid council tax of £1,320 in respect of the property, and also spent £2,560 on building a new extended porch. She spent £500 on a new washer-dryer to replace an old washing machine. A like for like replacement of the old washing machine would have cost £350.

Required

(a)   Calculate Flick's taxable income for the tax year 2017/18.   **(11 marks)**

(b)   List the advantages and disadvantages for the partnership of choosing 30 April as its accounting date rather than 5 April.   **(4 marks)**

(Total = 15 marks)

111 Josie (12/12) (amended)   27 mins

On 30 June 2017 Josie ceased self-employment. On 1 August 2017 she commenced employment with Typo plc. The following information is available for the tax year 2017/18:

Self-employment

(1)   Josie's trading profits for the final two periods of trading were as follows:

	£
Year ended 30 April 2017	95,260
Two-month period ended 30 June 2017	10,440

There were no capital allowances.

(2)   Josie has unused overlap profits brought forward of £41,700.

Employment

(1)   Josie is paid a salary of £15,100 per month by Typo plc. The salary is paid on the last day of each calendar month.

(2)   During August 2017 Typo plc paid £11,649 towards Josie's removal expenses when she permanently moved to take up her new employment with the company as she did not live within a reasonable commuting distance. The £11,649 covered both her removal expenses and the legal costs of acquiring a new main residence.

(3)   On 1 September 2017 Typo plc provided Josie with an interest-free loan of £39,600 that she used to renovate her new main residence. This loan was still outstanding at 5 April 2018.

(4)   During the period from 1 August 2017 to 5 April 2018, Josie was provided with free meals in Typo plc's staff canteen. The total cost of these meals to the company was £1,340. The canteen is available to all of the company's employees.

(5)   During the period from 1 October 2017 to 5 April 2018, Typo plc provided Josie with a diesel powered motor car with an official CO_2 emission rate of 104 grams per kilometre. The motor car, which has a list price of £14,400, cost Typo plc £13,900. Typo plc does not provide Josie with any fuel for private journeys.

Other information

(1)   During the tax year 2017/18 Josie received interest of £1,200 from a holding of £24,000 5% Treasury Stock 2025 and dividends of £7,200.

(2)   During the tax year 2017/18 Josie made gift aid donations totalling £4,400 (net) to national charities.

Required

Calculate Josie's income tax liability for the tax year 2017/18.

Note. You should indicate by the use of zero any items that are non-taxable/exempt from tax.   **(15 marks)**

(Total = 15 marks)

112 Richard (A) (12/13) (amended)

27 mins

(a) On 6 April 2017, Richard commenced in self-employment, running a restaurant. Richard's statement of profit or loss for the year ended 5 April 2018 is as follows:

	Note	£	£
Gross profit			73,440
Expenses			
Motor expenses	1	7,660	
Property expenses	2	16,200	
Repairs and renewals	3	6,420	
Other expenses	4	10,960	
			(41,240)
Net profit			32,200

Notes

1 *Motor expenses*

Motor expenses are as follows:

	£
Cost of running Richard's motor car	4,710
Cost of running a motor car used by the restaurant's chef	2,670
Parking fines incurred by Richard	280
	7,660

Richard's motor car is used 70% for private journeys and the chef's motor car is used 20% for private journeys.

2 *Property expenses*

Richard lives in an apartment which is situated above the restaurant, and one-fifth of the total property expenses of £16,200 relate to this apartment.

3 *Repairs and renewals*

Repairs and renewals are as follows:

	£
Decorating the restaurant	5,100
Decorating the apartment	1,320
	6,420

The property was in a usable state when it was purchased.

4 *Other expenses*

The figure of £10,960 for other expenses includes legal fees of £2,590 in connection with the purchase of the restaurant property. The remaining expenses are all allowable.

Additional information

Advertising

Richard spent £800 in March 2017 on newspaper advertisements prior to opening the restaurant.

Plant and machinery

The following motor cars were purchased during the year ended 5 April 2018:

	Date of purchase	Cost	CO_2 emission rate
		£	
Motor car [1]	6 April 2017	14,000	114 grams per kilometre
Motor car [2]	6 April 2017	16,800	103 grams per kilometre

Motor car [1] is used by Richard and motor car [2] is used by the restaurant's chef.

Required

Calculate Richard's tax adjusted trading profit for the year ended 5 April 2018.

Notes

1   Your computation should commence with the net profit figure of £32,200, and should list all of the items referred to in notes (1) to (4), indicating by the use of zero (0) any items which do not require adjustment.

2   In answering this part of the question you are not expected to take account of any of the information provided in part (b) below. **(8 marks)**

(b)   Richard had three employees working for him in his restaurant during the tax year 2017/18 as follows:

(1)   A chef who was employed throughout the tax year 2017/18 on a gross annual salary of £46,000. The chef was provided with a petrol powered motor car (see the plant and machinery information in part (a) above) throughout the tax year. The list price of the motor car is the same as its cost. Richard did not provide any fuel for private journeys.

(2)   A part-time waitress who was employed for 20 hours per week throughout the tax year 2017/18 on a gross annual salary of £8,000.

(3)   An assistant chef who was employed for 8 months from 6 August 2017 to 5 April 2018 on a gross monthly salary of £2,200.

Required

Calculate the employer's Class 1 and Class 1A national insurance contributions which Richard would have incurred in respect of his employees' earnings and benefit for the tax year 2017/18.

Note. You are not expected to calculate the national insurance contributions suffered by the employees or by Richard in respect of his self-employment. **(7 marks)**

(Total = 15 marks)

113 John (06/13) (amended)   27 mins

John is employed by Surf plc. The following information is available for the tax year 2017/18:

(1)   During the tax year 2017/18, John was paid gross remuneration of £208,318. John was promoted at the start of 2017/18 and in 2016/17 his adjusted income was below £150,000.

(2)   During the tax year 2017/18, John contributed £18,000 into Surf plc's HM Revenue & Customs' registered occupational pension scheme. The company contributed a further £12,000 on his behalf. Both John and Surf plc have made exactly the same contributions for the previous five tax years.

(3)   During 2014 Surf plc provided John with a loan which was used to purchase a yacht. The amount of loan outstanding at 6 April 2017 was £84,000. John repaid £12,000 of the loan on 31 July 2017, and then repaid a further £12,000 on 31 December 2017. He paid loan interest of £270 to Surf plc during the tax year 2017/18. The taxable benefit in respect of this loan is calculated using the average method.

(4)   During the tax year 2017/18, John made personal pension contributions up to the maximum amount of available annual allowances, including any unused amounts brought forward from previous years. These contributions were in addition to the contributions he made to Surf plc's occupational pension scheme (see note (2)). John has not made any personal pension contributions in previous tax years.

(5)   John owns a holiday cottage which is let out as a furnished holiday letting, although the letting does not qualify as a trade under the furnished holiday letting rules. The property business profit for the year ended 5 April 2018 was £16,730 before the deduction of interest. John paid loan interest of £5,000 for the year in respect of a loan to buy this property.

Required

(a)   Calculate John's income tax liability for the tax year 2017/18.   **(12 marks)**

(b)   State **THREE** tax advantages of a rental property qualifying as a trade under the furnished holiday letting
        rules.   **(3 marks)**

                                                                              (Total = 15 marks)

---

114 Ronald (06/14) (amended)   **27 mins**

Ronald is employed and also self-employed. Ronald has tried to prepare his own income tax computation for the
tax year 2017/18, but he has found it more difficult than expected. Although the sections which Ronald has
completed are correct, there are a significant number of omissions. The omissions are marked as outstanding
(O/S). The partly completed income tax computation is as follows:

RONALD – INCOME TAX COMPUTATION 2017/18

	Note	£
Trading income	1	O/S
Employment income		65,065
Property business profit	2	O/S
Building society interest		1,260
Dividends		O/S
		O/S
Personal allowance		(11,500)
Taxable income		O/S
Income tax		
Non-savings income: £33,500 @ 20%		6,700
Non-savings income: O/S @ 40%		O/S
Savings income: £500 @ 0%		0
Savings income: O/S @ 40%		O/S
Dividend income: O/S @ 0%		0
Dividend income: £800 @ 32.5%		260
O/S		
Income tax liability		O/S
Tax suffered at source		
PAYE		(9,130)
Income tax payable		O/S

Notes

1   *Trading profit*

      Ronald commenced self-employment on 1 January 2017. He had a tax adjusted trading profit of £3,840 for
      the 4-month period ended 30 April 2017, and £12,060 for the year ended 30 April 2018. These figures are
      before taking account of capital allowances.

      The only item of plant and machinery owned by Ronald is his motor car, which cost £18,000 on
      1 September 2017.

      The motor car has a CO_2 emission rate of 142 grams per kilometre, and 70% of the mileage driven by
      Ronald is for private journeys.

2   *Property business profit*

      Ronald owns a freehold shop. The shop was purchased on 1 October 2017, and during October 2017 Ronald
      spent £8,400 replacing the building's roof. The shop was not usable until this work was carried out, and this
      fact was represented by a reduced purchase price.

On 1 December 2017, the property was let to a tenant, with Ronald receiving a premium of £12,000 for the grant of a 30-year lease. The monthly rent is £960 payable in advance, and during the period 1 December 2017 to 5 April 2018 Ronald received five rental payments.

Due to a fire, £8,600 was spent on replacing the roof of the shop during February 2018. Only £8,200 of this was paid for by Ronald's property insurance.

Ronald paid insurance of £480 in respect of the property. This was paid on 1 October 2017 and is for the year ended 30 September 2018.

Other information

Ronald did not make any personal pension contributions during the tax year 2017/18. He has never been a member of a pension scheme.

Required

(a)   Calculate the income tax payable by Ronald for the tax year 2017/18.   **(11 marks)**

(b)   Advise Ronald why the maximum gross amount of tax relievable personal pension scheme contribution which he could have made for the tax year 2017/18 is £40,000, and the method by which tax relief would have been given if he had made this amount of contribution.   **(4 marks)**

(Total = 15 marks)

115 Wai (06/15)   **27 mins**

Wai is employed as a sales manager by Qaz plc, and the following information is available in respect of the tax year 2017/18:

(1)   During the tax year 2017/18, Wai was paid a gross monthly salary of £10,200.

(2)   In addition to her salary, Wai has been paid the following bonuses:

Amount £	Date of payment	Date of entitlement	In respect of the six-month period ended
4,600	25 April 2017	31 March 2017	31 December 2016
8,100	20 August 2017	3 July 2017	30 June 2017
2,900	3 May 2018	15 April 2018	31 December 2017

(3)   During the period 6 April to 31 August 2017, Wai used her private motor car for both private and business journeys. She was reimbursed by Qaz plc at the rate of 55p per mile for the following mileage:

	Miles
Normal daily travel between home and Qaz plc's offices	2,420
Travel between home and the premises of Qaz plc's clients (none of the clients' premises were located near the offices of Qaz plc)	8,580
Travel between home and a temporary workplace (the assignment was for ten weeks)	2,860
Total mileage reimbursed by Qaz plc	13,860

(4)   During the period 1 September 2017 to 5 April 2018, Qaz plc provided Wai with a petrol powered motor car which has a list price of £11,590, and an official CO_2 emission rate of 86 grams per kilometre. Qaz plc does not provide Wai with any fuel for private journeys.

(5)   During January 2018, Wai spent 10 nights overseas on company business. Qaz plc paid Wai a daily allowance of £10 to cover the cost of personal incidental expenses, such as telephone calls to her family.

(6)   Throughout the tax year 2017/18, Qaz plc allowed Wai the use of two mobile telephones. The telephones had each cost £400 when purchased by the company in March 2017.

(7)   Throughout the tax year 2017/18, Qaz plc provided Wai with living accommodation. The company had purchased the property on 1 June 2014 for £142,000, and it has been provided to Wai since 1 February 2016. Improvements costing £24,200 were made to the property during October 2014, and further improvements costing £9,800 were made during August 2017. The annual value of the property is £4,828.

Qaz plc does not payroll employee benefits.

Required

(a)   Calculate Wai's taxable income for the tax year 2017/18.   **(12 marks)**

(b)   Briefly outline the information to be included in PAYE forms P60 and P11D, and state the dates by which they should have been provided to Wai for the tax year 2017/18.

   Note. Your answer should be confined to the details which are relevant to Wai, although no figures are required.   **(3 marks)**

                                                                                              (Total = 15 marks)

116 Samson and Delilah (Sep/Dec 15) (amended)   27 mins

Samson and Delilah are a married couple. They are both employed by Rope plc, and Delilah is also a partner in a partnership. The following information is available in respect of the tax year 2017/18:

Samson

During the tax year 2017/18, Samson was paid a gross annual salary of £112,000 in respect of his employment with Rope plc.

Delilah

(1)   During the tax year 2017/18, Delilah was paid a gross annual salary of £184,000 in respect of her employment with Rope plc.

(2)   Throughout the tax year 2017/18, Rope plc provided Delilah with a petrol powered motor car which has a list price of £67,200, and an official CO_2 emission rate of 177 grams per kilometre. Rope plc does not provide Delilah with any fuel for private journeys. Delilah was unable to drive her motor car for a period during the tax year 2017/18 because of a skiing accident, and during this period Rope plc provided her with a chauffeur at a total cost of £9,400.

(3)   Rope plc provided all its employees with a hamper of groceries costing £42 each in December 2017.

(4)   Delilah spent £70 in July 2017 on travelling by train to visit a customer of Rope plc. This amount was reimbursed by Rope plc in August 2017.

(5)   During the tax year 2017/18, Delilah donated £250 (gross) per month to charity under the payroll deduction scheme operated by Rope plc.

(6)   Delilah has been in partnership with Esther and Felix for a number of years. The partnership's tax adjusted trading profit for the year ended 31 December 2017 was £93,600. Esther is paid an annual salary of £8,000, with the balance of profits being shared 40% to Delilah, 30% to Esther and 30% to Felix.

(7)   During the tax year 2017/18, Delilah paid interest of £6,200 (gross) on a personal loan taken out to purchase her share in the partnership.

(8)   During the tax year 2017/18, Delilah made charitable gift aid donations totalling £4,864 (net).

Joint income – Building society deposit account

Samson and Delilah have savings in a building society deposit account which is in their joint names. During the tax year 2017/18, they received building society interest totalling £9,600 from this joint account.

Required

(a)   Calculate Samson and Delilah's respective income tax liabilities for the tax year 2017/18.

   Note. The following mark allocation is provided as guidance for this requirement:

   Samson (4 marks)

   Delilah (9 marks)   **(13 marks)**

(b)   Calculate Samson's income tax saving for the tax year 2017/18 if the building society deposit account had been in Delilah's sole name instead of in joint names for the entire year.   **(2 marks)**

                                                                                              (Total = 15 marks)

117 Patience (Mar/Jun 16)   27 mins

Patience retired on 31 December 2017, and on that date ceased employment and self-employment. The following information is available in respect of the tax year 2017/18:

Employment

(1)   Patience was employed by a private school as a teacher. From 6 April to 31 December 2017, she was paid a salary of £3,750 per month.

(2)   During the period 6 April to 31 December 2017, Patience contributed 6% of her monthly gross salary of £3,750 into her employer's HM Revenue & Customs (HMRC) registered occupational pension scheme. Patience's employer contributed a further 10% on her behalf.

(3)   During the period 6 April to 30 June 2017, Patience's granddaughter was provided with a free place at the private school run by Patience's employer. The normal fee payable would have been £4,600. The additional marginal expense of providing the place for the grandchild was £540.

(4)   On 25 June 2017, Patience was given a clock valued at £600 as an award for her 25 years of teaching at her employer's school. She has not previously received any similar awards.

(5)   Patience's employer provided her with an interest-free loan so that she could purchase a season ticket for the train to work. The balance of the loan outstanding at 6 April 2017 was £8,000, and Patience repaid the loan in full on 31 December 2017.

Self-employment

(1)   Patience was self-employed as a private tutor. Her trading profit for the year ended 31 July 2017 was £14,800. This figure is **after** taking account of capital allowances.

(2)   Patience's trading profit for the final five-month period of trading from 1 August to 31 December 2017 was £6,900. This figure is **before** taking account of capital allowances.

(3)   The tax written down value of the capital allowances main pool at 1 August 2017 was £2,200. On 10 August 2017, Patience purchased a laptop computer for £1,700.

         On the cessation of trading, Patience personally retained the laptop computer. Its value on 31 December 2017 was £1,200. The remainder of the items included in the main pool were sold for £800 on 31 December 2017.

(4)   Patience has unused overlap profits brought forward of £3,700.

Personal pension contributions

During the period 6 April to 31 December 2017, Patience contributed a total of £3,600 (net) into a personal pension scheme.

Pension income

During the period 1 January to 5 April 2018, Patience received the state pension of £1,450, a pension of £6,000 from her employer's occupational pension scheme, and a private pension of £3,300. These were the total gross amounts received.

Property

Patience owned two properties which were let out unfurnished until both properties were sold on 31 December 2017. The following information is available in respect of the two properties:

	Property one	Property two
	£	£
Rent received during the tax year 2017/18	3,600	7,200
Sale proceeds on 31 December 2017	122,000	98,000
Allowable revenue expenditure during the tax year 2017/18 (no finance costs)	(4,700)	(2,600)
Purchase cost	(81,400)	(103,700)

Patience has never occupied either of the two properties as her main residence.

Required

Calculate Patience's income tax and capital gains tax liabilities for the tax year 2017/18.

Notes

1   You should indicate by the use of zero (0) any items which are not taxable or deductible.

2   The following mark allocation is provided as guidance for this question:

Income tax (13 marks)
Capital gains tax (2 marks)

(Total = 15 marks)

118 Petula (Mar/Jun 17)   27 mins

Petula has been employed as a sales manager by Downtown plc since 6 April 2010. The following information is available in respect of the tax year 2017/18:

(1)   During the tax year 2017/18, Petula was paid a gross annual salary of £230,000.

(2)   In addition to her salary, Petula has been paid the following bonuses by Downtown plc:

Amount £	Date of payment	Date of entitlement	In respect of the six-month period ended
21,200	30 April 2017	1 April 2017	31 December 2016
18,600	31 October 2017	1 October 2017	30 June 2017
22,400	30 April 2018	1 April 2018	31 December 2017

(3)   During the tax year 2017/18, Petula used her private motor car for both private and business journeys. The total mileage driven by Petula throughout the tax year was 26,000 miles, with all of this mileage reimbursed by Downtown plc at the rate of 60p per mile. However, only 21,000 miles were in the performance of Petula's duties for Downtown plc.

(4)   Petula pays an annual professional subscription of £630 which is relevant to her employment with Downtown plc. Petula also pays an annual subscription membership fee of £1,840 to a golf club which she uses to entertain Downtown plc's clients. Downtown plc does not reimburse Petula for either of these costs.

(5)   During the tax year 2017/18, Petula paid interest of £140 on a personal loan taken out on 6 April 2017 to purchase a computer for sole use in her employment with Downtown plc.

(6)   Each tax year since 6 April 2010 (including the tax year 2017/18), Downtown plc has contributed £25,000 into the company's HM Revenue and Customs' registered money purchase occupational pension scheme on Petula's behalf. Petula has never personally made any pension contributions. Petula's adjusted income for 2016/17 was below £150,000.

(7)   Petula owns a freehold house which was let out furnished throughout the tax year 2017/18. The total amount of rent received during the tax year was £12,000.

During August 2017, Petula purchased a new washer-dryer for the property at a cost of £730. This was a replacement for an old washing machine which was scrapped, with nil proceeds. The cost of a similar washing machine would have been £420.

During November 2017, Petula purchased a new dishwasher for the property at a cost of £580. The property did not previously have a dishwasher.

The other expenditure on the property for the tax year 2017/18 amounted to £1,640, none of which is loan interest, and all of this is allowable.

(8)   During the tax year 2017/18, Petula rented out one furnished room of her main residence. During the year, she received rent of £8,900 and incurred allowable expenditure of £2,890 in respect of the room. Petula always uses the most favourable basis as regards the tax treatment of the furnished room.

(9)   On 1 July 2017, Petula purchased £250,000 (nominal value) of gilts paying interest at the rate of 3% for £300,000. Interest is paid half-yearly on 30 June and 31 December based on the nominal value. Petula sold the gilts on 31 October 2017 for £302,500 (including accrued interest).

Required

(a)   Calculate Petula's taxable income for the tax year 2017/18.

Note. Your computation should list all of the items referred to in notes (1) to (9), indicating with the use of zero (0) any items which are not taxable or deductible.   **(12 marks)**

(b)   Advise Petula of the total amount of her unused pension annual allowances which are available to carry forward to the tax year 2018/19.   **(3 marks)**

(Total = 15 marks)

Questions 119 to 157 cover chargeable gains for individuals, the subject of Chapters 13 to 16 of the BPP Study Text for Taxation (TX – UK).

MCQ bank – Chargeable gains for individuals 1   18 mins

119   Which **TWO** of the following are exempt assets for CGT purposes?

     (1)   Vintage Rolls Royce motor car worth £30,000
     (2)   Painting worth £20,000
     (3)   Shares held in an individual savings account
     (4)   Shop used by a sole trader in his business

     ○   1 and 2
     ○   1 and 3
     ○   2 and 4
     ○   2 and 3   **(2 marks)**

120   Trudy sold a house in November 2017. She had never lived in the house. Her chargeable gain on the sale was £25,300. Trudy has taxable income of £21,420 in the tax year 2017/18. The house does not qualify for entrepreneurs' relief.

     What is Trudy's capital gains tax liability for the tax year 2017/18 assuming that she has no other disposals in that year?

     ○   £2,712
     ○   £3,920
     ○   £5,876
     ○   £1,592   **(2 marks)**

121   Clive purchased a 10-acre plot of land in May 2010 for £80,000. In January 2018, Clive sold 3 of the acres for £36,000 with expenses of sale amounting to £1,000. The market value of the remaining 7 acres of land in January 2018 was £90,000.

     What is Clive's chargeable gain on the disposal of the three acres of land in the tax year 2017/18?

     ○   £12,600
     ○   £13,143
     ○   £11,000
     ○   £12,143   **(2 marks)**

122   James has the following gains and losses arising from disposals of chargeable assets:

Tax year	2015/16 £	2016/17 £	2017/18 £
Gains	2,000	4,000	13,900
Losses	(14,000)	(2,000)	(2,000)

     The allowable loss carried forward to 2018/19 will be:

     ○   £0
     ○   £2,000
     ○   £11,400
     ○   £100   **(2 marks)**

123   Ellen purchased an antique vase for £1,500. In October 2017 she sold the vase for £7,000.

What is Ellen's chargeable gain on the sale of the vase?

○   £0
○   £1,000
○   £1,667
○   £5,500   (2 marks)

(Total = 10 marks)

CBE style OTQ bank – Chargeable gains for individuals 2

36 mins

124   Harold bought a painting for £8,500. In December 2017 he sold the painting for £5,000.

What is Harold's allowable loss on the sale of the painting?

£	

(2 marks)

125   Angela purchased a house and lived in it for three years. The house was then unoccupied for five years because Angela went to work outside the UK. She then lived in the house for two years. Angela then went to live with her sister and the house was unoccupied for four years. Angela then lived in the house for the last one year of ownership.

How many years of Angela's 15-year period of ownership of the house will be exempt for the purposes of principal private residence relief?

Select...   ▼
14½ years
14 years
13½ years
15 years

(2 marks)

126   Sascha owned a factory which had always been used in her business. She sold the factory on 14 May 2017 and realised a gain of £60,000. On 12 August 2017, she purchased a 20-year lease on a warehouse using all the proceeds from the sale of the factory. A claim for relief for replacement of business assets was made. The warehouse will continue to be used in Sascha's trade until it is sold on 14 October 2027.

When will the deferred gain of £60,000 become chargeable to capital gains tax?

○   12 August 2017
○   14 May 2027
○   12 August 2027
○   14 October 2027   (2 marks)

127 Louise has two chargeable gains from the disposal of shares in the tax year 2017/18:

£8,000 – claim made for entrepreneurs' relief

£13,100 – claim not made for entrepreneurs' relief

Louise has taxable income of £34,000 in the tax year 2017/18.

What is Louise's capital gains tax liability for the tax year 2017/18?

£ [   ]   **(2 marks)**

---

128 Neil bought 1,000 shares in G plc for £1,500 in October 2004. In November 2006, there was a 1 for 2 bonus issue when the shares had a market value of £2.40 each. In July 2011, there was a 3 for 1 rights issue when the shares had a market value of £3 but were offered to existing shareholders for £2.70 each. Neil took up his full entitlement to shares under the rights issue. Neil sold all of his shares in G plc in February 2018.

What is the cost of the shares sold in February 2018?

£ [   ]   **(2 marks)**

---

129 On 10 January 2018, a freehold property owned by Winifred was damaged by a fire. The property had been purchased on 29 May 2003 for £73,000. Winifred received insurance proceeds of £37,200 on 23 February 2018, and she spent a total of £41,700 during March 2018 restoring the property. Winifred has elected to disregard the part disposal.

What is the base cost of the restored freehold property for capital gains tax purposes?

O   £68,500
O   £77,500
O   £114,700
O   £35,800   **(2 marks)**

---

130 On 31 March 2018, Jessica sold a copyright for £28,800. The copyright had been purchased on 1 April 2012 for £21,000 when it had an unexpired life of 15 years.

What is Jessica's chargeable gain in respect of the disposal of the copyright?

O   £0
O   £20,400
O   £16,200
O   £7,800   **(2 marks)**

---

131 For the tax year 2017/18, Nog has a chargeable gain of £23,800 and a capital loss of £10,400. She has unused capital losses of £6,100 brought forward from the tax year 2016/17.

What amount of capital losses can Nog carry forward to the tax year 2018/19?

£ [   ]   **(2 marks)**

---

132 Alice is in business as a sole trader. On 13 May 2017, she sold a freehold warehouse for £184,000, and this resulted in a chargeable gain of £38,600. Alice purchased a replacement freehold warehouse on 20 May 2017 for £143,000. Where possible, Alice always makes a claim to roll over gains against the cost of replacement assets. Both buildings have been, or will be, used for business purposes by Alice.

What is the base cost of the replacement warehouse for capital gains tax purposes?

£ [   ]   **(2 marks)**

133   Larry is a sole trader who made a disposal of a factory on 31 July 2017.

Match the earliest date and the latest date that Larry can make an acquisition of a new qualifying business asset and claim replacement of business asset (rollover) relief.

1 August 2014		31 July 2018
1 August 2016		31 July 2020

Earliest date	

Latest date		(2 marks)

(Total = 20 marks)

CBE style OT case – Nim (06/09) (amended)   18 mins

This objective test question contains question types which will only appear in a computer-based exam, but this question provides valuable practice for all students whichever version of the exam they are taking.

The following scenario relates to Questions 134 to 138.

Nim disposed of the following assets during the tax year 2017/18:

(1)   On 20 July 2017 Nim made a gift of 10,000 £1 ordinary shares in Kapook plc to his daughter. On that date the shares were quoted on the stock exchange at £3.70–£3.80. Nim has made the following purchases of shares in Kapook plc:

19 February 2004	8,000 shares for £16,200
6 June 2009	1 for 2 rights issue at £3.65 per share
24 July 2017	2,000 shares for £5,800

Nim's total shareholding was less than 5% of Kapook plc, and so holdover relief is not available.

(2)   On 13 August 2017 Nim transferred his entire shareholding of 5,000 £1 ordinary shares in Jooba Ltd, an unquoted company, to his wife. On that date the shares were valued at £28,200. Nim's shareholding had been purchased on 11 January 2010 for £16,000.

(3)   On 26 November 2017 Nim sold an antique table for net proceeds of £8,700 after deducting the sale costs of £300. The antique table had been purchased for £5,200.

Other information

Nim has unused capital losses of £15,800 brought forward from the tax year 2016/17.

134   What are the deemed proceeds of the shares in Kapook plc sold on 20 July 2017?

○   £37,000
○   £37,250
○   £37,500
○   £38,000   (2 marks)

135   What is the total cost of the shares in Kapook plc sold on 20 July 2017?

○   £26,333
○   £28,500
○   £25,667
○   £20,533   (2 marks)

136 Which **TWO** of the following statements about capital gains tax for Nim and his wife are correct?

☐ Nim's wife will take the Jooba Ltd shares at market value at the date of the transfer.

☐ Nim will have deemed proceeds on the transfer of the Jooba Ltd shares to his wife so that neither a gain nor a loss will arise.

☐ The transfer of the Jooba Ltd shares is exempt from capital gains tax because it is between spouses.

☐ Nim's wife will not be able to transfer her annual exempt amount to Nim. **(2 marks)**

137 What is the gain on the sale of the antique table on 26 November 2017?

Select... ▼
£4,500
£5,000
£3,500
£800

(2 marks)

138 Assuming that Nim had chargeable gains of £20,000 in the tax year 2017/18, what is the amount of the loss brought forward from 2016/17 which will be carried forward to 2018/19?

£ [   ] **(2 marks)**

(Total = 10 marks)

Aloi, Bon and Dinah (06/11) (amended)   18 mins

The following scenario relates to Questions 139 to 143.

On 15 October 2017 Alphabet Ltd, an unquoted trading company, was taken over by XYZ plc. Prior to the takeover Alphabet Ltd's share capital consisted of 100,000 £1 ordinary shares, and under the terms of the takeover the shareholders received for each £1 ordinary share in Alphabet Ltd either cash of £6 per share or one £1 ordinary share in XYZ plc worth £6.50. The following information is available regarding three of the shareholders of Alphabet Ltd:

Aloi

Aloi has been the managing director of Alphabet Ltd since the company's incorporation on 1 January 2011, and she accepted XYZ plc's cash alternative of £6 per share in respect of her shareholding of 60,000 £1 ordinary shares in Alphabet Ltd. Aloi had originally subscribed for 50,000 shares in Alphabet Ltd on 1 January 2011 at their par value, and purchased a further 10,000 shares on 20 May 2012 for £18,600.

On 6 February 2018 Aloi sold an investment property, and this disposal resulted in a chargeable gain against which her annual exempt amount will be set.

For the tax year 2017/18 Aloi has taxable income of £60,000. All her income tax has previously been collected under PAYE so she has not received a notice to file a return for the tax year 2017/18 and so is required to give notice of her chargeability to capital gains tax to HMRC.

Bon

Bon has been the sales director of Alphabet Ltd since 1 February 2017, having not previously been an employee of the company, although she had been a shareholder since 1 March 2016. She accepted XYZ plc's share alternative of one £1 ordinary share for each of her 25,000 £1 ordinary shares in Alphabet Ltd. Bon had purchased her shareholding on 1 March 2016 for £92,200.

On 4 March 2018 Bon made a gift of 10,000 of her £1 ordinary shares in XYZ plc to her brother. On that date the shares were quoted on the stock exchange at £7.10 – £7.14. Holdover (gift) relief is not available in respect of this disposal.

Dinah

Dinah has been an employee of Alphabet Ltd since 1 May 2016. She accepted XYZ plc's share alternative of one £1 ordinary share for each of her 3,000 £1 ordinary shares in Alphabet Ltd. Dinah had purchased her shareholding on 20 June 2015 for £4,800.

On 13 November 2017 Dinah sold 1,000 of her £1 ordinary shares in XYZ plc for £6,600.

Dinah died on 5 April 2018, and her remaining 2,000 £1 ordinary shares in XYZ plc were inherited by her daughter. On that date these shares were valued at £15,600.

For the tax year 2017/18 Dinah had taxable income of £12,000.

139   Which **TWO** of the following statements are correct about Bon and Dinah's entitlement to entrepreneurs' relief on their disposals of shares in Alphabet Ltd?

   (1)   Alphabet Ltd was not Bon's personal company for the requisite time before disposal.
   (2)   Bon was not an officer or employee of Alphabet Ltd for the requisite time before disposal.
   (3)   Dinah was not an officer or employee of Alphabet Ltd for the requisite time before disposal.
   (4)   Alphabet Ltd was not Dinah's personal company for the requisite time before disposal.

   ○   1 and 3
   ○   2 and 3
   ○   1 and 4
   ○   2 and 4   (2 marks)

140   What is Aloi's capital gains tax liability on the disposal of her shares in Alphabet Ltd assuming that the gain qualifies for entrepreneurs' relief?

   ○   £31,000
   ○   £52,452
   ○   £29,140
   ○   £81,592   (2 marks)

141   What are the latest dates by which Aloi must:

   (1)   Give notice of her chargeability to capital gains tax for the tax year 2017/18 to HMRC?
   (2)   Pay her capital gains liability for the tax year 2017/18 in order to avoid interest and penalties?

	Notification	*Payment*
○	5 October 2018	31 January 2019
○	31 December 2018	31 January 2019
○	5 October 2018	31 July 2019
○	31 December 2018	31 July 2019

                                                                                                  (2 marks)

142   What is the chargeable gain arising on Bon's gift of her shares in XYZ plc to her brother?

   ○   £34,320
   ○   £6,200
   ○   £34,220
   ○   £61,200   (2 marks)

143   What is Dinah's capital gains tax liability for the tax year 2017/18?

   ○   £630
   ○   £0
   ○   £900
   ○   £1,098   (2 marks)

                                                                               (Total = 10 marks)

CBE style OT case – Ginger, Innocent and Nigel (06/13) (amended)

18 mins

This objective test question contains question types which will only appear in a computer-based exam, but this question provides valuable practice for all students whichever version of the exam they are taking.

The following scenario relates to Questions 144 to 148.

You should assume that today's date is 1 March 2018.

Ginger

Ginger has a holding of 10,000 £1 ordinary shares in Nutmeg Ltd, an unquoted trading company, which she had purchased on 13 February 2005 for £2.40 per share. The current market value of the shares is £6.40 per share, but Ginger intends to sell some of the holding to her daughter at £4.00 per share during March 2018. Ginger and her daughter will elect to hold over any gain as a gift of a business asset.

For the tax year 2017/18, Ginger will not make any other disposals, and has therefore not utilised her annual exempt amount. She has a loss brought forward from 2016/17 of £(1,800).

Innocent and Nigel

Innocent and Nigel, a married couple, both have shareholdings in Cinnamon Ltd, an unquoted trading company with a share capital of 100,000 £1 ordinary shares.

Innocent has been the managing director of Cinnamon Ltd since the company's incorporation on 1 July 2007, and she currently holds 20,000 shares (with matching voting rights) in the company. These shares were subscribed for on 1 July 2007 at their par value.

Nigel has never been an employee or a director of Cinnamon Ltd, and he currently holds 3,000 shares (with matching voting rights) in the company. These shares were purchased on 23 April 2011 for £46,200.

Either Innocent or Nigel will sell 2,000 of their shares in Cinnamon Ltd during March 2018 for £65,000, but are not sure which of them should make the disposal. For the tax year 2017/18, both Innocent and Nigel have already made disposals which will fully utilise their annual exempt amounts, and they will each have taxable income of £80,000.

144   What is the chargeable gain per share that Ginger will make on her disposal of shares in Nutmeg Ltd to her daughter?

    O   £4.00
    O   £1.60
    O   £2.40
    O   £0

                                                       (2 marks)

145   If the chargeable gain per share on Ginger's disposal of shares in Nutmeg Ltd had been £1.54 per share, what would be the maximum number of shares that Ginger could have sold to her daughter without incurring a charge to capital gains tax?

    O   2,046
    O   7,207
    O   8,506
    O   3,275

                                                       (2 marks)

146   Which **TWO** of the following statements about entrepreneurs' relief are correct?

    ☐   Entrepreneurs' relief is only available on shareholdings owned by a director.

    ☐   There is a lifetime limit of £10,000,000 for entrepreneurs' relief.

    ☐   Entrepreneurs' relief is only available on shareholdings if they are held in a trading company.

    ☐   The conditions for entrepreneurs' relief in relation to a shareholding must be satisfied for five years before the disposal.   **(2 marks)**

147 What would Innocent's capital gains tax liability be if she sold her shares in Cinnamon Ltd during March 2018?

£ [   ]

(2 marks)

148 What would Nigel's capital gains tax liability be if he sold his shares in Cinnamon Ltd during March 2018?

£ [   ]

(2 marks)

(Total = 10 marks)

CBE style OT case – Jerome (Mar/Jun 16) (amended)   18 mins

This objective test question contains question types which will only appear in a computer-based exam, but this question provides valuable practice for all students whichever version of the exam they are taking.

The following scenario relates to Questions 149 to 153.

Jerome made the following disposals of assets to family members during the tax year 2017/18:

(1)   On 28 May 2017, Jerome sold a house to his wife for £140,000. The value of the house at that date was £187,000. Jerome's uncle had originally purchased the house on 14 July 1995 for £45,900. The uncle died on 12 June 2004, and the house was inherited by Jerome. On that date, the house was valued at £112,800. Jerome has never occupied the house as his main residence.

(2)   On 24 June 2017, Jerome made a gift of his entire 12% holding of 12,000 £1 ordinary shares in Reward Ltd, an unquoted trading company, to his son. The market value of the shares on that date was £98,400. The shares had been purchased on 15 March 2006 for £39,000. On 24 June 2017, the market value of Reward Ltd's chargeable assets was £540,000, of which £460,000 was in respect of chargeable business assets. Jerome and his son will elect to hold over the gain on this gift of a business asset.

(3)   On 7 November 2017, Jerome made a gift of an antique bracelet valued at £12,200 to his granddaughter. The antique bracelet had been purchased on 1 September 2001 for £2,100.

(4)   On 29 January 2018, Jerome made a gift of 9 acres of land valued at £78,400 to his brother. He had originally purchased 10 acres of land on 3 November 2005 for £37,800. The market value of the unsold acre of land as at 29 January 2018 was £33,600. The land has never been used for business purposes.

149 What is the base cost of the house for capital gains tax purposes for Jerome's wife?

- ○ £45,900
- ○ £187,000
- ○ £112,800
- ○ £140,000

(2 marks)

150 What is the amount of hold over relief that can be claimed on the gift of the Reward Ltd shares?

£ [   ]

(2 marks)

151   Match the latest date for submission of the election to hold over the gain on the gift of the Reward Ltd shares and person(s) who must make the election.

31 January 2019		Jerome

5 April 2022		Jerome and his son

Latest date for election	

Person(s) making election		**(2 marks)**

152   What is the amount of the chargeable gain on the disposal of the antique bracelet?

Select... ▼
£10,100
£3,900
£10,333
£10,000

(2 marks)

153   What is the amount of the chargeable gain on the disposal of the nine acres of land?

    O   £66,200
    O   £40,600
    O   £44,380
    O   £51,940   **(2 marks)**

(Total = 10 marks)

154 Jorge (12/11) (amended)   **18 mins**

Jorge disposed of the following assets during the tax year 2017/18:

(1)   On 30 June 2017 Jorge sold a house for £308,000. The house had been purchased on 1 January 2000 for £93,000. On 10 June 2006, Jorge had incurred legal fees of £5,000 in relation to a boundary dispute with his neighbour. Throughout the 210 months of ownership the house had been occupied by Jorge as follows:

Months
34	Occupied
18	Unoccupied – Travelling overseas
24	Unoccupied – Required to work overseas by his employer
11	Occupied
30	Unoccupied – Required to work elsewhere in the United Kingdom by his employer
22	Unoccupied – Travelling overseas
26	Unoccupied – Required to work elsewhere in the United Kingdom by his employer
17	Occupied
12	Unoccupied – Required to work overseas by his employer
13	Unoccupied – Travelling overseas
3	Unoccupied – Lived with sister
210	

Jorge let the house out during all of the periods when he did not occupy it personally. Throughout the period 1 January 2000 to 30 June 2017 Jorge did not have any other main residence.

(2) On 30 September 2017 Jorge sold a copyright for £80,300. The copyright had been purchased on 1 October 2015 for £70,000 when it had an unexpired life of 10 years.

(3) On 6 October 2017 Jorge sold a painting for £5,400. The painting had been purchased on 18 May 2012 for £2,200.

(4) On 29 October 2017 Jorge sold a motor car for £10,700. The motor car had been purchased on 21 December 2014 for £14,600.

Required

Calculate Jorge's taxable gains for the tax year 2017/18. **(10 marks)**

(Total = 10 marks)

155 Winston (06/12) (amended) 18 mins

(a) On 19 May 2017 Winston disposed of a painting, and this resulted in a chargeable gain of £46,560. For the tax year 2017/18 Winston has taxable income of £20,900 after the deduction of the personal allowance.

Winston is considering the sale of a business that he has run as a sole trader since 1 July 2008. The business will be sold for £260,000, and this figure, along with the respective cost of each asset, is made up as follows:

	Sale proceeds £	Cost £
Freehold shop	140,000	80,000
Freehold warehouse	88,000	102,000
Net current assets	32,000	32,000
	260,000	

The freehold warehouse has never been used by Winston for business purposes.

Required

(i) Assuming that Winston does not sell his sole trader business, calculate his capital gains tax liability for the tax year 2017/18. **(3 marks)**

(ii) Calculate Winston's capital gains tax liability for the tax year 2017/18 if he sold his sole trader business on 25 March 2018. **(4 marks)**

(b) On 3 December 2017 Renaldo sold two acres of land at auction for gross proceeds of £92,000. The auctioneers' commission was 5% of the sale price.

Renaldo's wife's father had originally purchased three acres of land on 4 August 2002 for £19,500. He died on 17 June 2009, and the land was inherited by Renaldo's wife. On that date the three acres of land were valued at £28,600.

Renaldo's wife transferred the land to Renaldo on 14 November 2012. On that date the three acres of land were valued at £39,000. The market value of the unsold acre of land as at 3 December 2017 was £38,000.

Required

Compute Renaldo's chargeable gain in respect of the disposal on 3 December 2017. **(3 marks)**

(Total = 10 marks)

156 Mick (06/14) (amended)

18 mins

Mick disposed of the following assets during the tax year 2017/18:

(1)   On 19 May 2017, Mick sold a freehold warehouse for £522,000. The warehouse was purchased on 6 August 2003 for £258,000, and was extended at a cost of £99,000 during April 2005. In January 2009, the floor of the warehouse was damaged by flooding and had to be replaced at a cost of £63,000. The warehouse was sold because it was surplus to the business's requirements as a result of Mick purchasing a newly built warehouse during 2016. Both warehouses have always been used for business purposes in a wholesale business run by Mick as a sole trader.

(2)   On 24 September 2017, Mick sold 700,000 £1 ordinary shares in Rolling Ltd, an unquoted trading company, for £3,675,000. He had originally purchased 500,000 shares in Rolling Ltd on 2 June 2007 for £960,000. On 1 December 2012, Rolling Ltd made a 3 for 2 bonus issue. Mick has been a director of Rolling Ltd since 1 January 2007.

Required

(a)   Assuming that no reliefs are available, calculate the chargeable gain arising from each of Mick's asset disposals during the tax year 2017/18.

Note. You are not required to calculate the taxable gains or the amount of tax payable.   **(4 marks)**

(b)   State which capital gains tax reliefs might be available to Mick in respect of each of his disposals during the tax year 2017/18, and what further information you would require in order to establish if the reliefs are actually available and to establish any restrictions as regards the amount of relief.

Note. For this part of the question you are not expected to perform any calculations.   **(6 marks)**

(Total = 10 marks)

157 Ruby (Sep/Dec 15)

18 mins

You should assume that today's date is 1 March 2018.

(a)   On 27 August 2017, Ruby disposed of a residential investment property and this resulted in a chargeable gain of £46,000.

For the tax year 2017/18 Ruby has taxable income of £19,315.

Required

Calculate Ruby's capital gains tax liability for the tax year 2017/18 if this is her only disposal in that tax year.

(2 marks)

(b)   In addition to the disposal already made on 27 August 2017, Ruby is going to make one further disposal during the tax year 2017/18. The disposal will be of either Ruby's holding of £1 ordinary shares in Pola Ltd, or her holding of 50p ordinary shares in Aplo plc.

Shareholding in Pola Ltd

Pola Ltd is an unquoted trading company in which Ruby has a 10% shareholding. The shareholding was purchased on 14 July 2008 for £23,700 and could be sold for £61,000. Ruby has been an employee of Pola Ltd since 2006.

Shareholding in Aplo plc

Aplo plc is a quoted trading company in which Ruby has a shareholding of 40,000 50p ordinary shares. Ruby received the shareholding as a gift from her father on 27 May 2011. On that date, the shares were quoted on the stock exchange at £2.12–£2.18. The shareholding could be sold for £59,000.

Neither entrepreneurs' relief nor holdover relief is available in respect of this disposal.

Required

Calculate Ruby's revised capital gains tax liability for the tax year 2017/18, if she also disposes of either (1) her shareholding in Pola Ltd; or alternatively (2) her shareholding in Aplo plc.

Note. The following mark allocation is provided as guidance for this requirement:

Pola Ltd (4½ marks)

Aplo plc (3½ marks)   **(8 marks)**

(Total = 10 marks)

PART D INHERITANCE TAX

Questions 158 to 197 cover inheritance tax, the subject of Chapter 18 of the BPP Study Text for Taxation (TX – UK).

MCQ bank – Inheritance tax 1
18 mins

158 Gillian owned a 70% shareholding in R Ltd, an unquoted investment company. On 23 July 2017, she gave a 20% shareholding in R Ltd to her son. The values of shareholdings in R Ltd on 23 July 2017 were as follows:

	£
100% shareholding	600,000
70% shareholding	350,000
50% shareholding	200,000
20% shareholding	80,000

What is the diminution in value of Gillian's estate as a result of her gift on 23 July 2017?

○ £150,000
○ £270,000
○ £80,000
○ £120,000
(2 marks)

159 Joel and Sunita were a married couple. Sunita died in July 2008 and 65% of her nil rate band of £312,000 (2008/09) was unused. Joel died in May 2017. He had made a potentially exempt transfer (after all available exemptions) of £75,000 in August 2013. Joel left his estate to his sister. Any relevant elections were made.

What is the nil rate band available to set against Joel's death estate?

○ £325,000
○ £452,800
○ £461,250
○ £536,250
(2 marks)

160 On 7 July 2012, Paul made a gross chargeable transfer (after all exemptions) of £260,000. On 19 December 2017 he gave £190,000 to a trust. Paul agreed to pay any lifetime inheritance tax (IHT) due.

How much IHT will be payable by Paul on the December 2017 transfer of value?

○ £28,250
○ £31,250
○ £29,750
○ £23,800
(2 marks)

161 Donald made the following transactions in the tax year 2017/18:

(1) A gift of £2,000 to his granddaughter on the occasion of her marriage.

(2) A sale of a vase to his friend, Alan, for £1,000 which both Donald and Alan believed to be the market value of the vase. The vase was later valued by an auction house as worth £20,000 at the date of the sale.

Ignoring the annual exemption, what is the total value of potentially exempt transfers made by Donald as a result of these gifts?

○ £21,000
○ £0
○ £2,000
○ £19,000
(2 marks)

162   Kirstin gave shares worth £150,000 to a trust on 15 September 2008 and shares worth £600,000 to her brother on 10 July 2014. The nil rate band in 2008/09 was £312,000 and in 2014/15 it was £325,000. Kirstin died on 23 October 2017.

Ignoring the annual exemption, what is the inheritance tax payable on Kirstin's death in relation to her lifetime transfers?

○   £170,000
○   £88,000
○   £136,000
○   £134,080   (2 marks)

(Total = 10 marks)

CBE style OTQ bank – Inheritance tax 2   36 mins

163   Mary made the following gifts in the tax year 2017/18:

(1)   £1,000 on the first day of each month for nine months to her grandson to pay university living expenses. Mary used income surplus to her living requirements to make these payments.

(2)   £100 to her grandnephew on his birthday and a further £250 to the same grandnephew as a Christmas gift.

Ignoring the annual exemption, what is the total value of potentially exempt transfers made by Mary as a result of these gifts?

○   £9,350
○   £100
○   £9,000
○   £350   (2 marks)

164   Daniel owned all 1,000 shares in Q Ltd, an unquoted investment company. On 10 October 2017, Daniel gave 300 of his shares in Q Ltd to his daughter. The values of the shares on 10 October 2017 were as follows:

% shareholding	Value per share
	£
76–100	150
51–75	120
26–50	90
1–25	30

What is the diminution in value of Daniel's estate as a result of his gift on 10 October 2017?

Select...   ▼
£123,000
£27,000
£66,000
£18,000

(2 marks)

165 Susanna died on 19 November 2017. Her estate consisted of her main residence worth £300,000 (on which there was secured a repayment mortgage of £220,000) and investments and cash totalling £385,000. Susanna left her estate equally to her son and daughter. She was divorced from her husband. Susanna had not made any lifetime transfers of value.

How much inheritance tax will be payable on Susanna's estate?

£ [   ]   (2 marks)

166 Rodney died on 13 August 2017. In his will he left £200 in cash to each of his five nephews, investments held in ISAs valued at £350,000 to his daughter, and the residue of his estate, which amounted to £520,000, to his wife.

What is the chargeable estate for inheritance tax purposes?

£ [   ]   (2 marks)

167 Ruth made a chargeable lifetime transfer of £750,000 on 18 June 2017. Ruth died on 10 July 2017.

Match the dates by which the lifetime inheritance tax and the inheritance tax arising as a result of Ruth's death will be paid.

31 December 2017		31 January 2018

30 April 2018		30 April 2018

Lifetime tax	

| Death tax | | (2 marks)
|---|---|

168 Benjamin died on 30 November 2017 leaving an estate valued at £890,000. Inheritance tax of £276,000 was paid in respect of the estate. Under the terms of his will, Benjamin left £260,000 to his wife, a specific legacy of £120,000 (free of tax) to his brother, and the residue of the estate to his grandchildren.

What is the amount of inheritance received by Benjamin's grandchildren?

Select...   ▼
£614,000
£510,000
£354,000
£234,000

(2 marks)

169   Heng is a wealthy 45 year old who would like to reduce the potential inheritance tax liability on her estate when she dies.

Which of the following actions will or will not achieve Heng's aim of reducing the potential inheritance tax liability on her estate when she dies?

Changing the terms of her will so that the residue of her estate goes to her grandchildren rather than her children	WILL ACHIEVE	WILL NOT ACHIEVE
Making lifetime gifts to trusts up to the value of the nil rate band every seven years	WILL ACHIEVE	WILL NOT ACHIEVE
Changing the terms of her will so that the residue of her estate goes to her husband rather than her children	WILL ACHIEVE	WILL NOT ACHIEVE
Making lifetime gifts to her grandchildren early in life	WILL ACHIEVE	WILL NOT ACHIEVE

(2 marks)

170   Chan died on 8 December 2017, having made a lifetime cash gift of £500,000 to a trust on 16 October 2016. Chan paid the inheritance tax arising from this gift.

Match the due date payment of the additional inheritance tax arising from the gift made to the trustees and the persons who are responsible for paying this tax.

8 June 2018	30 June 2018

The trustees	The personal representatives of Chan's estate

Due date	

Persons responsible	

(2 marks)

171   Nadia died on 6 December 2017. Her death estate included her main residence which was valued at £350,000 on which there was secured an outstanding repayment mortgage of £180,000. Nadia will leave her entire estate to her three children.

Nadia is a widow. Her husband died in 2009 leaving his entire estate to Nadia.

What amount of residence nil rate band will be available in computing inheritance tax on Nadia's death estate?

O   £100,000
O   £170,000
O   £200,000
O   £350,000

172   Rachel is aged 85 and in poor health. She is keen to minimise the inheritance tax due on her death estate
       which is likely to have a value of about £1.2 million. Her will currently leaves her main residence (valued at
       £300,000) to her brother and the residue of her estate to her son. Rachel has never been married.

       Complete the following sentence by matching the correct response in each space.

       The inheritance tax liability on Rachel's estate will [   ] by [   ] if she leaves her

       main residence to her son rather than her brother.

increase	decrease
£40,000	£100,000

(Total = 20 marks)

Ning (06/12) (amended)   18 mins

The following scenario relates to Questions 173 to 177.

You should assume that today's date is 19 March 2018.

Ning owns the following assets:

(1)   Two investment properties respectively valued at £674,000 and £442,000. The first property has an
       outstanding repayment mortgage of £160,000, and the second property has an outstanding endowment
       mortgage of £92,000.

(2)   Vintage motor cars valued at £172,000.

(3)   Investments in Individual Savings Accounts valued at £47,000, National Savings & Investments savings
       certificates valued at £36,000, and government stocks (gilts) valued at £69,000.

Ning owes £22,400 in respect of a personal loan from a bank, and she has also verbally promised to pay legal fees
of £4,600 incurred by her nephew. Her reasonable funeral expenses will amount to £5,500.

Ning's husband died on 12 March 2007, and 70% of his inheritance tax nil rate band was not used.

On 14 August 2006 Ning had made a gift of £90,000 to her daughter, and on 7 November 2016 she made a gift of
her main residence, worth £220,000, to her son. These amounts are after taking account of any available
exemptions.

The nil rate band for the tax year 2006/07 is £285,000.

173   What is the net value for the two properties in (1) which will be included in the calculation of Ning's
       chargeable estate were she to die on 20 March 2018?

       ○   £1,024,000
       ○   £956,000
       ○   £856,000
       ○   £864,000   **(2 marks)**

174   What is the value of the assets in (2) and (3) which will be included in the calculation of Ning's chargeable
       estate were she to die on 20 March 2018?

       ○   £172,000
       ○   £0
       ○   £324,000
       ○   £152,000   **(2 marks)**

175 What is the total amount of deductions (ignoring mortgage debts) which will be taken into account in the calculation of Ning's chargeable estate were she to die on 20 March 2018?

    ○   £5,500
    ○   £32,500
    ○   £10,100
    ○   £27,900   **(2 marks)**

176 What is the amount of Ning's own nil rate band for calculating the inheritance tax payable in respect of her estate were she to die on 20 March 2018?

    ○   £325,000
    ○   £105,000
    ○   £15,000
    ○   £205,000   **(2 marks)**

177 What is the amount of Ning's husband's nil rate band that Ning's personal representatives could claim were she to die on 20 March 2018 and by when should the claim be made?

	Amount	Claim
○	£227,500	By 31 March 2020
○	£227,500	By 30 September 2018
○	£199,500	By 31 March 2020
○	£199,500	By 30 September 2018

          (2 marks)

          (Total = 10 marks)

CBE style OT case – Jimmy (06/11) (amended)   **18 mins**

This objective test question contains question types which will only appear in a computer-based exam, but this question provides valuable practice for all students whichever version of the exam they are taking.

The following scenario relates to Questions 178 to 182.

Jimmy died on 14 February 2018. He had used up his nil rate band at the date of his death by making the following gifts during his lifetime:

(1) On 2 August 2016 Jimmy made a cash gift to his grandson as a wedding gift when he got married.

(2) On 9 September 2016 Jimmy gave 200 shares valued at £5 each in J Ltd, an unquoted investment company, to his daughter. Before the gift, Jimmy owned 5,100 shares valued at £30 each in J Ltd. After the gift Jimmy owned 4,900 shares valued at £20 each in J Ltd.

(3) On 14 November 2016 Jimmy made a cash gift of £800,000 to a trust. Jimmy paid the inheritance tax arising from this gift. Additional inheritance tax was payable on this transfer as a result of Jimmy's death.

At the date of his death Jimmy owned assets valued at £980,000. He did not own a main residence at his death. Under the terms of his will Jimmy left £200,000 to his wife and the residue of his estate to his son.

The nil rate band for the tax year 2016/17 was £325,000.

178 What was the total amount of the exemptions that were deducted in computing the potentially exempt transfer made on 2 August 2016?

    ○   £3,000
    ○   £8,500
    ○   £6,000
    ○   £11,000   **(2 marks)**

179 What is the diminution in value in Jimmy's estate as a result of his gift on 9 September 2016?

Select... ▼
£55,000
£4,000
£6,000
£1,000

(2 marks)

180 What was the amount of the inheritance tax paid by Jimmy as a result of his gift made on 14 November 2016?

£ [ ]

(2 marks)

181 Match the due date for payment of the additional inheritance tax on the gift made on 14 November 2015 as a result of Jimmy's death and by whom should it be paid.

| 14 August 2018 | | Trustees of trust |

| 31 August 2018 | | Executors of Jimmy's estate |

| Due date | |

| By whom paid | |

(2 marks)

182 What is the inheritance tax chargeable on Jimmy's death estate as a result of his death on 14 February 2018?

£ [ ]

(2 marks)

(Total = 10 marks)

CBE style OT case – Zoe and Luke (06/15) (amended)   18 mins

This objective test question contains question types which will only appear in a computer-based exam, but this question provides valuable practice for all students whichever version of the exam they are taking.

The following scenario relates to Questions 183 to 187.

Zoe and Luke are brother and sister who died within a few months of each other.

Zoe

Zoe died on 17 February 2018.

She had always used her annual exemption in April each year and had made the following additional gifts during her lifetime:

(1) On 21 March 2011, Zoe made a cash gift of £633,000 to a trust. Zoe paid the inheritance tax (IHT) arising from this gift. The nil rate band for the tax year 2010/11 is £325,000.

(2) On 17 August 2014, Zoe made a further cash gift of £200,000 to the trust. The trustees paid the IHT arising from the gift. The nil rate band for the tax year 2014/15 is £325,000.

Luke

Luke died on 10 October 2017. He was survived by two adult children, a son and a daughter. Luke's wife had died on 25 July 2008.

On 7 March 2016, Luke had made a cash gift of £270,000 to his daughter as a wedding gift when she got married.

Luke had also paid his son's university tuition fees in each of September 2015, 2016 and 2017, making the payments directly to the university. He was advised that these payments were exempt from inheritance tax under the normal expenditure out of income exemption.

On her death, Luke's wife had left £240,000 to their daughter and the remainder of her estate to Luke. She made no lifetime transfers. The nil rate band for the tax year 2008/09 was £312,000.

183   Which **TWO** of the following statements about Luke's payment of his son's university tuition fees are correct?

☐   The payments could be exempt without any cash limit under the normal expenditure out of income exemption.

☐   The payments could not be exempt under the normal expenditure out of income exemption because they were paid directly to the university and not to his son.

☐   The payments must have been reported each tax year to HM Revenue & Customs in Luke's income tax return to qualify for the normal expenditure out of income exemption.

☐   The payments must have left Luke with sufficient income to maintain his usual standard of living to qualify for the normal expenditure out of income exemption.   **(2 marks)**

184   What is the amount of the gross chargeable transfer made by Zoe on 21 March 2011?

○   £702,500
○   £710,000
○   £694,600
○   £756,200   **(2 marks)**

185   What is the additional IHT which will be payable, as a result of Zoe's death, in respect of the transfer made on 17 August 2014, assuming that the nil rate band has been completely used by the gross chargeable transfer made by Zoe on 21 March 2011?

Select...   ▼
£40,000
£80,000
£24,000
£64,000

(2 marks)

186   What is the value of the potentially exempt transfer made by Luke on 7 March 2016?

£ [   ]   **(2 marks)**

187   What is the amount of Luke's wife's nil rate band which could be transferred and used in calculating the IHT on Luke's death?

○   £75,000
○   £72,000
○   £312,000
○   £325,000   **(2 marks)**

(Total = 10 marks)

CBE style OT case – Marcus (Sep/Dec 15) (amended)   18 mins

This objective test question contains question types which will only appear in a computer-based exam, but this question provides valuable practice for all students whichever version of the exam they are taking.

The following scenario relates to Questions 188 to 192.

Marcus died on 10 March 2018. He had been married to his wife, Barbara, for many years. He had made the following gifts during his lifetime:

(1)   On 14 January 2008, Marcus made a chargeable lifetime transfer of £315,000 to a trust. The trustees paid the lifetime inheritance tax which arose in respect of this gift.

(2)   On 3 January 2015, Marcus made a chargeable lifetime transfer to another trust. In addition to the gift, Marcus paid the related lifetime inheritance tax on this gift. The gross chargeable lifetime transfer amounted to £491,250.

(3)   On 17 March 2015, Marcus made a gift (a potentially exempt transfer) of 30,000 £1 ordinary shares in Scarum Ltd, an unquoted investment company, to his daughter.

Before the transfer, Marcus owned all of Scarum Ltd's issued share capital of 100,000 £1 ordinary shares. On 17 March 2015, Scarum Ltd's shares were worth £5 each for a holding of 30%, £9 each for a holding of 70%, and £12 each for a holding of 100%.

(4)   On 29 June 2016, Marcus gave a plot of land worth £100,000 to Barbara. Marcus had bought the land in 2008 for £80,000.

The nil rate band for the tax year 2007/08 is £300,000, and for the tax year 2014/15 it is £325,000.

Under the terms of his will, Marcus left his entire estate to Barbara. Barbara has not made any gifts during her lifetime. She is intending to remarry.

Ignore the inheritance tax annual exemption.

188   What was the amount of the lifetime inheritance tax paid by the trustees (if any) as a result of the gift made on 14 January 2008?

£	

(2 marks)

189   What was the amount of the lifetime inheritance tax paid by Marcus as a result of the gift made on 3 January 2015?

- ○   £120,312
- ○   £33,250
- ○   £96,250
- ○   £41,562

(2 marks)

190   What was the amount of the taper relief deductible from the additional inheritance tax due as a result of the death of Marcus on the gift made on 3 January 2015?

Select...   ▼
£154,000
£38,500
£13,300
£53,200

(2 marks)

191　What was the amount of the potentially exempt transfer made by Marcus on 17 March 2015?

- ○　£360,000
- ○　£270,000
- ○　£150,000
- ○　£570,000　　　　　　　　　　　　　　　　　　　　　　　　　　　**(2 marks)**

192　Which **TWO** of the following statements about Marcus and Barbara for inheritance tax purposes are correct?

☐　There is no liability for inheritance tax on the transfer of Marcus's estate to Barbara because they are treated together as a single chargeable person for inheritance tax.

☐　If Barbara remarries, any unused nil rate band on her death can be transferred to her spouse if they survive her.

☐　The gift of the land on 29 June 2016 by Marcus to Barbara is a potentially exempt transfer of £80,000.

☐　The transfer of Marcus's estate to Barbara on his death is an exempt transfer.　　**(2 marks)**

(Total = 10 marks)

193 Pere and Phil (06/13) (amended)　　　　　　　　　**18 mins**

On 23 August 2011, Pere made a gift of a house valued at £420,000 to his son, Phil. This was a wedding gift when Phil got married. The nil rate band for the tax year 2011/12 is £325,000.

Pere

Pere died on 20 March 2018 at which time his estate was valued at £880,000. Under the terms of his will, Pere divided his estate equally, before inheritance tax, between his wife and his son, Phil. Pere had not made any gifts during his lifetime except for the gift of the house to Phil. Pere did not own a main residence.

Phil

Phil sold the house which he received as a wedding gift from Pere, his father, on 5 April 2018. The following information relates to the property:

	£
Net sale proceeds after costs of disposal	495,700
Cost of new boundary wall around the property (there was previously no boundary wall)	(5,200)
Cost of replacing the property's chimney	(2,800)

Phil has taxable income (after deduction of the personal allowance) of £9,950 in 2017/18. The house was never occupied by Phil.

Required

(a)　Calculate the inheritance tax that will be payable as a result of Pere's death.　　**(6 marks)**
(b)　Calculate Phil's capital gains tax liability for the tax year 2017/18.　　**(4 marks)**

(Total = 10 marks)

194 Afiya (12/13) (amended)　　　　　　　　　　　　　**18 mins**

Afiya died on 29 November 2017. She had made the following gifts during her lifetime:

(1)　On 14 September 2016, Afiya made a gift of 6,500 £1 ordinary shares in Cassava Ltd, an unquoted investment company, to her daughter.

Before the transfer Afiya owned 8,000 shares out of Cassava Ltd's issued share capital of 10,000 £1 ordinary shares. On 14 September 2016, Cassava Ltd's shares were worth £3 each for a holding of 15%, £7 each for a holding of 65%, and £8 each for a holding of 80%.

(2) On 27 January 2017, Afiya made a cash gift of £400,000 to a trust. Afiya paid the inheritance tax arising from this gift.

On 29 November 2017, Afiya's estate was valued at £623,000 including her main residence which was valued at £90,000. Her executors paid funeral expenses of £3,000 on 12 January 2018. Under the terms of her will Afiya left £150,000 cash to her husband, a specific legacy of £40,000 to her sister, and the residue of the estate to her children.

The nil rate band for the tax year 2016/17 is £325,000.

Required

(a) Calculate the inheritance tax which will be payable as a result of Afiya's death. **(9 marks)**
(b) Calculate the amount of the inheritance which will be received by Afiya's children. **(1 mark)**

(Total = 10 marks)

195 Kendra (06/14) (amended)   18 mins

You should assume that today's date is 1 January 2018.

Kendra, aged 93, is unfortunately in poor health with just a few months left to live. She has made no lifetime gifts.

Kendra owns the following assets:

(1) An investment property valued at £970,000. The property has never been occupied by Kendra, and if it were disposed of during the tax year 2017/18 the disposal would result in a chargeable gain of £174,000.

(2) Building society deposits of £387,000.

(3) Investments in Individual Savings Accounts (ISAs) valued at £39,000 and savings certificates from National Savings & Investments (NS&I) valued at £17,000.

(4) A life assurance policy on her own life. The policy has an open market value of £210,000, and proceeds of £225,000 will be received following Kendra's death.

None of the above valuations are expected to change in the near future. The cost of Kendra's funeral will be £12,800. She also has an outstanding unsecured loan of £1,200 which is due to be repaid on her death.

Under the terms of her will, Kendra has left her entire estate to her children.

The nil rate band of Kendra's husband was fully utilised when he died 10 years ago.

For the tax year 2017/18, Kendra will pay income tax at the higher rate.

Required

(a) Calculate the inheritance tax which would be payable if Kendra were to die on 31 March 2018. **(5 marks)**

(b) Advise Kendra why it would not be beneficial to make an immediate lifetime gift of the property valued at £970,000 to her children.

Notes

1 Your answer should take account of both the capital gains tax and the inheritance tax implications of making the gift.

2 For this part of the question you should ignore the capital gains tax annual exempt amount and inheritance tax annual exemptions. **(3 marks)**

(c) Advise Kendra why it might be beneficial for inheritance tax purposes to change the terms of her will so that part of her estate was instead left to her grandchildren rather than her children. **(2 marks)**

(Total = 10 marks)

196 James (Mar/Jun 16)

18 mins

James died on 22 January 2018. He had made the following gifts during his lifetime:

(1) On 9 October 2010, a cash gift of £35,000 to a trust. No lifetime inheritance tax was payable in respect of this gift.

(2) On 14 May 2016, a cash gift of £420,000 to his daughter.

(3) On 2 August 2016, a gift of a property valued at £260,000 to a trust. No lifetime inheritance tax was payable in respect of this gift because it was covered by the nil rate band. By the time of James's death on 22 January 2018, the property had increased in value to £310,000.

On 22 January 2018, James's estate was valued at £870,000. James did not own a main residence. Under the terms of his will, James left his entire estate to his children.

The nil rate band of James's wife was fully utilised when she died 10 years ago.

The nil rate band for the tax years 2010/11 and 2016/17 is £325,000.

Required

(a) Calculate the inheritance tax which will be payable as a result of James's death, and state who will be responsible for paying the tax. **(6 marks)**

(b) Explain why it might have been beneficial for inheritance tax purposes if James had left a portion of his estate to his grandchildren rather than to his children. **(2 marks)**

(c) Explain why it might be advantageous for inheritance tax purposes for a person to make lifetime gifts even when such gifts are made within seven years of death.

Notes

1 Your answer should include a calculation of James's inheritance tax saving from making the gift of property to the trust on 2 August 2016 rather than retaining the property until his death.

2 You are not expected to consider lifetime exemptions in this part of the question. **(2 marks)**

(Total = 10 marks)

197 Alan

18 mins

Assume that it is 1 December 2017.

Alan acquired quoted shares in Crimson plc in August 2011 at a cost of £375,000. He is now considering whether to give the shares to his daughter, Julie, in the near future or to retain the shares and give them to Julie under the terms of his will. You should assume that Alan will die on 1 April 2021 and that the inheritance tax nil rate band in 2020/21 will be £325,000.

Lifetime gift to Julie

Alan would give the shares to Julie on 10 December 2017 when they are expected to have a value of £450,000. Neither capital gains tax gift relief nor entrepreneurs' relief will be available on this disposal. Alan is a higher rate taxpayer and has no other chargeable assets.

Alan's only previous lifetime transfer was a gift to a trust in December 2013 which resulted in a gross chargeable transfer (after all exemptions) of £55,000.

Gift in will to Julie

Alan would give the shares to Julie on his death in his will when they are expected to have a value of £500,000.

Alan's other assets in his estate would be reduced to a value of nil by his debts so that the gift to Julie would be the only chargeable transfer on his death.

Required

(a) (i) Calculate the capital gains tax payable if the shares in Crimson plc are gifted on 10 December 2017.

(2 marks)

(ii) Calculate the inheritance tax payable if the shares in Crimson plc are gifted on 10 December 2017 and Alan dies on 1 April 2021. **(4 marks)**

(b) (i) State the capital gains tax implications of Alan's death in relation to his shareholding in Crimson plc if he retains the shares until his death. **(1 mark)**

(ii) Calculate the inheritance tax payable if Alan dies on 1 April 2021 and the shares in Crimson plc are left in his will to Julie. **(2 marks)**

(c) Based on your answers in parts (a) and (b), advise Alan whether it would be more tax advantageous to gift the shares in Crimson plc to Julie on 10 December 2017 or to retain them until his death on 1 April 2021 and pass them to Julie in his will. **(1 mark)**

(Total = 10 marks)

PART E CORPORATION TAX LIABILITIES

Questions 198 to 238 cover corporation tax liabilities, the subject of Chapters 19 to 23 of the BPP Study Text for Taxation (TX – UK).

CBE style OTQ bank – Corporation tax liabilities   36 mins

198   Jet Ltd has deducted some items in its statement of profit or loss for the year ended 31 December 2017.

Identify, by clicking on the relevant boxes in the table below, whether each of the following items of expenditure are allowable or not allowable for computing Jet Ltd's taxable trading profit.

Legal expenses relating to the acquisition of a new 40-year lease on its factory	ALLOWABLE	NOT ALLOWABLE
Cost of arranging a new bank loan to purchase machinery for trade	ALLOWABLE	NOT ALLOWABLE
Write off of an irrecoverable loan to a former employee	ALLOWABLE	NOT ALLOWABLE
Donation to local charity with mention of Jet Ltd's support in programme for fundraising concert (not a qualifying charitable donation)	ALLOWABLE	NOT ALLOWABLE

(2 marks)

199   Rat Ltd started trading on 1 December 2016 and prepared its first set of accounts to 31 March 2018.

What will Rat Ltd's accounting periods be for the period of account to 31 March 2018?

- ○   4 months to 31 March 2017, 12 months to 31 March 2018
- ○   4 months to 5 April 2017, nearly 12 months to 31 March 2018
- ○   12 months to 30 November 2017, 4 months to 31 March 2018
- ○   16 months to 31 March 2018   (2 marks)

200   Xeon Ltd has included a deduction in its accounting profit of £3,200 in respect of the annual leasing cost for a car, which has a recommended list price of £16,000 and CO_2 emissions of 140 g/km. The lease of the car started on 1 April 2017 and the car has been used for the whole of the 12-month period ended 31 March 2018.

When preparing the adjusted profit for tax purposes what is the allowable deduction in respect of the leasing cost in the year ended 31 March 2018?

£ [   ]   (2 marks)

201 Kit Ltd was incorporated and started trading on 1 July 2017 and prepared its first set of accounts to 31 December 2017. During the six-month accounting period to 31 December 2017, it purchased two vehicles:

		£
28 November 2017	Motor car [1] (CO$_2$ emissions 146 g/km)	15,400
2 December 2017	Motor car [2] (CO$_2$ emissions 111 g/km)	30,400

Motor car [1] is used 20% for private purposes by a director of Kit Ltd.

What are the capital allowances to which Kit Ltd is entitled for the period to 31 December 2017?

Select... ▼
£4,122
£3,352
£6,704
£3,229

(2 marks)

202 Eminal Ltd purchased 50,000 shares in Vesterama Ltd for £3.50 a share on 6 June 2002 (retail price index (RPI) = 176.2). On 6 June 2017 (RPI = 270.6), Eminal Ltd sold 15,000 shares in Vesterama Ltd for £70,000. Eminal Ltd prepares accounts to 31 December each year.

What is Eminal Ltd's chargeable gain or capital loss for the year ended 31 December 2017?

○ £10,627
○ £159
○ £0
○ £17,500

(2 marks)

203 Cook plc prepares accounts to 31 December each year. For the year ended 31 December 2016 taxable total profits (after deduction of a £1,000 qualifying charitable donation) were £25,000. For the year ended 31 December 2017 the company made an adjusted trading loss of £40,000 and had other taxable income of £10,000 and made no qualifying charitable donation.

What is the maximum amount of the loss of the accounting period ended 31 December 2017 that the company can claim to carry back to the accounting period ended 31 December 2016?

£ _____

(2 marks)

204 Deal Ltd has the following results:

	12 months to 31 March 2017 £	9 months to 31 December 2017 £	12 months to 31 December 2018 £
Trading profits/(losses)	45,000	40,000	(160,000)
Property business profits	18,000	15,500	5,000

The company wishes to claim relief for its loss as early as possible.

What is the unused loss carried forward at 31 December 2018?

£ _____

(2 marks)

205 Retry Ltd has the following results for the year ended 31 March 2018:

	£
Trading loss	(15,000)
Interest income	2,000
Qualifying charitable donation	(5,000)
Capital loss	(4,000)

What is the maximum amount that Retry Ltd could surrender as group relief?

£ [   ]

(2 marks)

206 The Daffodil plc group of companies has the following structure.

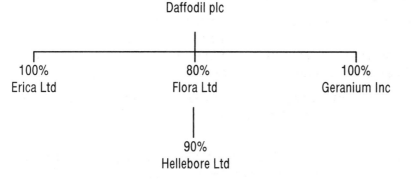

All companies are resident in the UK except Geranium Inc.

Identify, by clicking on the relevant boxes in the table below, the companies to which Erica Ltd could surrender a trading loss.

Daffodil plc	Geranium Inc
Flora Ltd	Hellebore Ltd

(2 marks)

207 The Pine plc group of companies has the following structure.

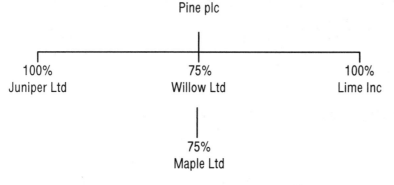

All companies are resident in the UK except Lime Inc.

Identify, by clicking on the relevant boxes in the table below, the companies to which Maple Ltd could transfer a capital loss.

Pine plc	Willow Ltd
Juniper Ltd	Lime Inc

(2 marks)

(Total = 20 marks)

CBE style OT case – Luna Ltd (06/15) (amended)   18 mins

This objective test question contains question types which will only appear in a computer-based exam, but this question provides valuable practice for all students whichever version of the exam they are taking.

The following scenario relates to Questions 208 to 212.

Luna Ltd had the following transactions in shares during the year ended 31 March 2018:

(1)   On 29 November 2017, Luna Ltd sold its entire shareholding of £1 ordinary shares in Pluto plc for £53,400. Luna Ltd had originally purchased these shares in Pluto plc on 14 June 2008 for £36,800.

(2)   On 30 November 2017, Luna Ltd sold 10,000 of its shares in Neptune plc for £26,000. Luna Ltd had originally purchased 16,000 shares in Neptune plc on 10 May 2010 for £32,000.

(3)   On 10 December 2017, Luna Ltd acquired shares under a rights issue in Saturn plc. Luna Ltd had originally purchased 5,000 £1 ordinary shares in Saturn plc for £7,500 in August 2011. There was a 1 for 1 bonus issue in July 2013 when the shares were worth £1.75 each. The December 2017 rights issue was on a 1 for 4 basis and the cost of the rights issue shares was £2.25 per share.

(4)   On 12 February 2018, Luna Ltd's shareholding in Asteroid plc was taken over by Comet plc. Luna Ltd had originally purchased 10,000 £1 ordinary shares in Asteroid plc and their indexed cost on 12 February 2018 was £33,000.

Under the terms of the takeover, for each of its £1 ordinary shares in Asteroid plc, Luna Ltd received £6.50 in cash plus one £1 ordinary share in Comet plc. Immediately after the takeover, Comet plc's £1 ordinary shares were quoted at £4.50.

Retail price indices (RPIs) are as follows:

June 2008	216.8
May 2010	223.6
November 2017	273.8

208   Identify, by clicking on the relevant boxes in the table below, whether each of the following statements concerning the indexation allowance is true or false.

	TRUE	FALSE
Indexation allowance can reduce a gain to nil but not create a loss		
Indexation allowance can increase an unindexed loss		

(2 marks)

209   What is Luna Ltd's chargeable gain on the sale of Pluto plc shares on 29 November 2017?

£ [   ]   (2 marks)

210   What is the indexed cost of Luna Ltd's holding in Neptune Ltd immediately after the sale on 30 November 2017?

- ○   £12,000
- ○   £39,184
- ○   £24,490
- ○   £14,694

(2 marks)

211 What is the unindexed cost of Luna Ltd's holding in Saturn plc immediately after the rights issue on 10 December 2017?

- ○ £13,125
- ○ £11,875
- ○ £10,313
- ○ £21,875

(2 marks)

212 What is the cost that was used to compute Luna Ltd's chargeable gain on the takeover of Asteroid plc on 12 February 2018?

£ [   ]

(2 marks)

(Total = 10 marks)

Tay Ltd   18 mins

The following scenario relates to Questions 213 to 217.

Tay Ltd prepares accounts to 31 March each year. In the year to 31 March 2018, it had the following events relating to chargeable assets:

(1) Received insurance proceeds of £180,000 in December 2017 as the result of the destruction of a freehold warehouse in a flood in that month. The warehouse originally cost £140,000 and had an indexed cost in December 2017 of £155,000. Tay Ltd purchased a new warehouse for £162,000 in March 2018.

(2) Received shares and cash on the takeover of Grey Ltd. Tay Ltd had acquired 20,000 shares in Grey Ltd. The shares had an indexed cost in September 2017 of £96,000 when Grey Ltd was taken over by Kline plc. On the takeover, Tay Ltd received one £1 ordinary share in Kline plc worth £4 per share and £2 in cash for each one share held in Grey Ltd.

(3) Sold a piece of machinery which it had used in its trade for £9,000 in July 2017. The machinery had an indexed base cost in July 2017 of £3,500. Capital allowances had been claimed on the machinery.

(4) Sold a plot of land, which it had held as an investment, for £45,000 in October 2017. The land had been acquired in June 2007 for £20,000. Tay Ltd had spent £2,000 on draining the land in January 2011. The indexation factor from June 2007 to October 2017 was 0.316 and from January 2011 to October 2017 was 0.192.

In the year to 31 March 2019, Tay Ltd will dispose of an investment property which will realise a loss. The company wants to know how this loss can be relieved.

213 What is the base cost of the new warehouse purchased in March 2018?

- ○ £162,000
- ○ £155,000
- ○ £144,000
- ○ £140,000

(2 marks)

214 What was the chargeable gain or allowable loss arising on the takeover of Grey Ltd?

- ○ £8,000 gain
- ○ £24,000 gain
- ○ £16,000) gain
- ○ £(24,000) loss

(2 marks)

215 What was the chargeable gain (if any) arising on the disposal of the machinery?

    ○   £0
    ○   £5,500
    ○   £2,500
    ○   £5,000   **(2 marks)**

216 What was the chargeable gain arising on the disposal of the plot of land?

    ○   £16,680
    ○   £16,048
    ○   £16,296
    ○   £15,732   **(2 marks)**

217 Which **TWO** of the following statements about the use of the capital loss in the year ended 31 March 2019 are correct?

    (1)   The capital loss can be carried back against chargeable gains made in the year ended 31 March 2018.
    (2)   The capital loss can be set against chargeable gains made in the year ended 31 March 2019.
    (3)   The capital loss can be set against total profits in the year ended 31 March 2019.
    (4)   The capital loss can be carried forward and set against the first available chargeable gains.

    ○   1 and 2
    ○   1 and 3
    ○   2 and 4
    ○   3 and 4   **(2 marks)**

        (Total = 10 marks)

CBE style OT case – Hyde plc group   **18 mins**

This objective test question contains question types which will only appear in a computer-based exam, but this question provides valuable practice for all students whichever version of the exam they are taking.

The following scenario relates to Questions 218 to 222.

The Hyde plc group has the following structure:

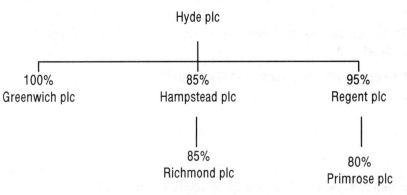

All the group companies prepared accounts to 31 March 2018. However, Greenwich plc intends to change its accounting date to 31 December and will prepare accounts to 31 December 2018.

Hyde plc and Greenwich plc are in a group relief group.

In the year ended 31 March 2018, Greenwich plc had the following results:

	£
Trading loss	(68,000)
Capital loss	(4,000)
Interest income	3,000
Qualifying charitable donations	(5,000)

Greenwich plc will surrender the maximum amount possible for the year ended 31 March 2018 to Hyde plc under group relief.

In the year ended 31 March 2018, Hyde plc had the following results:

	£
Trading loss	(8,000)
Chargeable gain	48,000
Interest income	12,000
Qualifying charitable donations	(1,500)

Greenwich plc will make a trading loss in the period ended 31 December 2018 and will surrender the maximum amount possible to Hyde plc under group relief.

Regent plc and Primrose plc are in a chargeable gains group. In the year to 31 March 2018, Regent plc sold a factory to Primrose plc for £250,000. The market value of the factory at that date was £300,000. Regent plc had acquired the factory for £100,000. The indexation factor between the date of acquisition and the date of disposal is 0.200.

218   Identify, by clicking on the relevant boxes in the table below, which of the following companies are also members of the Hyde plc group for group relief purposes.

Hampstead plc	Regent plc
Richmond plc	Primrose plc

(2 marks)

219   What is the maximum amount that Greenwich plc could surrender as group relief of the year ended 31 March 2018?

- ○   £68,000
- ○   £70,000
- ○   £73,000
- ○   £77,000

(2 marks)

220   What are the maximum available taxable total profits of Hyde plc that could be group relieved for the year ended 31 March 2018?

Select...   ▼
£58,500
£2,500
£52,000
£50,500

(2 marks)

221 Which **TWO** of the following statements about group relief claims between Hyde plc and Greenwich plc are correct?

☐ A claim for group relief will be ineffective unless Greenwich plc gives a notice of consent.

☐ If Hyde plc pays Greenwich plc an amount up to the amount of the loss surrendered, the payment will be deducted from the group relief.

☐ A claim for group relief between Greenwich plc and Hyde plc will be available against the whole of the taxable total profits of Hyde plc for the year to 31 March 2019.

☐ The claim for group relief would be made on Hyde plc's corporation tax return. **(2 marks)**

222 What is base cost of the factory acquired by Primrose plc in August 2017?

○ £100,000
○ £120,000
○ £250,000
○ £300,000 **(2 marks)**

(Total = 10 marks)

223 Do-Not-Panic Ltd (06/08) (amended)   18 mins

Do-Not-Panic Ltd is a trading company. The company commenced trading on 1 January 2017 and its results for the 15-month period ended 31 March 2018 are summarised as follows:

(1) The trading profit as adjusted for tax purposes is £285,000. This figure is before taking account of capital allowances.

(2) Do-Not-Panic Ltd purchased a new car with CO_2 emissions of 67 g/km for £9,000 on 10 August 2017, machinery for £8,000 on 19 October 2017 and office equipment for £5,000 on 20 February 2018.

(3) Do-Not-Panic Ltd bought some loan stock on 1 January 2018 as an investment. Interest of £9,500 was received on 31 March 2018 which was also the amount accrued to that date.

(4) On 21 December 2017 Do-Not-Panic Ltd disposed of some investments and this resulted in a capital loss of £4,250. On 28 March 2018 the company made a further disposal and this resulted in a chargeable gain of £39,000.

(5) A qualifying charitable donation of £2,000 was paid on 22 February 2018.

Required

Calculate Do-Not-Panic Ltd's corporation tax liabilities in respect of the 15-month period ended 31 March 2018 and advise the company by when these should be paid. **(10 marks)**

(Total = 10 marks)

224 Problematic Ltd (06/10) (amended)

18 mins

Problematic Ltd sold the following assets during the year ended 31 March 2018:

(1) On 14 June 2017 16,000 £1 ordinary shares in Easy plc were sold for £54,400. Problematic Ltd had originally purchased 15,000 shares in Easy plc on 26 June 2005 for £12,600. On 28 September 2008 Easy plc made a 1 for 3 rights issue. Problematic Ltd took up its allocation under the rights issue in full, paying £2.20 for each new share issued. The relevant retail prices indexes (RPIs) are as follows:

June 2005	192.2
September 2008	218.4
June 2017 (assumed)	270.6

(2) On 28 January 2018 a freehold factory was sold for £171,000. The indexed cost of the factory on that date was £127,000. Problematic Ltd has made a claim to hold over the gain on the factory against the cost of a replacement leasehold factory under the rollover relief (replacement of business assets) rules. The leasehold factory has a lease period of 20 years, and was purchased on 10 December 2017 for £154,800. The two factory buildings have always been used entirely for business purposes.

Required

(a) Calculate Problematic Ltd's chargeable gains for the year ended 31 March 2018. **(9 marks)**

(b) Advise Problematic Ltd of the carried forward indexed base cost of the leasehold factory. **(1 mark)**

(Total = 10 marks)

225 Volatile Ltd (12/09) (amended)

18 mins

Volatile Ltd commenced trading on 1 July 2013. The company's results for its first five periods of trading are as follows:

	Period ended 31 December 2013 £	Year ended 31 December 2014 £	Year ended 31 December 2015 £	Period ended 30 September 2016 £	Year ended 30 September 2017 £
Trading profit/(loss)	44,000	(73,800)	95,200	78,700	(186,800)
Property business profit	9,400	6,600	6,500	–	–
Chargeable gain/(loss)	5,100	–	(2,000)	11,700	–
Qualifying charitable donations	(800)	(1,000)	(1,200)	–	–

Required

(a) State the factors that will influence a company's choice of loss relief claims.

   Note. You are not expected to consider group relief. **(2 marks)**

(b) Assuming that Volatile Ltd claims relief for its trading losses as early as possible, calculate the company's taxable total profits for the six-month period ended 31 December 2013, each of the years ended 31 December 2014 and 2015 and the nine-month period ended 30 September 2016. Your answer should also clearly identify the amount of any unrelieved trading losses as at 30 September 2017. **(8 marks)**

(Total = 10 marks)

226 Acebook Ltd (12/12) (amended)

18 mins

(a)   Explain how limited companies can obtain relief for capital losses.   **(3 marks)**

Note. You are not expected to explain how groups of companies can obtain relief for capital losses.

(b)   On 10 March 2018 Acebook Ltd sold its entire shareholding of 50p ordinary shares in Oogle plc for £3.20 per share. The company had originally purchased 8,000 shares in Oogle plc on 28 June 2003 for £25,200. On 31 October 2006 Oogle plc made a 2 for 1 bonus issue. Then, on 14 February 2008, Oogle plc made a 1 for 5 rights issue. Acebook Ltd took up its allocation under the rights issue in full, paying £4.30 for each new share issued.

Indexation factors are as follows:

June 2003 to October 2006	0.105
June 2003 to February 2008	0.166
June 2003 to March 2018 (assumed)	0.525
October 2006 to February 2008	0.055
October 2006 to March 2018 (assumed)	0.379
February 2008 to March 2018 (assumed)	0.307

Required

Calculate Acebook Ltd's chargeable gain on the disposal on 10 March 2018.   **(7 marks)**

(Total = 10 marks)

---

227 Black Ltd (12/11) and Gastron Ltd (06/09) (amended)

18 mins

(a)   Black Ltd owns 100% of the ordinary share capital of White Ltd. The results of Black Ltd and White Ltd for the year ended 31 March 2018 are as follows:

	Black Ltd £	White Ltd £
Trading profit/(loss)	396,800	(351,300)
Property business profit	21,100	26,700
Capital loss	–	(17,200)
Qualifying charitable donations	(4,400)	(5,600)

As at 1 April 2017 Black Ltd had unused trading losses of £57,900, and unused capital losses of £12,600, whilst White Ltd had unused trading losses of £21,800.

Required

Advise Black Ltd as to the maximum amount of group relief that can be claimed from White Ltd in respect of its losses for the year ended 31 March 2018. Clearly identify any losses that cannot be surrendered by White Ltd as part of the group relief claim.

Note. You are not expected to calculate either company's corporation tax liability.   **(5 marks)**

(b)   Gastron Ltd is a manufacturing company. In the year to 31 March 2018 Gastron Ltd had taxable total profits of £600,000. The taxable total profits included a chargeable gain of £74,800 on the sale of a 1% shareholding. This figure is after taking account of indexation.

Gastron Ltd owns 100% of the ordinary share capital of Culinary Ltd. On 13 February 2018 Culinary Ltd sold a freehold factory and this resulted in a capital loss of £66,000. For the year ended 31 March 2018 Culinary Ltd made no other disposals.

(i)   Explain the group relationship that must exist in order for two or more companies to form a group for chargeable gains purposes.   **(2 marks)**

(ii)   Explain why it would be beneficial for Gastron Ltd and Culinary Ltd to make a joint election to transfer the whole of the capital gain on Gastron Ltd's disposal of shares to Culinary Ltd.   **(1 mark)**

(iii) Explain what two other taxation consequences arise as a result of companies being in a chargeable gains group.   **(2 marks)**

(Total = 10 marks)

228 Jogger Ltd (A) (12/08) (amended)   27 mins

Jogger Ltd is a manufacturing company. The company's summarised statement of profit or loss for the year ended 31 March 2018 is as follows:

	Note	£	£
Operating profit	1		156,482
Income from investments			
Bank interest	3	8,460	
Loan interest	4	24,600	
Income from property	5	144,000	
Dividends		45,000	
			222,060
Profit from sale of non-current assets			
Disposal of shares	6		102,340
Profit before taxation			480,882

Notes

1   *Operating profit*

Depreciation of £58,840 has been deducted in arriving at the operating profit of £156,482.

2   *Plant and machinery*

On 1 April 2017 the tax written down values of plant and machinery were as follows:

	£
Main pool	26,600
Special rate pool	18,800

The following transactions took place during the year ended 31 March 2018:

		Cost/(proceeds) £
20 July 2017	Sold a special rate pool motor car	(11,700)
31 July 2017	Purchased motor car CO$_2$ emissions 105 g/km	11,800
15 August 2017	Purchased new motor car CO$_2$ emissions 65 g/km	9,000
30 September 2017	Purchased machinery	500,000
15 December 2017	Purchased computer system	12,500
14 March 2018	Sold a lorry	(8,600)

The motor car sold on 20 July 2017 for £11,700 originally cost more than this amount. The computer system purchased on 15 December 2017 has a predicted working life of 6 years and any relevant election has been made. The lorry sold on 14 March 2018 for £8,600 originally cost £16,600.

3   *Bank interest received*

The bank interest was received on 31 March 2018. The bank deposits are held for non-trading purposes.

4   *Loan interest receivable*

The loan was made for non-trading purposes on 1 July 2017. Loan interest of £16,400 was received on 31 December 2017, and interest of £8,200 was accrued at 31 March 2018.

5   *Income from property*

Jogger Ltd lets out an unfurnished freehold office building that is surplus to requirements. The office building was let throughout the year ended 31 March 2018. On 1 April 2017 Jogger Ltd received a premium of £100,000 for the grant of a 10-year lease, and the annual rent of £44,000 which is payable in advance.

6   *Profit on disposal of shares*

The profit on disposal of shares is in respect of a shareholding that was sold in December 2017 for £150,000. The shares were acquired in August 2006 at a cost of £47,660. The retail price index (RPI) in August 2006 was 199.2 and is assumed to be 274.8 in December 2017.

Required

(a) Calculate Jogger Ltd's tax adjusted trading loss for the year ended 31 March 2018.

Notes

1   Your computation should start with the operating profit of £156,482.
2   You should assume that the company claims the maximum available capital allowances.
3   Ignore VAT.   **(8 marks)**

(b) Assuming that Jogger Ltd claims relief for its trading loss against total profits, calculate the company's corporation tax liability for the year ended 31 March 2018.   **(7 marks)**

                                                       (Total = 15 marks)

229 Mice Ltd (06/10) (amended)   **27 mins**

Mice Ltd commenced trading on 1 July 2014 as a manufacturing company. The company prepares accounts to 31 March, and its results for the first three periods of trading were as follows:

	Period ended 31 March 2015	Year ended 31 March 2016	Year ended 31 March 2017
	£	£	£
Trading profit	83,200	24,700	51,200
Property business profit	2,800	7,100	12,200
Qualifying charitable donations	(1,000)	(1,500)	–

The following information is available in respect of the year ended 31 March 2018:

Trading loss

Mice Ltd expects to make a trading loss of £180,000.

Property business income

Mice Ltd lets out three freehold office buildings that are surplus to requirements.

The first office building was let throughout the year ended 31 March 2018 at a quarterly rent of £3,200, payable in advance. Mice Ltd paid business rates of £2,200 and insurance of £460 in respect of this property for the year ended 31 March 2018. During June 2017 Mice Ltd repaired the existing car park for this property at a cost of £1,060 and then subsequently enlarged the car park at a cost of £2,640.

The second office building was let on 1 April 2017 to a tenant, with Mice Ltd receiving a premium of £18,000 for the grant of an eight-year lease. The company also received the annual rent of £6,000 which was payable in advance. Mice Ltd paid insurance of £310 in respect of this property for the year ended 31 March 2018.

The third office building was purchased by Mice Ltd on 1 January 2018 and it will be empty until 31 March 2018. The building is to be let from 1 April 2018 at a monthly rent of £640, and on 15 March 2018 Mice Ltd received three months' rent in advance. On 1 January 2018 Mice Ltd paid insurance of £480 in respect of this property for

the year ended 31 December 2018, and during February 2018 spent £680 on advertising for tenants. Mice Ltd paid loan interest of £1,800 in respect of the period 1 January 2018 to 31 March 2018 on a loan that was taken out to purchase this property.

Loan interest received

On 1 July 2017 Mice Ltd made a loan for non-trading purposes. Loan interest of £6,400 was received on 31 December 2017 and £3,200 will be accrued at 31 March 2018.

Chargeable gain

On 20 December 2017 Mice Ltd sold a piece of freehold land which it acquired in August 2012 at a cost of £28,000. The gross proceeds of sale were £36,229 before legal and selling costs of 5% of the gross proceeds.

The relevant retail price indexes (RPIs) are as follows:

August 2012	243.0
December 2017	274.8

Required

(a) Calculate Mice Ltd's property business profit for the year ended 31 March 2018. **(8 marks)**

(b) Assuming that Mice Ltd claims relief for its trading loss as early as possible, calculate the company's taxable total profits for the nine-month period ended 31 March 2015, and each of the years ended 31 March 2016, 2017 and 2018. **(7 marks)**

(Total = 15 marks)

230 Molten-Metal plc (06/11) (amended)   27 mins

Molten-Metal plc is a manufacturing company. The following information is available for the year ended 31 March 2018:

Trading profit

The tax adjusted trading profit for the year ended 31 March 2018 is £2,170,144. This figure is before making any deductions required for:

(1) Interest payable
(2) Capital allowances

Interest payable

During the year ended 31 March 2018 Molten-Metal plc paid loan stock interest of £22,500. Loan stock interest payable of £3,700 was accrued at 31 March 2018, with the corresponding accrual at 1 April 2017 being £4,200. The loan is used for trading purposes.

The company also incurred a loan interest expense of £6,800 in respect of a loan that is used for non-trading purposes.

Capital expenditure account

The following items of expenditure have been debited to the capital expenditure account during the year ended 31 March 2018:

1 May 2017	Purchase of a secondhand freehold office building for £428,000. This figure included £31,000 for a ventilation system and £42,000 for a lift. Both the ventilation system and the lift are integral to the office building.
26 June 2017	Purchase of machinery for £186,600. During June 2017 a further £7,700 was spent on building alterations that were necessary for the installation of the machinery.
8 August 2017	A payment of £41,200 for the construction of a new decorative wall around the company's premises.

27 August 2017	Purchase of movable partition walls for £22,900. Molten-Metal plc uses these to divide up its open plan offices, and the partition walls are moved around on a regular basis.
18 November 2017	Purchase of a motor car costing £24,000. This motor car has a CO_2 emission rate of 145 grams per kilometre. This car is used only for business purposes.
28 January 2018	Purchase of a computer costing £2,500. This computer has an expected working life of five years. Any relevant election will be made in respect of this asset.
11 March 2018	Purchase of two motor cars each costing £17,300. Each motor car has a CO_2 emission rate of 110 grams per kilometre. One motor car is used by the factory manager, and 60% of the mileage is for private journeys. The other motor car is used as a pool car.

Written down value

On 1 April 2017 the tax written down value of plant and machinery in Molten-Metal plc's main pool was £87,800.

Interest receivable

Molten-Metal plc made a loan for non-trading purposes on 1 August 2017. Loan interest of £9,800 was received on 31 January 2018, and £3,100 was accrued at 31 March 2018.

The company also received bank interest of £2,600 during the year ended 31 March 2018. The bank deposits are held for non-trading purposes.

Required

Calculate Molten-Metal plc's corporation tax liability for the year ended 31 March 2018. Ignore VAT. **(15 marks)**

(Total = 15 marks)

231 Starfish Ltd (A) (12/11) (amended)   27 mins

Starfish Ltd, a retailing company, commenced trading on 1 December 2013. The company initially prepared accounts to 31 March, but changed its accounting date to 31 December by preparing accounts for the nine-month period ended 31 December 2017. Starfish Ltd ceased trading on 31 March 2018.

Starfish Ltd's results for each of its periods of account up to 31 December 2017 are as follows:

	Tax adjusted trading profit/(loss) £	Bank interest £	Qualifying charitable donations £
Four-month period ended 31 March 2014	(12,600)	600	(800)
Year ended 31 March 2015	64,200	1,400	(1,000)
Year ended 31 March 2016	53,900	1,700	(900)
Year ended 31 March 2017	14,700	0	(700)
Nine-month period ended 31 December 2017	49,900	0	(600)

The company's summarised statement of profit or loss for its final three-month period of trading ended 31 March 2018 is as follows:

	Note	£	£
Gross profit			16,100
Expenses			
Depreciation		25,030	
Donations	1	1,650	
Impairment loss	2	2,000	
Legal fees	3	9,370	
Other expenses	4	168,050	
			(206,100)
Loss before taxation			(190,000)

Notes

1   *Donations*

Donations were made to the following:

	£
A political party	900
A national charity (qualifying charitable donation)	750
	1,650

2   *Impairment loss*

On 31 March 2018 Starfish Ltd wrote off an impairment loss of £2,000 in respect of a trade debt.

3   *Legal fees*

Legal fees were in connection with the following:

	£
Court action for a misleading advertisement	2,020
Issue of 6% loan notes (to raise finance for trading) that was subsequently cancelled	7,350
	9,370

4   *Other expenses*

Other expenses are as follows:

	£
Entertaining customers	3,600
Counselling services provided to employees who were made redundant	8,400
Balance of expenditure (all allowable)	156,050
	168,050

5   *Plant and machinery*

On 1 January 2018 the tax written down values of the company's plant and machinery were as follows:

	£
Main pool	23,600
Special rate pool	13,200

The special rate pool consists of a motor car which has CO_2 emissions of 190 grams per kilometre. The motor car was used 30% privately by a director of Starfish Ltd.

On 10 January 2018 Starfish Ltd purchased a laptop computer for £3,120. This figure is inclusive of value added tax (VAT). Starfish Ltd is registered for VAT.

On 31 March 2018 the company sold all of the items included in the main pool for £31,200, the laptop computer for £1,800, and the motor car for £9,600. These figures are inclusive of VAT where applicable. None of the items included in the main pool was sold for more than its original cost, and all of the items were standard rated.

Required

(a) Calculate Starfish Ltd's tax adjusted trading loss for the three-month period ended 31 March 2018.

Note. Your computation should commence with the loss before taxation figure of £190,000, and should also list all of the items referred to in notes (1) to (4) indicating by the use of zero (0) any items that do not require adjustment. **(10 marks)**

(b) Assuming that Starfish Ltd claims relief for its trading losses on the most beneficial basis, calculate the company's taxable total profits for the four-month period ended 31 March 2014, the years ended 31 March 2015, 2016 and 2017 and the nine-month period ended 31 December 2017. **(5 marks)**

(Total = 15 marks)

232 Greenzone Ltd (A) (06/13) (amended)   27 mins

(a) Greenzone Ltd is a trading company. The company's summarised statement of profit or loss for the year ended 31 March 2018 is as follows:

	Note	£	£
Gross profit			404,550
Operating expenses			
Depreciation		28,859	
Repairs and renewals	1	28,190	
Other expenses	2	107,801	
			(164,850)
Operating profit			239,700

Notes

1   *Repairs and renewals*

Repairs and renewals are as follows:

	£
Repainting the exterior of the company's office building	8,390
Extending the office building in order to create a new reception area	19,800
	28,190

2   *Other expenses*

Other expenses are as follows:

	£
Entertaining UK customers	3,600
Entertaining overseas customers	1,840
Political donations	740
Donation to a charity where Greenzone Ltd received free advertising in the charity's newsletter	
This was not a qualifying charitable donation	430
Gifts to customers (pens costing £30 each, not displaying Greenzone Ltd's name)	660
Gifts to customers (clocks costing £65 each and displaying Greenzone Ltd's name)	910
Balance of expenditure (all allowable)	99,621
	107,801

3   *Plant and machinery*

On 1 April 2017 the tax written down values of Greenzone Ltd's plant and machinery were as follows:

	£
Main pool	48,150
Special rate pool	9,200

The following motor cars were purchased new during the year ended 31 March 2018:

	Date of purchase	Cost £	CO$_2$ emission rate
Motor car [1]	10 April 2017	10,800	72 grams per kilometre
Motor car [2]	10 June 2017	20,400	110 grams per kilometre

The following motor cars were sold during the year ended 31 March 2018:

	Date of sale	Proceeds £	Original cost £
Motor car [3]	8 March 2018	9,100	8,500
Motor car [4]	8 March 2018	12,400	18,900

The original cost of motor car [3] has previously been added to the main pool, and the original cost of motor car [4] has previously been added to the special rate pool.

Required

Calculate Greenzone Ltd's tax adjusted trading profit for the year ended 31 March 2018.

Note. Your computation should commence with the operating profit figure of £239,700, and should also list all of the items referred to in notes (1) and (2), indicating by the use of zero (0) any items that do not require adjustment. **(10 marks)**

(b) Greenzone Ltd has held shares in four trading companies for many years. All four companies prepare accounts to 31 March. The following information is available for the year ended 31 March 2018:

	Are Ltd	Be Ltd	Can Ltd	Doer Co
Residence	UK	UK	UK	Overseas
Percentage ordinary shareholding	60%	40%	90%	70%
Trading profit/(loss)	£(74,800)	£68,900	£(64,700)	£22,600
Dividends paid to Greenzone Ltd	£36,180	£35,100	£29,400	£16,650

Required

(i) State, giving reasons, which of the four trading companies are treated as related 51% group companies with Greenzone Ltd and how this affects the way Greenzone Ltd pays its corporation tax liability for the year ended 31 March 2018. **(3 marks)**

(ii) Calculate the maximum amount of group relief that Greenzone Ltd can claim for the year ended 31 March 2018. **(2 marks)**

(Total = 15 marks)

233 Softapp Ltd (12/13) (amended) 27 mins

Softapp Ltd is a trading company. The company's summarised statement of profit or loss for the year ended 31 March 2018 is as follows:

	Note	£
Operating profit	1	711,475
Other income		
Rental income receivable	2	30,000
Loan interest receivable	3	8,100
Profit on disposal of shares	4	64,900
Finance costs		
Interest payable	5	(67,200)
Profit before taxation		747,275

Notes

1 *Operating profit*

Depreciation of £10,170 and amortisation of leasehold property of £2,500 have been deducted in arriving at the operating profit of £711,475.

2 *Rental income*

Softapp Ltd let out a warehouse surplus to its requirements on 1 October 2017, the monthly rent of £5,000 being payable in advance on the first of each calendar month. The rent due on 1 March 2018 was not received due to the business failure of the tenant. Half of the unpaid rent was received on 10 April 2018 and the rest is irrecoverable.

3 *Loan interest receivable*

The loan was made for non-trading purposes on 1 July 2017. Loan interest of £5,600 was received on 31 December 2017, and interest of £2,500 was accrued at 31 March 2018.

4   *Profit on disposal of shares*

The profit on disposal of shares is in respect of the sale of Softapp Ltd's entire (2%) shareholding in Networked plc on 28 February 2018 for proceeds of £94,661. The shares were acquired on 15 July 2013 at a cost of £30,000. The retail price index (RPI) for July 2013 was 249.7 and the RPI for February 2018 is assumed to be 275.8.

5   *Interest payable*

The interest payable is in respect of the company's 4% loan stock. Interest of £33,600 was paid on 30 September 2017 and again on 31 March 2018. The loan stock was used to finance the company's trading activities.

Additional information

Leasehold property

On 1 January 2018, Softapp Ltd acquired a leasehold office building, paying a premium of £100,000 for the grant of a 10-year lease. The office building was used for business purposes by Softapp Ltd throughout the period 1 January to 31 March 2018.

Plant and machinery

The tax written down value of Softapp Ltd's plant and machinery as at 1 April 2017 was nil.

On 1 September 2017, Softapp Ltd purchased computer equipment at a cost of £175,000.

During October 2017 Softapp Ltd had an extension constructed adjacent to its existing freehold office building, which is used by the company's employees as a staff room.

The total cost of £100,000 for the extension is made up as follows:

	£
Integral to building	
Building costs of extension	61,000
Heating system	3,600
Ventilation system	4,600
Not integral to building	
Furniture and furnishings	29,400
Refrigerator and microwave cooker	1,400
	100,000

Required

Calculate Softapp Ltd's corporation tax liability for the year ended 31 March 2018.

Note. Your computation should commence with the operating profit figure of £711,475.   **(15 marks)**

(Total = 15 marks)

234 Long Ltd group (A) (06/14) (amended)   27 mins

Long Ltd owns 100% of the ordinary share capital of both Wind Ltd and Road Ltd. Long Ltd and Road Ltd run freight transport businesses, whilst Wind Ltd provides transport related insurance services.

Long Ltd's shareholding in Wind Ltd was acquired on 1 April 2012 and the shareholding in Road Ltd was acquired on 15 January 2017 when that company was incorporated. Long Ltd and Wind Ltd have prepared accounts for the year ended 31 March 2018, whilst Road Ltd has prepared accounts for the period 1 January 2018 (when the company commenced trading) to 31 March 2018. The following information is available:

Long Ltd

(1)   The operating profit for the year ended 31 March 2018 is £817,820. Depreciation of £10,170 has been deducted in arriving at this figure.

(2)   On 1 April 2017, the tax written down value of the plant and machinery main pool was £44,800. On 10 June 2017, Long Ltd purchased a lorry for £36,800 and a motor car for £15,700. The motor car has a CO_2 emission rate of 122 grams per kilometre. The motor car is used by the managing director of Long Ltd, and 40% of the mileage is for private journeys.

(3)   On 29 July 2017, Long Ltd disposed of a 2% shareholding in an unconnected company. The disposal resulted in a capital loss of £21,300.

(4)   During the year ended 31 March 2018, Long Ltd received a dividend of £41,400 from Wind Ltd, and dividends totalling £32,000 from unconnected companies.

Wind Ltd

(1)   The operating profit for the year ended 31 March 2018 is £59,490. Depreciation of £5,000 has been deducted in arriving at this figure.

(2)   On 1 April 2017, the tax written down value of the plant and machinery main pool was £900. There were no additions or disposals during the year ended 31 March 2018.

(3)   On 18 August 2017, Wind Ltd disposed of a 1% shareholding in an unconnected company. The disposal resulted in a chargeable gain of £29,800. This figure is after taking account of indexation.

Road Ltd

(1)   The operating loss for the three-month period ended 31 March 2018 is £26,100. Donations of £2,800 have been deducted in arriving at this figure. The donations consist of political donations of £400, and qualifying charitable donations of £2,400.

(2)   On 3 October 2017, Road Ltd purchased a new motor car for £11,600. The motor car has a CO_2 emission rate of 65 grams per kilometre.

(3)   For the three-month period ended 31 March 2018, loan interest receivable was £4,300. The loan was made for non-trading purposes.

Other information

(1)   Long Ltd, Wind Ltd and Road Ltd do not have any other shareholdings in any other company.

(2)   Road Ltd is not expected to be profitable for the foreseeable future.

Required

(a)   On the assumption that any available reliefs are claimed on the most beneficial basis, calculate the corporation tax liabilities of Long Ltd and Wind Ltd for the year ended 31 March 2018, and of Road Ltd for the three-month period ended 31 March 2018.   **(11 marks)**

(b)   Explain whether or not Long Ltd is a large company for the purpose of paying corporation tax by instalments for the year ended 31 March 2018.   **(4 marks)**

                                                                    (Total = 15 marks)

235 Retro Ltd (06/15)

Retro Ltd's summarised statement of profit or loss for the year ended 31 March 2018 is as follows:

	Note	£	£
Gross profit			127,100
Operating expenses			
Depreciation		27,240	
Gifts and donations	1	2,300	
Impairment loss	2	1,600	
Leasing costs	3	4,400	
Other expenses	4	205,160	
			(240,700)
Finance costs			
Interest payable	5		(6,400)
Loss before taxation			(120,000)

Notes

1   *Gifts and donations*

Gifts and donations are as follows:

	£
Gifts to employees (food hampers costing £60 each)	720
Gifts to customers (calendars costing £8 each and displaying Retro Ltd's name)	480
Political donations	420
Qualifying charitable donations	680
	2,300

2   *Impairment loss*

On 31 March 2018, Retro Ltd wrote off an impairment loss of £1,600 relating to a trade debt. This was in respect of an invoice which had been due for payment on 10 November 2017.

3   *Leasing costs*

The leasing costs of £4,400 are in respect of a motor car lease which commenced on 1 April 2017. The leased motor car has CO_2 emissions of 145 grams per kilometre.

4   *Other expenses*

The figure of £205,160 for other expenses includes a fine of £5,100 for a breach of health and safety regulations, and legal fees of £4,860 in connection with the defence of Retro Ltd's internet domain name. The remaining expenses are all fully allowable.

5   *Interest payable*

The interest payable is in respect of the company's 5% loan notes which were repaid on 31 July 2017. Interest of £9,600 was paid on 31 July 2017, and an accrual of £3,200 had been provided for at 1 April 2017. The loan notes were issued in order to finance the company's trading activities.

Additional information

Plant and machinery

On 1 April 2017, the tax written down value of the plant and machinery main pool was £39,300.

The following new vehicles were purchased during the year ended 31 March 2018:

	Date of purchase	Cost £	CO_2 emission rate
Motor car [1]	8 June 2017	14,700	124 grams per kilometre
Delivery van	3 August 2017	28,300	162 grams per kilometre
Motor car [2]	19 October 2017	12,400	66 grams per kilometre

Previous results

Retro Ltd commenced trading on 1 September 2015. The company's results for its two previous periods of trading are as follows:

	Year ended 31 August 2016 £	Period ended 31 March 2017 £
Tax adjusted trading profit	56,600	47,900
Bank interest receivable	1,300	0
Qualifying charitable donations paid	(540)	(330)

Future results

Retro Ltd is expected to return to profitability in the year ended 31 March 2019 and to continue to be profitable in subsequent years.

Required

(a) Calculate Retro Ltd's tax adjusted trading loss for the year ended 31 March 2018.

Note. Your computation should commence with the loss before taxation figure of £120,000, and should also list all of the items referred to in notes (1) to (5), indicating by the use of zero (0) any items which do not require adjustment. **(9 marks)**

(b) Assuming that Retro Ltd claims relief for its trading loss as early as possible, calculate the company's taxable total profits for the year ended 31 August 2016 and for the seven-month period ended 31 March 2017. **(4 marks)**

(c) Identify the amount of unrelieved trading loss which Retro Ltd will have at 31 March 2018, and state how this can be relieved. **(2 marks)**

(Total = 15 marks)

236 Lucky Ltd (Sep/Dec 15) (amended) 27 mins

Lucky Ltd was incorporated on 20 July 2017, and commenced trading on 1 December 2017. The following information is available for the four-month period 1 December 2017 to 31 March 2018:

(1) The operating profit for the 4-month period ended 31 March 2018 is £432,600. Advertising expenditure of £4,700 (incurred during September 2017), depreciation of £14,700, and amortisation of £9,000 have been deducted in arriving at this figure.

The amortisation relates to a premium which was paid on 1 December 2017 to acquire a leasehold warehouse on a 12-year lease. The amount of premium assessed on the landlord as income was £46,800. The warehouse was used for business purposes by Lucky Ltd throughout the period ended 31 March 2018.

(2) Lucky Ltd purchased the following assets during the period 20 July 2017 to 31 March 2018:

		£
19 August 2017	Computer	6,300
22 January 2018	Integral features	41,200
31 January 2018	Office equipment	32,900
17 March 2018	Motor car	12,800

The integral features of £41,200 are in respect of expenditure on electrical systems, a ventilation system and lifts which are integral to a freehold office building owned by Lucky Ltd.

The motor car has a CO_2 emission rate of 62 grams per kilometre.

(3) Lucky Ltd made a loan to another company for non-trading purposes on 1 February 2018. Loan interest income of £700 was accrued at 31 March 2018.

Lucky Ltd will make a company car available to its chief executive officer. The car will be purchased, rather than leased, and will be made available to the chief executive officer in December 2018 onwards.

Required

(a)   State when an accounting period starts for corporation tax purposes.   **(2 marks)**

(b)   Calculate Lucky Ltd's corporation tax liability for the four-month period ended 31 March 2018.

Note. Your computation should commence with the operating profit of £432,600, and should also indicate by the use of zero (0) any items referred to in the question for which no adjustment is required.   **(9 marks)**

(c)   Advise Lucky Ltd as to how long it must retain the records used in preparing its self-assessment corporation tax return for the four-month period ended 31 March 2018, and the potential consequences of not retaining the records for the required period.   **(2 marks)**

(d)   Advise Lucky Ltd on the effects of the company car on its taxable total profits for the year ended 31 March 2019.   **(2 marks)**

(Total = 15 marks)

---

237 Jump Ltd (Mar/Jun 2016)   27 mins

Jump Ltd's summarised statement of profit or loss for the three-month period ended 31 March 2018 is as follows:

	Note	£	£
Revenue			264,900
Operating expenses			
Depreciation		8,100	
Employee costs	1	189,700	
Lease of motor car	2	1,200	
Professional fees	3	7,800	
Other expenses	4	202,800	
			(409,600)
Operating loss			(144,700)
Bank interest receivable			0
Loss before taxation			(144,700)

Notes

1   *Employee costs*

Employee costs are as follows:

	£
Employee training courses	3,400
Employee pension contributions paid	11,600
Cost of annual staff party (for eight employees)	1,500
Balance of expenditure (all allowable)	173,200
	189,700

2   *Lease of motor car*

The lease is in respect of a motor car with CO_2 emissions of 189 grams per kilometre.

3   *Professional fees*

Professional fees are as follows:

	£
Accountancy	2,200
Legal fees in connection with the issue of share capital	3,800
Legal fees in connection with the renewal of a 20-year property lease	1,800
	7,800

4   *Other expenses*

Other expenses are as follows:

	£
Entertaining UK customers	1,700
Entertaining overseas customers	790
Political donations	800
Balance of expenditure (all allowable)	199,510
	202,800

Additional information

Plant and machinery

On 1 January 2018, the tax written down values of Jump Ltd's plant and machinery were as follows:

	£
Main pool	12,100
Special rate pool	5,700

The following motor cars were sold during the three-month period ended 31 March 2018:

	Date of sale	Proceeds	Original cost
		£	£
Motor car [1]	7 January 2018	9,700	9,300
Motor car [2]	29 March 2018	6,100	13,200

The original cost of motor car [1] was added to the special rate pool when it was purchased, and the original cost of motor car [2] was added to the main pool when it was purchased.

Previous results

Jump Ltd's results for its two previous periods of trading are as follows:

	Year ended 31 May 2017	Period ended 31 December 2017
	£	£
Tax adjusted trading profit	78,600	42,400
Bank interest receivable	1,200	0

Group companies

Jump Ltd owns 80% of the ordinary share capital of Hop Ltd and 60% of the ordinary share capital of Skip Ltd.

Hop Ltd commenced trading on 1 August 2017, and for the eight-month period ended 31 March 2018 has taxable total profits of £63,000.

Skip Ltd has been trading for several years and has taxable total profits of £56,000 for the year ended 31 March 2018.

Required

(a) Calculate Jump Ltd's tax adjusted trading loss for the three-month period ended 31 March 2018.

Notes

1   Your computation should commence with the operating loss figure of £144,700, and should list all of the items referred to in notes (1) to (4), indicating by the use of zero (0) any items which do not require adjustment.

2   You should assume that the company claims the maximum available capital allowances.   **(10 marks)**

(b) (i) State the main factor which will influence Jump Ltd's choice of loss relief or group relief claims.

(1 mark)

(ii) Advise Jump Ltd as to the maximum amount of its trading loss which can be relieved against its total profits for the year ended 31 May 2017 and the seven-month period ended 31 December 2017.

(2 marks)

(iii) Advise Jump Ltd as to the maximum amount of its trading loss which can be surrendered as group relief.

(2 marks)

(Total = 15 marks)

238 Online Ltd (Mar/Jun 2017) 27 mins

The following information is available in respect of Online Ltd for the year ended 31 March 2018:

Operating profit

Online Ltd's operating profit for the year ended 31 March 2018 is £896,700. Depreciation of £21,660 and amortisation of leasehold property of £9,000 (see the leasehold property note below) have been deducted in arriving at this figure.

Leasehold property

On 1 April 2017, Online Ltd acquired a leasehold office building, paying a premium of £90,000 for the grant of a 10-year lease. The office building was used for business purposes by Online Ltd throughout the year ended 31 March 2018.

Plant and machinery

On 1 April 2017, the tax written down values of plant and machinery were as follows:

	£
Main pool	56,700
Special rate pool	12,400

The following transactions took place during the year ended 31 March 2018:

		Costs/(proceeds) £
14 May 2017	Sold a motor car	(18,100)
18 July 2017	Sold all items included in the special rate pool	(9,300)
27 January 2018	Purchased a motor car	13,700

The motor car sold on 14 May 2017 for £18,100 was originally purchased during the year ended 31 March 2017 for £17,200. This expenditure was added to the main pool.

The motor car purchased on 27 January 2018 for £13,700 has a CO_2 emission rate of 90 grams per kilometre. The motor car is used as a pool car by the company's employees.

Qualifying charitable donations

During the year ended 31 March 2018, Online Ltd made qualifying charitable donations of £6,800. These were not included in arriving at the operating profit above.

Disposal of shareholding in Network plc

On 20 March 2018, Online Ltd sold its entire shareholding of £1 ordinary shares in Network plc for £90,600. Online Ltd had originally purchased 40,000 shares (less than a 1% shareholding) in Network plc on 24 June 2010 for £49,300. On 7 October 2013, Online Ltd sold 22,000 of the shares for £62,200.

Indexation factors are as follows:

June 2010 to October 2013	0.124
June 2010 to March 2018	0.233
October 2013 to March 2018	0.097

Brought forward losses

As at 1 April 2017, Online Ltd had the following brought forward amounts of unused losses:

	£
Capital loss	3,278
Property business loss	12,500

Planned acquisition

Online Ltd currently does not have any 51% group companies. However, Online Ltd is planning to acquire a 60% shareholding in Offline Ltd in the near future. Offline Ltd is profitable and will pay regular dividends to Online Ltd.

Required

(a)   Calculate Online Ltd's taxable total profits for the year ended 31 March 2018.   **(13 marks)**

(b)   Briefly explain how the acquisition of Offline Ltd will affect the calculation and payment of Online Ltd's corporation tax liability in future years.   **(2 marks)**

(Total = 15 marks)

PART F VALUE ADDED TAX

Questions 239 to 299 cover value added tax, the subject of Chapters 24 and 25 of the BPP Study Text for Taxation (TX – UK).

MCQ bank – Value added tax 1

18 mins

239 Jerome is a value added tax (VAT) registered trader who received an order for goods with a 10% deposit on 18 August 2017. The goods were despatched on 26 August 2017 and an invoice was sent on 2 September 2017. The balancing 90% of the payment was received on 10 September 2017.

What are the tax points for the deposit and the balancing payment if Jerome does not use the cash accounting scheme?

	Deposit	Balancing payment	
O	18 August 2017	10 September 2017	
O	26 August 2017	26 August 2017	
O	18 August 2017	2 September 2017	
O	2 September 2017	10 September 2017	**(2 marks)**

240 Alma runs a financial services business making exempt supplies. Barry runs a children's clothing shop making zero rated supplies. Chris runs an adult clothing shop making standard rated supplies.

Who is making taxable supplies and therefore can reclaim input VAT?

- O   Alma and Barry
- O   Alma and Chris
- O   Barry and Chris
- O   Chris only **(2 marks)**

241 Light Ltd is registered for value added tax (VAT). On 1 January 2018 Light Ltd purchased a motor car costing £18,400 (inclusive of VAT) for the use of its managing director for business and private purposes. The private use is estimated to be 40%. The managing director is provided with free petrol for business and private mileage which cost Light Ltd £625 (exclusive of VAT). Light Ltd wishes to use the fuel scale charge: the relevant quarterly VAT inclusive scale charge is £361.

What is Light Ltd's VAT repayment in respect of the motor car and the fuel for the quarter ended 31 March 2018?

- O   £1,905
- O   £3,132
- O   £65
- O   £44 **(2 marks)**

242 Nora Ltd prepared a value added tax (VAT) return for the quarter ended 31 May 2017 which showed net VAT payable of £2,500.

By which dates should this return have been submitted to HM Revenue & Customs (HMRC) and the payment made to HMRC?

	Return submitted	Payment	
O	30 June 2017	30 June 2017	
O	7 July 2017	7 July 2017	
O	7 July 2017	30 June 2017	
O	30 June 2017	7 July 2017	**(2 marks)**

243 Mick is a value added tax (VAT) registered trader who prepares quarterly VAT returns to 31 March, 30 June, 30 September and 31 December each year. Mick's accounts are prepared annually to 30 September. Mick made a supply of goods amounting to £6,000 on 22 September 2017 with a due date of payment of 10 October 2017. The customer has defaulted on the payment and Mick has written the debt off in his accounts. He does not use the cash accounting scheme.

Which quarterly VAT return is the earliest in which relief for the impaired debt may be claimed?

- ○ VAT quarter ended 31 December 2017
- ○ VAT quarter ended 31 March 2018
- ○ VAT quarter ended 30 June 2018
- ○ VAT quarter ended 30 September 2018 **(2 marks)**

(Total = 10 marks)

CBE style OTQ bank – Value added tax 2   36 mins

244 Karen is a sole trader and is registered for value added tax (VAT). In October 2017, Karen sold goods for £8,000 exclusive of VAT. The sale was standard rated. Karen's invoice states that there is a discount of 8% on sales if invoices are paid within 21 days. The invoice for the supply was actually paid 25 days after it was issued.

How much VAT should Karen have added to the sale price of £8,000?

£ [   ] **(2 marks)**

245 Olive is a sole trader who is registered for value added tax (VAT). On 10 October 2017 she purchased a motor car for £12,000 (inclusive of VAT) to use for business and private purposes. The private use is estimated to be 30%. On 1 December 2017, the motor car was damaged in an accident and the repairs amounted to £2,000 (inclusive of VAT).

What is the input tax Olive can recover in relation to the motor car for the quarter ended 31 December 2017?

£ [   ] **(2 marks)**

246 Price Ltd incurred the following expenditure (inclusive of value added tax) in the quarter to 31 December 2017:

	£
New car for salesman (20% private use)	14,040
New motor van	10,320
Entertaining UK customers	4,200
Entertaining overseas customers	3,600

How much input tax can be recovered by Price Ltd for the quarter to 31 December 2017?

Select... ▼
£5,360
£4,192
£3,020
£2,320

(2 marks)

247 Ben has been in business for three years. Due to an upturn in trade, he applied to register for value added tax (VAT) with effect from 1 October 2017. Prior to registration, he had incurred the following VAT expenditure:

	£
Legal fees on an invoice dated 13 January 2017	500
Accountancy fees on an invoice dated 5 September 2017	30
Inventory of spare parts acquired in past two years and still held on 30 September 2017	240

What is the total pre-registration input tax that Ben can recover in respect of these items?

£ [   ]

(2 marks)

---

248 In the first year of trading to 31 December 2016 Scott's taxable turnover was £5,000 per month.

For the first seven months of 2017 his turnover was as follows:

	£
January 2017	8,400
February 2017	8,600
March 2017	8,800
April 2017	9,600
May 2017	10,000
June 2017	10,200
July 2017	10,300

You have advised Scott that he is compulsorily required to be registered for value added tax (VAT).

From what date will Scott be registered for VAT under compulsory registration?

- ○ 30 July 2017
- ○ 1 August 2017
- ○ 30 June 2017
- ○ 1 July 2017

(2 marks)

---

249 During the quarter ended 31 December 2017, Rachel makes purchases of office items for her business of £5,700 and spends £420 entertaining UK customers. Her sales for the period are £35,250. All figures are inclusive of value added tax (VAT) and standard rated.

What is Rachel's total VAT liability for the quarter ended 31 December 2017?

£ [   ]

(2 marks)

---

250 Charlie, a UK value added tax (VAT) registered trader, made a supply of goods in February 2018 to a customer in France who is VAT registered there.

What rate of VAT will Charlie charge on this sale?

- ○ 0%
- ○ 20%
- ○ 1/6
- ○ 5%

(2 marks)

251 Which **TWO** of the following are features of the value added tax (VAT) cash accounting scheme?

☐ Date of payment or receipt determines the VAT period in which the transaction is dealt with

☐ Only need to submit an annual VAT return

☐ Gives automatic impairment loss relief (bad debt relief)

☐ Payments on account of VAT are required throughout the quarter **(2 marks)**

252 Queen Ltd is registered for value added tax (VAT) and uses the flat rate scheme. In its VAT quarter ended 30 June 2017 it had a tax inclusive turnover of £120,000. This comprises of standard rated sales of £85,000, zero rated sales of £25,000 and exempt sales of £10,000. The flat rate scheme percentage for the company's trading sector is 9.5%.

The VAT payable by Queen Ltd for the quarter ended 30 June 2017 is:

O   £11,400
O   £10,450
O   £8,075
O   £9,025 **(2 marks)**

253 Match the thresholds for a business to join and to leave the value added tax (VAT) flat rate scheme.

Tax exclusive annual taxable turnover up to £150,000		Tax inclusive annual taxable turnover up to £150,000
Tax exclusive annual turnover up to £230,000		Tax inclusive annual turnover up to £230,000

Join scheme

Leave scheme **(2 marks)**

(Total = 20 marks)

CBE style OT case – Anne (06/09) (amended)   18 mins

This objective test question contains question types which will only appear in a computer-based exam, but this question provides valuable practice for all students whichever version of the exam they are taking.

The following scenario relates to Questions 254 to 258.

Anne runs a retail clothing shop. She is registered for value added tax (VAT) and is in the process of completing her VAT return for the quarter ended 30 November 2017.

The following information is available (all figures are exclusive of VAT):

(1) Cash sales amounted to £42,000, of which £28,000 was in respect of sales of adult clothing (standard rated) and £14,000 was in respect of sales of children's clothing (zero rated).

(2) Sales invoices totalling £12,000 were issued in respect of credit sales. These sales were all standard rated. Anne states on her invoice that there is a 5% discount for payment within one month of the date of the sales invoice. 90% of the customers pay within this period. The sales figure of £12,000 is stated before any deduction for the 5% discount.

(3) Purchase and expense invoices totalling £19,200 were received from VAT registered suppliers. This figure is made up as follows:

	£
Standard rated purchases and expenses	11,200
Zero rated purchases	6,000
Exempt expenses	2,000
	19,200

Anne pays all of her purchase and expense invoices two months after receiving the invoice.

(4) On 30 November 2017 Anne wrote off two impairment losses that were in respect of standard rated credit sales. The first impairment loss was for £300, and was in respect of a sales invoice due for payment on 15 July 2017. The second impairment loss was for £800, and was in respect of a sales invoice due for payment on 10 April 2017.

Anne does not use the cash accounting scheme but she is considering using the scheme.

254 What is the amount of output tax on cash sales payable by Anne for the quarter ended 30 November 2017?

£ [   ]

(2 marks)

255 What is the amount of output tax on credit sales payable by Anne for the quarter ended 30 November 2017, taking into account impairment loss relief?

○ £2,052
○ £2,400
○ £2,280
○ £2,292

(2 marks)

256 What is the amount of input tax recoverable by Anne for the quarter ended 30 November 2017?

£ [   ]

(2 marks)

257 Which **TWO** of the following statements about the cash accounting scheme are correct?

[ ] Anne will be permitted to join the scheme if her expected taxable turnover for the next 12 months does not exceed £1,350,000.

[ ] Anne must pay her 90% of the previous year's net VAT liability during the year by means of nine monthly payments commencing at the end of the fourth month of the year.

[ ] Anne will be permitted to join the scheme if she is up to date with her VAT payments but not necessarily up to date with her VAT returns.

[ ] If the value of Anne's taxable supplies exceeds £1,600,000 in the 12 months to the end of a VAT period she must leave the scheme immediately.

(2 marks)

258 Identify, by clicking on the relevant boxes in the table below, whether each of the following statements are the advantages of Anne using the cash accounting scheme.

Reduced amount of output VAT payable	ADVANTAGE	NOT ADVANTAGE
Automatic impairment loss relief (bad debt relief)	ADVANTAGE	NOT ADVANTAGE
Only one VAT return each year	ADVANTAGE	NOT ADVANTAGE
Output VAT on 10% of credit sales will be accounted for up to 1 month later than at present	ADVANTAGE	NOT ADVANTAGE

(2 marks)

(Total = 10 marks)

Auy and Bim (06/10) (amended)   18 mins

The following scenario relates to Questions 259 to 263.

Auy and Bim have been in partnership since 6 April 2006 and have been registered for value added tax (VAT) since that date.

In the year ended 5 April 2018 the partnership's summarised statement of profit or loss shows sales revenue of £140,762, which is exclusive of output VAT of £25,600, and expenses of £60,200 which are exclusive of recoverable input VAT of £180 for motor expenses and £140 for other expenses.

The partnership has recently started invoicing for its services on new payment terms, and the partners are concerned about output VAT being accounted for at the appropriate time.

The partnership is considering using the flat rate scheme. The relevant flat rate scheme percentage for the partnership's trade is 14%.

259 Which **TWO** of the following statements about the tax point are correct?

(1) The basic tax point for services is the date that services commence.

(2) If the VAT invoice is issued within 14 days after the basic tax point and payment has not been received before the basic tax point, the invoice date becomes the tax point.

(3) The tax point determines the VAT period in which output tax must be accounted for and credit for input tax will be allowed.

(4) If the VAT invoice is issued and payment is received before the basic tax point, the actual tax point is the later of those two dates.

○ 1 and 2
○ 2 and 3
○ 1 and 4
○ 2 and 4   (2 marks)

260 What is the total amount of VAT paid by the partnership to HM Revenue & Customs for the year ended 5 April 2018?

○ £25,600
○ £25,420
○ £25,280
○ £25,460   (2 marks)

261   Which **TWO** of the following statements about the flat rate scheme are correct?

      (1)   Businesses using the scheme must still issue VAT invoices to their VAT registered customers.

      (2)   Under the scheme, businesses calculate VAT by applying a fixed percentage to their standard rate income only.

      (3)   Businesses using the scheme cannot reclaim any input tax suffered.

      (4)   A 1% reduction off the flat rate percentage can always be made by businesses in the first year that they use the flat rate scheme.

      ○   1 and 2
      ○   2 and 4
      ○   2 and 3
      ○   1 and 3   **(2 marks)**

262   What are the conditions that the partnership must satisfy in order to join and continue to use the VAT flat rate scheme?

	Join	*Continue to use*
○	Expected taxable turnover (excluding VAT) for the next 12 months does not exceed £230,000.	Until its total turnover (including VAT) for the previous year exceeds £1,350,000
○	Expected taxable turnover (excluding VAT) for the next 12 months does not exceed £150,000.	Until its total turnover (including VAT) for the previous year exceeds £230,000
○	Expected taxable turnover (excluding VAT) for the next 12 months does not exceed £150,000.	Until its total turnover (including VAT) for the previous year exceeds £1,350,000
○	Expected taxable turnover (excluding VAT) for the next 12 months does not exceed £230,000.	Until its total turnover (including VAT) for the previous year exceeds £230,000

                                                                                        (2 marks)

263   What is the amount of VAT that would have been paid to HM Revenue & Customs if the partnership had used the flat rate scheme to calculate the amount of VAT payable for the year ended 5 April 2018?

      ○   £23,291
      ○   £19,707
      ○   £22,971
      ○   £28,152   **(2 marks)**

                                                                        (Total = 10 marks)

Aston (06/11) (amended)

18 mins

The following scenario relates to Questions 264 to 268.

Aston commenced self-employment on 1 August 2017 providing consultancy services. His sales revenue has been as follows:

		Standard rated £	Zero rated £
2017	August	6,300	–
	September	6,400	–
	October	21,900	4,800
	November	11,700	–
	December	17,100	–
2018	January	14,800	2,200
	February	4,200	–
	March	31,500	3,300
	April	44,600	6,600

Where applicable, the above figures are stated exclusive of value added tax (VAT). Aston only supplies services and all of his supplies are to VAT registered businesses. He does not offer any discount for prompt payment.

Aston wants advice about when he will need to submit his VAT returns and pay the associated VAT due.

The following is a sample of the new sales invoice that Aston is going to issue to his customers:

SALES INVOICE

Aston
111 Long Road
London W1 9MG
Telephone 0207 123 3456

Customer: Faster Motors plc
Address: 22 Short Lane
Manchester M1 8MB

Invoice Date 6 June 2018
Tax Point   6 June 2018

Description of services
Business advice

	£
Total price (excluding VAT)	12,000.00
Total price (including VAT)	14,400.00

You have advised Aston that he also needs to include the rate of VAT for each supply and the amount of VAT payable.

Aston sometimes receives supplies of standard rated services from VAT registered businesses situated elsewhere within the European Union. Aston wants to know how he should account for these services for VAT purposes.

Because of the complexity of the VAT legislation, Aston is concerned that despite his best efforts he will incorrectly treat a standard rated supply as zero rated, thus understating the amount of VAT payable. He wants to know if such an error will result in a penalty, and if so how much the penalty will be.

264 On what date was Aston liable to be registered for VAT and from what date should Aston's business be registered for VAT?

	Liable for registration	Date of registration
O	28 February 2018	28 February 2018
O	31 January 2018	1 March 2018
O	31 January 2018	28 February 2018
O	28 February 2018	1 March 2018

(2 marks)

265 When must Aston submit his VAT returns and pay the associated VAT?

	Submission	Payment
O	One month after the end of the VAT period	One month after the end of the VAT period
O	One month after the end of the VAT period	One month and seven days after the end of the VAT period
O	One month and seven days after the end of the VAT period	One month and seven days after the end of the VAT period
O	One month and seven days after the end of the VAT period	One month after the end of the VAT period **(2 marks)**

266 Which **TWO** pieces of information must Aston show on his new sales invoices in order for them to be valid for VAT purposes in addition to those about which you have already advised him?

(1) Date for payment
(2) Aston's VAT registration number
(3) HMRC reference number
(4) An identifying number (invoice number)

O 1 and 2
O 2 and 4
O 2 and 3
O 1 and 3 **(2 marks)**

267 Which **TWO** of the following statements about when and how Aston should account for VAT in respect of the supplies of services he receives from VAT registered businesses situated elsewhere within the European Union are correct?

(1) The transaction is entered on Aston's VAT return as an output and an input.

(2) The tax point is the earlier of the 15th day of the month following that in which the service is completed and the date it is paid for.

(3) Supplies of services from VAT registered businesses situated elsewhere within the European Union are always zero rated for the customer.

(4) The service is treated as being supplied in the UK since this is where Aston is situated.

O 1 and 3
O 2 and 4
O 1 and 4
O 2 and 3 **(2 marks)**

268 Assuming that Aston incorrectly treats a standard rated supply as zero rated with the result that the amount of VAT payable is understated, what is the maximum amount of penalty that is likely to be charged by HM Revenue & Customs and the minimum penalty that could be charged as a result of a subsequent unprompted disclosure?

	Maximum penalty	Minimum penalty for unprompted disclosure
O	70% of the VAT underpaid	15% of the VAT underpaid
O	70% of the VAT underpaid	0% of the VAT underpaid
O	30% of the VAT underpaid	15% of the VAT underpaid
O	30% of the VAT underpaid	0% of the VAT underpaid

(2 marks)

(Total = 10 marks)

Starfish Ltd (B) (12/11) (amended)   18 mins

The following scenario relates to Questions 269 to 273.

Starfish Ltd, a retailing company, ceased trading on 31 March 2018 and deregistered from value added tax (VAT) on that date.

The following information relates to the company's final VAT return for the quarter ended 31 March 2018:

(1)   Cash sales revenue amounted to £41,160, of which £38,520 was in respect of standard rated sales and £2,640 was in respect of zero rated sales.

(2)   Sales invoices totalling £2,000 were issued in respect of credit sales revenue. This figure is exclusive of VAT, and the sales were all standard rated. Starfish Ltd states on its invoices that it offers all of its credit sale customers a 4% discount for payment within 14 days of the date of the sales invoice. 60% of the customers paid within this period.

(3)   In addition to the above sales revenue, Starfish Ltd sold its remaining inventory on 31 March 2018 for £28,800.

(4)   There were no purchases of inventory during the period.

(5)   Standard rated expenses amounted to £69,960, of which £4,320 was in respect of entertaining UK customers.

(6)   Starfish Ltd wrote off an impairment loss on 31 March 2018 in respect of a sales invoice (exclusive of VAT) that was due for payment on 8 August 2017. Output VAT of £384 was originally paid in respect of this sale.

(7)   On 31 March 2018 the company sold all of its machinery for £31,200 and a motor car for £9,600. The motor car was used 30% privately by a director of Starfish Ltd.

Unless otherwise stated, all of the above figures are inclusive of VAT where applicable.

Starfish Ltd did not use the cash accounting scheme for VAT.

269   What is the amount of output tax on credit sales payable by Starfish Ltd for the quarter ended 31 March 2018?

    O   £384
    O   £480
    O   £390
    O   £325   (2 marks)

270 What is the amount of output tax, other than on credit sales, payable by Starfish Ltd for the quarter ended 31 March 2018?

- ○ £16,420
- ○ £11,620
- ○ £11,220
- ○ £10,000 **(2 marks)**

271 What is the amount of input tax recoverable by Starfish Ltd for the quarter ended 31 March 2018?

- ○ £12,744
- ○ £11,324
- ○ £10,940
- ○ £11,276 **(2 marks)**

272 From which date would default interest be payable if Starfish Ltd is late in paying the VAT for the quarter ended 31 March 2018?

- ○ 30 April 2018
- ○ 7 May 2018
- ○ 14 May 2018
- ○ 31 March 2018 **(2 marks)**

273 Which of the following would be the consequences for VAT if Starfish Ltd had instead sold its entire business as a going concern to a single VAT registered purchaser?

- ○ Output VAT would have been due on the sale of the inventory or the sale of the non-current assets but would be payable by the purchaser.

- ○ No output VAT would have been due on the sale of the inventory but would have been due on the sale of the non-current assets.

- ○ No output VAT would have been due on the sale of the non-current assets but would have been due on the sale of the inventory.

- ○ No output VAT would have been due on the sale of the inventory or the sale of the non-current assets. **(2 marks)**

(Total = 10 marks)

CBE style OT case – Greenzone Ltd (B) (06/13) (amended)
18 mins

This objective test question contains question types which will only appear in a computer-based exam, but this question provides valuable practice for all students whichever version of the exam they are taking.

The following scenario relates to Questions 274 to 278.

Greenzone Ltd owns 60% of Are Ltd, 40% of Be Ltd, 90% of Can Ltd and 70% of Doer Inc. All the companies are UK resident except for Doer Inc which also does not have a fixed establishment in the UK.

The following information is available in respect of Greenzone Ltd's value added tax (VAT) for the quarter ended 31 March 2018:

(1) Output VAT of £38,210 was charged in respect of sales. This figure includes output VAT of £400 on a deposit received on 29 March 2018, which is in respect of a contract that is due to commence on 20 April 2018.

(2) In addition to the above, Greenzone Ltd charged output VAT of £4,330 on sales to Can Ltd. Greenzone Ltd does not have group registration.

(3) The managing director of Greenzone Ltd is provided with free fuel for his company motor car. The total cost of fuel for the motor car for the quarter is £500 and 60% of the total mileage is private mileage.
Greenzone Ltd wishes to use the fuel scale charge. The relevant quarterly scale charge is £320. Both these figures are inclusive of VAT.

(4) Input VAT of £12,770 was incurred in respect of expenses (excluding the fuel in (3)). This figure includes the following input VAT:

	£
Entertaining UK customers	210
Entertaining overseas customers	139
Repainting the exterior of the company's office building	1,678
Extending the office building in order to create a new reception area	3,300

274   What is the amount of output VAT charged on the sales in (1) and (2) for the quarter to 31 March 2018?

- ○   £42,540
- ○   £38,210
- ○   £42,140
- ○   £37,810   **(2 marks)**

275   What is the net amount of VAT payable or recoverable for the provision of the fuel for the managing director's company motor car in (3)?

- ○   £20 payable
- ○   £36 recoverable
- ○   £53 payable
- ○   £30 recoverable   **(2 marks)**

276   What is the amount of input VAT that can be recovered on the expenses in (4)?

£ [   ]   **(2 marks)**

277   Identify, by clicking on the relevant boxes in the table below, which of the following companies (apart from Can Ltd) could be registered in a VAT group with Greenzone Ltd.

ARE LTD	BE LTD	DOER INC

(2 marks)

278   Which **TWO** of the following statements about VAT group registration are correct?

- ☐   Each VAT group must appoint a representative member which accounts for the group's output tax and input tax.
- ☐   Each VAT group must appoint a representative member which is solely liable for paying the group VAT liability.
- ☐   All eligible companies must be part of the group registration.
- ☐   Any supply of goods or services by a member of the group to another member of the group is disregarded for VAT purposes.   **(2 marks)**

(Total = 10 marks)

CBE style OT case – Long Ltd group (B) (06/14) (amended)

18 mins

This objective test question contains question types which will only appear in a computer-based exam, but this question provides valuable practice for all students whichever version of the exam they are taking.

The following scenario relates to Questions 279 to 283.

Long Ltd owns 100% of the ordinary share capital of both Wind Ltd and Road Ltd. Long Ltd and Road Ltd run freight transport businesses, whilst Wind Ltd provides transport related insurance services.

Long Ltd, Wind Ltd and Road Ltd are not registered as a group for value added tax (VAT) purposes, but such a registration is being considered, with Long Ltd being the representative member.

The following VAT information is available for the quarter ended 31 March 2018:

Long Ltd

(1)   All of Long Ltd's sales are standard rated for VAT.

(2)   Output VAT of £52,640 was charged in respect of sales. This figure includes output VAT of £1,760 on a deposit received on 28 December 2017. The deposit was in respect of a contract which was completed on 6 January 2018, with a sales invoice being issued on 20 January 2018.

(3)   In addition to the above, Long Ltd also charged output VAT of £1,940 on sales to Wind Ltd and output VAT of £960 on sales to Road Ltd.

(4)   Input VAT of £14,720 was incurred in respect of expenses.

(5)   In addition to the above, Long Ltd has discovered that it has not been claiming for the input VAT of £18 which it has paid each month since 1 January 2012 for the hire of a photocopier.

Wind Ltd

(1)   All of Wind Ltd's sales are exempt from VAT.

(2)   Input VAT of £7,330 was incurred in respect of expenses. This includes input VAT of £1,940 incurred on purchases from Long Ltd.

Road Ltd

(1)   All of Road Ltd's sales are zero rated for VAT.

(2)   Road Ltd registered for VAT on 1 January 2018 and this is the company's first VAT return.

(3)   Input VAT of £3,120 was incurred in respect of expenses. This includes input VAT of £960 incurred on purchases from Long Ltd.

(4)   In addition to the above, Road Ltd incurred input VAT in respect of advertising expenditure as follows:

	£
April 2017	640
November 2017	380
	1,020

279   What is the amount of output tax payable by Long Ltd for the quarter ended 31 March 2018?

£ [   ]

(2 marks)

280 What is the amount of input tax recoverable by Long Ltd for the quarter ended 31 March 2018?

    ○   £14,720
    ○   £14,774
    ○   £14,882
    ○   £15,638   **(2 marks)**

281 What is the amount of input tax recoverable by Wind Ltd for the quarter ended 31 March 2018?

£	

(2 marks)

282 What is the amount of input tax recoverable by Road Ltd for the quarter ended 31 March 2018?

Select... ▼
£3,120
£4,140
£3,500
£3,760

(2 marks)

283 Which **TWO** of the following statements about the Long Ltd group and VAT group registration are correct?

☐ If Wind Ltd and Road Ltd were both owned by the same individual they would not be able to be included in a group registration.

☐ Supplies of goods or services to Road Ltd from outside the group will be treated as a supply to Long Ltd.

☐ Each company in the Long Ltd group must join the VAT group if group registration is applied for.

☐ The supplies by Long Ltd to Wind Ltd and Road Ltd would be disregarded for VAT purposes.

(2 marks)

(Total = 10 marks)

CBE style OT case – Zim (06/15) (amended)   18 mins

This objective test question contains question types which will only appear in a computer-based exam, but this question provides valuable practice for all students whichever version of the exam they are taking.

The following scenario relates to Questions 284 to 288.

Zim has been registered for value added tax (VAT) since 1 April 2006. The following information is available for the year ended 31 March 2018:

(1) Sales invoices totalling £126,000 were issued, of which £115,200 were in respect of standard rated sales and £10,800 were in respect of zero rated sales. Zim's customers are all members of the general public.

(2) Purchase invoices totalling £49,200 were received, of which £43,200 were in respect of standard rated purchases and £6,000 were in respect of zero rated purchases.

(3) On 31 March 2018, Zim wrote off two impairment losses which were in respect of standard rated sales. The first impairment loss was for £780, and was in respect of a sales invoice which had been due for payment on 15 August 2017. The second impairment loss was for £660, and was in respect of a sales invoice which had been due for payment on 15 September 2017.

(4) During the year ended 31 March 2018, Zim spent £2,600 on mobile telephone calls, of which 40% related to private calls.

(5) During the year ended 31 March 2018, Zim spent £1,560 on entertaining customers, of which £240 was in respect of overseas customers.

All of the above figures are inclusive of VAT where applicable.

Zim does not use either the cash accounting scheme or the flat rate scheme. If he did use the flat rate scheme the relevant percentage for his business is 12%.

284   What is the net amount of VAT payable on the sales in (1) and the purchases in (2)?

£	

(2 marks)

285   What is the amount of input VAT which can be recovered on the impairment losses in (3)?

- ○   £0
- ○   £110
- ○   £130
- ○   £240

(2 marks)

286   What is the amount of input VAT which can be recovered on the expenditure on the mobile phone calls in (4) and entertaining customers in (5)?

	Mobile phone	*Customers*
○	£0	£220
○	£0	£40
○	£260	£220
○	£260	£40

(2 marks)

287   Match the thresholds for Zim to be able to join and to be required to leave the flat rate scheme.

Taxable turnover excluding VAT not more than £150,000 in next 12 months		Total turnover including VAT not more than £230,000 in next 12 months
Taxable turnover including VAT not more than £150,000 in next 12 months		**Total turnover excluding VAT more than £230,000 in previous 12 months**

Join	

Leave	

(2 marks)

288   How much VAT would Zim have paid in the year to 31 March 2018 if he had been in the flat rate scheme for the whole of that year?

Select... ▼
£15,120
£13,860
£13,824
£9,216

(2 marks)

(Total = 10 marks)

CBE style OT case – Smart Ltd (Sep/Dec 15) (amended) 18 mins

This objective test question contains question types which will only appear in a computer-based exam, but this question provides valuable practice for all students whichever version of the exam they are taking.

The following scenario relates to Questions 289 to 293.

Smart Ltd commenced trading on 1 September 2017. The company's sales for the first four months of trading were as follows:

2017	£
September	26,000
October	47,000
November	134,000
December	113,000

On 1 November 2017, the company signed a contract valued at £86,000 for completion during November 2017.

All of the above figures are stated exclusive of value added tax (VAT). Smart Ltd only supplies services and all of the company's supplies are standard rated.

Smart Ltd allows its customers 60 days' credit when paying for services, and it is concerned that some customers will default on the payment of their debts. The company pays its purchase invoices as soon as they are received.

Smart Ltd does not use either the VAT cash accounting scheme or the annual accounting scheme.

Smart Ltd is concerned about the penalties that could be charged if it makes a careless error in its VAT return resulting in underpaid VAT.

289   Match the dates from which Smart Ltd was required to register for VAT and by when it was required to notify HM Revenue & Customs (HMRC) of the registration.

1 November 2017	30 December 2017

30 November 2017	31 December 2017

Register	

Notification		(2 marks)

290 Identify, by clicking on the relevant boxes in the table below, which of the following statements about how and when Smart Ltd will have to submit its quarterly VAT returns and pay any related VAT liability are true or false.

Smart Ltd must file its VAT returns online.	TRUE	FALSE
Smart Ltd can choose whether to pay the VAT which is due electronically or by cheque.	TRUE	FALSE
The deadline for paying any VAT which is due is one month after the end of each quarter.	TRUE	FALSE
The deadline for filing the VAT return is one month and seven days after the end of each quarter.	TRUE	FALSE

(2 marks)

291 Which **TWO** of the following statements about the tax point for Smart Ltd's supplies of services are correct?

☐ The basic tax point is the date on which the invoice is issued.

☐ The basic tax point is the date on which services are completed.

☐ If a customer pays for services before the basic tax point, the payment date will be the tax point.

☐ If a customer pays for services after the basic tax point, the payment date will be the tax point.

(2 marks)

292 Which **TWO** of the following statements are advantages for Smart Ltd to use the VAT cash accounting scheme?

(1) The scheme will provide automatic relief for an impairment loss should a customer default on the payment of a debt.

(2) Only one VAT return will be required each year so there are fewer occasions to trigger a default surcharge.

(3) There will be reduced VAT administration as Smart Ltd will not be required to issue invoices to its customers.

(4) Output VAT will be accounted for 60 days later than at present, because the scheme will result in the tax point becoming the date when payment is received from customers.

O 1 and 2
O 2 and 3
O 1 and 4
O 2 and 4

(2 marks)

293 What is the maximum amount of penalty that could be charged by HMRC if Smart Ltd makes a careless error in its VAT return resulting in underpaid VAT and the minimum penalty that could be charged as a result of a subsequent prompted disclosure?

	Maximum penalty	Minimum penalty for prompted disclosure
O	70% of the VAT underpaid	15% of the VAT underpaid
O	70% of the VAT underpaid	0% of the VAT underpaid
O	30% of the VAT underpaid	15% of the VAT underpaid
O	30% of the VAT underpaid	0% of the VAT underpaid (2 marks)

(Total = 10 marks)

294 Jogger Ltd (B) (12/08) (amended) 18 mins

Jogger Ltd is a manufacturing company and has been registered for value added tax (VAT) since 1 April 2011. From that date until 30 June 2016 the company's VAT returns were all submitted on time. Since 1 July 2016 the company's VAT returns have been submitted as follows:

Quarter ended	VAT paid £	Submitted
30 September 2016	42,700	One month late
31 December 2016	41,200	On time
31 March 2017	38,900	One month late
30 June 2017	28,300	On time
30 September 2017	49,100	On time
31 December 2017	63,800	On time
31 March 2018	89,100	Two months late

Jogger Ltd always pays any VAT that is due at the same time as the related return is submitted.

Required

(a) State, giving appropriate reasons, the default surcharge consequences arising from Jogger Ltd's submission of its VAT returns for the quarter ended 30 September 2016 to the quarter ended 31 March 2018 inclusive, at the times stated. You may assume that Jogger Ltd is not a small business for the purposes of the default surcharge regime. **(6 marks)**

(b) Advise Jogger Ltd why it might be beneficial to use the VAT annual accounting scheme, and state the conditions that it will have to satisfy before being permitted to do so. **(4 marks)**

(Total = 10 marks)

295 Flick (B) (06/12) (amended) 18 mins

On 1 January 2018, Flick commenced in partnership with Art running a small cinema.

The partnership voluntarily registered for value added tax (VAT) on 1 January 2018, and immediately began using the flat rate scheme to calculate the amount of VAT payable. The relevant flat rate scheme percentage for the partnership's trade is 12%.

For the quarter ended 31 March 2018 the partnership had standard rated sales of £59,700, and these were all made to members of the general public. For the same period standard rated expenses amounted to £27,300. Both figures are stated inclusive of VAT.

The partnership has two private boxes in its cinema that can be booked on a special basis by privileged customers. Such customers can book the boxes up to two months in advance, at which time they have to pay a 25% deposit. An invoice is then given to the customer on the day of the screening of the film, with payment of the balance of 75% required within seven days. For VAT purposes, the renting out of the cinema boxes is a supply of services.

Required

(a) Explain whether or not it was beneficial for the partnership to have used the VAT flat rate scheme for the quarter ended 31 March 2018.

Notes

1   Your answer should be supported by appropriate calculations.

2   You should ignore the 1% reduction from the flat rate that is available during the first year of VAT registration. **(3 marks)**

(b) Explain whether or not it was financially beneficial for the partnership to have voluntarily registered for VAT from 1 January 2018.

Note. Your answer should be supported by appropriate calculations. **(3 marks)**

(c) Advise the partnership as to when it should account for output VAT on the renting out of its private boxes to privileged customers. **(4 marks)**

(Total = 10 marks)

296 Richard (B) (12/13) (amended)　　　18 mins

On 6 April 2017, Richard commenced in self-employment, running a restaurant.

Richard's sales since the commencement of trading have been as follows:

April to July 2017	£10,500 per month
August to November 2017	£15,000 per month
December 2016 to March 2018	£21,500 per month

These figures are stated exclusive of value added tax (VAT). Richard's sales are all standard rated.

As a trainee Chartered Certified Accountant you have advised Richard in writing that he should be registered for VAT, but he has refused to register because he thinks his net profit is insufficient to cover the additional cost which would be incurred.

Required

(a) Explain from what date Richard was required to be compulsorily registered for VAT and the VAT implications of continuing to trade after this date without registering.

Note. You are not expected to explain the VAT penalties arising from late VAT registration. **(4 marks)**

(b) Briefly explain from an ethical viewpoint the issues you, as a trainee Chartered Certified Accountant, should consider in order for your firm to deal with Richard's refusal to register for VAT. **(2 marks)**

(c) State the circumstances in which a trader can issue a simplified (or less detailed) VAT invoice, when such an invoice should be issued, and **FIVE** pieces of information which such an invoice must show where the supply is entirely standard rated. **(4 marks)**

(Total = 10 marks)

297 Clueless Ltd (A) (12/12) (amended)　　　18 mins

Clueless Ltd is a manufacturing company. It is registered for value added tax (VAT), but currently does not use any of the special VAT schemes. The company has annual standard rated sales of £1,200,000 and annual standard rated expenses of £550,000. Both these figures are exclusive of VAT and are likely to remain the same for the foreseeable future. Clueless Ltd is up to date with all of its tax returns, including those for corporation tax, PAYE and VAT. It is also up to date with its corporation tax, PAYE and VAT payments. However, the company often incurs considerable overtime costs due to its employees working late in order to meet tax return filing deadlines.

Clueless Ltd pays its expenses on a cash basis, but allows customers two months' credit when paying for sales. The company does not have any impairment losses.

Clueless Ltd is planning to purchase some new machinery at a cost of £22,000 (exclusive of VAT). The machinery can either be purchased from an overseas supplier situated outside the European Union, or from a VAT registered supplier situated in the European Union. Clueless Ltd is not a regular importer and so is unsure of the VAT treatment for this purchase.

Required

(a) Explain why Clueless Ltd is entitled to use both the VAT cash accounting scheme and the VAT annual accounting scheme, and why it will probably be beneficial for the company to use both schemes. **(6 marks)**

(b) Explain when and how Clueless Ltd will have to account for VAT in respect of the new machinery if it is purchased from:

(i) A supplier situated outside the European Union
(ii) A VAT registered supplier situated elsewhere within the European Union **(4 marks)**

(Total = 10 marks)

298 Garfield (Mar/Jun 16) 18 mins

Garfield has been registered for valued added tax (VAT) since 1 April 2011. Garfield has previously completed his VAT returns himself, but for the quarter ended 31 March 2018 there are some items for which he is unsure of the correct VAT treatment.

Garfield's partly completed VAT computation for the quarter ended 31 March 2018 is shown below. All of the completed sections of the computation are correct, with the omissions marked as outstanding (O/S).

	Note	£
Output VAT		
Sales (all standard rated)		22,500
Discounted sale	1	O/S
Equipment	2	O/S
Fuel scale charge		60
Input VAT		
Purchases (all standard rated)		(11,200)
Motor car (purchased on 1 January 2018)		0
Equipment	2	O/S
Impairment losses	3	O/S
Entertaining – UK customers		0
– Overseas customers	4	O/S
Motor expenses	5	O/S
VAT payable		O/S

Unless otherwise stated, all of the figures in the following notes are stated exclusive of VAT.

Notes

1 *Discounted sale*

On 10 February 2018, a sales invoice for £4,300 was issued by Garfield in respect of a standard rated supply. To encourage this previously late paying customer to pay promptly, Garfield offered a 10% discount for payment within 14 days of the date of the sales invoice. The customer paid within the 14-day period.

This invoice has not been taken into account in calculating the output VAT figure of £22,500, and this is the only sale for which Garfield has offered a prompt payment discount.

2 *Equipment*

During the quarter ended 31 March 2018, Garfield acquired some new equipment at a cost of £12,400 from a VAT registered supplier situated in the European Union.

3   *Impairment losses*

On 31 March 2018, Garfield wrote off three impairment losses. Details are as follows:

Amount	Invoice date	Payment due date
£1,400	30 July 2017	29 August 2017
£2,700	12 September 2017	12 October 2017
£1,900	4 October 2017	3 November 2017

4   *Entertaining*

During the quarter ended 31 March 2018, Garfield spent £960 on entertaining overseas customers. This figure is inclusive of VAT.

5   *Motor expenses*

The motor car purchased on 1 January 2018 is used by Garfield 60% for business mileage. During the quarter ended 31 March 2018, Garfield spent £1,008 on repairs to the motor car and £660 on fuel for both his business and private mileage. Both of these figures are inclusive of VAT.

Additional information

Garfield does not use the cash accounting scheme, the annual accounting scheme or the flat rate scheme, but has read that the use of these schemes can be beneficial for small businesses such as his.

Garfield's VAT exclusive annual turnover is currently £450,000, and this is expected to steadily decrease over the coming years. He pays for most of his purchases and expenses on a cash basis, but allows many of his customers 30 days' credit when paying for sales.

Required

(a)   Calculate the amount of value added tax (VAT) payable by Garfield for the quarter ended 31 March 2018.

(7 marks)

(b)   State which VAT schemes Garfield is currently permitted to use, and explain, with supporting reasons, which **ONE** of the available schemes would appear to be the most beneficial for him to use.

Notes

1   Your answer should be confined to the information given in the question.
2   You are not expected to explain how any of the schemes operate.   **(3 marks)**

(Total = 10 marks)

299 Zhi (Mar/Jun 17)   18 mins

You should assume that today's date is 15 December 2017.

Zhi has been self-employed since 2000, preparing accounts to 31 December. On 1 December 2017, Zhi purchased a new freehold warehouse for £164,000 for use in his business, but this purchase has resulted in Zhi having cash flow problems. He has various tax payments becoming due over the next two months, and would like to reduce or postpone these payments as much as possible.

Income tax and national insurance contributions (NICs)

Zhi's income tax liabilities and class 4 NICs for the tax years 2015/16, 2016/17, and 2017/18 are, or are forecast to be:

	2015/16	2016/17	2017/18
	£	£	£
Income tax liability	25,200	27,600	18,000
Class 4 NICs	4,084	4,204	3,724

Zhi has not made any claims to reduce his payments on account.

Capital gains tax (CGT)

Zhi has a CGT liability of £12,940 becoming due for payment on 31 January 2018. This is in respect of a freehold office building which was sold for £210,000 on 10 December 2016, resulting in a chargeable gain of £76,000. The office building had always been used for business purposes by Zhi.

Zhi is a higher rate taxpayer. No claim has been made for rollover relief.

Value added tax (VAT)

Zhi has forecast that he will have to pay VAT of £20,200 on 7 February 2018 to HM Revenue and Customs (HMRC) in respect of the VAT quarter ended 31 December 2017.

On 12 December 2017, Zhi despatched goods relating to an exceptionally large credit sale of standard rated goods of £45,600 (inclusive of VAT). He has not yet issued a sales invoice for this sale.

Because the customer is unlikely to pay until 28 February 2018, Zhi is considering not issuing a sales invoice until 1 February 2018.

PAYE and NICs

Zhi will have to pay PAYE and NICs of £5,724 electronically on 22 January 2018 to HMRC in respect of his two employees for the tax month running from 6 December 2017 to 5 January 2018.

This includes amounts for bonuses which Zhi was planning to pay to his two employees on 1 January 2018, but could delay payment until 10 January 2018. The bonuses are in respect of the year ended 31 December 2017, and they will be treated as being received on whichever is the date of payment.

The first employee has a gross annual salary of £20,000 and is to be paid a bonus of £1,500. The second employee has a gross annual salary of £55,000 and is to be paid a bonus of £5,000.

Required

(a) Calculate the amount by which Zhi can claim to reduce his self-assessment income tax and NICs due for payment on 31 January 2018 without incurring interest or penalties. **(2 marks)**

(b) Calculate the amount by which Zhi's CGT liability due for payment on 31 January 2018 will be reduced if he makes a claim for rollover relief based on the warehouse purchased on 1 December 2017 for £164,000. **(3 marks)**

(c) Explain whether Zhi can reduce the amount of VAT payable on 7 February 2018 by not issuing a sales invoice for the credit sale of £45,600 until 1 February 2018, and, if so, by how much the payment will be reduced. **(2 marks)**

(d) Calculate the amount by which Zhi's PAYE and NICs due on 22 January 2018 will be reduced if he delays the payment of employee bonuses until 10 January 2018, and state when the postponed amount will be payable.

Note. Your calculations should be based on annual income tax and NIC thresholds. **(3 marks)**

(Total = 10 marks)

Answers

MCQ bank – The UK tax system and its administration 1

1   **2 and 4**

Inheritance tax is a progressive tax as the proportion of the wealth that is taxable increases as wealth increases (the amount covered by the nil rate band is charged at 0% and the remainder at 20% or 40%). It is also a redistributive tax as it redistributes wealth.

Inheritance tax is a direct tax and it is not an environmental tax.

2   **2 and 3**

Statutes (Acts of Parliament) and Statutory Instruments have legal force.

HMRC publications such as Revenue and Customs Briefs and Extra Statutory Concessions do not have legal force.

3   **By the Upper Tribunal**

The Upper Tribunal deals with complex cases which either involve an important issue of tax law or a large financial sum.

4   **Notify by 5 October 2018, payment by 31 January 2019**

The chargeable gain arises in the tax year 2017/18 and so Daren must notify HMRC of his chargeability within six months from the end of the tax year. The tax liability must be paid by 31 January following the end of the tax year. There are no payments on account for capital gains tax.

5   **£742**

Potential Lost Revenue is the tax payable of £2,120 (40% × £5,300).

The minimum penalty for a prompted, deliberate, but not concealed error is 35% × PLR which is £742.

6   **£1,524**

Due date 1 April 2018, paid 31 July 2018 so four months late. Interest is

4/12 × 2.75% × £166,250   £1,524

7   **Year ended 31 December 2020**

The profit threshold for being a large company is £1,500,000/2 = £750,000 since there is one related 51% group company. This threshold is first exceeded in the year ended 31 December 2019 but a company is not required to pay its corporation tax by instalments in the first year that it is large unless its profits exceed £10,000,000, as reduced by related 51% group companies. Mammoth Ltd is also a large company in the year ended 31 December 2020 and so must pay its corporation tax liability by quarterly instalments for that year.

8   Value added tax neither type, Inheritance tax capital tax, National insurance contributions revenue tax

9   **£406,600**

	£
Unconnected company	5,200
Group dividend	0
Non-51% group dividend	1,400
Taxable total profits	400,000
Profits	406,600

10   Paper return 31 October 2018, Online tax return 31 January 2019

CBE style OTQ bank – The UK tax system and its administration 2

11

Submission	31 January 2019

Notification	30 April 2020

As the return is filed after the due filing date of 31 January 2019, the notification must be made by the quarter day following the first anniversary of the actual filing date.

12 £5,148

	£
Income tax £(12,500 – 10,000 payments on account)	2,500
Class 2 NIC	148
Class 4 NIC £(2,500 – 2,000 payments on account)	500
Capital gains tax	2,000
Amount to pay on 31 January 2019	5,148

13 £28

£10,000 is paid by the due date of 1 January 2019. The balance of £12,400 is one month late so the interest on late paid tax is £12,400 × 2.75% × 1/12 = £28.

14 £50,000 due on 14 May 2018

The amount of each of the first 3 instalments is 3/10 × £500,000 = £150,000. The final instalment is the remaining liability of £500,000 – (3 × £150,000) = £50,000, and is due on the 14th day of the 4th month of the next accounting period.

15 £100

There is a £100 penalty for late return which is submitted within 3 months of the due date (here 12 months after the end of the period to which the return relates).

16 Tax evasion is illegal, whereas tax avoidance involves the minimisation of tax liabilities by the use of any lawful means.

17 10%

The due date for payment was 31 January 2018. The penalty date is 30 days after the due date for the tax. There is a penalty of 5% of the unpaid tax for failing to pay by the penalty date plus a further penalty of 5% of the unpaid tax as the payment is more than 5 months after the penalty date but not more than 11 months after the penalty date.

18 Amendment 31 January 2019, Compliance check 10 August 2018

Willard may amend his return for 2016/17 within 12 months after the filing date which for this purpose is taken to be 31 January 2018 (not the paper filing date of 31 October 2017, even though he has made a paper return). HMRC must give written notice of its intention to start a compliance check by the first anniversary of the actual filing date as the return was delivered on or before the due filing date, so in this case the notice must be given by 10 August 2018.

19   Start a compliance check enquiry into the return

> **Examining team's comments.** This question tested candidates' knowledge of how HMRC can make a determination of the amount of tax that a taxpayer is liable to. Perhaps not surprisingly, more than 40% of candidates opted for 'start a compliance check enquiry into the return' – possibly because a compliance check was the most well-known of the options. However, the correct answer (a determination) was the second most popular choice. Although this style of question can be answered very quickly, it does not mean that it doesn't warrant any thought. Realising that a compliance check by its very nature involves a submitted return, could have easily ruled this option out.

20   £52

> **Examining team's comments.** This question tested candidates' ability to calculate late payment interest where an excessive claim has been made to reduce a payment on account. Answers were spread fairly evenly over the four choices, indicating that many candidates simply made an educated guess. Although not an easy question, taking a careful approach with amounts and dates would probably have achieved the correct answer. The most important point was the £6,000 payment on 30 September 2018, which was two months late. The final payment was made on time. Therefore, £7,800 was late for two months (31 July to 30 September 2018) and £1,800 (£7,800 - £6,000) was late for four months (1 October 2016 to 31 January 2019). The interest amounts at 2.75% are £36 and £16, making a total of £52. An alternative working would have been £6,000 late for two months (£27) and £1,800 late for six months (£25).This question demonstrates just how much care needs to be taken with dates when calculating interest payable on late tax payments.

Domingo and Fargo

> **Text references.** Chapter 17 deals with self-assessment for individuals.
>
> **Top tips.** Note the difference between record keeping requirements for taxpayers in business and those not in business.
>
> **Easy marks.** There were easy marks in question 21 for the requirements for filing tax returns.

21   Domingo 31 October 2018, Fargo 31 January 2019

22   Domingo 31 January 2020, Fargo 31 January 2024

Domingo was not in business during 2017/18, so his records must be retained until one year after 31 January following the tax year, which is 31 January 2020.

Fargo was in business during 2017/18, so all of his records (both business and non-business) must be retained until five years after 31 January following the tax year, which is 31 January 2024.

23   £3,000

24   Balancing payment and first payment on account 31 January 2019, second payment on account 31 July 2019

25   Interest £1,800 × 2.75% × 4/12 = £16

The answer £49 is the interest for a whole year.

Penalty £1,800 @ 5% = £90 (balancing payment not more than five months after the penalty date).

CBE style OT case – Joe (A)

26   The code number for Joe, if he was only entitled to a personal allowance, would be 1150L and Joe's tax code will be applied to his salary when calculating the amount of income tax that has to be paid each month under the PAYE system.

Joe's tax code can be adjusted for unpaid tax on income from earlier years. HMRC may issue amended tax codes during the tax year.

27

Date	31 December 2017

Employer	Firstly plc

Form P45 will show Joe's taxable earnings and income tax deducted up to the date of leaving, together with his tax code at the date of leaving.

28   31 May 2018 by Secondly plc

Form P60 will be prepared by Secondly plc at the end of the tax year. It will show Joe's taxable earnings, income tax deducted, final tax code, national insurance contributions, and Secondly plc's name and address.

29

Date	6 July 2018

Information	Cash equivalents of the benefits

30   £400

Secondly plc has over 250 employees so the penalty is £400.

CBE style OT case – Ernest

31

Tax evasion is illegal	**TRUE**	
Both tax evasion and tax avoidance are illegal		**FALSE**
Tax avoidance involves any legal method of reducing the taxpayer's tax burden	**TRUE**	
Tax evasion always involves providing HM Revenue & Customs with false information		**FALSE**

Tax evasion does not necessarily involve providing HM Revenue & Customs (HMRC) with false information. It could include this situation where Ernest is evading tax by not providing HMRC with information to which it is entitled.

32 Ernest should be advised to disclose details of the capital gain to HMRC. If Ernest does not disclose the gain to HMRC, your firm would be obliged to report under the money laundering regulations.

Your firm should also consider ceasing to act for Ernest. If it does cease to act, your firm should notify HMRC that it no longer acts for him although your firm should not provide any reason for this.

33 £12,600

The maximum penalty for an error which is deliberate but not concealed is 70% of potential lost revenue which is £18,000 × 70% = £12,600.

34 £6,300

The minimum penalty for prompted disclosure of an error which is deliberate but not concealed is 35% of potential lost revenue which is £18,000 × 35% = £6,300.

35 £247

The due date for payment was 31 January 2018 so the payment is six months late. The interest payable is therefore £18,000 × 2.75% × 6/12 = £247.

CBE style OTQ case – Thai Curry Ltd

Text references. Chapter 23 deals with corporation tax administration. Chapter 17 contains material on the common penalty regime for errors.

Top tips. Remember that some elements of tax administration are the same for both individuals and companies such as penalties for errors. However, you need to watch out for circumstances where they are different such as the penalties for late filing.

Easy marks. Make sure you know due dates for returns and tax payments.

36 31 March 2019

The CT return must be submitted one year after the end of the period of account ie by 31 March 2019.

37 £3,462

As the return is more than three months late the fixed penalty is £200. As the return is more than six months late there is also a tax geared penalty of 10% × unpaid tax, ie £32,624 × 10% = £3,262. The total amount of penalties is therefore £(200 + 3,262) = £3,462.

38 £32,624 on 1 January 2019

As the company is not large since its profits are below the profit threshold of £1,500,000 it must pay its corporation tax by nine months and one day after the accounting period, ie by 1 January 2019.

39   An internal review is a less costly and more effective way to resolve disputes informally than a formal appeal.

HMRC must usually carry out the review within 45 days.

An internal review is a less costly and more effective way to resolve disputes informally than a formal appeal and HMRC must usually carry out the review within 45 days. The internal review will be made by an objective HMRC review officer not previously connected with the case. After the review conclusion is notified, the company has 30 days to appeal to the Tax Tribunal.

40

Complex track	Upper tier

Standard track	First tier

41 John

Text references. Self-assessment for individuals is covered in Chapter 17. The UK tax system is the subject of Chapter 1.

Top tips. There are a number of penalties based on Potential Lost Revenue so you need to be able to explain what this is.

Easy marks. There were some easy marks for the date for notification and the date by which the compliance check needed to be started.

				Marks
(a)	(i)	Date for notification	1	
		Maximum penalty	1	
		Minimum penalty	1	
				3
	(ii)	Compliance check notification date	1	
		Random basis	1	
		Other reasons	1	
				3
(b)	(i)	Saving		1
	(ii)	Charitable support		1
	(iii)	Capital gains reliefs		
		Plant and machinery	1	
			1	
				2
				10

(a)   (i)   **Notification of chargeability**

John should have given notice to HM Revenue & Customs (HMRC) of his chargeability to income tax for 2016/17 by 5 October 2017.

The maximum penalty for careless late notification is 30% of the Potential Lost Revenue (PLR) to HMRC which will be John's tax payable on the return for 2016/17.

However, if John tells HMRC of his failure to notify within 12 months and John has no reason to believe HMRC has discovered, or is about to discover, the error (unprompted disclosure) as appears to be the case here, the penalty can be reduced by HMRC to 0%.

(ii)   **Compliance check**

If HMRC intends to carry out a compliance check enquiry into John's 2016/17 tax return, it will have to notify him by the first anniversary of the actual filing date.

HMRC has the right to carry out a compliance check enquiry as regards the completeness and accuracy of any return and some returns are selected for a compliance check enquiry at random.

Other returns are selected for a particular reason; for example, if HMRC believes that there has been an underpayment of tax due to the taxpayer's failure to comply with tax legislation.

(b)   (i)   Saving is encouraged by offering individuals tax incentives such as income tax and capital gains tax exemptions on new individual savings accounts and income tax relief on pension contributions.

(ii)   Charitable support is encouraged by giving individuals income tax relief on donations made through the gift aid scheme or by payroll deduction.

(iii)   Entrepreneurs are encouraged to build their own businesses through various capital gains tax reliefs such as entrepreneurs' relief.

Investment in plant and machinery is encouraged through capital allowances.

42 Sugar plc

> **Text references.** Chapter 19 deals with computing the corporation tax liability. Chapter 23 includes payment of tax by companies.
>
> **Top tips.** The rules on related 51% group companies are still relatively new and so are highly topical.
>
> **Easy marks.** The calculation of the corporation tax liability in part (c) was straightforward.

Marking scheme

			Marks
(a)	Definition	1	
	Honey plc	½	
	Molasses plc	½	
	Treacle plc	1	
			3
(b)	*Year ended 31 March 2018*		
	Profit limit	½	
	Taxable total profits	½	
	Dividends	1	
	Profits, therefore large	½	
	Year ended 31 March 2019		
	Taxable total profits = profits, therefore large	½	
			3
(c)	*Year ended 31 March 2018*		
	Corporation tax	½	
	Date payable	½	
	Year ended 31 March 2019		
	Corporation tax	½	
	Instalments	½	
	Dates payable	2	
			4
			10

(a)   A company B is a related 51% group company of another company A, if A is a 51% subsidiary of B (B owns more than 50% of A's ordinary shares directly or indirectly) or B is a 51% subsidiary of A or both A and B are 51% subsidiaries of another company. Honey plc is not a related 51% group company of Sugar plc because Sugar plc only directly owns 45% of the ordinary shares of Honey plc. Molasses plc is a related 51% group company of Sugar plc because Sugar plc directly owns 75% of the ordinary shares of Molasses plc. Treacle plc is a related 51% group company of Sugar plc because Sugar plc indirectly owns 75% × 70% = 52.5% of the ordinary shares of Treacle plc.

(b)   *Year ended 31 March 2018*

Sugar plc has two related 51% group companies (Molasses plc and Treacle plc) at the end of the previous accounting period. The profit limit is therefore £1,500,000/3 = £500,000. Sugar plc's profits for the year to 31 March 2018 are:

	£
Taxable total profits	470,000
Dividends from non-group companies	50,000
Profits	520,000

Sugar plc is therefore a large company in the year to 31 March 2018.

Year ended 31 March 2019

The profit limit is the same and Sugar plc's taxable total profits of £600,000 are also its profits for these purposes. Sugar plc is therefore a large company in the year to 31 March 2019.

(c)   *Year ended 31 March 2018*

	£
Corporation tax liability	
£470,000 × 19%	89,300

Since this is the first year that Sugar plc is a large company, its corporation tax liability will be due in one amount on 1 January 2019.

Year ended 31 March 2019

	£
Corporation tax liability	
£600,000 × 19%	114,000

This is payable in four equal instalments of £28,500. The instalments will be due on 14 October 2018, 14 January 2019, 14 April 2019 and 14 July 2019.

MCQ bank – Income tax and NIC liabilities 1

43 Sofia only

> **Examining team's comments.** As Hamza spent only 42 days in the UK he meets the automatic overseas test despite having a home in the UK, and no other home. Sofia doesn't meet any of the automatic overseas tests but she is automatically UK resident due to the home test. The vast majority of candidates chose the option Both Hamza and Sofia.

44 £2,500

	£
£3,000 @ 20%	600
£(5,000 – 3,000) = £2,000 @ 0% (starting rate band)	0
£1,000 @ 0% (savings income nil rate band)	0
£(12,500 – 2,000 – 1,000) = £9,500 @ 20%	1,900
Tax liability	2,500

The answer £2,900 does not apply the starting rate band. The answer £2,700 does not apply the savings income nil rate band. The answer £3,100 applies 20% to all income.

45 £300

	£
Rental income £150 × 52	7,800
Less rent a room limit	(7,500)
	300

Luke should elect for the 'alternative basis' under rent a room relief, rather the normal basis which would give taxable property business income of £(150 – 20) = £130 × 52 = £6,760.

46 £2,250

	£
Taxable income	12,400
Tax	
£12,400 × 20%	2,480
Less transferred personal allowance tax reducer £1,150 × 20%	(230)
Income tax liability	2,250

The answer £180 assumes that Delia can transfer her full personal allowance to Mike. The answer £1,330 deducts £1,150 as a tax reducer. The answer £2,480 is Mike's income tax liability with no transfer.

47 £3,300

			£
Use	£3,600 × 20%		720
Gift	Current market value	£1,000	
	or		
	Original value	£3,600	
	less use:		
	2016/17 £720 × 5/12	(300)	
	2017/18	(720)	
		£2,580	
	The greater amount is taken		2,580
Total benefits 2017/18			3,300

Note that the value of the asset when first provided to any employee is used rather than the value when first provided to John.

The answer £2,880 assumes the first year of provision was taxed in full. The answer £1,720 uses the lower value for the gift rather than the higher value. The answer £1,833 uses the value of £2,000 when the asset was provided to John.

48   £59,800

	£
£(33,500 + 10,000) = £43,500 @ 20%	8,700
£(150,000 + 10,000) = £(160,000 − 43,500) = £116,500 @ 40%	46,600
£(170,000 − 160,000) = £10,000 @ 45%	4,500
Tax liability	59,800

The answer £60,300 does not adjust the higher rate limit. The answer £62,300 does not adjust either the basic rate limit or the higher rate limit. The answer £54,700 deducts the personal allowance.

49   £538

	£
Net income	57,000
Less personal pension contributions (gross)	(2,000)
Adjusted net income	55,000
Less threshold	(50,000)
Excess	5,000
÷ £100	50
Child benefit income tax charge: 1% × £1,076 × 50	538

The answer £1,076 assumes there is full recovery of child benefit. The answer £430 is the child benefit times 40%. The answer £753 does not adjust for pension contributions.

50   £22,500

The bonus received on 30 September 2017 is taxable in 2017/18 as the receipts basis applies to employment income.

The gratuity received on 1 December 2017 is taxable as employment income in 2017/18 as it is a reward of the employment even though it was not received from the employer.

51   £4,600

CO_2 emission (rounded down)	105
Base figure	(95)
	10
Divided by 5	2
Starting percentage	18
Diesel addition	3
Final percentage	23
Benefit £20,000 (list price) × 23%	£4,600

The answer £3,600 uses actual cost (not list price) and there is no diesel addition. The answer £4,140 uses actual cost. The answer £4,000 does not use the diesel addition.

52   £8,450

	£	£
Basic benefit		
Annual value		8,000
Additional benefit		
Market value	93,000	
Less limit	(75,000)	
	18,000	
Additional benefit £18,000 × 2.5%		450
Total benefits 2017/18		8,450

The value of the accommodation when occupied by Jonas is not relevant as fewer than six years have elapsed since purchase when Jonas first moves in.

The answer £8,850 uses £109,000 as the cost of the accommodation. The answer £10,325 does not deduct the limit of £75,000. The answer £8,000 is the basic benefit.

CBE style OTQ bank – Income tax and NIC liabilities 2

53

Marion	£333

Gerald	£167

Marion

	£
Accrued interest deemed received 31.12.17 taxable savings income £20,000 × 5% × 4/12	333

Gerald

	£
Interest received 31.12.17 £20,000 × 5% × 6/12	500
Less relief for accrued interest (amount taxable on Marion) £20,000 × 5% × 4/12	(333)
Taxable savings income	167

54 Travel from office to visit a client

Travel from home to visit a trade fair relevant to the employer's business

Travel from home to a workplace to which an employee has been seconded for 36 months does not qualify as travel to a temporary workplace as the secondment exceeds 24 months. Travel from home to a permanent place of work is not a qualifying travel expense.

55 £55,000

	£
2017/18 annual allowance	40,000
2016/17 annual allowance £(40,000 – 25,000)	15,000
	55,000

The annual allowance for 2014/15 and 2015/16 are not available as Troy was not a member of a pension scheme in those years.

The answer £40,000 is the current year annual allowance. The answer £135,000 brings forward allowances from all three previous tax years. The answer £35,000 restricts the current year allowance to £10,000.

56 Interest on an NS&I Investment account

Interest on UK government stocks ('gilts').

Premium bond prizes and dividends on shares held in an Individual Savings Account are exempt.

57 £3,800

The replacement of an equivalent model of sofa is allowable as a deduction. It is restricted by the amount of proceeds realised by selling the first sofa.

£(4,000 – 200)   £3,800

The answer £5,500 allows the full cost of the enhancement of furniture. The answer £5,300 allows the cost of the enhancement of furniture less the proceeds of the first sofa. The answer £4,000 is the cost of the replacement sofa.

58 £1,640

The grant of a new short lease and the purchase of freehold premises are capital and therefore the legal fees on them are not deductible.

The legal fees concerning the employment contract and debt collection are deductible £(720 + £920) = £1,640

59 £5,400

Depreciation and customer entertaining are not deductible and must be added back. The amount added back is therefore £(3,000 + 2,400) = £5,400.

Staff entertaining is fully deductible (the £150 limit applies to the taxable benefit for the employees).

60 £20,375

	£
Cash sales	41,000
Invoice sales £(4,000 – 1,500)	2,500
Less: cash expenses	(20,200)
motoring expenses 6,500 × 45p	(2,925)
Taxable trading income 2017/18	20,375

61 £968

The motor car will be treated as a special rate item and will therefore be entitled to writing down allowance at 8%. The allowance will be restricted because of the private use. The total amount due is: £22,000 × 8% × 4,950/9,000 = £968

62 £84,208

	AIA £	Main pool £	Allowances £
p/e 5.4.18			
Plant	95,000		
AIA £200,000 × 5/12	(83,333)		83,333
Transfer to pool	11,667	11,667	
WDA @ 18% × 5/12		(875)	875
TWDV c/f		10,792	
Allowances			84,208

The answer £68,367 time apportions from the date of acquisition rather than the length of the period of account. The answer £85,433 does not time apportion the WDA. The answer £95,000 is the unrestricted annual investment allowance.

CBE style OTQ bank – Income tax and NIC liabilities 3

63   £400

	Main pool £	Allowances £
y/e 5.4.18		
TWDV b/f	12,000	
Disposal (limit to cost)	(11,600)	
	400	
WDA – small pool	(400)	400
TWDV c/f	0	

64

Start date	6 April 2017

End date	5 April 2018

2017/18 is the second year of trading. There is no accounting date ending in this year so the actual basis applies.

65   £13,000

First tax year (2015/16): Actual basis 1.2.16 to 5.4.16

Second tax year (2016/17): First 12 months of trading 1.2.16 to 31.1.17

Third tax year (2017/18): Current year basis 1.12.16 to 30.11.17

Periods of overlap 1.2.16 to 5.4.16 and 1.12.16 to 31.1.17

	£
2/10 × £30,000	6,000
2/12 × £42,000	7,000
	13,000

66   £19,000

	£
y/e 31.12.17	18,000
p/e 31.3.18	3,000
Less overlap profits	(2,000)
	19,000

67

2016/17	£3,000

2017/18	£9,600

	£
2016/17 Actual basis 1.1.17 to 5.4.17	
£9,000 × 3/9	3,000
2017/18 First 12 months 1.1.17 to 31.12.17	
£(9,000 – 3,000)	6,000
£14,400 × 3/12	3,600
	9,600

68 £6,000

	2016/17	2017/18
	£	£
Trading profit	16,000	0
Investment income	3,000	3,000
Total income	19,000	3,000
Less loss relief	(19,000)	(0)
Net income	0	3,000
Less personal allowance	0	(3,000)
Net income	0	0

Loss to carry forward to 2018/19 is £(25,000 – 19,000) = £6,000

A claim should not be made to set the loss against investment income in 2017/18 since this is covered by the personal allowance for that year. It is not possible to restrict the set off of the loss in 2016/17 to preserve the personal allowance.

69 £44,150

	£
1.8.16 to 31.8.16 1/12 × £96,000 × 1/2	4,000
1.9.16 to 31.7.17 Salary 11/12 × £9,000	8,250
1.9.16 to 31.7.17 Profit share	
(11/12 × £[96,000 – 8,250]) × 2/5	31,900
	44,150

70

Robin and Stuart each	£48,000

Tania	£5,600

Robin and Stuart

CYB y/e 31.12.17 £96,000 × 1/2 = £48,000

Tania

Actual basis 1.1.18 – 5.4.18 £112,000 × 1/5 × 3/12 = £5,600

71 £151

	£
Class 2 contributions 14 × £2.85	40
Class 4 contributions £(9,400 – 8,164) × 9%	111
Total contributions	151

72 £300

	£
Class 4 contributions £([13,500 – 2,000] – 8,164) × 9%	300

CBE style OT case – Ann, Basil and Chloe

> **Text references.** Pensions are covered in Chapter 5. The computation of taxable income and the income tax liability are dealt with in Chapter 2.
>
> **Top tips.** Remember that higher rate tax relief for personal pension contributions made by higher rate taxpayers is given by increasing the basic rate limit.
>
> **Easy marks.** There were some easy marks in question 75 for working out a basic tax liability.

73 Individuals can always make gross pension contributions of £3,600 in 2017/18 even if they do not have any relevant earnings in that tax year.

Relevant earnings relate both to contributions to personal pension schemes and to occupational pension schemes.

Unused relevant earnings cannot be carried forward. Relevant earnings include trading income, employment income and income from furnished holiday lettings.

74

Employer contributions do not count towards the annual allowance.		**FALSE**
The annual allowance can be carried forward for three years to the extent that it is unused in the tax year.	**TRUE**	
The annual allowance is available even if the individual is not a member of a pension scheme in a tax year and so can be carried forward.		**FALSE**
If tax-relievable pension contributions exceed the annual allowance, there is a charge to income tax.	**TRUE**	

75 £15,200

The available annual allowance is £(40,000 + 20,000) = £60,000 and so there is no annual allowance charge for the tax year 2017/18. The basic rate band limit is £(33,500 + 49,000) = £82,500 so all of Anne's taxable income is within the basic rate band.

Tax £76,000 × 20%	£15,200

76 £6,000

The annual allowance must be tapered because Basil's adjusted income before any deduction for the pension contribution is more than £150,000. Basil is still a higher rate taxpayer because his higher rate limit is lifted by the gross pension contribution.

Annual allowance £40,000 − [½ × £(160,000 − 150,000)]	£35,000
Excess pension contribution over annual allowance £(50,000 − 35,000) @ 40%	£6,000

77   £720

Maximum personal pension contribution is £3,600 since Chloe has no relevant earnings. The pension tax relief is therefore £3,600 × 20% = £720. This relief will have been given at source. The remaining £4,600 contribution is not given tax relief.

Ae, Bee, Cae, and Eu

Text references. Partnerships are covered in Chapter 11. Assessable trading income is dealt with in Chapter 9 and capital allowances are covered in Chapter 8.

Top tips. Remember that there is no annual investment allowance nor writing down allowance in the final period of account.

Easy marks. There were easy marks in question 80 for working out the trading income assessment.

78   £32,500

	£
2016/17	
Second year, short period of account (first 12 months trading)	
1 July 2015 to 30 April 2016	
£54,000 × ½	27,000
1 May 2016 to 30 June 2016	
£66,000 × ½ × 2/12	5,500
	32,500

79   £21,750

	£
Y/e 30 April 2018 – Cae joined 1 July 2017	
1 July 2017 to 30 April 2018	
£87,000 × 10/12 = 72,500 × 1/3	24,167
First year	
Actual basis 1 July 2017 – 5 April 2018	
£24,167 × 9/10	21,750

80   £61,200

	£
2018/19	
CYB y/e 30.6.18 Trading income	62,775
Less CAs	(1,575)
	61,200

81   £3,108

	£
p/e 30.9.19	
TWDV b/f	5,883
Addition	2,400
Disposal	(5,175)
BA	3,108

82   £57,908

	£
2019/20	
y/e 30.6.19 £(57,600 – 1,292)	56,308
p/e 30.9.19 £(14,400 – 3,000)	11,400
Less overlap profits	(9,800)
	57,908

CBE style OT case – Rosie and Sam

Text references. Personal pensions are covered in Chapter 5. The income tax treatment of investments is covered in Chapter 2 and the capital gains tax implications of investments are dealt with in Chapter 13.

Top tips. Remember that there is useful information contained in the Tax Tables provided in the examination. For question 83, the annual allowance amounts were vital and could be found in the Tax Tables. For question 86 the annual limit for ISAs is also in the Tax Tables.

Easy marks. There were easy marks in question 85 for identifying the tax consequences of flexible access drawdown.

83   £34,000

Rosie was a member of a pension scheme for 2016/17, so the annual allowance for that year is available but the annual allowance is not available for carry forward from 2014/15. Her adjusted income for the tax years 2016/17 and 2017/18 are greater than £210,000 so her annual allowances for both tax years are tapered to £10,000.

She has unused allowances of £(40,000 – 26,000) = £14,000 from 2015/16, and £10,000 from 2016/17, so the available annual allowances for 2017/18 are therefore £(10,000 (2017/18) + 14,000 + 10,000) = £34,000.

84   Charge at **45%** on excess contributions

The annual allowance charge is calculated by taxing the excess contribution as an extra amount of income received by Rosie and so is charged at her highest rate of income tax.

85   Lump sum: up to 25% of fund can be taken as tax-free lump sum

Rest of fund: taxable as pension income when received

86   £19,000

The ISA amount 2017/18 is £20,000. Sam has already invested £6,000 in the tax year 2017/18, so can invest a further £(20,000 – 6,000) = £14,000. He can also replace the £5,000 withdrawn in October 2017 so the total amount he can now invest is £(14,000 + 5,000) = £19,000.

87

Premium bonds	Exempt from both income tax and capital gains tax

Government securities	Chargeable to income tax, exempt from capital gains tax

CBE style OTQ case – Fang and Hong

Text references. The basis of assessment for sole traders is covered in Chapter 9. Relief for pre-trading expenditure is described in Chapter 7 and capital allowances in Chapter 8. Trading losses are dealt with in Chapter 10.

Top tips. It is important to identify the relevant tax years when dealing with the basis of assessment.

Easy marks. The identification of relief for overlap profits in question 89 should have been easy marks.

88

2015/16	£30,640

2016/17	£45,960

Tax year	Basis of assessment	£
2015/16	Actual – 1 August 2015 to 5 April 2016	
	£45,960 × 8/12	30,640
2016/17	12 months to accounting date in tax year	
	y/e 31 July 2016	45,960

89   Against trading income on cessation

90   Trading expenditure: treated as incurred on 1 August 2015

Computer equipment: addition for capital allowances purposes based on its market value at 1 August 2015

91   £31,000

	£
Trading profit	29,700
Less trading loss brought forward	(2,600)
	27,100
Property business profit	3,900
	31,000
Less trading loss carried back	(31,000)
Net income	0

If your choice was £19,500, you restricted the loss relief to keep the personal allowance in charge which is not permitted.

92   The trading loss is first set against general income of the tax year 2016/17 and only any excess loss is set against chargeable gains of that year.

The amount of chargeable gains for the tax year 2016/17 is computed ignoring the annual exempt amount for the purposes of this relief.

Both capital losses of the tax year 2016/17 and brought forward losses are taken into account for the purposes of this relief. Hong cannot specify the amount to be set against chargeable gains, so her annual exempt amount for the tax year 2016/17 may be wasted.

CBE style OT case – Chi

Text references. Chapter 2 covers the computation of taxable income and the income tax liability. National insurance contributions are the subject of Chapter 12. The cash basis of assessment is dealt with in Chapter 7.

Top tips. If the cash basis is used there are no capital allowances on the office equipment but the expenditure is instead deducted in the same way as a revenue expense.

Easy marks. The computation of income tax in question 93 should have been easy marks. There were some easy marks in question 97 for identifying cash receipts and payments.

93   £9,900

	£
Trading income/net income	53,000
Less personal allowance	(11,500)
Taxable income	41,500
Tax	
£33,500 @ 20%	6,700
£8,000 (41,500 – 33,500) @ 40%	3,200
	9,900

94   £3,475

	£
£(45,000 – 8,164) = £36,836 @ 9%	3,315
£(53,000 – 45,000) = £8,000 @ 2%	160
Total Class 4 contributions	3,475

95   The trader can deduct capital expenditure on plant and machinery (other than motor cars) as business expenses rather than using capital allowances.

A trader can start to use the cash basis if his receipts for the tax year do not exceed £150,000.

Accounts can be prepared to any date in the tax year as for the normal basis of assessment. Cash basis traders cannot offset losses against other income or gains; they can only carry them forward against profits of the cash basis trade.

96   £5,300

	£
10,000 miles @ 45p	4,500
3,200 miles @ 25p	800
	5,300

Capital allowances are not relevant, since purchases of equipment are deducted as an expense. The running and capital costs of owning a motor car are replaced by the deduction based on statutory mileage allowances.

97   Revenue £70,900, other expenses £7,300

Revenue £(72,500 – 1,600)   £70,900

98 Bayle (A)

Marking scheme

				Marks
(a)		Monthly thresholds	½	
		Employee's Class 1 NIC	1½	
		Employer's Class 1 NIC	2	
				4
(b)	(i)	*Trading income assessments*		
		2017/18	1½	
		2018/19	2½	
				4
	(ii)	*NIC*		
		Class 2 NIC	½	
		Class 4 NIC	1	
		Bayle	½	
				2
				10

(a)   The monthly employee's and employer's thresholds are both £680 (£8,164/12).

Fyle will pay employee's Class 1 NIC for 2017/18 of £1,258 (£(3,300 − 680) = £2,620 @ 12% × 4).

Bayle will not pay employer's Class 1 NIC for 2017/18 since the employment allowance will cover the contributions of £1,446 (£(3,300 − 680) = £2,620 @ 13.8% × 4).

Tutorial note

The alternative approach using the annual earnings threshold and then taking 4/12ths of an annual NIC figure is acceptable.

(b)   (i)   **Trading income assessments**

Fyle's trading income assessment for 2017/18 is £14,400 calculated as follows:

	£
Profit share for period 1.12.17 to 30.9.18 (10 months)	
£216,000 × 10/12 × 20%	36,000
Basis period (1st year − actual) 1.12.17 to 5.4.18 (4 months)	
£36,000 × 4/10	14,400

The assessment for 2018/19 is £44,000 calculated as follows:

	£
Profit share for period 1.12.17 to 30.9.18 (10 months)	
£216,000 × 10/12 × 20%	36,000
Profit share for period 1.10.18 to 30.9.19 (12 months)	
£240,000 × 20%	48,000

		£
Basis period (2nd year – first 12 months of trading)		
1.12.17 to 30.9.18		36,000
1.10.18 to 30.11.18		
£48,000 × 2/12		8,000
		44,000

(ii) **NIC**

Fyle will pay Class 2 NIC for 2017/18 of £(2.85 × 18) = £51.

He will pay Class 4 NIC for 2017/18 of £(14,400 – 8,164) = 6,236 @ 9% = £561.

There are no NIC implications for Bayle.

Tutorial note

Any reasonable estimate of the number of weeks for Class 2 contributions is acceptable.

99 Michael and Sean

Text references. Chapter 10 deals with trading losses.

Top tips. Remember that if a taxpayer claims loss relief against general income, the benefit of the personal allowance may be lost.

Easy marks. There were some easy marks for identifying the possible loss relief claims.

		Marks
Michael		
Early years relief against total income		1
Claims		1
Rate of tax saved	– 2013/14	1
	– 2014/15	1
Carry forward		½
Sean		
Available loss		1
Terminal loss relief		1
Claims		1
Rates of tax saved		1
Relief against total income		1½
		10

Michael

The loss of £25,230 for 2016/17 can be claimed against general income for the 3 preceding years, under early years loss relief, earliest year first, since it is incurred in the first 4 years of trading.

The loss relief claim will therefore be £19,365 in 2013/14 and £(25,230 – 19,365) = £5,865 in 2014/15.

For 2013/14 this will waste Michael's personal allowance, with the balance of the claim of £(19,365 – 11,500) = £7,865 saving income tax at the basic rate of 20%.

For 2014/15 Michael has income of £(52,095 – 11,500 – 33,500) = £7,095 subject to income tax at the higher rate of 40%, so the claim of £5,365 will save tax at the higher rate.

Alternatively, Michael could have carried the trading loss forward against future trading profits, but the trading profit of £9,665 for 2017/18 is covered by the personal allowance, and there is no information regarding future trading profits.

Tutorial note

A claim for loss relief against general income for 2016/17 and/or 2015/16 is not possible since Michael does not have any income for either of these years.

Sean

The unused overlap profits brought forward are added to the loss for the year ended 31 December 2017, so the total loss for 2017/18 is £(23,100 + 3,600) = £26,700.

The whole of the loss can be claimed as a terminal loss since it is for the final 12 months of trading. The claim is against trading income for the year of the loss (2017/18 – nil) and the 3 preceding years, latest first.

The terminal loss claim will therefore be £3,700 in 2016/17, £18,900 in 2015/16 and £(26,700 – 3,700 – 18,900) = £4,100 in 2014/15.

The property business profits are sufficient to utilise Sean's personal allowance for each year, so the loss relief claims will save income tax at the basic rate of 20%.

Alternatively, Sean could have initially claimed loss relief against his general income for 2017/18 and/or 2016/17, but this would have wasted his personal allowance in those years.

100 Samantha

Text references. Chapter 10 deals with trading losses.

Top tips. You should use the standard layout for losses: set up the columns and lines required and then slot in the numbers. A loss memorandum is also useful as a double check that you have used the losses correctly.

Easy marks. There were easy marks for setting out the trading income and gains stated in the question and using the personal allowance and annual exempt amount.

Marking scheme

			Marks
(a)	Rate of tax	1	
	Timing of relief	1	
	Waste of personal allowance/annual exempt amount	1	
			3
(b)	Trading income	½	
	Trading loss relief carried forward	1	
	Building society interest	½	
	Trading loss relief against general income	1	
	Personal allowance	½	
	Gains	½	
	Capital loss relief carried forward	1	
	Trading loss relief against gains	1	
	Annual exempt amount	1	
			7
			10

(a) Factors that will influence an individual's choice of loss relief claim are:

(i) The rate of income tax or capital gains tax at which relief will be obtained, with preference being given to income charged at the additional rate of 45%, then the higher rate of 40%

(ii) The timing of the relief obtained, with a claim against general income/capital gains of the current year or preceding year resulting in earlier relief than a carry forward claim against future trading profits

(iii) The extent to which the income tax personal allowance and the capital gains tax annual exempt amount will be wasted by using a claim against general income/capital gains

(b) **Samantha – Taxable income**

	2015/16 £	2016/17 £	2017/18 £	2018/19 £
Trading income	7,290	42,600	0	18,285
Less trading loss relief carried forward	(0)	(0)	(0)	(7,000)
	7,290	42,600	0	11,285
Building society interest	0	6,100	3,800	2,130
	7,290	48,700	3,800	13,415
Less trading loss relief against general income (N)	(0)	(48,700)	(0)	(0)
Net income	7,290	0	3,800	13,415
Less personal allowance	(7,290)	(0)	(3,800)	(11,500)
Taxable income	0	0	0	1,915

Samantha – Taxable gains

	2015/16 £	2016/17 £	2017/18 £	2018/19 £
Gains	21,100	23,300	0	14,100
Less trading loss relief against gains (note)	(0)	(23,300)	(0)	(0)
	21,100	0	0	14,100
Less capital loss carried forward	(0)	(0)	(0)	(2,800)
	21,100	0	0	11,300
Less annual exempt amount	(11,300)	(0)	(0)	(11,300)
Taxable gains	9,800	0	0	0

Note. Loss relief has been claimed against general income and gains for 2016/17 since this gives relief at the earliest date and at the highest rates of tax. No claim should be made to set the loss against general income in 2017/18 since this is already covered by the personal allowance for that year.

Trading loss memorandum

	£
Loss 2017/18	79,000
Less: used 2016/17 (income)	(48,700)
used 2016/17 (gains)	(23,300)
Available for c/f	7,000
Less used 2018/19	(7,000)
Loss unused	0

101 Martin

Text references. Chapter 9 deals with basis of assessment.

Top tips. It is important to follow the requirements carefully as they will lead you through the computations so that you can reach a conclusion for part (e).

Easy marks. You should have been able to identify that the actual basis applied for the tax year 2016/17 whichever accounting date was chosen.

Marks

(a)	p/e 5 April 2017	½
	y/e 5 April 2018	1
	y/e 5 April 2019	½
		2
(b)	2016/17	1
	2017/18	½
	2018/19	½
		2
(c)	p/e 30 April 2017	½
	y/e 30 April 2018	1½
		2
(d)	2016/17	1
	2017/18	1
	2018/19	1
		3
(e)	Explanation	1
		10

(a) **Martin's taxable profits for the periods of account ending 5 April 2017, 5 April 2018 and 5 April 2019**

Period of account	Working	Taxable profits
		£
1.1.17 – 5.4.17	£3,000 × 3	9,000
6.4.17 – 5.4.18	£3,000 × 3 + £4,000 × 6 + £5,000 × 3	48,000
6.4.18 – 5.4.19	£5,000 × 12	60,000

(b) **Martin's taxable income for the tax years 2016/17, 2017/18 and 2018/19 if he chooses 5 April**

Year	Basis period	Taxable profits
		£
2016/17	1.1.17 – 5.4.17 – actual basis	9,000
2017/18	6.4.17 – 5.4.18 – current year basis	48,000
2018/19	6.4.18 – 5.4.19 – current year basis	60,000
Total		117,000

(c) **Martin's taxable profits for the periods of account ending 30 April 2017 and 30 April 2018**

Period of account	Working	Taxable profits
		£
1.1.17 – 30.4.17	£3,000 × 4	12,000
1.5.17 – 30.4.18	£3,000 × 2 + £4,000 × 6 + £5,000 × 4	50,000

(d) **Martin's taxable income for the tax years 2016/17, 2017/18 and 2018/19 if he chooses 30 April**

Year	Basis period	Working	Taxable profits
			£
2016/17	1.1.17 – 5.4.17: actual basis	£12,000 × 3/4	9,000
2017/18	1.1.17 – 31.12.17: first 12 months	£12,000 + £50,000 × 8/12	45,333
2018/19	1.5.17 – 30.4.18: current year basis		50,000
Total			104,333

(e) If Martin chooses 30 April as his accounting date, £(117,000 – 104,333) = £12,667 less trading income will be taxable in the tax years 2016/17, 2017/18 and 2018/19 than if he chooses 5 April.

102 Lucy

Marking scheme

	Marks
Employee	
Income tax payable	1½
Class 1 NIC	1½
Income	1
Self-employed	
Income tax payable	2
Classes 2 and 4 NIC	2
Income	1½
Determination of working pattern with higher disposable income	½
	10

Disposable income if Lucy is employee

Income tax	£
Employment income/net income	35,000
Less personal allowance	(11,500)
Taxable income	23,500
Income tax @ 20%	4,700

Class 1 NIC	£
Salary	35,000
Less employee's threshold	(8,164)
	26,836
Class 1 NIC @ 12%	3,220

Disposable income	£
Salary	35,000
Less: income tax	(4,700)
Class 1 NIC	(3,220)
travel costs	(1,500)
	25,580

Disposable income if Lucy is self-employed

Income tax	£
Fees received	35,000
Less fixed rate mileage 4,600 @ 45p per mile	(2,070)
Trading income/net income	32,930
Less personal allowance	(11,500)
Taxable income	21,430
Income tax @ 20%	4,286

Classes 2 and 4 NIC	£	£
Class 2 NIC £2.85 × 52		148
Class 4 NIC		
Trading income	32,930	
Less lower limit	(8,164)	
	24,766	
Class 4 NIC @ 9%		2,229
Total NICs		2,377

Disposable income	£
Fees received	35,000
Less: income tax	(4,286)
Classes 2 and 4 NICs	(2,377)
travel costs 4,600 @ 40p	(1,840)
	26,497

Lucy will therefore have a higher disposable income by £(26,497 – 25,580) = £917 if she undertakes the self-employed work arrangement.

103 Daniel, Francine and Gregor

Text references. Partnerships are the subject of Chapter 11. Employment benefits are covered in Chapter 4. Trading losses are dealt with in Chapter 10.

Top tips. In part (a) it is important to realise that Daniel is treated as commencing a trade and therefore his trading income assessment for 2017/18 is on an actual basis. In part (c), remember that a trading loss can be relieved against total income in the tax year of the loss and the preceding tax year and can also be extended against chargeable gains.

Easy marks. There were some easy marks in part (b) for dealing with the interest paid by Francine on her loan.

Examining team's comments. This question had three separate scenarios, of which the first and third were fairly well answered and the second was less well answered.

The first scenario in part (a) involved three individuals who were in partnership, preparing accounts to 31 October annually. A fourth partner joined mid-way through an accounting period and the requirement was to calculate the new partner's trading income assessment for his first tax year as a partner. Although many candidates demonstrated satisfactory knowledge here, a large number wasted a significant amount of time by also performing calculations for the three existing partners, despite the requirement only concerning the new partner.

The second scenario in part (b) involved an employee who was provided with a beneficial loan part-way through the tax year. The loan was subsequently increased before the end of the tax year. The basic idea behind this question was that candidates had to calculate the benefit using the average method (they were instructed to use this method), with the interest actually paid to the employer being calculated on a strict basis. However, many candidates failed to read the requirement carefully and thus ignored the instruction to use the average basis when calculating the taxable benefit. In addition, many candidates failed to use proper workings and accordingly became confused mid-way through their calculations.

The third scenario in part (c) involved a self-employed taxpayer who had made a trading loss in the tax year. On the assumption that the taxpayer relieved his trading loss as early as possible, the requirement was to calculate the amount of trading loss carried forward to the next tax year. Once again, many candidates' workings were not well laid out. Many candidates prepared tax computations for both years for which figures were provided, before realising that all that was required was a loss memorandum. The set off of the brought forward capital loss against the current year chargeable gain was also often overlooked.

			Marks
(a)	1 May 2017 to 31 October 2017	1½	
	1 November 2017 to 5 April 2018	1½	
			3
(b)	Average loan	1½	
	Interest paid	1½	
			3
(c)	2016/17 claim against total income	1	
	2017/18 claim against total income	1	
	claim against chargeable gain	1½	
	Loss carried forward	½	4
			10

(a) **Daniel – Trading income assessment 2017/18**

	£
1 May 2017 to 31 October 2017	
£96,000 × ¼ × 6/12	12,000
1 November 2017 to 5 April 2018	
£180,000 × ¼ × 5/12	18,750
	30,750

Tutorial note

Daniel joined as a partner on 1 May 2017, so the commencement rules apply to him for 2017/18. The basis period is the 11-month period from 1 May 2017 to 5 April 2018.

(b) **Francine – Beneficial loan 2017/18**

	£	£
$\dfrac{96,000 + (96,000 + 14,000)}{2} \times 2.5\% \times 8/12$		1,717
Interest paid £96,000 at 1.5% × 2/12	240	
£110,000 at 1.5% × 6/12	825	
		(1,065)
Taxable benefit		652

(c) **Gregor – Trading loss carried forward**

	£
Trading loss	68,800
2016/17 – Claim against total income	
£(14,700 + 4,600 + 1,300)	(20,600)
2017/18 – Claim against total income	(900)
– Claim against chargeable gain (working)	(14,500)
Loss carried forward to 2018/19	32,800

Working: Claim against chargeable gain

The loss relief claim against the chargeable gain is restricted to £14,500 (chargeable gain of £17,400 less the capital loss brought forward of £2,900).

Tutorial note

Gregor can claim loss relief against his total income and chargeable gains for 2016/17 and 2017/18.

104 George

Text references. Employment income is covered in Chapter 3. National insurance contributions are dealt with in Chapter 12.

Top tips. Use your tax tables for all the national insurance limits and rates.

Easy marks. There were some easy marks in part (a) for working out the income tax liability and in part (c) the comparison of the national insurance contributions gets some easy credit even if you have made errors in the main calculations.

Examining team's comments. In part (a), most candidates missed the fact that the taxpayer would not incur any significant expenses in respect of the contract and would not be taking any significant financial risk. Many candidates incorrectly gave the payment of tax under PAYE for the previous year as an indicator.

Part (b) was well answered, but many candidates produced extremely long answers for what should have been a simple set of workings. For example, the capital allowance was simply a 100% annual investment allowance on the purchase of a new asset and did not require a detailed capital allowances computation.

In part (c), as regards the payment aspect, most candidates just referred to PAYE without any further relevant detail. Very few appreciated that the due date under the self-employed basis was simply 31 January following the tax year – payments on account not being required because the previous year's tax liability was collected under PAYE.

Marking scheme

				Marks
(a)	Factors indicative of employment (½ mark each)			2
(b)	Income		½	
	Capital allowances		1	
	Personal allowance		½	
	Income tax		½	
	Class 2		½	
	Class 4		1	
				4
(c)	(i)	PAYE	1	
		Self-assessment	1	
				2
	(ii)	Class 1	1½	
		Additional NIC	½	
				2
				10

(a) The contract is for a relatively long period of time.
George is required to do the work personally.
Xpee plc exercises control over George via the weekly meetings and instructions.
George will not incur any significant expenses in respect of the contract.
George will only be working for Xpee plc.
George is not taking any significant financial risk.

Note. Four items only required.

(b)   **George – Income tax liability 2017/18**

	£
Income	40,000
Capital allowances – annual investment allowance	(3,600)
Trading income	36,400
Less personal allowance	(11,500)
Taxable income	24,900

Income tax
£24,900 × 20%   4,980

George – National insurance contributions 2017/18

Class 2 national insurance contributions will be £148 (52 × £2.85).

Class 4 national insurance contributions will be £2,541 (28,236 (36,400 – 8,164) × 9%).

(c)   (i)   If George is treated as employed in respect of his contract with Xpee plc, then the company will be required to deduct tax under PAYE every time that George is paid during 2017/18.

If treated as self-employed, George's income tax liability for 2017/18 would not be payable until 31 January 2019.

(ii)   If George is treated as employed in respect of his contract with Xpee plc, then his Class 1 national insurance contributions for 2017/18 will be £3,820 (31,836 (40,000 – 8,164) at 12%).

The additional amount of national insurance contributions which he will suffer for 2017/18 is therefore £1,131 (3,820 – 148 – 2,541).

Tutorial note

For income tax purposes, capital allowances will reduce employment income in the same way that they are deducted in calculating the trading profit. However, there is no deduction for capital allowances when it comes to calculating Class 1 national insurance contributions.

105 Joe (B)

Marking scheme

		Marks
Salary – Firstly plc		½
Occupational pension scheme contributions		1
Bonus		½
Salary – Secondly plc		½
Personal pension contributions		½
Beneficial loan	– Average method	1½
	– Strict method	1½
Workplace nursery		1
Home entertainment system	– Use	1½
	– Acquisition	1½
Living accommodation		2
Furniture		1½
Running costs		½
Childcare vouchers		1
		15

Joe – Employment income 2017/18

	£
Salary – Firstly plc (6,360 × 9)	57,240
Pension contributions (57,240 × 6%) (N2)	(3,434)
	53,806
Bonus (N1)	0
Salary – Secondly plc (6,565 × 3)	19,695
Beneficial loan (W1)	1,479
Workplace nursery (N3)	0
Home entertainment system – Use (W2)	660
– Acquisition (W2)	3,860
Living accommodation (W3)	6,750
Furniture (W3)	816
Running costs	1,900
Childcare vouchers (W4)	936
Employment income	89,902

Workings

1   *Loan benefit*

The benefit of the beneficial loan using the average method is £1,583 ((120,000 + 70,000)/2 = 95,000 at 2.5% × 8/12).

Using the strict method the benefit is £1,479 ((120,000 at 2.5% × 3/12) + (70,000 at 2.5% × 5/12)).

Joe will therefore elect to have the taxable benefit calculated according to the strict method.

2   *Home entertainment system*

The benefit for the use of the home entertainment system is £660 (4,400 × 20% × 9/12).

The benefit for the acquisition of the home entertainment system is the market value of £3,860, as this is greater than £3,740 (4,400 – 660).

3   *Living accommodation and furniture*

The benefit for the living accommodation is the higher of the annual value of £2,600 (10,400 × 3/12) and the rent paid of £6,750 (2,250 × 3).

The benefit for the use of the furniture is £816 (16,320 × 20% × 3/12).

4   *Childcare vouchers*

The exemption for childcare vouchers is £28 per week since Joe is a higher rate employee. The benefit for the provision of the vouchers is therefore £936 ((100 – 28) = 72 × 13).

Notes

1   The bonus of £12,000 will have been treated as being received during 2016/17 as Joe became entitled to it during that tax year.

2   The personal pension contributions will increase Joe's basic rate tax limit and are therefore irrelevant as regards the calculation of employment income.

3   The provision of a place in a workplace nursery does not give rise to a taxable benefit.

106 Sammi

Text references. Chapter 4 deals with employment benefits. National insurance contributions are covered in Chapter 12. Computing taxable total profits and computing corporation tax are dealt with in Chapter 19.

Top tips. Use headings to show the examining team which of the two options you are dealing with.

Easy marks. There were easy marks for computing the car benefit and computing the national insurance contributions.

Marking scheme

		Marks
(a)	*Company motor car*	
	Car benefit	2
	Income tax	1
	NIC implications	½
	Additional director's remuneration	
	Income tax	½
	Class 1 NIC	1
		5
(b)	*Company motor car*	
	Class 1A NIC	1
	Allowable leasing costs	1
	Corporation tax saving	1
	Additional director's remuneration	
	Class 1 NIC	1
	Corporation tax saving	1
		5

				Marks
(c)	*Sammi*			
	Director's remuneration	– Net of tax income	1	
		– Overall result	1	
	Conclusion		1	
	Smark Ltd			
	Director's remuneration		1	
	Conclusion		1	
				$\frac{5}{15}$

(a) **Sammi – Company motor car**

The list price used in the car benefit calculation is £80,000. The relevant percentage is restricted to a maximum of 37% (18% + 41% (300 – 95 = 205/5) = 59%).

Sammi will therefore be taxed on a car benefit of £29,600 (80,000 × 37%).

Sammi's marginal rate of income tax is 45%, so her additional income tax liability for 2017/18 will be £13,320 (29,600 at 45%).

There are no national insurance contribution implications for Sammi.

Tutorial note

There is no fuel benefit as fuel is not provided for private journeys.

Sammi – Additional director's remuneration

Sammi's additional income tax liability for 2017/18 will be £12,150 (27,000 at 45%).

The additional employee's Class 1 NIC liability will be £540 (27,000 at 2%).

Tutorial note

Sammi's director's remuneration exceeds the upper earnings limit of £45,000, so her additional Class 1 NIC liability is at the rate of 2%.

(b) **Smark Ltd – Company motor car**

The employer's Class 1A NIC liability in respect of the car benefit will be £4,085 (29,600 at 13.8%).

The motor car has a CO_2 emission rate in excess of 130 grams per kilometre, so only £23,486 (27,630 less 15%) of the leasing costs are allowed for corporation tax purposes.

Smark Ltd's corporation tax liability will be reduced by £5,238 (23,486 + 4,085 = 27,571 at 19%).

Smark Ltd – Additional director's remuneration

The employer's Class 1 NIC liability in respect of the additional director's remuneration will be £3,726 (27,000 at 13.8%).

Smark Ltd's corporation tax liability will be reduced by £5,838 (27,000 + 3,726 = 30,726 at 19%).

(c) **More beneficial alternative for Sammi**

Under the director's remuneration alternative, Sammi will receive additional net of tax income of £14,310 (27,000 – 12,150 – 540).

However, she will have to lease the motor car at a cost of £27,630, so the overall result is additional expenditure of £13,320 (27,630 – 14,310).

If Sammi is provided with a company motor car then she will have an additional tax liability of £13,320, so she is in exactly the same financial position.

Most beneficial alternative for Smark Ltd

The net of tax cost of paying additional director's remuneration is £24,888 (27,000 + 3,726 – 5,838).

This is more beneficial than the alternative of providing a company motor car since this has a net of tax cost of £26,477 (27,630 + 4,085 – 5,238).

107 Simon

Marking scheme

			Marks
(a)	Subject matter	½	
	Length of ownership	½	
	Frequency of transactions	½	
	Work done	½	
	Circumstances of realisation	½	
	Profit motive	½	
			3
(b)	Income	½	
	Acquisition of house	½	
	Legal fees on acquisition	½	
	Renovation costs	½	
	Legal fees on sale	½	
	Loan interest	1	
	Personal allowance	½	
	Income tax liability	1	
	Class 4 NICs	1½	
	Class 2 NICs	1½	
			8
(c)	Sale proceeds	½	
	Legal fees on sale	½	
	Cost of house	½	
	Legal fees on acquisition	½	
	Enhancement expenditure	½	
	Loan interest – not allowable	½	
	Annual exempt amount	½	
	Capital gains tax liability	½	
			4
			15

(a) **Badges of trade**

Subject matter

Some assets are commonly held as investments for their intrinsic value, for example an individual may buy shares for dividend income produced by them or may buy a painting to enjoy it as a work of art. A subsequent disposal of an investment asset usually produces a capital gain. Where the subject matter of a transaction is not an investment asset, any profit on resale is usually a trading profit.

Length of ownership

If items purchased are sold soon afterwards, this indicates trading transactions.

Frequency of transactions

Transactions which may, in isolation, be of a capital nature will be interpreted as trading transactions where their frequency indicates the carrying on of a trade.

Work done

When work is done to make an asset more marketable, or steps are taken to find purchasers, this is likely to be indicative of trading.

Circumstances of realisation

A forced sale, for example to realise funds for an emergency, is not likely to be treated as trading.

Motive

The absence of a profit motive will not necessarily preclude a tax charge as trading income, but its presence is a strong indication that a person is trading.

(b)   **Simon – Income tax and NICs for 2017/18 if trading**

	£	£
Income		260,000
Less: costs incurred		
house	127,000	
legal fees on acquisition	1,800	
renovation	50,000	
legal fees on sale	2,600	
loan interest		
£150,000 × 6% × 4/12	3,000	
		(184,400)
Trading income/Net income		75,600
Less personal allowance		(11,500)
Taxable income		64,100
Income tax		
£33,500 @ 20%		6,700
£30,600 @ 40%		12,240
Income tax liability		18,940
Class 4 NICs		
£(45,000 – 8,164) = £36,836 @ 9%		3,315
£(75,600 – 45,000) = £30,600 @ 2%		612
Total Class 4 NICs		3,927
Class 2 NICs		
£2.85 × 19 weeks (N)		54

Note. Marks were awarded for any reasonable attempt at calculating the number of weeks. ½ mark was deducted if 52 weeks were used.

(c)   **Simon – Capital gains tax 2017/18 if not trading**

	£	£
Sale proceeds		260,000
Less legal fees on sale		(2,600)
Net proceeds of sale		257,400
Less: cost of house	127,000	
legal fees on acquisition	1,800	
renovation	50,000	
loan interest (N)	0	
		(178,800)
Chargeable gain		78,600
Less annual exempt amount		(11,300)
Taxable gain		67,300

Capital gains tax

	£
£33,500 @ 18%	6,030
£(67,300 – 33,500) = 33,800 @ 28%	9,464
Capital gains tax liability	15,494

Note. The loan interest is a revenue expense and so is not allowable in computing the chargeable gain.

108 Na

> **Text references.** Assessment of trading profits is covered in Chapter 9. Adjustment of trading profit is in Chapter 7. The computation of taxable income and the income tax liability is dealt with in Chapter 2.
>
> **Top tips.** As you deal with each adjustment to profit, tick it off in the question – this method should ensure that you do not miss out any item and thus lose marks.
>
> **Easy marks.** The computation of the income tax liability in part (c) should have been easy marks.

Marking scheme

			Marks
(a)	First tax year trading profits	1	
	Second tax year trading profits	1½	
	Third tax year trading profits	½	
	Overlap profits	2	
			5
(b)	Net profit	½	
	Depreciation	½	
	Motor expenses	1	
	Legal fees	½	
	Property expenses	1	
	Own consumption	1	
	Fine	½	
	Trade subscription	½	
	Private telephone	1	
	Capital allowances	½	
			7
(c)	Trading profit	½	
	Individual savings account interest (exempt)	½	
	Dividends	½	
	Personal allowance	½	
	Income tax liability	1	
			3
			15

(a) **Na – Trading profits 2014/15, 2015/16 and 2016/17**

Year	Basis period	Working	Taxable profits £
2014/15	1.1.15 – 5.4.15	£25,200 × 3/6	12,600
2015/16	1.1.15 – 31.12.15(N)	£25,200 + £21,600 × 6/12	36,000
2016/17	1.7.15 – 30.6.16		21,600

Note. Because the accounting period ending in the second tax year is less than 12 months, the basis period for that year is the first 12 months of trading.

Overlap profits

Overlap period	Working	Overlap profits £
1.1.15 – 5.4.15	£25,200 × 3/6	12,600
1.7.15 – 31.12.15	£21,600 × 6/12	10,800

(b) **Na – Tax adjusted trading profit for year ended 30 June 2017**

	£	£
Net profit		23,000
Add: depreciation	2,635	
motor expenses – private use	1,925	
7,000/8,000 × £2,200		
professional fees – lease (N)	1,260	
property expenses – private use	4,300	
1/3 × £12,900		
purchases – goods taken for own use (selling price)	450	
other expenses – fine	480	
other expenses – trade subscription	0	
		11,050
		34,050
Less: telephone – business use 20% × £1,200	240	
capital allowances	810	(1,050)
Tax adjusted trading profit		33,000

Note. Legal expenses relating to the **grant** of a short lease are not allowable.

(c) **Na – Income tax liability for 2017/18**

	Non-savings income £	Dividend income £	Total £
Trading income (part (b))	33,000		
UK dividends		1,200	
Net income (ISA interest is exempt)	33,000	1,200	34,200
Less personal allowance	(11,500)		
Taxable income	21,500	1,200	22,700

	£
Income tax	
Non-savings income	
£21,500 @ 20%	4,300
Dividend income	
£1,200 @ 0%	0
Tax liability	4,300

109 Bayle (B)

Text references. Adjustment of profit is dealt with in Chapter 7. Employment income is covered in Chapter 3. Taxable income and the income tax liability are dealt with in Chapter 2.

Top tips. You must start your adjustment of profit computation with the net profit. Don't forget to include any items which do not require adjustment (such as the impairment loss) with a zero.

Easy marks. There were plenty of easy marks for the adjustment of profit computation with standard items such as gifts to customers which should have been well known.

		Marks
(a)	Impairment loss	½
	Gifts to customers	1
	Donations to political parties	½
	Lease of motor car	1
	Personal tax advice	½
	Property expenses	1
	Parking fines	½
	Professional subscription	½
	Golf membership fee	½
		6
(b)	Trading profits	½
	Employment income: salary	½
	Employment income: bonus payments	1
	Interest from savings certificates	½
	Interest from government stock	2
	Dividends	½
	Personal allowance	½
	Income tax	2½
	Tax suffered at source	1
		9
		15

(a) **Bayle – Trading profit for the year ended 30 September 2017**

		£
Net profit		173,302
Add: impairment loss		0
gifts to customers	– Clocks	3,300
	– Bottles of champagne	2,480
donations to political parties		2,900
lease of motor car £4,345 × 15%		652
personal tax advice		600
property expenses £46,240 × 2/5		18,496
parking fines		520
professional subscriptions		0
golf club membership fee		960
Taxable trading profit		203,210

Tutorial notes

1 The recovered impairment loss will have been allowed as a deduction when originally written off, so the recovery is now taxable. Therefore no adjustment is required.

2 Gifts to customers are only an allowable deduction if they cost less than £50 per recipient per tax year, are not of food, drink, tobacco or vouchers for exchangeable goods and carry a conspicuous advertisement for the trader making the gift.

3 The motor car has a CO_2 emission rate in excess of 130 grams per kilometre, so 15% of the leasing costs are not allowed.

(b)   Bayle – Income tax computation 2017/18

	Non-savings income £	Savings income £	Dividend income £	Total £
Trading profit (from (a) above)	203,210			
Employment income £(42,000 + 6,000)	48,000			
Interest from savings certificates (exempt)		0		
Interest from gilts (W)		3,600		
Dividends			11,000	
Net income	251,210	3,600	11,000	265,810
Less personal allowance	(0)	(0)	(0)	
Taxable income	251,210	3,600	11,000	265,810

Working

	£
Interest received 30.6.17	
£160,000 × 3% × 6/12	2,400
Accrued interest deemed received 31.12.17 for period 1.7.17 to 30.9.17	
£160,000 × 3% × 3/12	1,200
Total taxable as savings income	3,600

Tax	£
£(33,500 + 5,000) = 38,500 @ 20%	7,700
£(150,000 + 5,000 − 38,500) = 116,500 @ 40%	46,600
£(251,210 + 3,600 − 116,500 − 38,500) = 99,810 @ 45%	44,914
£5,000 @ 0%	0
£(11,000 − 5,000) = 6,000 @ 38.1%	2,286
Income tax liability	101,500
Tax suffered at source	
PAYE £48,000 @ 45%	(21,600)
Income tax payable	79,900

Tutorial notes

1   The bonus payment of £6,000 that Bayle became entitled to on 10 March 2017 will have been treated as being received during 2016/17.

2   Interest received on maturity of savings certificates issued by National Savings & Investments is exempt.

3   No personal allowance is available as Bayle's adjusted net income of £260,810 (£265,810 less gift aid donation of £5,000) exceeds £123,000.

4   The basic rate and the higher rate limits are increased by the gross gift aid donation of £5,000.

5   The savings income nil rate band is not available to additional rate taxpayers.

110 Flick (A)

Marking scheme

			Marks
(a)	Salary		½
	Living accommodation	– Annual value	½
		– Additional benefit	2
	Trading profit	– Profit share	2
		– Assessment	1
		– Capital allowances	2
	Property business profit	– Rent receivable	½
		– Council tax	½
		– Porch	½
		– Washer-dryer	1
	Personal allowance		½
			11
(b)	Interval		1
	Tax planning		1
	Basis period rules more complicated		1
	Profit assessed in the year of cessation		1
			4
			15

(a) **Flick – Taxable income 2017/18**

		Non-savings income
		£
Employment income		
Salary		28,030
Living accommodation	– Annual value	4,600
	– Additional benefit (W1)	1,750
		34,380
Trading profit (W2)		8,220
Property income (W3)		6,250
Net income		48,850
Less personal allowance		(11,500)
Taxable income		37,350

Workings

1 *Living accommodation additional benefit*

	£
Market value	145,000
Less limit	(75,000)
	70,000
Additional benefit £70,000 × 2.5%	1,750

Tutorial note

Since the property was acquired more than six years before being provided to Flick, the market value at the date it was provided to her is used as the cost of providing the benefit, instead of the original cost.

2 *Trading profit*

First work out the capital allowances for the partnership.

	Motor car	Allowances @ 60%
	£	£
Purchase	18,750	
WDA @ 8% × 4/12	(500)	300
TWDV c/f	18,250	

Tutorial note

The partnership's motor car has CO_2 emissions over 130 g/km and therefore qualifies for writing down allowance at the rate of 8%.

Flick's share of the partnership's trading profit for the period ended 30 April 2018 is then calculated as follows.

	£
Trading profit	29,700
Less capital allowances	(300)
	29,400
Less salary paid to Art £6,000 × 4/12	(2,000)
Profits available for profit sharing	27,400
Profit share for Flick £27,400 × 40%	10,960
Flick's trading income for 2017/18 £10,960 × 3/4	8,220

Tutorial note

Flick's basis period for 2017/18 is 1 January 2018 to 5 April 2018 since this is her first year of trading.

3 *Property business profit*

	£	£
Rent receivable £660 × 12		7,920
Less: council tax	1,320	
porch	0	
washer-dryer	350	
		(1,670)
		6,250

Tutorial note

The cost of building the porch is not allowable as it is capital expenditure. Only the cost of a like for like replacement of the washing machine is allowable, not the improvement of the washer-dryer.

(b) Advantages

The interval between earning profits and paying the related tax liability will be 11 months longer. This can be particularly beneficial where profits are rising.

It will be possible to calculate taxable profits well in advance of the end of the tax year, making it much easier to implement tax planning and make pension contributions.

Disadvantages

The application of the basis period rules is more complicated.

The amount of profit assessed in the year of cessation could potentially be quite high as the basis period will be up to 23 months in length. Although overlap profits are deductible, these might be insignificant if the opening years' profits are low.

111 Josie

Text references. Computing trading income is covered in Chapter 7 and the basis of assessment for trading income in Chapter 9. Employment income is dealt with in Chapters 3 and 4. Taxable income and the income tax computation are dealt with in Chapter 2.

Top tips. Be careful with employment benefits which are provided for only part of a tax year as they must be pro-rated. Follow the instructions in the question, using a zero to indicate any items which are non-taxable or exempt.

Easy marks. There were easy marks for common employment benefits. The income tax computation should also have been a familiar topic.

Marking scheme

	Marks
Trading income	
Profit for year ended 30 April 2017	½
Profit for period ended 30 June 2017	½
Overlap profits	1
Employment income	
Salary	1
Removal expenses	1
Beneficial loan	1½
Staff canteen	½
Car benefit – Percentage	1½
– Benefit	1
Investment income	
Gilt interest	1
Dividends	½
Taxable income	
Personal allowance not available	1
Tax payable	
Increase in limits for gift aid donations	1
Tax liability	3
	15

Josie – Income tax computation 2017/18

	Non-savings income £	Savings income £	Dividend income £	Total £
Trading income (W1)	64,000			
Employment income (W2)	126,610			
Gilt interest		1,200		
Dividends			7,200	
Net income	190,610	1,200	7,200	199,010
Less personal allowance (N)	(0)			(0)
Taxable income	190,610	1,200	7,200	199,010

Tax

	£
On non-savings income	
£39,000 (W4) @ 20%	7,800
£116,500 @ 40%	46,600
£155,500 (W6)	
£35,110 @ 45%	15,799
£190,610	
On savings income	
£1,200 @ 45% (no nil rate band for additional rate taxpayer)	540
On dividend income	
£5,000 @ 0%	0
£2,200 (7,200 – 5,000) @ 38.1%	838
Income tax liability	71,577

Tutorial notes

1   Only £8,000 of the relocation costs is exempt.

2   No personal allowance is available as Josie's adjusted net income of £(199,010 – 5,500) = £193,510 exceeds £123,000.

Workings

1   *Trading income*

	£
Year ended 30 April 2017	
Trading profit	95,260
Period ended 30 June 2017	
Trading profit	10,440
Less overlap profits	(41,700)
Trading income	64,000

2   *Employment income*

	£
Salary £15,100 × 8	120,800
Removal expenses £(11,649 – 8,000)	3,649
Loan £39,600 @ 2.5% × 7/12	577
Staff canteen (exempt)	0
Car benefit (W3)	1,584
Employment income	126,610

3   *Car benefit*

Amount by which CO_2 emissions exceed base level: (100 (rounded down) − 95) = 5 ÷ 5 = 1. Car benefit percentage is 1 + 18 + 3 (diesel supplement) = 22%.

Car available from 1 October 2017 to 5 April 2018 = 6 months.

Car benefit is £14,400 (list price) × 22% × 6/12 = £1,584.

4   *Tax rate limits*

Josie's basic and higher rate tax limits are increased by (£4,400 × 100/80) = £5,500 to £(33,500 + 5,500) = £39,000 and £(150,000 + 5,500) = £155,500.

112 Richard (A)

Text references. The adjustment of profit is covered in Chapter 7 and capital allowances in Chapter 8. National insurance contributions are the subject of Chapter 12.

Top tips. Don't forget to deduct the employment allowance in part (b).

Easy marks. The adjustment of profit in part (a) should have yielded good marks. The national insurance computations in part (b) were not too difficult.

		Marks
(a)	*Adjustment of profit*	
	Motor expenses: Richard	1
	Motor expenses: chef	½
	Parking fines	½
	Property expenses	1
	Decorating: restaurant	½
	Decorating: apartment	½
	Other expenses	½
	Advertising: pre-trading expenditure	1
	Capital allowances: motor car [1] addition	½
	motor car [2] addition	½
	motor car [2] WDA	½
	motor car [1] WDA	1
		8
(b)	Class 1: chef	1
	waitress	½
	assistant chef: monthly threshold	1
	assistant chef: NICs	1½
	employment allowance	1
	Class 1A: car benefit percentage	1
	car benefit	½
	NICs	½
		7
		15

(a) **Richard – Trading profit for the year ended 5 April 2018**

	£
Net profit per accounts	32,200
Add: motor expenses – Richard £4,710 × 70% (private use)	3,297
motor expenses – chef	0
parking fines for Richard	280
property expenses – apartment £16,200 × 1/5 (private use)	3,240
decorating – restaurant	0
decorating – apartment (private use)	1,320
other expenses – legal fees (capital)	2,590
	42,927
Less: advertising: pre-trading expenditure	(800)
capital allowances (W)	(3,780)
Tax adjusted trading profit	38,347

Tutorial note

The redecoration of the restaurant is a trading expense since the property was in a usable state when it was purchased.

The advertising is pre-trading expenditure incurred within seven years before commencement and is treated as having been made on 6 April 2017.

Working: Capital allowances

Additions	Main pool £	Private use motor car £	Allowances £
Motor car [1]		14,000	
Motor car [2]	16,800		
WDA @ 18%	(3,024)		3,024
WDA @ 18%		(2,520) × 30%	756
TWDV c/f	13,776	11,480	
Allowances			3,780

Tutorial note

Both motor cars have CO_2 emissions between 76 and 130 grams per kilometre, and therefore qualify for writing down allowances at the rate of 18%. The private use of a motor car by an employee is irrelevant, since such usage will be assessed on the employee as a benefit.

(b) **Richard – National insurance contributions (NIC) as employer**

Class 1 employer's contributions

	£
Chef: £(46,000 – 8,164) = £37,836 × 13.8%	5,221
Waitress less than employer's threshold	0
Assistant chef: £(2,200 – 680(W)) = £1,520 × 13.8% × 8	1,678
	6,899
Less employment allowance	(3,000)
Total Class 1 employer's contributions	3,899

Working: Monthly employer's threshold

£8,164 ÷ 12 = £680

Tutorial note

The alternative approach for the assistant chef using the annual earnings threshold and then taking 8/12ths of an annual NIC figure is acceptable.

Class 1A contributions

£3,192 (W) × 13.8%   £440

Working: Car benefit

Amount by which CO_2 emissions exceed base level: (100 (rounded down) − 95) = 5/5 = 1.
Car benefit percentage is 1 + 18 = 19%.

Car benefit is £16,800 (list price) × 19% = £3,192.

113 John

Text references. Chapter 2 deals with the computation of taxable income and the income tax liability. Pensions are covered in Chapter 5. Employment income is dealt with in Chapters 3 and 4. Property income is the subject of Chapter 6.

Top tips. Make sure you distinguish between occupational pension contributions (which are given tax relief at all rates by being deducted in the computation of employment income) and personal pension contributions (which are given basic rate relief by the taxpayer making a net contribution and higher and additional rate relief by increasing the basic rate and higher rate limits).

Easy marks. The inclusion of salary, deduction of occupational pension contributions and calculation of the tax liability should have been straightforward in part (a).

Marking scheme

		Marks
(a)	Remuneration	½
	Occupational pension contributions	1
	Beneficial loan	
	Outstanding loan at end of tax year	1
	Average loan	1
	Interest paid	½
	Property business profit	½
	Deduction of interest × 75%	1
	Personal allowance – not available	½
	Personal pension contributions	
	Unused allowances	1½
	Available allowance 2017/18	1½
	Increase in basic and higher rate limits	1
	Tax liability	
	Basic rate	½
	Higher rate	½
	Finance costs tax reducer	1
		12
(b)	One for each relevant point (maximum of three)	3
		15

(a)   **John – Income tax computation 2017/18**

	Non-savings income £
Employment income	
Remuneration	208,318
Less occupational pension contributions	(18,000)
	190,318
Beneficial loan (W1)	1,530
Property business income (W2)	12,980
Net income	204,828
Less personal allowance	(0)
Taxable income	204,828

Tutorial note

No personal allowance is available as John's adjusted net income of £(204,828 – 10,000 (W3)) = £194,828 exceeds £123,000.

Tax

	£
£43,500 (W3) @ 20%	8,700
£116,500 (160,000 (W3) – 43,500) @ 40%	46,600
£44,828 (204,828 – 160,000) @ 45%	20,173
	75,473
Less: finance costs tax reducer £5,000 × 25% × 20%	(250)
Income tax liability	75,223

Workings

1   *Beneficial loan*

John repaid £(12,000 + 12,000) = £24,000 of the loan during 2017/18, so the outstanding balance at 5 April 2018 is £(84,000 – 24,000) = £60,000.

The benefit calculated using the average method (specified in the question) is as follows:

	£
$\dfrac{84,000+60,000}{2} \times 2.5\%$	1,800
Less interest paid	(270)
Taxable benefit	1,530

2   *Property business income*

	£
Profit before interest	16,730
Less: finance costs restricted to £5,000 × 75%	(3,750)
Property business income	12,980

3   *Effect of personal pension contributions on tax limits*

John has adjusted income which is higher than £150,000 in the tax year 2017/18 so his annual allowance is reduced (tapered) for 2017/18 by £1 for every £2 the adjusted income exceeds £150,000. However, the annual allowance is not reduced to less than £10,000.

Unused allowances can be carried forward for three years.

The maximum gross personal pension contribution possible in 2017/18 is as follows:

	£
2017/18(tapered)	
Adjusted income = £(204,828 + 18,000 + 12,000) = £234,828	
which is at least £210,000 so minimum annual allowance applies	10,000
2016/17	
No tapering required as adjusted income below £150,000	40,000
2015/16, 2014/15 (2 × £40,000)	80,000
Occupational pension contributions already made	
£(18,000 + 12,000) × 4	(120,000)
Personal pension contribution allowable	10,000

John's basic and higher rate limits will be increased by this gross personal pension contributions to £(33,500 + 10,000) = £43,500 and £(150,000 + 10,000) = £160,000.

Tutorial note

Adjusted income for an employee is net income plus employee pension contributions to occupational pension schemes under net pay arrangements plus employer contributions to occupational pension schemes and/or personal pension schemes. Tapering of the annual allowance only applies from 2016/17.

(b) **Furnished holiday lettings**

Any three from:

(1) There is no restriction on finance costs.

(2) Furniture and equipment purchased for use in the furnished holiday letting will qualify for capital allowances instead of replacement furniture relief.

(3) The profit from the furnished holiday letting will qualify as relevant earnings for pension tax relief purposes.

(4) Capital gains tax entrepreneurs' relief, relief for replacement of business assets and gift relief for business assets will potentially be available on a disposal of the furnished holiday letting.

114 Ronald

Text references. Assessable trading income is covered in Chapter 9 and capital allowances in Chapter 8. Property business income is the subject of Chapter 6. The computation of taxable income and the income tax liability will be found in Chapter 2. Pensions are the subject of Chapter 5.

Top tips. You could work out the amount of dividend income by adding back the dividend nil rate band of £5,000 to the dividend included in the computation.

Easy marks. There were some easy marks in part (a) for working out the income tax liability as the question outlined the computation required and the rates of tax.

Marks

(a)	Trading profit p/e 30 April 2017: assessable trading profit	½
	Trading profit p/e 30 April 2018: capital allowances	1½
	Trading profit p/e 30 April 2018: assessable trading profit	1
	Property business income: premium assessable	1
	Property business income: rent receivable	1
	Property business income: roof replacement	1
	Property business income: roof repairs	1
	Property business income: insurance	1
	Dividends	1
	Figures given	1
	Tax @ 40%	1
		11
(b)	No annual allowances for previous years	1
	Annual allowance 2017/18	1
	Basic rate relief	1
	Higher rate relief	1
		4
		15

(a) **Ronald – Income tax computation 2017/18**

	Non-savings income	Savings income	Dividend income	Total
	£	£	£	£
Trading income (W1)	11,592			
Employment income	65,065*			
Property business income (W2)	8,240			
Building society interest		1,260*		
Dividends £(800 + 5,000)			5,800	
Net income	84,897	1,260	5,800	91,957
Less personal allowance	(11,500)*			
Taxable income	73,397	1,260	5,800	80,457

	£
Income tax	
Non-savings income	
£33,500 @ 20%	6,700*
£39,897 (73,397 – 33,500) @ 40%	15,959
Savings income	
£500 @ 0%	0*
£760 (1,260 – 500) @ 40%	304
Dividend income	
£5,000 @ 0%	0*
£800 (5,800 – 5,000) @ 32.5%	260*
Income tax liability	23,223
Tax suffered at source	
PAYE	(9,130)*
Income tax payable	14,093

* Figures provided in question

Tutorial note

The amount of dividends are not given, but as the dividend nil rate band of £5,000 is available and only £800 is being taxed at the higher rate, the total dividends must be £(5,000 + 800) = £5,800.

Workings

1   *Trading profit*

	£	£
Period ended 30 April 2017		3,840
Period ended 30 April 2018	12,060	
Capital allowances £18,000 × 8% × 30%	(432)	
	11,628	
× 8/12		7,752
		11,592

2   *Property business income*

	£	£
Premium received		12,000
Less £12,000 × 2% × (30 – 1)		(6,960)
		5,040
Rents receivable £960 × 4		3,840
		8,880
Roof replacement	0	
Roof repairs £(8,600 – 8,200)	400	
Insurance £480 × 6/12	240	
		(640)
Property business profit		8,240

Tutorial note

The initial replacement cost of the shop's roof is not deductible, being capital in nature, as the building was not in a usable state when purchased and this fact was reflected in the reduced purchase price.

(b)   Ronald was not a member of a pension scheme prior to 2017/18, so the annual allowances for 2014/15, 2015/16 and 2016/17 are not available.

Although net relevant earnings are £(11,592 + 65,065) = £76,657, the maximum amount of tax relievable personal pension contribution is effectively restricted to the annual allowance of £40,000 for 2017/18.

Personal pension contributions are made net of basic rate tax, so Ronald would have paid £32,000 (£40,000 less 20%) to the pension company.

Higher rate tax relief would have been given by increasing Ronald's basic rate tax limit for 2017/18 by £40,000, being the gross amount of the pension contribution.

115 Wai

Marking scheme

			Marks
(a)	Salary	½	
	Bonus	1	
	Mileage allowance		
	Reimbursement	½	
	Ordinary commuting	½	
	Travel to clients	½	
	Temporary workplace	½	
	Tax-free amount @ 45p	½	
	Tax-free amount @ 25p	½	
	Car benefit		
	Percentage	½	
	Benefit	1	
	Incidental expenses	½	
	Mobile telephone	1	
	Living accommodation		
	Annual value	½	
	Additional benefit		
	Cost	½	
	Improvements	1	
	Limit	1	
	Benefit	½	
	Personal allowance	1	
			12
(b)	Form P60 contents	1½	
	Date	½	
	Form P11D contents	½	
	Date	½	
			3
			15

(a) **Wai – Taxable income 2017/18**

		£
Employment income		
Salary (10,200 × 12)		122,400
Bonus		8,100
Mileage allowance (W1)		2,763
Car benefit (W2)		1,149
Incidental expenses (overseas, up to £10 per night – exempt)		0
Mobile telephone (400 × 20%)		80
Living accommodation – Annual value		4,828
– Additional benefit (W3)		2,280
		141,600
Less personal allowance		(0)
Taxable income		141,600

Tutorial notes

1 The bonus of £4,600 will have been treated as being received during 2016/17 as Wai became entitled to it during that tax year. Similarly, the bonus of £2,900 will be treated as received during 2018/19.

2 The exemption for mobile telephones does not apply to the second telephone.

3 No personal allowance is available as Wai's adjusted net income of £141,600 exceeds £123,000.

Workings

1 *Mileage allowance*

	Miles	£
Reimbursement (13,860 at 55p)		7,623
Business mileage		
Ordinary commuting	0	
Travel to clients' premises	8,580	
Temporary workplace	2,860	
	11,440	
Tax-free amount		
10,000 miles at 45p		(4,500)
1,440 miles at 25p		(360)
Taxable benefit		2,763

Tutorial note

Travel to the temporary workplace qualifies as business mileage because the 24-month limit was not exceeded.

2 *Car benefit*

The relevant percentage for the car benefit is 17% because the motor car has CO_2 emissions between 76 and 94 grams per kilometre.

The motor car was available during the period 1 September 2017 to 5 April 2018, so the benefit for 2017/18 is £1,149 (11,590 × 17% × 7/12).

3 *Living accommodation additional benefit*

The benefit is based on the cost of the property plus subsequent improvements incurred before the start of the tax year.

	£
Cost	142,000
Improvements (prior to 6 April 2017 only)	24,200
	166,200
Limit	(75,000)
	91,200

The additional benefit is therefore £2,280 (91,200 at 2.5%).

(b) **Form P60**

Form P60 will show Wai's taxable earnings, income tax deducted, final tax code, national insurance contributions (NIC), and Qaz plc's name and address.

This form should have been provided to Wai by 31 May 2018.

Form P11D

Form P11D will detail the expenses and benefits provided to Wai.

This form should have been provided to Wai by 6 July 2018.

116 Samson and Delilah

Text references. The income tax computation is covered in Chapter 2. Chapters 3 and 4 deal with employment income and taxable and exempt benefits. Partnerships are the subject of Chapter 11.

Top tips. Trivial benefits (not exceeding £50) were new in Finance Act 2016 and are still highly examinable.

Easy marks. There were some easy marks for dealing with the car benefit and computing income tax.

Examining team's comments. Part (a) of the question was a typical income tax liability calculation (for both the husband and wife), and it was generally very well answered. Part (b) of the question involved income tax planning, requiring a calculation of the husband's income tax saving for the tax year if the building society deposit account had been in his wife's sole name instead of in joint names for the entire year. Given that the husband's personal allowance restriction would be reduced, the answer was simply the amount of interest (after deducting the savings income nil rate band of £500) at 60%. However, half page answers were quite common. Once again, working at the margin (where appropriate) could have saved an enormous amount of time.

Marking scheme

		Marks
(a)	*Samson*	
	Salary	½
	Building society interest	½
	Personal allowance	1
	Income tax	2
	Delilah	
	Salary	½
	Payroll giving	1
	Car benefit	1
	Chauffeur	½
	Hamper	½
	Business travel	½
	Trading profit	1
	Building society interest	½
	Deductible interest	1
	Personal allowance not available	½
	Income tax	2
		13
(b)	Transfer part of account from Samson to Delilah	2
		15

(a) **Samson – Income tax computation 2017/18**

	Non-savings income £	Savings income £	Total £
Employment income – Salary	112,000		
Building society interest £9,600/2		4,800	
Net income	112,000	4,800	116,800
Less personal allowance (W)	(3,100)		
Taxable income	108,900	4,800	113,700

Income tax

	£
£33,500 × 20%	6,400
£75,400 (108,900 – 33,500) × 40%	30,160
£500 × 0% (savings rate nil rate band)	0
£4,300 (4,800 – 500) × 40%	1,720
Income tax liability	38,280

Working

Samson's adjusted net income exceeds £100,000, so his personal allowance of £11,500 is reduced to £3,100 (11,500 – 8,400 ((116,800 – 100,000)/2)).

Delilah – Income tax computation 2017/18

	Non-savings income £	Savings income £	Total £
Employment income (W1)	213,248		
Trading profit £85,600 (93,600 – 8,000) × 40%	34,240		
Building society interest £9,600/2		4,800	
Total income	247,488	4,800	252,288
Less interest paid	(6,200)		
Net income/taxable income	241,288	4,800	246,088

Workings

1   *Employment income*

	£
Salary	184,000
Less charitable payroll deductions £250 × 12	(3,000)
	181,000
Car benefit (W2)	22,848
Chauffeur	9,400
Hamper	0
Reimbursement of travel to visit client	0
Employment income	213,248

2   *Car benefit*

The relevant percentage for the car benefit is 34% (18% + (175 – 95)/5).

The motor car was available throughout 2017/18 so the benefit is £22,848 (67,200 × 34%).

Income tax	£
£39,580 (W) × 20%	7,916
£116,500 (156,080 – 39,580) × 40%	46,600
£90,008 (246,088 – 156,080) × 45%	40,504
Income tax liability	95,020

Working

Delilah's basic and higher rate tax limits are increased by £4,864 × $\frac{100}{80}$ = £6,080 to £39,580 (33,500 + 6,080) and £156,080 (150,000 + 6,080) in respect of the charitable gift aid donations.

Tutorial notes

1   The car benefit does not cover the cost of a chauffeur, so this is an additional benefit.

2   The hamper is a trivial benefit as it does not exceed £50.

3   There is an automatic exemption for reimbursement of business expenses such as the train travel by Delilah (which would be a taxable benefit under general principles) provided that the expense would have been a deductible expense for the employee.

4   The loan interest paid of £6,200 is deductible because the loan was used by Delilah for a qualifying purpose.

5   No personal allowance is available as Delilah's adjusted net income of £240,008 (246,088 – 6,080) exceeds £123,000.

6   No savings income nil rate band is available as Delilah is an additional rate taxpayer.

(b)   If the building society deposit account had been in Delilah's sole name instead of in joint names for the entire year, this would have saved Samson income tax of £2,680 (£500 × 20% + £4,300 × 60%).

Tutorial note

Samson's effective marginal rate on the savings income covered by the savings income nil rate band (£500) is 20%. This is 40% of half of the £500 (ie 20% of the whole of the £500) of the savings income which was used to restrict the personal allowance. Samson's effective marginal rate of income tax on the savings income not covered by the savings income nil rate band (ie £4,800 – 500 = £4,300) is 60%. This is 40% (the higher rate) plus 40% of half (ie 20% of the whole) of the remaining £4,300 of savings income which was used to restrict the personal allowance.

117 Patience

Text references. Employment income is covered in Chapters 3 and 4 and national insurance contributions in Chapter 12. Assessable trading income is covered in Chapter 9 and capital allowances in Chapter 8. Property business income is the subject of Chapter 6. The computation of taxable income and the income tax liability will be found in Chapter 2. Pensions are the subject of Chapter 5.

Top tips. There are no writing down allowances or annual investment allowance in the final year of trading. Remember that gains on the disposal of residential property are taxed at 18% and 28% if they are not covered by the annual exempt amount and principal private residence relief.

Easy marks. Recognising the exempt benefits and mentioning them in your answer is important to get some easy marks.

Examining team's comments. Two aspects to this question caused particular difficulty. Firstly, many candidates treated the pension income (state pension, employer's occupational pension scheme and a private pension) as exempt income. Secondly, the format in which information was given for two properties caused a certain amount of confusion, with the information relevant for income tax and the capital gains tax details being shown within the one table; candidates being required to separate out the relevant information for income tax and capital gains tax purposes. Here figures were often duplicated with, for example, revenue expenditure being (correctly) deducted as an expense in calculating the property business profit, but then also (incorrectly) deducted in calculating chargeable gains.

		Marks
Salary		1
Pension contribution	Patience	½
Pension contribution	Employer	½
School place		1
Long-service award		½
Beneficial loan		½
Trading income	y/e 31.7.17	½
	p/e 31.12.17	½
	Overlap relief	1
Capital allowances	TWDV brought forward	½
	Laptop	½
	Disposal proceeds	1
	Balancing allowance	½
Property business profit	Rent received	½
	Expenditure	½
Pension income		1
Personal allowance		½
Increase basic rate limit		1
Income tax liability		1
Capital gains	Property one	½
	Property two	½
	Annual exempt amount	½
	CGT payable	½
		15

Patience – Income tax computation 2017/18

		£
Employment income		
Salary £3,750 × 9		33,750
Pension contributions	Patience £33,750 × 6%	(2,025)
	Employer	0
		31,725
School place		540
Long-service award		0
Beneficial loan		0
Trading income (W1)		16,100
Pension income £(1,450 + 6,000 + 3,300)		10,750
Property business income (W3)		3,500
Net income		62,615
Less personal allowance		(11,500)
Taxable income		51,115

Income tax

	£
£38,000 (W4) × 20%	7,600
£13,115 (51,115 – 38,000) × 40%	5,246
Income tax liability	12,846

Tutorial notes

1   An employer contribution to a pension scheme is not a taxable benefit.

2   The taxable benefit on the provision of the school place is the additional marginal cost to the employer, not the normal fee payable.

3   A non-cash long-service award is not a taxable benefit if it is for a period of service of at least 20 years, and the cost of the award does not exceed £50 per year of service.

4   There is no taxable benefit if beneficial loans do not exceed £10,000 during the tax year.

Workings

1   *Trading income*

	£	£
Year ended 31 July 2017		14,800
Period ended 31 December 2017	6,900	
Balancing allowance (W2)	(1,900)	
		5,000
		19,800
Relief for overlap profits		(3,700)
		16,100

2   *Capital allowances*

	Main pool	Allowances
	£	£
WDV brought forward	2,200	
Addition – Laptop computer	1,700	
Proceeds £(1,200 + 800)	(2,000)	
Balancing allowance	(1,900)	1,900

3   *Property business income*

	£
Rent received £(3,600 + 7,200)	10,800
Expenditure £(4,700 + 2,600)	(7,300)
Property business income	3,500

4   *Basic rate limit*

Patience's basic rate tax limit is increased by £4,500 to £38,000 (33,500 + 4,500 (3,600 × 100/80)) in respect of the personal pension contributions.

Patience – Capital gains tax computation 2017/18

		£	£
Property one	Disposal proceeds	122,000	
	Less cost	(81,400)	
			40,600
Property two	Disposal proceeds	98,000	
	Less cost	(103,700)	
			(5,700)
Net chargeable gains			34,900
Less annual exempt amount			(11,300)
Taxable gains			23,600
Capital gains tax			
£23,600 × 28%			6,608

118 Petula (Mar/Jun 17)

Marking scheme

			Marks
(a)	Salary		½
	Bonuses		1
	Mileage allowance:	reimbursed	½
		first 10,000 miles	½
		remaining miles	½
	Pension contributions		½
	Professional subscription		½
	Golf club membership		½

				Marks
Property income:	rent receivable		½	
	washing machine		1	
	dishwasher		1	
	other expenses		½	
	furnished room		1	
Savings income			2	
Interest paid			1	
Personal allowance			½	
				12
(b)	2017/18 annual allowance used in 2017/18		1	
	2014/15 annual allowance used in 2017/18		½	
	2015/16 annual allowance carried forward to 2018/19		½	
	2016/17 annual allowance carried forward to 2018/19		1	3
				15

(a) **Petula – Taxable income 2017/18**

	£
Employment income	
Salary	230,000
Bonuses (18,600 + 22,400)	41,000
Mileage allowance (W1)	8,350
Pension contributions	0
	279,350
Less Professional subscription	(630)
Less Golf club membership	0
	278,720
Property income (W2)	11,340
Savings income (250,000 at 3% × 4/12)	2,500
Less Interest paid	(140)
	292,420
Less Personal allowance	0
Taxable income	292,420

Tutorial notes

1   The bonus of £21,200 will have been treated as being received during 2016/17 because Petula became entitled to it during that tax year.

2   Under the accrued income scheme, Petula must include the accrued interest from the gilts as savings income for 2017/18, even though she has not received any actual interest.

3   No personal allowance is available because Petula's adjusted net income of £292,420 exceeds £123,000.

Workings

1   *Mileage allowance*

	£
Reimbursement (26,000 at 60p)	15,600
Tax free amount	
10,000 miles at 45p	(4,500)
11,000 miles at 25p	(2,750)
Taxable benefit	8,350

2   *Property income*

		£
Rent receivable		12,000
Replacement furniture relief		
	Washing machine	(420)
	Dishwasher	0
Other expenses		(1,640)
		9,940
Furnished room (8,900 – 7,500)		1,400
Property income		11,340

Tutorial notes

1   No relief is given for that part of the cost of the washer-dryer which represents an improvement over the original washing machine. Relief is therefore restricted to the cost of a similar washing machine.

2   No relief is available for the cost of the dishwasher because this is an initial cost rather than the cost of a replacement.

3   Claiming rent-a-room relief in respect of the furnished room is more beneficial than the normal basis of assessment (8,900 – 2,890 = £6,010).

(b)   *Annual allowances carried forward to 2018/19*

First work out the annual allowance used in 2017/18, remembering to use the current tax year allowance first and then the previous three tax years, earlier years first:

	£
Used in 2017/18	
Annual allowance 2017/18 (N1)	10,000
Brought forward from 2014/15	
£(40,000 – 25,000)	15,000
Annual allowance used in 2017/18	25,000

Then work out the remaining annual allowances carried forward to 2018/19:

	£
Carried forward from 2015/16	
£(40,000 – 25,000)	15,000
Carried forward from 2016/17 (N2)	
£(40,000 – 25,000)	15,000
Annual allowance carried forward to 2018/19	30,000

Notes

1   Petula's adjusted income for 2017/18 exceeds £210,000 so she is only entitled to the minimum annual allowance for this tax year.

2   Tapering of the annual allowance does not apply in 2016/17 as Petula's adjusted income did not exceed £150,000 in that year. The tax year 2016/17 was the first year in which the annual allowance was tapered.

MCQ bank – Chargeable gains for individuals 1

119   1 and 3

Motor vehicles suitable for private use and investments held in individual savings accounts (ISAs) are both exempt assets.

120   £2,712

	£
Chargeable gain	25,300
Less annual exempt amount	(11,300)
Taxable gains	14,000

Tax

	£
£(33,500 – 21,420) = 12,080 × 18% (residential property)	2,174
£(14,000 – 12,080) = 1,920 × 28% (residential property)	538
Total capital gains tax	2,712

The answer £3,920 uses 28% throughout. The answer £5,876 does not deduct the annual exempt amount. The answer £1,592 uses the rates of 10% and 20%.

121   £12,143

The amount of the cost attributable to the part sold is:

$$\frac{£36,000}{£36,000 + £90,000} \times £80,000 = £22,857$$

	£
Proceeds £(36,000 – 1,000)	35,000
Less cost (see above)	(22,857)
Gain	12,143

The answer £12,600 uses the net proceeds in the part disposal fraction. The answer £13,143 ignores the cost of disposal. The answer £11,000 uses 3/10 as the part disposal fraction.

122   £11,400

	2015/16	2016/17	2017/18	
	£	£	£	
Gains	2,000	4,000	13,900	
Losses	(14,000)	(2,000)	(2,000)	
	(12,000)	2,000	11,900	
c/f	12,000	12,000	(600) c/f	11,400
			11,300 AEA	

Current period losses must be set against current period gains. Brought forward losses are only set against current period gains in so far as they bring them down to the annual exempt amount.

123   £1,667

	£
Proceeds	7,000
Less cost	(1,500)
Gain	5,500

The maximum gain is 5/3 × £(7,000 – 6,000) = £1,667.

The chargeable gain is the lower of £5,500 and £1,667, so it is £1,667.

The answer £1,000 is the excess over £6,000. The answer £0 assumes the chattel is an exempt asset.

CBE style OTQ bank – Chargeable gains for individuals 2

124   £2,500

		£
Deemed proceeds		6,000
Less cost		(8,500)
Loss		(2,500)

125   14½ years

	Exempt years	Chargeable years	Total years
Actual occupation	3		3
Deemed occupation – any time employed overseas	5		5
Actual occupation	2		2
Deemed occupation – up to 3 years any reason	3		3
Unoccupied		½	½
Last 18 months of ownership	1½	–	1½
Totals	14½	½	15

126   12 August 2027

When a depreciating asset is purchased to replace a non-depreciating asset the gain on the sale is deferred until the earliest of:

The sale of the depreciating asset – 14 October 2027

Ceasing to use the depreciating asset in a business – not applicable here

The ten-year anniversary of the purchase of the depreciating asset – 12 August 2027

127   £1,160

Gains subject to entrepreneurs' relief are taxed at 10%. Other gains will be reduced by the annual exempt amount and then taxed, in this case at 20%, because Louise has taxable income in excess of the basic rate limit of £33,500. The capital gains tax (CGT) payable is therefore:

Tax	£
£8,000 × 10%	800
£(13,100 – 11,300) = 1,800 × 20%	360
Total CGT	1,160

128   £13,650

	Number	Cost £
Purchase October 2004	1,000	1,500
Bonus issue November 2006		
1 for 2 bonus issue	500	0
	1,500	1,500
Rights issue July 2011		
3 for 1 rights issue @ £2.70	4,500	12,150
	6,000	13,650
Disposal February 2018	(6,000)	(13,650)

129 £77,500

	£
Cost	73,000
Enhancement expenditure	41,700
Less insurance proceeds	(37,200)
Cost of restored property	77,500

130 £16,200

	£
Proceeds	28,800
Less cost £21,000 × 9/15	(12,600)
Chargeable gain	16,200

A copyright is a wasting asset and so the cost is written down over its life on a straight-line basis.

131 £4,000

	£
Gain	23,800
Less current year loss	(10,400)
Net current year gain	13,400
Less loss brought forward (balancing amount)	(2,100)
	11,300
Less annual exempt amount	(11,300)
Taxable gain	0
Loss carried forward £(6,100 – 2,100)	4,000

132 £143,000

The proceeds not reinvested in the new asset are £(184,000 – 143,000) = £41,000. Since this is greater than the gain of £38,600, no rollover relief is available. The cost of the replacement warehouse is therefore £143,000.

133

Earliest date	1 August 2016

Latest date	31 July 2020

CBE style OT case – Nim

134 £37,500

The shares in Kapook plc are valued at 3.70 + ½ × (3.80 – 3.70) = £3.75 so the deemed disposal proceeds are 10,000 × £3.75 = £37,500.

Make sure you learn this rule!

135 £26,333

The disposal is first matched against the purchase on 24 July 2017 (this is within the following 30 days) and then against the shares in the share pool. The cost of the shares disposed of is, therefore, £26,333 (5,800 + 20,533).

Share pool	No. of shares	Cost
	£	£
Purchase 19 February 2004	8,000	16,200
Purchase 6 June 2009 1 for 2 @ £3.65 per share	4,000	14,600
	12,000	30,800
Disposal 20 July 2017 £30,800 × 8,000/12,000	(8,000)	(20,533)
Balance c/f	4,000	10,267

The answer £28,500 treats the rights issue as separate holding and disposes of it in priority to the 2004 shares. The answer £25,667 is a disposal of 10,000 shares from the pool only. The answer £20,533 is the pool disposal only.

136 Nim will have deemed proceeds on the transfer of the Jooba Ltd shares to his wife so that neither a gain nor a loss will arise on the transfer.

Nim's wife will not be able to transfer her annual exempt amount to Nim.

Nim's wife will take the Jooba Ltd shares with a cost equal to the deemed proceeds ie the original cost to Nim. The spouse exemption applies for inheritance tax, not capital gains tax.

137 £3,500

	£
Net proceeds	8,700
Less cost	(5,200)
Gain	3,500

The maximum gain is 5/3 × £([8,700 + 300] – 6,000) = £5,000. The chargeable gain is the lower of £3,500 and £5,000, so it is £3,500.

138 £7,100

The set off of the brought forward capital losses is restricted to £8,700 (20,000 – 11,300) so that chargeable gains are reduced to the amount of the annual exempt amount. Capital losses carried forward are therefore £(15,800 – 8,700) = £7,100.

Aloi, Bon and Dinah

Text references. Entrepreneurs' relief is dealt with in Chapter 15. Shares are covered in Chapter 16. Transfers on death, computing chargeable gains and the calculation of capital gains tax will be found in Chapter 13.

Top tips. Par value means the face value of the shares. Aloi therefore had a cost of £50,000 for her first 50,000 £1 shares in Alphabet Ltd.

Easy marks. The dates in question 141 should have been well known.

---

139 2 and 4

Bon only became a director on 1 February 2017, so this qualifying condition was not met for one year prior to the date of disposal. Her shareholding of 25% (25,000/100,000 × 100) satisfies the minimum required holding of 5% for Alphabet Ltd to be her personal company and this qualifying condition was met for one year prior to the date of disposal.

Dinah was an employee for more than one year prior to the disposal but her shareholding of 3% (3,000/100,000 × 100) is less than the minimum required holding of 5%.

140 £29,140

	£
Gain qualifying for entrepreneurs' relief	
Ordinary shares in Alphabet Ltd	
Proceeds of sale (60,000 × £6)	360,000
Less cost £(50,000 + 18,600)	(68,600)
Gain	291,400
CGT @ 10% on £291,400	29,140

141 Notification 5 October 2018, payment 31 January 2019

142 £34,320

	£
Deemed proceeds of sale (10,000 × £7.12 (W1))	71,200
Less cost (W2)	(36,880)
Gain	34,320

Workings

1 The shares in XYZ plc are valued at 7.10 + ½ × (7.14 − 7.10) = £7.12.

2 Following the takeover, Bon received 25,000 shares in XYZ plc. The cost of the original shareholding is passed on to the new shareholding so the cost attributable to the 10,000 shares sold is £36,880 (92,200 × 10,000/25,000).

143 £0

There is no CGT liability on the sale of the XYZ plc shares as the gain of £5,000 (6,600 − (4,800 × 1,000/3,000)) is less than the annual exempt amount.

The transfer of the XYZ plc shares on Dinah's death is an exempt disposal.

CBE style OT case – Ginger, Innocent and Nigel

> **Text references.** Chapter 13 covers the basics of computing chargeable gains. Chapter 15 deals with business reliefs.
>
> **Top tips.** In questions 147 and 148 think why the disposals by Innocent and Nigel would give rise to different capital gains tax liabilities. Are there different rates of capital gains tax? When do those rates apply?
>
> **Easy marks.** There were easy marks in question 145 for working out the number of shares that could be sold without incurring a charge to CGT.

144 £1.60

The disposal is at an undervalue, so only the gift element of the gain can be deferred under gift relief. The consideration paid for each share will be immediately chargeable to capital gains tax to the extent that it exceeds the allowable cost. The chargeable amount is therefore £(4.00 – 2.40) = £1.60 per share.

145 8,506

Ginger's annual exempt amount for 2017/18 is £11,300 and she has a loss of £(1,800) brought forward from 2016/17. She can therefore sell (13,100/1.54) = 8,506 shares to her daughter without this resulting in any capital gains tax liability for 2017/18.

146 There is a lifetime limit of £10,000,000 for entrepreneurs' relief.

Entrepreneurs' relief is only available on shareholdings if they are held in a trading company.

The individual can be an officer (eg a director) or an employee of the company in which the shares are held. The conditions for entrepreneurs' relief must be satisfied for one year before the disposal.

147 £6,300

Innocent makes disposal

	£
Disposal proceeds	65,000
Less cost	(2,000)
Gain	63,000
CGT on £63,000 @ 10%	6,300

148 £6,840

Nigel makes disposal

	£
Disposal proceeds	65,000
Less cost (£46,200 × 2,000/3,000)	(30,800)
Gain	34,200
CGT on £34,200 @ 20%	6,840

CBE style OT case – Jerome

> **Text references.** Computing chargeable gains is dealt with in Chapter 13. Chattels are covered in Chapter 14. Business reliefs are the subject of Chapter 15.
>
> **Top tips.** If you are dealing with the disposal of a chattel, do not assume that the 5/3 rule always applies. Test it against the actual gain.
>
> **Easy marks.** There were some easy marks for identifying the base cost of the house for Jerome's wife in question 149 and for the administrative aspects of the election to hold over the gain on the Reward Ltd shares in question 151.

149 £112,800

The disposal of the house does not give rise to a gain or a loss because it is a transfer between spouses. The base cost of the house for Jerome's wife is therefore Jerome's base cost which was the value of the house at the uncle's death.

150 £50,600

	£
Deemed proceeds	98,400
Less cost	(39,000)
Gain before hold over relief	59,400

Hold over relief is restricted to £50,600 (£59,400 × 460,000/540,000), being the proportion of chargeable business assets to chargeable assets.

151

Latest date for election	5 April 2022

Person(s) making election	Jerome and his son

152 £10,100

	£
Proceeds	12,200
Less cost	(2,100)
Chargeable gain	10,100

The maximum gain is 5/3 × £(12,200 – 6,000) = £10,333. The chargeable gain is the lower of £10,330 and £10,100, so it is £10,100.

If your choice was £3,900 make sure you don't confuse the rules on gains and the rules on losses – the deemed proceeds are only £6,000 for computing the restricted loss.

153 £51,940

	£
Proceeds	78,400
Less cost (W)	(26,460)
Chargeable gain	51,940

Working

The amount of the cost attributable to the part sold is:

$$\frac{£78,400}{£78,400 + £33,600} \times £37,800 = £26,460$$

154 Jorge

Marking scheme

	Marks
House	
Proceeds	½
Cost	½
Enhancement expenditure	½
Period of exemption	3
Principal private residence exemption	1
Letting exemption	1
Copyright	
Proceeds	½
Cost	1½
Painting	½
Motor car	½
Annual exempt amount	½
	10

Jorge – Taxable gains computation 2017/18

	£
House (W1)	0
Copyright (W4)	24,300
Painting – exempt as proceeds and cost £6,000 or less	0
Motor car – exempt asset so loss not allowable	0
Chargeable gains	24,300
Less annual exempt amount	(11,300)
Taxable gains	13,000

Workings

1 House

	£
Proceeds	308,000
Less cost	(93,000)
Less enhancement expenditure (defending title to property)	(5,000)
Gain	210,000
Less: principal private residence exemption (W2)	(188,000)
letting exemption (W3)	(22,000)
Gain after exemptions	0

2   *Principal private residence exemption*

	Exempt months	Chargeable months	Total months
Actual occupation	34		34
Deemed occupation – up to 3 years any reason	18		18
Deemed occupation – any time employed overseas	24		24
Actual occupation	11		11
Deemed occupation – up to 4 years working elsewhere in UK	30		30
Deemed occupation – up to 3 years any reason balance (36 – 18) = 18, (22 – 18) = 4 chargeable	18	4	22
Deemed occupation – up to 4 years working elsewhere in UK balance (48 – 30) = 18, (26 – 18) = 8 chargeable	18	8	26
Actual occupation	17		17
Working overseas (12 – [18 – 3 – 13]) = 10 chargeable		10	10
Last 18 months – always treated as period of occupation	18		18
Totals	188	22	210

Principal private residence exemption £210,000 × 188/210	£188,000

Tutorial note

In calculating the principal private residence exemption, any periods of absence while working overseas, a maximum of four years' absence while working elsewhere in the UK, and a maximum of three years' absence for any reason are treated as deemed occupation, usually provided that they are preceded and followed by a period of actual occupation. The second period working overseas is therefore not a period of deemed occupation as it was not followed by a period of actual occupation.

Alternative approach

An alternative approach to calculate the chargeable months as follows:

Total period of ownership		210
Less actual occupation (34 + 11 + 17)		(62)
Deemed occupation	– any reason up to 3 years	(36)
	– employed overseas without limit	(24)
	– working in UK up to 4 years	(48)
Last 18 months – always treated as period of occupation		(18)
Chargeable months		22

3   *Letting exemption*

Lowest of:

(i)	Gain in letting period £210,000 × 22/210	£22,000
(ii)	Gain exempt under PPR (W2)	£188,000
(iii)	Maximum exemption	£40,000

Therefore letting exemption is	£22,000

4   *Copyright*

	£
Proceeds	80,300
Less cost £70,000 × 8/10 (N)	(56,000)
Gain	24,300

Tutorial note

The copyright is a wasting asset. The cost of £70,000 must therefore be depreciated based on an unexpired life of 10 years at the date of acquisition and an unexpired life of 8 years at the date of disposal.

155 Winston

Text references. Chapter 13 covers transfers on death, computing chargeable gains, transfers between spouses, part disposals and CGT liability. Chapter 15 includes entrepreneurs' relief.

Top tips. Losses on assets not qualifying for entrepreneurs' relief and the annual exempt amount should be deducted to produce the lowest CGT liability. This means that they should be deducted from gains taxed at 20% in priority to gains taxed at 10%.

Easy marks. The calculation of capital gains tax in part (a)(i) was straightforward.

Marking scheme

			Marks	
(a)	(i)	Annual exempt amount	1	
		Unused basic rate band	½	
		Capital gains tax	1½	
				3
	(ii)	Freehold shop	½	
		Painting	½	
		Capital loss	1	
		Annual exempt amount	½	
		Capital gains tax	1½	
				4
(b)		Net proceeds	1	
		Cost – probate value taken over on transfer from spouse	1	
		Apportionment of cost	1	
				3
				10

(a) (i) **Winston – CGT liability 2017/18**

	£
Chargeable gain on painting	46,560
Less annual exempt amount	(11,300)
Taxable gain	35,260

CGT liability: £(33,500 – 20,900) = 12,600 @ 10%	1,260
£(35,260 – 12,600) = 22,660 @ 20%	4,532
	5,792

(ii) **Winston – Revised CGT liability 2017/18**

	£
Gain qualifying for entrepreneurs' relief	
Gain on freehold shop £(140,000 – 80,000)	60,000
Gain not qualifying for entrepreneurs' relief	
Painting	46,560
Less allowable loss on warehouse £(102,000 – 88,000)	(14,000)
Net gain	32,560
Less annual exempt amount	(11,300)
Taxable gain	21,260

	£
CGT liability: £60,000 @ 10%	6,000
£21,260 @ 20%	4,252
	10,252

Tutorial notes

1   The capital loss on the sale of the freehold warehouse and the annual exempt amount are set against the chargeable gain from the sale of the painting as this saves CGT at the higher rate of 20%. Although the warehouse is being sold with the business, it was never actually used in the business, and so this aspect of the sale does not qualify for entrepreneurs' relief. If it had been used in the business, the loss of £14,000 would have been deducted from the gain on the shop to give a net gain on sale of the business of £46,000. CGT would then be charged on £46,000 at 10%.

2   The unused basic rate tax band of £12,600 is effectively used by the gain qualifying for entrepreneurs' relief of £60,000 even though this has no effect on the 10% tax rate.

(b)   **Renaldo – Chargeable gain 3 December 2017**

	£
Gross proceeds	92,000
Less auctioneers' commission (cost of disposal) £92,000 × 5%	(4,600)
Net proceeds	87,400
Less cost £28,600 × $\dfrac{92,000}{92,000 + 38,000}$	(20,240)
Chargeable gain	67,160

Tutorial notes

1   The cost of the land is £28,600 which is the value when Renaldo's father in law died. Renaldo would have taken over this cost when his wife transferred the land to him.

2   The gross proceeds of sale are used in the part disposal fraction.

156 Mick

Text references. The computation of chargeable gains for individuals is covered in Chapter 13. Shares are the subject of Chapter 16. Business reliefs are dealt with in Chapter 15.

Top tips. In part (b) you need to think about how you would use replacement of business asset relief and entrepreneurs' relief to identify the missing information.

Easy marks. The share pool in part (a) should have scored easy marks.

		Marks
(a)	*Warehouse*	
	Disposal proceeds	½
	Cost	½
	Extension	½
	Floor	½
	Shares in Rolling Ltd	
	Disposal proceeds	½
	Purchase	½
	Bonus issue	½
	Disposal cost	½
		4

(b) *Warehouse*

Replacement of business assets relief	1
Acquisition date of new warehouse	1
Cost of new warehouse	1
Shares in Rolling Ltd	
Entrepreneurs' relief	1
Rolling Ltd share capital	1
Previous claims	1
	6
	10

(a) **Mick – Chargeable gains 2017/18**

Freehold warehouse

	£	£
Disposal proceeds		522,000
Less: cost	258,000	
enhancement expenditure: extension	99,000	
enhancement expenditure: floor	0	
		(357,000)
Chargeable gain		165,000

Tutorial note

The cost of replacing the warehouse's floor is revenue expenditure as the floor is a subsidiary part of the property.

Shares in Rolling Ltd

	£
Disposal proceeds	3,675,000
Less cost (W)	(537,600)
Chargeable gain	3,137,400

Working: Share pool

	Number	Cost £
Purchase June 2007	500,000	960,000
Bonus issue December 2012		
500,000 × 3/2	750,000	0
Disposal September 2017	1,250,000	960,000
960,000 × 700,000/1,250,000	(700,000)	(537,600)
Balance carried forward	550,000	422,400

(b) **Freehold warehouse**

Replacement of business assets relief (rollover relief) may be available in respect of the chargeable gain arising on the disposal of the freehold warehouse.

The acquisition date of the replacement warehouse is required, since relief will only be available if this is after 19 May 2016 (one year before the date of disposal).

The cost of the replacement warehouse is required, since relief will be restricted if the sale proceeds of £522,000 have not been fully reinvested.

Shares in Rolling Ltd

Entrepreneurs' relief may be available in respect of the chargeable gain arising on the disposal of the shares in Rolling Ltd.

Details of Rolling Ltd's share capital are required, since relief will only be available if Mick had the minimum required holding (and voting rights) of 5%.

Details of any previous entrepreneurs' relief claims made by Mick are required, since there is a lifetime limit of £10 million of gains.

157 Ruby

Text references. The computation of chargeable gains and capital gains tax is covered in Chapter 13. Business reliefs are the subject of Chapter 15 and shares are dealt with in Chapter 16.

Top tips. The annual exempt amount should be set against gains which do not qualify for entrepreneurs' relief in priority to those which do qualify for the relief.

Easy marks. There were easy marks in part (a) for a basic computation of capital gains tax.

Examining team's comments. Part (a) of the question was well answered.

In part (b), the main problem was that candidates did not appreciate that both disposals would impact on the capital gains tax payable in respect of the disposal of the investment property. The disposal of the shares in the unquoted trading company (qualifying for entrepreneurs' relief) would utilise the remaining basic rate tax band, meaning that the 28% rate was now applicable. The capital loss arising on the disposal of the shares in the quoted trading company would be offset against the chargeable gain on the investment property. Another common problem was the 50p nominal value of the shares in the quoted trading company. This did not impact on the calculation of the capital loss, although many candidates incorrectly divided their cost figure by two.

Marking scheme

			Marks
(a)	Annual exempt amount	½	
	CGT at 18%	1	
	CGT at 28%	½	
			2
(b)	*Pola Ltd*		
	Disposal proceeds	½	
	Cost	½	
	Investment property	½	
	Annual exempt amount (best use)	1	
	CGT at 10%	1	
	CGT at 28%	1	
	Aplo plc		
	Disposal proceeds	½	
	Cost	1½	
	Investment property	½	
	Annual exempt amount	½	
	CGT at 18%	½	
			8
			10

(a) Ruby's CGT liability

	£
Chargeable gain on investment property	46,000
Less annual exempt amount	(11,300)
	34,700

Capital gains tax

	£
£14,185 (33,500 – 19,315) @ 18% (residential property)	2,553
£20,515 (34,700 – 14,185) @ 28% (residential property)	5,744
	8,297

(b) Choice of disposal

Shareholding in Pola Ltd

	Entrepreneurs' relief £	No entrepreneurs' relief £
Pola Ltd shares £(61,000 – 23,700)	37,300	
Investment property (part (a))		46,000
Less annual exempt amount (best use)		(11,300)
	37,300	34,700

Capital gains tax

	Entrepreneurs' relief £	No entrepreneurs' relief £
£37,300 @ 10%	3,730	
£34,700 @ 28%		9,716
Total CGT £(3,730 + 9,716)		13,446

Shareholding in Aplo plc

	£
Aplo plc shares £59,000 – (40,000 × £2.15(W))	(27,000)
Investment property (part (a))	46,000
Less annual exempt amount	(11,300)
Taxable gain	7,700

Capital gains tax

	£
£7,700 @ 18%	1,386

Working: The Aplo plc shares are valued at £2.12 + ½ × (£2.18 – £2.12) = £2.15.

MCQ bank – Inheritance tax 1

158 £150,000

	£
Before the gift: 70% shareholding	350,000
After the gift: 50% shareholding	(200,000)
Transfer of value	150,000

The answer £270,000 is the difference between a 70% shareholding and a 20% shareholding. The answer £80,000 is the value of a 20% shareholding. The answer £120,000 is 20% of a 100% shareholding.

159 £461,250

	£
Sunita's unused nil rate band £325,000 × 65%	211,250
Joel's nil rate band	325,000
	536,250
Less used against Joel's PET now chargeable	(75,000)
Available nil rate band to set against Joel's death estate	461,250

Sunita's nil rate band is increased pro-rata to that available at the time of Joel's death.

The answer £325,000 does not involve a spouse transfer and does not take account of the PET. The answer £452,800 transfers 65% of £312,000. The answer £536,250 does not deduct the PET.

160 £29,750

	£
Gift	190,000
Less AE × 2 (17/18 + 16/17 b/f)	(6,000)
	184,000
Less nil rate band available £(325,000 – 260,000)	(65,000)
	119,000
IHT @ $^{20}/_{80}$	29,750

The answer £28,250 deducts annual exemptions from the earlier transfer. The answer £31,250 does not deduct annual exemptions from the current transfer. The answer £23,800 does not gross up ie uses a rate of 20%.

161 £0

The gift to the granddaughter is covered by the marriage exemption of £2,500 by a remoter ancestor.

The sale of the vase is not a transfer of value because there is no gratuitous intent as Donald and Alan believed that the vase was worth what Alan paid for it.

162 £136,000

	£
PET on 10.7.14 PET now chargeable	600,000
Less nil rate band available £(325,000 – 150,000)	(175,000)
	425,000
IHT @ 40%	170,000
Less taper relief (3 to 4 years) @ 20%	(34,000)
Death tax payable on lifetime transfer	136,000

The chargeable lifetime transfer on 15 September 2008 is cumulated with the later PET since it was made in the seven years before that transfer.

The answer £170,000 does not deduct taper relief. The answer £88,000 treats the earlier gift as exempt so the full nil rate band is available. The answer £134,080 deducts annual exemptions from the current transfer.

CBE style OTQ bank – Inheritance tax 2

163   £350

The gifts to the grandson are exempt as normal expenditure out of income because they are part of the normal expenditure of the donor, made out of income and left the donor with sufficient income to maintain her usual standard of living.

The small gifts exemption only applies to gifts up to £250 per donee per tax year. If gifts total more than £250 the whole amount is chargeable. Since the gifts to the grandnephew totalled £(100 + 250) = £350 in 2017/18, this exemption does not apply.

164   £66,000

	£
Before the gift: 100% shareholding 1,000 × £150	150,000
After the gift: 70% shareholding 700 × £120	(84,000)
Transfer of value	66,000

165   £24,000

	£
Main residence (net of mortgage) £(300,000 – 220,000)	80,000
Investments and cash	385,000
Chargeable death estate	465,000
Less: residence property nil rate band	
(lower of £80,000 and £100,000)	(80,000)
available nil rate band (no lifetime transfers)	(325,000)
	60,000
IHT @ 40%	24,000

The residence nil rate band applies because the main residence is left to direct descendents. Note that the residence nil rate band is the lower of the net value of the main residence and the maximum amount of £100,000 (2017/18).

166   £351,000

	£
Cash to nephews £200 × 5	1,000
ISA investments	350,000
Chargeable estate	351,000

The small gifts exemption only applies to lifetime transfers. The ISA exemption only applies for income tax and capital gains tax. The residue to the wife is covered by the spouse exemption.

167

Lifetime tax	30 April 2018

Death tax	31 January 2018

The due date for the lifetime tax is the later of 30 April just after the end of the tax year of the transfer and six months after the end of the month of the transfer. The due date for additional tax on death is six months from the end of the month of death.

168   £234,000

	£
Estate	890,000
Less: IHT	(276,000)
legacy to wife	(260,000)
legacy to brother	(120,000)
Residue to grandchildren	234,000

169

Changing the terms of her will so that the residue of her estate goes to her grandchildren rather than her children		**WILL NOT ACHIEVE**
Making lifetime gifts to trusts up to the value of the nil rate band every seven years	**WILL ACHIEVE**	
Changing the terms of her will so that the residue of her estate goes to her husband rather than her children	**WILL ACHIEVE**	
Making lifetime gifts to her grandchildren early in life	**WILL ACHIEVE**	

There will be the same amount of inheritance tax on the residue of the estate if it is left to Heng's children or grandchildren. However, if the estate is left to her husband the spouse exemption will apply. Heng could reduce the potential inheritance tax liability on her estate when she dies by making lifetime gifts to trusts up to the value of the nil rate band every seven years as these will reduce her assets and will not be cumulated if she survives seven years. She could also make lifetime gifts to her grandchildren early in life as these would be potentially exempt transfers and she is more likely to survive seven years the earlier in life she makes the gifts.

170

Due date	30 June 2018

Persons responsible	The trustees

> **Examining team's comments.** This question tested knowledge of when IHT will be payable and by whom. The correct answer was the trustees on 30 June 2018, which is six months following the month of death. More candidates selected this option than any of the others, but 'The personal representatives of Chan's estate on 30 June 2018' and 'The trustees on 8 June 2018' were both popular choices. This is fairly basic knowledge, and it is the type of question which should represent a very easy (and quick) two marks.

171   £170,000

Nadia is entitled to her husband's residence nil rate band (as it was unused at the date of his death). It is assumed to be £100,000 as her husband died before 6 April 2017. The maximum residence nil rate band is therefore £(100,000 + 100,000) = £200,000.

The residence nil rate band is the lower of the maximum residence nil rate band of £200,000 and the net value of the main residence of £(350,000 − 180,000) = £170,000 ie £170,000.

172   The inheritance tax liability on Rachel's estate will | **decrease** | by | **£40,000** | if she leaves her main residence to her son rather than her brother.

This is because the residence nil rate band will apply since Rachel will be leaving her main residence to a direct descendent. The available residence nil rate band is the lower of £100,000 and £300,000 ie £100,000. This gives a decrease in the inheritance tax liability of £100,000 × 40% = £40,000.

Ning

173 £956,000

	£
Property one	674,000
Less repayment mortgage	(160,000)
	514,000
Property two	442,000
	956,000

There is no deduction in respect of the endowment mortgage as this will be repaid upon death by the life assurance element of the mortgage.

174 £324,000

	£
Motor cars	172,000
Investments £(47,000 + 36,000 + 69,000)	152,000
	324,000

There are no exempt assets for inheritance tax.

175 £27,900

	£
Bank loan	22,400
Nephew's legal fees	0
Funeral expenses	5,500
	27,900

The promise to pay the nephew's legal fees is not deductible as it is purely gratuitous (not made for valuable consideration).

176 £105,000

The potentially exempt transfer on 14 August 2006 is exempt from inheritance tax as it was made more than seven years before 20 March 2018.

The potentially exempt transfer on 7 November 2016 will utilise £220,000 of the nil rate band, so only £(325,000 − 220,000) = £105,000 is available against the death estate. The residence nil rate band is not available as it cannot be used against lifetime gifts.

177 Amount £227,500, Claim by 31 March 2020

Ning's personal representatives could claim her deceased husband's unused nil rate band of £325,000 × 70% = £227,500. The time limit for the claim is two years from the end of the month of Ning's death ie by 31 March 2020.

CBE style OT case – Jimmy

Text references. Inheritance tax is dealt with in Chapter 18.

Top tips. Watch out for the spouse exemption – it applies both to lifetime gifts and on death.

Easy marks. There were easy marks in question 181 for identifying the date of payment of additional tax on the lifetime gift as a result of Jimmy's death and that it was payable by the donee of the gift (the trustees of the trust).

178 £8,500

	£
Marriage exemption	2,500
Annual exemption 2016/17	3,000
Annual exemption 2015/16 b/f	3,000
	8,500

The answer £3,000 is just the current year annual exemption. The answer £6,000 is the annual exemptions for the current year and the previous year. The answer £11,000 uses £5,000 as the marriage exemption.

179 £55,000

	£
Before the gift: 5,100 shares × £30	153,000
After the gift: 4,900 shares × £20	(98,000)
Diminution in value	55,000

The answer £4,000 is 200 shares at £20 each. The answer £6,000 is 200 shares at £30 each. The answer £1,000 is the actual value of the shares gifted which is 200 shares at £5 each.

180 £118,750

	£
Net transfer of value (Jimmy pays IHT)	800,000

IHT	£325,000	× 0% =	Nil
	£475,000	× 20/80 =	118,750
	£800,000		118,750

181

Due date	31 August 2018

By whom paid	Trustees of trust

182 £312,000

	£
Death estate	980,000
Less spouse exemption	(200,000)
Chargeable death estate	780,000
£780,000 × 40%	312,000

The nil rate band has been used up by the lifetime transfers (stated in question) so the chargeable death estate is all taxed at 40%.

CBE style OT case – Zoe and Luke

183 The payments could be exempt without any cash limit under the normal expenditure out of income exemption.

The payments must have left Luke with sufficient income to maintain his usual standard of living to qualify for the normal expenditure out of income exemption.

Payments can qualify for the normal expenditure out of income exemption even if they are not paid directly to the individual who benefits from them. The payments did not have been reported each tax year to HM Revenue & Customs in Luke's income tax return to qualify for the normal expenditure out of income exemption (they will be reported in the inheritance tax account submitted on Luke's death).

184 £710,000

	£
Net chargeable transfer (AEs already used)	633,000

IHT	
£325,000 × 0%	0
£308,000 × 20/80	77,000
£633,000	77,000

Gross chargeable transfer £(633,000 + 77,000)	710,000

The answer £702,500 deducts two annual exemptions. The answer £694,600 treats the transfer as a gross chargeable transfer so uses the rate of 20%. The answer £756,200 uses the death rate of 40%.

185 £24,000

	£
Gross chargeable transfer	200,000

IHT on death (nil rate band already used)	
£200,000 × 40%	80,000
Less taper relief (3 to 4 years) £80,000 × 20%	(16,000)
	64,000
Less lifetime tax £200,000 × 20%	(40,000)
Additional IHT payable	24,000

The answer £40,000 does not deduct taper relief. The answer £80,000 is the death tax without deducting taper relief or lifetime tax. The answer £64,000 does not deduct lifetime tax.

186 £259,000

		£
Gift		270,000
Less:	marriage exemption	(5,000)
	annual exemption 2015/16	(3,000)
	annual exemption 2014/15 b/f	(3,000)
Potentially exempt transfer		259,000

187 £75,000

	£
Unused nil rate band at wife's death £(312,000 – 240,000)	72,000
Amount to transfer £325,000 × 72,000/312,000	75,000

The answer £72,000 does not adjust for the change in the nil rate band between the death of Luke's wife and Luke. The answer £312,000 is the nil rate band at the date of Luke's wife's death. The answer £325,000 is the nil rate band at Luke's death.

CBE style OT case – Marcus

> **Text references.** Inheritance tax is dealt with in Chapter 18.
>
> **Top tips.** In question 192, do not mix up the rules for transfers between spouses for capital gains tax (no gain/no loss transfer) and inheritance tax (exempt transfer).
>
> **Easy marks.** There were some easy marks for a basic inheritance tax computation in question 188 provided that you remembered that the nil rate band at the date of the transfer should be used.

188 £3,000

			£
IHT	£300,000	× 0% =	Nil
	£15,000	× 20% =	3,000
	£315,000		3,000

189 £96,250

			£
IHT	£10,000	(325,000 – 315,000) × 0% =	Nil
	£481,250	× 20% =	96,250
	£491,250		96,250

Although Marcus pays the inheritance tax due, since the gross chargeable transfer is given, in order to work out the tax he pays, this is 20% of the excess over the available nil rate band.

The answer £120,312 grosses up (ie uses 20/80). The answer £33,250 uses the full nil rate band. The answer £41,562 uses the full nil rate band and grosses up.

190 £38,500

			£
IHT	£10,000	× 0% =	Nil
	£481,250	× 40% =	192,500
	£491,250		192,500
Taper relief (3 to 4 years) £192,500 @ 20%			38,500

The answer £154,000 is the tax payable after taper relief. The answer £13,300 does not take account of the brought forward transfer. The answer £53,200 is does not take account of the brought forward transfer and is the tax payable after taper relief.

191 £570,000

	£
Before: 100,000 × £12	1,200,000
After: 70,000 × £9	(630,000)
Potentially exempt transfer of value	570,000

The answer £360,000 is 30,000 shares at £12 each. The answer £270,000 is 30,000 shares at £9 each. The answer £150,000 is 30,000 shares at £5 each.

192 If Barbara remarries, any unused nil rate band on her death can be transferred to her spouse if they survive her.

The transfer of Marcus's estate to Barbara on his death is an exempt transfer.

Married couples (and registered civil partnerships) are not chargeable persons for inheritance tax (IHT) purposes, because each spouse (or civil partner) is taxed separately.

The gift of the land on 29 June 2016 by Marcus to Barbara is an exempt transfer.

193 Pere and Phil

Text references. Inheritance tax is dealt with in Chapter 18. Chargeable gains and the computation of capital gains tax are in Chapter 13. The points on distinguishing between revenue and capital expenditure are covered in Chapter 7.

Top tips. You don't need to know names of tax cases in the Taxation (TX – UK) exam, but you are expected to know, and be able to apply, the principles decided, as in part (b) here.

Easy marks. There were some easy marks in part (a) for using the exemptions.

Marking scheme

		Marks
(a)	Lifetime gift	
	Marriage exemption	1
	Annual exemption – current year	½
	Annual exemption – brought forward	½
	Potentially exempt transfer	½
	IHT @ 0%	½
	IHT @ 40%	½
	Taper relief	1
	Death estate	
	Spouse exemption	1
	IHT @ 40%	½
		6
(b)	Disposal proceeds	½
	Cost	1
	Enhancement	1
	Annual exempt amount	½
	Capital gains tax @ 18%	½
	Capital gains tax @ 28%	½
		4
		10

(a) **Pere – Inheritance tax (IHT) arising on death**

Lifetime transfer 23 August 2011

		£
Gift		420,000
Less:	marriage exemption	(5,000)
	annual exemption 2011/12	(3,000)
	annual exemption 2010/11 b/f	(3,000)
Potentially exempt transfer		409,000
IHT		
£325,000 @ 0%		0
£84,000 @ 40%		33,600
£409,000		
Less taper relief (6 to 7 years @ 80%)		(26,880)
IHT payable		6,720

Tutorial note

The potentially exempt transfer becomes chargeable as a result of Pere dying within seven years of making it.

Death estate

	£
Value of estate	880,000
Less spouse exemption £880,000/2	(440,000)
Chargeable estate	440,000
IHT on £440,000 @ 40%	176,000

(b) **Phil – Capital gains tax computation 2017/18**

		£
Net disposal proceeds		495,700
Less:	cost	(420,000)
	enhancement expenditure	(5,200)
Gain		70,500
Less annual exempt amount		(11,300)
Taxable gain		59,200

	£
CGT on £23,550 (33,500 – 9,950) @ 18%	4,239
CGT on £35,650 (59,200 – 23,550) @ 28%	9,982
	14,221

Tutorial notes

1 The cost of replacing the property's chimney is revenue expenditure because the chimney is a part of the house and so this is a repair to the house. The cost of the new boundary wall is capital expenditure because the wall is a separate structure which is not part of the house.

2 Because the house is residential property, the gain is taxed at 18% and 28% rather than 10% and 20%.

194 Afiya

Marking scheme

			Marks
(a)	*Lifetime transfers*		
	14 September 2016	Value of shares before transfer	1
		Value of shares after transfer	1
		Annual exemption 2016/17	½
		Annual exemption 2015/16 brought forward	½
	27 January 2017	Nil rate band	½
		Balance @ 20/80	½
	Additional liabilities arising on death		
	14 September 2016	Potentially exempt transfer now chargeable	1
	27 January 2017	Gross chargeable transfer	½
		Nil rate band	½
		Balance @ 40%	½
		Lifetime tax already paid	½
	Death tax		
	Value of estate		½
	Spouse exemption		½
	Residence nil rate band		½
	Charge @ 40%		½
			9
(b)	Residue of estate		1
			10

(a) **Afiya – Inheritance tax on death**

Lifetime transfers

14 September 2016

	£
Value of shares held before transfer 8,000 × £8	64,000
Less value of shares held after transfer 1,500 × £3	(4,500)
Transfer of value	59,500
Less: annual exemption 2016/17	(3,000)
annual exemption 2015/16 b/f	(3,000)
Potentially exempt transfer	53,500

27 January 2017

	£
Net chargeable transfer	400,000

IHT

	£
325,000 × 0%	0
75,000 × 20/80 (donor pays tax)	18,750
400,000	18,750

Gross chargeable transfer £(400,000 + 18,750)	418,750

Additional tax on lifetime transfer on death of donor

14 September 2016

Potentially exempt transfer of £53,500 becomes chargeable as donor dies within 7 years.

Within nil rate band at death, no tax to pay.

27 January 2017

Nil rate band available £(325,000 – 53,500) = £271,500.

	£
Gross chargeable transfer	418,750

IHT

	£
271,500 × 0%	0
147,250 × 40%	58,900
418,750	58,900
No taper relief (death within three years of transfer)	
Less lifetime tax paid	(18,750)
Additional tax payable on death	40,150

Death estate

	£
Assets at death	623,000
Less funeral expenses	(3,000)
Value of estate for IHT purposes	620,000
Less exempt legacy to spouse	(150,000)
Chargeable estate	470,000
Less residence nil rate band (lower of £90,000 and £100,000)	(90,000)
Taxable estate	380,000

IHT liability £380,000 × 40%	152,000

The nil rate band was used by lifetime transfers.

(b)   Afiya's children will inherit the residue of £(620,000 – 150,000 – 40,000 – 152,000) = £278,000.

195 Kendra

Marking scheme

		Marks
(a)	Property	½
	Building society deposits	½
	ISAs	½
	NS&I certificates	½
	Proceeds of life assurance policy	1
	Funeral expenses	½
	Loan	½
	Inheritance tax	1
		5
(b)	No IHT benefit	1½
	No CGT benefit	1½
		3
(c)	Skip a generation	1
	Avoids double charge to IHT	1
		2
		10

(a) Kendra – Inheritance tax on death

	£
Property	970,000
Building society deposits	387,000
Individual Savings Accounts	39,000
NS&I certificates	17,000
Proceeds of life policy	225,000
Gross estate	1,638,000
Less: funeral expenses	(12,800)
loan	(1,200)
Net estate	1,624,000

Inheritance tax	
£325,000 @ 0%	0
£1,299,000 @ 40%	519,600
Inheritance tax liability	519,600

(b) As the property is not expected to increase in value in the near future, there is no inheritance tax benefit in making a lifetime gift. Kendra would need to live for three more years for taper relief to be available.

Also, a lifetime gift would result in a capital gains tax liability of £48,720 (£174,000 at 28%) for 2017/18, whereas a transfer on death would be an exempt disposal.

(c)   It can be beneficial to skip a generation so that gifts are made to grandchildren rather than children, particularly if the children already have significant assets.

This avoids a further charge to inheritance tax when the children die. Gifts will then only be taxed once before being inherited by the grandchildren, rather than twice.

196 James

Text references. Chapter 18 deals with inheritance tax.

Top tips. When working out the inheritance death tax on the lifetime transfer, remember to look back seven years from the date of the lifetime transfer (not the date of death) to see whether there are any previous transfers to cumulate.

Easy marks. The nil rate band is used up on the first gift so the calculation of the inheritance tax on the CLT and death estate are easy.

Marking scheme

		Marks	
(a)	Potentially exempt transfer (after annual exemptions)	1	
	Nil rate band available	1½	
	Inheritance tax	½	
	Daughter to pay	½	
	Chargeable lifetime transfer	½	
	Inheritance tax	½	
	Trustees to pay	½	
	Death estate – IHT liability	½	
	James's personal representatives to pay	½	
			6
(b)	Avoidance of double taxation		2
(c)	Taper relief	½	
	Lifetime transfer values fixed	½	
	IHT saving	1	
			2
			10

(a)   **James – Inheritance tax arising on death**
Lifetime transfers within seven years of death
14 May 2016

			£
Gift			420,000
Less: annual exemption	2016/17		(3,000)
annual exemption	2015/16 b/f		(3,000)
Potentially exempt transfer			414,000
Inheritance tax liability		£296,000 (W) @ 0%	0
		£118,000 @ 40%	47,200
			47,200

James's daughter will be responsible for paying the inheritance tax of £47,200.

2 August 2016

	£
Chargeable lifetime transfer	260,000
Inheritance tax liability £260,000 @ 40%	104,000

The trustees will be responsible for paying the inheritance tax of £104,000.

Death estate

	£
Chargeable estate	870,000
Inheritance tax liability £870,000 @ 40%	348,000

The personal representatives of James's estate will be responsible for paying the inheritance tax of £348,000.

Working: Available nil rate band

			£	£
Nil rate band at date of death				325,000
Gift 9 October 2010			35,000	
Less:	annual exemption	2010/11	(3,000)	
	annual exemption	2009/10 b/f	(3,000)	(29,000)
Nil rate band available				296,000

(b) Skipping a generation avoids a further charge to inheritance tax when the children die. Gifts will then only be taxed once before being inherited by the grandchildren, rather than twice.

(c) Even if the donor does not survive for seven years, taper relief will reduce the amount of IHT payable after three years.

The value of potentially exempt transfers and chargeable lifetime transfers are fixed at the time they are made.

James therefore saved inheritance tax of £20,000 (£(310,000 – 260,000) @ 40%) by making the lifetime gift of property.

197 Alan

Marking scheme

				Marks
(a)	(i)	*CGT on lifetime gift*		
		Chargeable gain	1	
		Annual exempt amount	½	
		CGT payable	½	
				2
	(ii)	*IHT on lifetime gift*		
		Identify no lifetime tax on PET	½	
		Gift	½	
		Annual exemptions	1	
		Nil rate band at death	1	
		Death tax	½	
		Taper relief	½	
				4
(b)	(i)	CGT on death		1
	(ii)	*IHT on death*		
		Transfer of value	½	
		Nil rate band at death	1	
		Death tax	½	
				2
(c)		Conclusion		1
				10

(a) (i) **CGT payable on lifetime gift 10 December 2017**

	£
Proceeds (market value)	450,000
Less cost	(375,000)
Chargeable gain	75,000
Less annual exempt amount	(11,300)
Taxable gain	63,700
CGT on £63,700 @ 20% (higher rate taxpayer)	12,740

(ii) **IHT payable on lifetime gift 10 December 2017 if Alan dies on 1 April 2021**

Potentially exempt transfer (PET) on 10 December 2017. No lifetime inheritance tax.

Value of PET £450,000 less £3,000 (AE 2017/18) and £3,000 (AE 2016/17) = £444,000.

PET becomes chargeable when Alan dies within seven years.

Lifetime transfer of value of £55,000 in 7 years before 10 December 2017 (transfers after 10 December 2010). Nil rate band of £(325,000 – 55,000) = £270,000 available to compute death tax.

		£
£270,000 × 0%		0
£174,000 × 40%		69,600
£444,000		69,600
Less taper relief @ 20% (3 to 4 years)		(13,920)
Death tax payable		55,680

(b) (i) **CGT on death**

The transfer of the Crimson plc shares on Alan's death is an exempt disposal and Julie will take the shares at their value at Alan's death (probate value).

(ii) **IHT payable on death estate**

No lifetime transfers of value in seven years before 1 April 2021 (transfers after 1 April 2014). Nil rate band (at date of death) of £325,000 available.

Value of death estate is £500,000.

Death tax payable is:

	£
£325,000 × 0%	0
£175,000 × 40%	70,000
£500,000	70,000

(c) Based on the answers to parts (a) and (b), it would be more tax advantageous for Alan to gift the Crimson plc shares to Julie in his lifetime because this would result in an overall tax saving of:

£([12,740(CGT) + 55,680(IHT)] – [0(CGT) + 70,000(IHT)])   <u>£1,580</u>

Tutorial note

Mark will be awarded for any **sensible** conclusion based on your own answers in parts (a) and (b).

CBE style OTQ bank – Corporation tax liabilities

198

Legal expenses relating to the acquisition of a new 40-year lease on its factory		NOT ALLOWABLE
Cost of arranging a new bank loan to purchase machinery for trade	ALLOWABLE	
Write off of an irrecoverable loan to a former employee		NOT ALLOWABLE
Donation to local charity with mention of Jet Ltd's support in programme for fundraising concert (not a qualifying charitable donation)	ALLOWABLE	

Legal expenses in respect of leases are only allowable if they relate to the **renewal** of a short lease. The cost of arranging a bank loan for trade purposes is allowable. A debt written off in respect of a former employee is accounted for under the non-trade loan relationship rules as it does not relate to the trade of the company. A small donation to a local charity with publicity would normally be allowable as being for the purposes of the trade.

199   12 months to 30 November 2017, 4 months to 31 March 2018

If the company has a long period of account it is divided into one period of 12 months and one of the remainder.

200   £2,720

	£
Leasing cost	3,200
£3,200 × 15% disallowance	(480)
Allowable deduction	2,720

201   £3,352

	Main pool £	Special rate pool £	Allowances £
Additions	30,400	15,400	
WDA 8% × 6/12		(616)	616
18% × 6/12	(2,736)		2,736
TWDV c/f / Allowances	27,664	14,784	3,352

Do not forget to pro-rate writing down allowances in a short accounting period. No adjustment is made for private use by a director for a company.

The answer £4,122 uses 18% for both WDAs. The answer £6,704 is the full year's WDAs. The answer £3,229 adjusts for private use – this is a common mistake. Remember that there is never any private use by a company!

202   £0

	£
Proceeds	70,000
Less cost 15,000 × £3.50	(52,500)
Unindexed gain	17,500
Less indexation allowance	
$\frac{(270.6 - 176.2)}{176.2} \times £52,500 = £28,127$ restricted to	(17,500)
Indexed gain	0

203 £26,000

Cook plc must make a current year loss claim against total profits if it wishes to make a claim to carry a loss back. A company is permitted to carry back to 12 months only, against total profits (ie before qualifying charitable donations). Therefore the maximum carry back is the total profits in the year to 31 December 2016 ie £(25,000 + 1,000) = £26,000. This is less than the loss remaining, of £30,000, following the current year claim.

204 £83,750

	£
Loss	160,000
Less loss relief y/e 31.12.18	(5,000)
Less loss relief p/e 31.12.17 (40,000 + 15,500)	(55,500)
Less loss relief y/e 31.3.17 3/12 × (45,000 + 18,000)	(15,750)
Loss c/f	83,750

205 £18,000

	£
Trading loss	15,000
Excess qualifying charitable donation £(5,000 – 2,000)	3,000
Capital loss	0
Amount that can be surrendered as group relief	18,000

206

Daffodil plc	
Flora Ltd	

Group relief can be made to UK companies only, so not to Geranium Inc, and where there is a ≥75% direct and indirect holding by the controlling company. Daffodil plc only has a (80% × 90%) = 72% interest in Hellebore Ltd.

207

Pine plc	Willow Ltd
Juniper Ltd	

Losses can only be transferred to UK companies where there is a ≥75% direct interest at each level and >50% indirect holding by the top company. Pine plc has a (75% × 75%) = 56.25% interest in Maple Ltd.

CBE style OT case – Luna Ltd

208

	TRUE	
Indexation allowance can reduce a gain to nil but not create a loss	TRUE	
Indexation allowance can increase an unindexed loss		FALSE

Indexation allowance cannot increase or create a loss although it can reduce a gain to nil.

209 £6,925

	£
Proceeds	53,400
Less cost	(36,800)
	16,600
Less indexation allowance $\dfrac{273.8 - 216.8}{216.8} \times £36,800$	(9,675)
Gain	6,925

210 £14,694

	No. of shares	Indexed cost £
Acquisition	16,000	32,000
Indexed rise $\dfrac{273.8 - 223.6}{223.6} \times £32,000$		7,184
		39,184
Disposal	(10,000)	(24,490)
	6,000	14,694

211 £13,125

	No. of shares	Cost £
Acquisition	5,000	7,500
Bonus 1 for 1	5,000	0
	10,000	7,500
Rights 1 for 4 @ £2.25	2,500	5,625
	12,500	13,125

212 £19,500

$$£33,000 \times \dfrac{(£6.50 \times 10,000)}{(£6.50 \times 10,000) + (£4.50 \times 10,000)}$$ £19,500

Tay Ltd

Text references. Chargeable gains for companies is the subject of Chapter 20.

Top tips. The application of the rules for damaged assets in question 213 is similar to rollover relief for replacement of business assets.

Easy marks. The chattels rules in question 215 should have been well known.

213 £155,000

	£
Proceeds	180,000
Less indexed cost	(155,000)
Gain	25,000
Gain immediately chargeable £(180,000 − 162,000)	(18,000)
Deduction from base cost of new warehouse	7,000

The base cost of the new warehouse is £(162,000 − 7,000) = £155,000.

The answer £162,000 does not give any relief. The answer £144,000 deducts the gain immediately chargeable. The answer £140,000 uses the unindexed cost to work out the gain.

214 £8,000

	Market value £	Indexed cost £	Gain £
20,000 £1 ordinary shares @ £4 each	80,000	64,000	
£40,000 (20,000 × £2) cash	40,000	32,000	8,000
	120,000	96,000	

The answer £24,000 gain is the total gain if the acquisition of the shares was treated as a disposal. The answer £16,000 gain is the gain on the shares if the acquisition of the shares was treated as a disposal. The answer £(24,000) loss is the loss on cash if the nominal value of the shares of £1 is used for the apportionment.

215 £5,000

Although the general rule is that wasting chattels are exempt, there is an exception for assets used for the purpose of a trade in respect of which capital allowances have been or could have been claimed. The usual chattel rules therefore apply as follows:

	£
Proceeds	9,000
Less indexed cost	(3,500)
Gain	5,500

The maximum gain is 5/3 × £(9,000 − 6,000) = £5,000.

The chargeable gain is the lower of £5,500 and £5,000, so it is £5,000.

216 £16,296

	£
Proceeds	45,000
Less: cost	(20,000)
enhancement (drainage)	(2,000)
Unindexed gain	23,000
Less: indexation on cost £20,000 × 0.316	(6,320)
indexation on enhancement £2,000 × 0.192	(384)
Chargeable gain	16,296

The answer £16,680 does not index the enhancement. The answer £16,048 uses the indexation factor on cost for both cost and enhancement. The answer £15,732 indexes the unindexed gain using the indexation factor on cost.

217   2 and 4

The capital loss can be set against chargeable gains made in the year ended 31 March 2019 and the capital loss can be carried forward and set against the first available chargeable gains.

Capital losses cannot be carried back and cannot be set against profits other than chargeable gains.

CBE style OT case – Hyde plc group

Text references. Groups are the subject of Chapter 22.

Top tips. Make sure you know the difference between the rules for relationships between companies for group relief and those applying to chargeable gains groups.

Easy marks. The identification of the base cost of the factory in question 222 should have been easy marks if you remembered that transfers between chargeable gains group companies are on a no gain, no loss basis.

218

Hampstead plc	Regent plc
	Primrose plc

A company is in a group relief group where there is a ≥75% direct and indirect holding by the controlling company (Hyde plc). Hyde plc has a (95% × 80%) = 76% interest in Primrose Ltd but only has a (85% × 85%) = 72.25% interest in Richmond Ltd.

219   £70,000

	£
Trading loss	68,000
Excess qualifying charitable donations £(5,000 – 3,000)	2,000
Maximum group relief	70,000

220   £50,500

	£
Chargeable gain	48,000
Interest income	12,000
Trading loss	(8,000)
Qualifying charitable donations	(1,500)
Available taxable total profits	50,500

Hyde plc is assumed to use its own current year losses in working out the taxable total profits against which it may claim group relief, even if it does not in fact claim relief for current losses against total profits. Group relief is set against taxable total profits after all other reliefs for the current period such as qualifying charitable donations.

221   A claim for group relief will be ineffective unless Greenwich plc gives a notice of consent. The claim for group relief would be made on Hyde plc's corporation tax return.

Any payment by Hyde plc for group relief, up to the amount of the loss surrendered, is ignored for all corporation tax purposes. A claim for group relief between Greenwich plc and Hyde plc will be available against 9/12ths of the taxable total profits of Hyde plc for the year to 31 March 2019, since surrendered losses must be set against taxable total profits of a corresponding accounting period (1 April 2018 to 31 December 2018).

	£
Cost	100,000
Indexation allowance to date of transfer £100,000 × 0.200	20,000
Base cost for Primrose plc	120,000

The transfer of assets within a chargeable gains group is on a no gain / no loss basis including indexation to the date of the transfer.

223 Do-Not-Panic Ltd

Text references. Chapter 19 covers computing taxable total profits and the corporation tax liability. Payment of corporation tax is covered in Chapter 23.

Top tips. Split out the long period correctly into the 2 accounting periods. Remember it is always the first 12 months and then the balance (in this case 3 months). Watch out for an accounting period which spans 1 April 2017 as you will need to use two rates of corporation tax.

Easy marks. Allocating the figures between the two accounting periods should be straightforward.

Marking scheme

		Marks
Trading profit		1
Capital allowances	– year ended 31 December 2017	2
Capital allowances	– period ended 31 March 2018	1½
Interest income	– period ended 31 March 2018	½
Chargeable gains		1
Qualifying charitable donation – period ended 31 March 2018		½
Corporation tax	– year ended 31 December 2017	2
	– period ended 31 March 2018	½
Due dates		1
		10

Do-Not-Panic Ltd – Corporation tax liabilities for the 15-month period ended 31 March 2018

	Year ended 31 December 2017 £	Period ended 31 March 2018 £
Trading profit (12:3)	228,000	57,000
Capital allowances (W)	(17,000)	(5,000)
	211,000	52,000
Interest income (accruals basis)	–	9,500
Chargeable gains (39,000 – 4,250)	–	34,750
	211,000	96,250
Less qualifying charitable donation	–	(2,000)
Taxable total profits	211,000	94,250

		FY 2016/FY 2017 £	FY 2017 £
y/e 31.12.17			
FY 2016			
£211,000 × 3/12 × 20%		10,550	
FY 2017			
£211,000 × 9/12 × 19%		30,067	
Corporation tax for y/e 31.12.17		40,617	
p/e 31.3.18			
FY 2017			
£94,250 × 19%			17,907
Due dates		1 October 2018	1 January 2019

Working: Capital allowances

	FYA	AIA £	Main pool £	Allowances £
Y/e 31 December 2017				
Addition qualifying for AIA				
Machinery		8,000		
AIA		(8,000)		8,000
Transfer to main pool		0	0	
Addition not qualifying for AIA but qualifying for FYA				
Car	9,000			
FYA	(9,000)			9,000
Transfer to main pool	0		0	
Allowances				17,000
P/e 31 March 2018				
TWDV b/f			0	
Addition qualifying for AIA				
Equipment		5,000		
AIA £200,000 × 3/12 = £50,000 maximum		(5,000)		5,000
Transfer to main pool		0	0	
TWDV c/f			0	
Allowances				5,000

224 Problematic Ltd

Text references. Chargeable gains for companies are covered in Chapter 20.

Top tips. Make sure you use the three column proforma for the FA 1985 pool.

Easy marks. The base cost required in part (b) is easy provided you remember that the leasehold factory is a depreciating asset, and so do not reduce the base cost by rollover relief.

Marks

(a) **Easy plc**

FA 1985 pool – Purchase		½
– Rights issue		1
– Indexation		2
– Disposal		1
Chargeable gain		1½

Freehold factory

Disposal proceeds		½
Indexed cost		½
Rollover relief		2
		9

(b) **Leasehold factory**

		1
		10

(a) **Easy plc shares**

FA85 pool

	No. of shares	Cost £	Indexed cost £
Purchase 26.6.05	15,000	12,600	12,600
Index to September 2008			
$\dfrac{(218.4-192.2)}{192.2}\times £12,600$			1,718
Rights issue 1 for 3 @ £2.20	5,000	11,000	11,000
c/f	20,000	23,600	25,318
Index to June 2017			
$\dfrac{(270.6-218.4)}{218.4}\times £25,318$			6,051
			31,369
Sale	(16,000)	(18,880)	(25,095)
C/f	4,000	4,720	6,274

Gain	£
Proceeds	54,400
Less cost	(18,880)
	35,520
Less indexation £(25,095 – 18,880)	(6,215)
Chargeable gain	29,305

Freehold factory

	£
Proceeds	171,000
Less indexed cost	(127,000)
	44,000
Less gain deferred on purchase of leasehold factory £(44,000 – 16,200)	(27,800)
Chargeable gain (amount not reinvested £(171,000 – 154,800))	16,200

(b) The leasehold factory is a depreciating asset, so there is no adjustment to the base cost of £154,800.

Tutorial note

When a replacement asset is a depreciating asset then the gain is not rolled over by reducing the cost of the replacement asset. Instead, the gain is deferred until it crystallises on the earliest of:

- The disposal of the replacement asset
- The date the replacement asset is no longer used in the business
- Ten years after the acquisition of the replacement asset which in this case is 10 December 2027

225 Volatile Ltd

Text references. Corporation tax losses are covered in Chapter 21.

Top tips. Don't forget to set up a loss memorandum for each loss so that you can see how the loss is utilised.

Easy marks. You should have been able to state at least one of the principles of claiming loss relief in part (a).

Marking scheme

			Marks
(a)	Timing of relief	1	
	Loss of QCDs	1	
			2
(b)	Trading income	½	
	Property business income	½	
	Chargeable gains	1½	
	Loss relief – y/e 31 December 2014	2	
	Loss relief – y/e 30 September 2017	2½	
	Qualifying charitable donations	½	
	Unrelieved losses	½	
			8
			10

(a)   **Choice of loss relief**

The two factors that will influence a company's choice of loss relief claims are:

(i)   Timing of relief: both in terms of tax rate (the rate of corporation tax for financial year 2016 was 20% whereas for financial year 2017 it is 19%) and cash flow (saving tax sooner is beneficial for cash flow)

(ii) The extent to which relief for qualifying charitable donations might be lost

(b) **Volatile Ltd**

	P/e 31.12.13 £	Y/e 31.12.14 £	Y/e 31.12.15 £	P/e 30.9.16 £
Trading income	44,000	0	95,200	78,700
Less carry forward loss relief	(0)	(0)	(8,700)	(0)
	44,000	0	86,500	78,700
Property business income	9,400	6,600	6,500	0
Chargeable gains				
(11,700 – 2,000)	5,100	0	0	9,700
Total profits	58,500	6,600	93,000	88,400
Less current period loss relief	(0)	(6,600)	(0)	(0)
Less carry back loss relief	(58,500)		(23,250)	(88,400)
	0	0	69,750	0
Less qualifying charitable donations	(0)	(0)	(1,200)	(0)
Taxable total profits	0	0	68,550	0

Loss memorandum

	£
Loss in y/e 31.12.14	73,800
Less used y/e 31.12.14	(6,600)
Less used p/e 31.12.13	(58,500)
Less used y/e 31.12.15	(8,700)
Loss remaining unrelieved	0

	£
Loss in y/e 30.9.17	186,800
Less used p/e 30.9.16	(88,400)
Less: used y/e 31.12.15	
3 months to 31.12.15	
£93,000 × 3/12	(23,250)
Loss remaining unrelieved at 30.9.17	75,150

The loss of y/e 30.9.17 can be carried back against total profits of the previous 12 months ie against the 9-month period ending 30.9.16 and 3 months of the y/e 31.12.15.

226 Acebook Ltd

Text references. Capital losses are included in Chapter 21. Chargeable gains for companies are covered in Chapter 20.

Top tips. Use the three column proforma for the company's share pool and take care to add the indexation allowance to the cost in the pool to obtain the indexed cost.

Easy marks. Part (a) was a straightforward statement of the use of capital losses for companies.

		Marks
(a)	Set off against gains in same accounting period	1½
	Carry forward against first available gains	1½
		3
(b)	*Oogle plc shares*	
	Purchase June 2003	½
	Bonus issue October 2006	1
	Indexation to February 2008	1
	Rights issue February 2008	1½
	Indexation to March 2018	1
	Disposal proceeds	1
	Indexed cost	1
		7
		10

(a) When a limited company has a capital loss, it is first set off against any chargeable gains arising in the same accounting period.

Any remaining capital loss is then carried forward and set off against the first available chargeable gains of future accounting periods.

(b) **Acebook Ltd – Chargeable gain on disposal on 10 March 2018**

	No. of shares	Cost £	Indexed cost £
Purchase June 2003	8,000	25,200	25,200
Bonus issue October 2006 2:1	16,000		
	24,000		
Indexed rise to February 2008 0.166 × £25,200			4,183
Rights issue February 2008 1:5 @ £4.30	4,800	20,640	20,640
	28,800	45,840	50,023
Indexed rise to March 2018 0.307 × £50,023			15,357
			65,380
Disposal	(28,800)	(45,840)	(65,380)

The gain is computed as follows:

	£
Proceeds 28,800 × £3.20	92,160
Less indexed cost	(65,380)
Indexed gain	26,780

227 Black Ltd and Gastron Ltd

Marking scheme

				Marks
(a)	*Maximum potential claim by Black Ltd*			
	After losses brought forward used	1		
	Qualifying charitable donations	½		
	Maximum claim	½		
	Maximum surrender by White Ltd			
	Trading loss – current period only/maximum claim	1		
	Qualifying charitable donations	1		
	Capital losses	½		
	Maximum group relief claim that can be made	½		
				5
(b)	(i)	75% shareholding	1	
		50% effective interest	1	
				2
	(ii)	Set-off of capital loss		1
	(iii)	No gain no loss transfers	1	
		Rollover relief	1	
				2
				10

(a) **Black Ltd – Group relief claim for year ended 31 March 2018**

Maximum potential claim by Black Ltd

Black Ltd uses its own losses brought forward in working out the taxable total profits against which it may claim group relief.

Furthermore, group relief is against taxable total profits after all other reliefs for the current period (for example qualifying charitable donations).

The maximum potential claim by Black Ltd is therefore £(396,800 – 57,900 + 21,100 – 4,400) = £355,600.

Maximum potential surrender by White Ltd

White Ltd may surrender its current period trading losses of £351,300. Only current period losses are available for group relief so White Ltd's loss of £21,800 brought forward cannot be group relieved.

White Ltd may also surrender excess qualifying charitable donations (ie to the extent that they exceed total profits before taking account of any losses). Since the qualifying charitable donations of £5,600 do not exceed the total profits of £26,700, there is no excess.

It is not possible to surrender capital losses as part of a group relief claim.

The maximum potential surrender by White Ltd is therefore £351,300.

Maximum group relief claim

The maximum group relief claim is the lower of the claim that can be made by Black Ltd and the surrender that can be made by White Ltd ie £351,300.

(b) (i) Companies form a chargeable gains group if at each level in the group structure there is a 75% shareholding.

However, the parent company must also have an effective interest of over 50% in each group company.

(ii) The election will enable the capital loss of £66,000 to be set against the capital gain of £74,800 and so save tax in the current year. Otherwise the loss would have to be carried forward by Culinary Ltd and set against future gains.

Tutorial note

Alternatively, an election could have been made to transfer the loss of Culinary Ltd to Gastron Ltd to set against the gain. The overall corporation tax effect for the chargeable gains group would have been the same.

(iii) Companies in a chargeable gains group make intra-group transfers of chargeable assets without a chargeable gain or an allowable loss arising.

If a member of a chargeable gains group disposes of an asset eligible for chargeable gains rollover relief it may treat all of the group companies as a single unit for the purpose of claiming such relief.

228 Jogger Ltd (A)

Text references. Capital allowances are dealt with in Chapter 8. Corporation tax computation is dealt with in Chapter 19.

Top tips. Make sure you use the capital allowances proforma in part (a).

Easy marks. There were easy marks in part (b) for the corporation tax computation.

Marking scheme

			Marks
(a)	Operating loss	½	
	Depreciation	½	
	P&M	– AIA set against machinery in priority to SLA	1½	
		– FYA	1	
		– Main pool	1½	
		– Special rate pool	1½	
		– Short life asset	1½	
				8
(b)	Bank interest	½	
	Loan interest	1	
	Property business profit	2	
	Chargeable gain	2	
	Loss relief	1	
	Corporation tax	½	
			7
			15

(a) **Jogger Ltd – Trading loss y/e 31 March 2018**

	£
Operating profit	156,482
Add depreciation	58,840
	215,322
Less capital allowances (W)	(271,182)
Adjusted trading loss	(55,860)

Working: Plant and machinery

	AIA £	FYA £	Main pool £	Special rate pool £	SLA £	Allowances £
TWDV b/f			26,600	18,800		
Addition qualifying for AIA						
30.9.17 Machinery	500,000					
AIA	(200,000)		300,000			200,000
Addition qualifying for AIA but not claimed						
15.12.17 Computer					12,500	
Addition qualifying for FYA						
15.8.17 Car		9,000				
FYA		(9,000)				9,000
Addition not qualifying for AIA nor FYA						
31.7.17 Car			11,800			
Disposal						
20.7.17 Car				(11,700)		
				7,100		
14.3.18 Lorry		–	(8,600)			
			329,800			
WDA @ 18%			(59,364)		(2,250)	61,614
WDA @ 8%				(568)		568
TWDV c/f			270,436	6,532	10,250	
Allowances						271,182

(b) **Jogger Ltd – Corporation tax liability y/e 31 March 2018**

	£
Interest income (W1)	33,060
Property income (W2)	126,000
Chargeable gain (W3)	84,252
Total profits	243,312
Less loss relief	(55,860)
Taxable total profits	187,452
£187,452 × 19%	35,616

Workings

1 *Interest income*

		£
Bank interest receivable		8,460
Loan interest	– received 31.12.17	16,400
	– accrued 31.3.18	8,200
		33,060

2   *Property income*

	£
Premium received	100,000
Less 2% × (10 – 1) × £100,000	(18,000)
Taxable as property income	82,000
Add rental income accrued	44,000
	126,000

3   *Chargeable gain*

	£
Disposal proceeds	150,000
Less cost	(47,660)
	102,340
Less indexation allowance £47,660 × $\dfrac{274.8 - 199.2}{199.2}$	(18,088)
Gain	84,252

229 Mice Ltd

> **Text references.** Property business income is dealt with in Chapters 6 and 19. Losses for companies are in Chapter 21.
>
> **Top tips.** You should use the loss relief proforma in part (b).
>
> **Easy marks.** The calculation of property business profit in part (a) was straightforward and should have been easy marks.

Marking scheme

			Marks	
(a)	Lease premium received		1½	
	Rent receivable	– Property 1	1	
		– Property 2	½	
		– Property 3	½	
	Business rates		½	
	Repairs		1	
	Advertising		½	
	Insurance		1½	
	Loan interest		1	
				8
(b)	**Year ended 31 March 2018**			
	Property business profit		½	
	Loan interest		1½	
	Chargeable gain		1½	
	Loss relief		1	
	Other periods			
	Trading profit		½	
	Property business profit		½	
	Loss relief		1	
	Qualifying charitable donations		½	
				7
				15

(a) **Mice Ltd – Property business profit y/e 31 March 2018**

	£	£
Premium received for lease	18,000	
Less £18,000 × 2% × (8 – 1)	(2,520)	
Amount taxable as property business income		15,480
Property 1 rent accrued £3,200 × 4		12,800
Property 2 rent accrued		6,000
Property 3 rent accrued		0
Gross income accrued		34,280
Less: expenses accrued		
business rates	2,200	
repairs (N1)	1,060	
advertising	680	
insurance £(460 + 310 + (480 × 3/12))	890	
loan interest (N2)	0	
		(4,830)
Property business profit		29,450

Notes

1 The enlargement of the car park is capital expenditure which cannot be deducted when calculating the property business profit.

2 Interest paid in respect of a loan to purchase property is set off under the loan relationship rules.

(b) **Mice Ltd – Taxable total profits y/e 31 March 2018**

	£	£
Property business profit		29,450
Loan interest		
Received 31 December 2017	6,400	
Accrued 31 March 2018	3,200	
Paid on property 3 loan –		
1 January 2018 to 31 March 2018	(1,800)	
		7,800
Chargeable gain (W)		2,750
Total profits		40,000
Less current period loss relief		(40,000)
Taxable total profits		0

Working

	£
Net disposal proceeds 95% × £36,229	34,418
Less cost	(28,000)
	6,418
Less indexation allowance £28,000 × $\dfrac{274.8 - 243.0}{243.0}$ (= 0.131)	(3,668)
Gain	2,750

Mice Ltd – Taxable total profits for periods ending 31 March 2015, 2016 and 2017

	P/e 31.3.15	Y/e 31.3.16	Y/e 31.3.17
	£	£	£
Trading profit	83,200	24,700	51,200
Property business profit	2,800	7,100	12,200
Total profits	86,000	31,800	63,400
Less carry back loss relief	(0)	(0)	(63,400)
	86,000	31,800	0
Less qualifying charitable donation	(1,000)	(1,500)	(0)
Taxable total profits	85,000	30,300	0

There is no loss relief in the period to 31 March 2015 or the year ended 31 March 2016 because loss relief for a continuing business is restricted to 12 months before the loss making period.

230 Molten-Metal plc

Text references. Computing taxable total profits and the corporation tax liability is covered in Chapter 19. Capital allowances are covered in Chapter 8.

Top tips. This question has a lot of information for you to deal with. Study the layout of the suggested solution; in particular, note how detailed calculations are contained in Workings. Try to adopt this layout in your answers.

Easy marks. Working out the corporation tax liability was an easy half mark.

Marking scheme

	Marks
Trading profit	½
Loan stock interest payable	1½
P&M – Office building	½
– Ventilation system and lift	1
– AIA	1
– Machinery	½
– Building alterations	½
– Wall	½
– Partition walls	1
– AIA	1
– Main pool	2
– Special rate pool	1½
– Short life asset	1
Interest income	2
Corporation tax	½
	15

Molten-Metal plc – Corporation tax computation for the year ended 31 March 2018

	£	£
Trading profit		2,170,144
Less: loan stock interest payable £(22,500 + 3,700 – 4,200)	22,000	
capital allowances P&M (W1)	240,638	
		(262,638)
		1,907,506
Interest income (W2)		8,700
Taxable total profits		1,916,206
Corporation tax £1,916,206 @ 19%		364,079

Tutorial note

Interest paid in respect of a loan used for trading purposes is deductible in calculating the trading profit.

Workings

1   *Capital allowances*

	AIA	Main pool	Special rate pool	Short life asset	Allowances
	£	£	£	£	£
TWDVs c/f		87,800			
AIA additions					
Office building	0				
Ventilation system	31,000				
Lift	42,000				
	73,000				
AIA – 100%	(73,000)				73,000
Transfer balance to special rate pool	0		0		
Machinery	186,600				
Building alterations	7,700				
Wall	0				
Partition walls	22,900				
	217,200				
AIA	(127,000)				127,000
Transfer balance to main pool	90,200	90,200			
Other additions					
Computer				2,500	
Motor car			24,000		
Motor cars					
£17,300 × 2		34,600			
		212,600			
WDA @ 18%		(38,268)		(450)	38,718
WDA @ 8%			(1,920)		1,920
TWDVs c/f		174,332	22,080	2,050	
Allowances					240,638

Tutorial notes

1   The ventilation system and lift are both integral to a building and so are special rate pool expenditure. It is beneficial to claim the annual investment allowance of £200,000 initially against this expenditure, as it would otherwise only qualify for writing down allowance at the rate of 8%.

2   The building alterations were necessary for the installation of the machinery, and therefore qualify for capital allowances. Walls are specifically excluded, with the exception of partition walls which are movable and intended to be so moved.

3   The computer will be depooled by making the election and treated as a short life asset. The annual investment allowance should not be claimed against this asset as this will effectively disapply the depooling election.

4   The motor car acquired in November 2017 has CO_2 emissions over 130 grams per kilometre, and therefore qualifies for writing down allowances at the rate of 8% as part of the special rate pool.

5   The motor cars acquired in March 2018 have CO_2 emissions between 76 and 130 grams per kilometre, and therefore qualify for writing down allowances at the rate of 18% as part of the main pool. The private use of a motor car is irrelevant, since such usage will be assessed on the employee as a benefit.

2   *Interest income*

	£
Loan interest receivable £(9,800 + 3,100)	12,900
Bank interest receivable	2,600
	15,500
Less interest payable	(6,800)
Net interest income	8,700

231 Starfish Ltd (A)

Text references. Computing taxable total profits is covered in Chapter 19. Corporation tax losses are dealt with in Chapter 21.

Top tips. Make sure that you set out the computation of taxable total profits in part (b) using the standard layout, leaving space for losses carried forward against trading profits and losses carried back against total profits.

Easy marks. The adjustment of profit computation in part (a) was reasonably straightforward.

Marking scheme

			Marks	
(a)	Depreciation		½	
	Donations		1	
	Impairment loss		½	
	Legal fees		1	
	Entertaining customers		½	
	Counselling services		½	
	Plant and machinery	– WDV brought forward	1	
		– Addition	1½	
		– Main pool proceeds	2	
		– Motor car proceeds	1	
		– Balancing adjustments	½	
				10
(b)	Trading profit		½	
	Relief for 2014 loss	– Period ended 31 March 2014	½	
		– Carry forward	½	
	Bank interest		½	
	Relief for 2018 loss	– Year ended 31 March 2015	1	
		– Other periods	1	
	Qualifying charitable donations		1	
				5
				15

(a) **Starfish Ltd – Trading loss for the period ended 31 March 2018**

		£	£
Loss before taxation			(190,000)
Add:	depreciation	25,030	
	donation to political party	900	
	donation paid (qualifying charitable donation)	750	
	impairment loss	0	
	legal fees – misleading advertisement	2,020	
	– issue of loan notes	0	
	Entertaining customers	3,600	
	Counselling services	0	
			32,300
			(157,700)
Less capital allowances (W1)			(2,300)
Adjusted trading loss			(160,000)

Workings

1   *Capital allowances*

	Main pool £	Special rate pool £	Allowances £
TWDVs b/f	23,600	13,200	
Addition – computer (W2)	2,600		
	26,200		
Disposals (W3)	(27,500)	(9,600)	
Balancing charge	(1,300)		(1,300)
Balancing allowance		3,600	3,600
Total allowances			2,300

2   *Computer*

The input VAT on the computer is recoverable and so only the cost net of VAT is eligible expenditure which is £3,120 × 100/120 = £2,600.

3   *Disposal proceeds*

The output VAT charged on the disposals is not part of the proceeds for capital allowance purposes. The main pool proceeds are therefore £([31,200 + 1,800] × 100/120) = £27,500. There is no VAT charged on the sale of the car, as none was recovered on purchase (owing to private usage).

Tutorial notes

1   The cost of obtaining loan finance, even if abortive, is allowable as a trading loan relationship debit.

2   The costs of counselling services for redundant employees are deductible if they qualify for exemption from the employment income charge on employees.

3   The annual investment allowance and writing down allowances are not given for the period in which a trade ceases. Therefore the addition is simply added into the main pool.

(b) **Starfish Ltd – Taxable total profits**

	P/e 31.3.14 £	Y/e 31.3.15 £	Y/e 31.3.16 £	Y/e 31.3.17 £	P/e 31.12.17 £
Trading profit	0	64,200	53,900	14,700	49,900
Less c/f loss relief (N1)	0	(12,600)	0	0	0
	0	51,600	53,900	14,700	49,900
Bank interest	600	1,400	1,700	0	0
	600	53,000	55,600	14,700	49,900
Less c/b loss relief (N2)	(0)	(13,250)	(55,600)	(14,700)	(49,900)
	600	39,750	0	0	0
Less: qualifying charitable donations (N3)	(600)	(1,000)	(0)	(0)	(0)
Taxable total profits	0	38,750	0	0	0

Tutorial notes

1   Starfish Ltd would not have made a loss relief claim against total profits for the period ended 31 March 2014 as this would have wasted the £600 of relieved qualifying charitable donations for that period.

2   The trading loss for the period ended 31 March 2018 can be relieved against total profits for the three years immediately preceding the start of the loss making period since it is a terminal loss. The three-year year period is between 1 January 2015 and 31 December 2017. Relief is as follows:

	£
Loss of 3 month p/e 31.3.18	160,000
Less used in p/e 31.12.17	(49,900)
	110,100
Less used in y/e 31.3.17	(14,700)
	95,400
Less used in y/e 31.3.16	(55,600)
	39,800
Less used in y/e 31.3.15	
(restricted to 3/12 × £53,000)	(13,250)
Balance unrelieved	26,550

3   The qualifying charitable donations in the period ending 31 March 2018, and earlier years, are also unrelieved.

232 Greenzone Ltd (A)

Text references. Computing taxable total profits is covered in Chapter 19. The basics of adjustment of trading profit and capital allowances are dealt with in Chapters 7 and 8 respectively. Corporation tax administration, including the definition of related 51% group companies, will be found in Chapter 23. Look in Chapter 22 for details of group relief.

Top tips. Watch out for the special allowance on low emission motor cars.

Easy marks. There were plenty of easy marks for standard items in the adjustment of profit.

Marking scheme

			Marks	
(a)	Depreciation	½		
	Repainting	½		
	Reception area	½		
	Entertaining UK customers	½		
	Entertaining overseas customers	½		
	Political donations	½		
	Non-qualifying charitable donation	½		
	Pens	½		
	Clocks	½		
	Capital allowances deducted	½		
	Capital allowances			
	TWDVs b/f	1		
	Addition – motor car [2]	½		
	Disposal – motor car [3]	1		
	Disposal – motor car [4]	½		
	Balancing charge on special rate pool	½		
	WDA on main pool	½		
	Addition – motor car [1]	½		
	FYA	½		
			10	
(b)	(i)	Related 51% group company definition	½	
		Are Ltd and Can Ltd	½	
		Doer Co	½	
		Profit threshold	½	
		Group dividends	1	
			3	
	(ii)	Maximum group relief	2	
			15	

(a) **Greenzone Ltd – Trading profit for the year ended 31 March 2018**

		£
Operating profit		239,700
Add:	depreciation	28,859
	repainting office building	0
	new reception area	19,800
	entertaining UK customers	3,600
	entertaining overseas customers	1,840
	political donations	740
	non-qualifying charitable donation	0
	gifts to customers: pens	660
	clocks	910
		296,109
Less capital allowances (W)		(18,409)
Trading profit		277,700

Tutorial notes

1 The extension of the office building is not deductible as it is capital in nature. The building has been improved rather than repaired.

2 Gifts to customers are only an allowable expense if they cost less than £50 per recipient per year, are not of food, drink, tobacco or vouchers exchangeable for goods, and carry a conspicuous advertisement for the company.

Working: Capital allowances

	FYA £	Main pool £	Special rate pool £	Allowances £
TWDV brought forward		48,150	9,200	
Addition not qualifying for AIA/FYA				
Motor car [2]		20,400		
		68,550		
Disposals				
Motor car [3]		(8,500)		
Motor car [4]			(12,400)	
Balancing charge			3,200	(3,200)
		60,050		
WDA @ 18%		(10,809)		10,809
Addition qualifying for FYA				
Motor car [1]	10,800			
FYA @ 100%	(10,800)			10,800
WDV carried forward		49,241		
Allowances				18,409

Tutorial notes

1 Motor car [1] has CO_2 emissions up to 75 grams per kilometre and is a new car so therefore qualifies for the 100% first year allowance.

2 Motor car [2] has CO_2 emissions between 76 and 130 grams per kilometre and therefore is added to the main pool.

3 The disposal value for motor car [3] is restricted to the original cost figure of £8,500.

(b) **(i)** Greenzone Ltd has related 51% group companies if it directly or indirectly owns more than 50% of the ordinary shares of those companies.

Are Ltd and Can Ltd are therefore related 51% group companies.

For related 51% group companies purposes, it does not matter where a company is resident, so Doer Co is also a related 51% group company despite being resident overseas.

Greenzone Ltd has three related 51% group companies at the end of the previous accounting period, so that the profit threshold for determining whether the company must pay corporation tax by instalments is reduced to £(1,500,000/4) = £375,000.

The dividends from Are Ltd, Can Ltd and Doer Co are group dividends and are therefore not included in profits for this purpose.

(ii) The maximum amount of group relief that can be claimed is Can Ltd's trading loss of £64,700.

Tutorial note

Greenzone Ltd cannot claim group relief from Are Ltd as this company is not a 75% subsidiary.

The group relief claim is limited to the lower of Can Ltd's loss and Greenzone Ltd's taxable total profits (equal to trading profits of £277,700) ie Can Ltd's loss of £64,700.

233 Softapp Ltd

Text references. The computation of taxable total profits and the corporation tax liability is covered in Chapter 19.

Top tips. Watch out for the accruals basis in the computation of interest and property business income.

Easy marks. There were some easy marks for the calculation of capital allowances and property business income.

		Marks
Operating profit		½
Depreciation		½
Amortisation		½
Deduction for lease premium:	premium received	½
	amount not assessed on landlord	1
	deduction for trader	1½
Loan stock interest		1
Capital allowances:	building costs	½
	heating system	½
	ventilation system	½
	AIA on special rate pool expenditure	1
	computer equipment	½
	furniture and furnishings	½
	fridge and cooker	½
	AIA on main rate pool expenditure	½
	WDA	½
Chargeable gain:	proceeds	½
	cost	½
	indexation allowance	1
Property business income		1
Interest income		1
Corporation tax		½
		15

Softapp Ltd – Corporation tax computation for the year ended 31 March 2018

		£
Operating profit		711,475
Add:	depreciation	10,170
	amortisation	2,500
		724,145
Less:	deduction for lease premium (W1)	(2,050)
	loan stock interest payable (trading loan relationship)	(67,200)
	capital allowances (W2)	(202,520)
Trading profit		452,375
Property business income (W3)		27,500
Chargeable gain (W4)		61,525
Interest income (non-trading loan relationships) £(5,600 + 2,500)		8,100
Taxable total profits		549,500

Corporation tax liability	
£549,500 × 19%	104,405

Workings

1   *Deduction for lease premium*

The amount assessed on the landlord is £82,000, calculated as follows:

	£
Premium	100,000
Less £100,000 × 2% × (10 – 1)	(18,000)
Assessable as property business income on landlord	82,000

This is deductible by a business tenant over the life of the lease so the deduction for Softapp Ltd for the year ended 31 March 2018 is £(82,000/10 × 3/12) = £2,050.

2   *Capital allowances*

	AIA £	Main pool £	Special rate pool £	Allowances £
Additions qualifying for AIA				
Building costs	0			
Heating system	3,600			
Ventilation system	4,600			
	8,200			
AIA (part)	(8,200)			8,200
Transfer to SR pool	0		0	
Computer equipment	175,000			
Furniture and furnishings	29,400			
Fridge and cooker	1,400			
	205,800			
AIA (balance)	(191,800)			191,800
Transfer to main pool	14,000	14,000		
WDA @ 18%		(2,520)		2,520
TWDVs c/f		11,480	0	
Allowances				202,520

Tutorial notes

1   The expenditure which is integral to the building is special rate pool expenditure.

2   It is beneficial to claim the annual investment allowance of £200,000 against this expenditure in priority to main pool expenditure, as it would otherwise only qualify for writing down allowance at the rate of 8% in the special rate pool.

3   *Property business income*

	£
Rental income receivable	30,000
Less irrecoverable rent £5,000 × 1/2	(2,500)
Property business income	27,500

4   *Chargeable gain*

	£
Proceeds	94,661
Less cost	(30,000)
Unindexed gain	64,661
Less indexation allowance	
$\dfrac{(275.8 - 249.7)}{249.7} \times £30,000$	(3,136)
Indexed gain	61,525

234 Long Ltd group (A)

Text references. The computation of taxable total profits and the corporation tax liability are covered in Chapter 19. Groups of companies are covered in Chapter 22.

Top tips. A capital loss transferred between group companies can only be set against a capital gain, whereas a trading loss transferred between group companies is deducted in computing taxable total profits.

Easy marks. There were some easy marks for computing the corporation tax.

Marking scheme

	Marks
(a) *Long Ltd*	
Depreciation	½
Capital allowances	
TWDV b/f	½
Lorry	½
AIA	½
Motor car	½
WDA	½
Group relief	1½
Wind Ltd	
Amortisation	½
Capital allowances	1
Chargeable gain after loss relief	1½
Corporation tax	½
Road Ltd	
Trading loss	½
Donations	½
Capital allowances	½
Corporation tax computation	
Interest income	½
Qualifying charitable donations	½
Corporation tax	½
	11

(a) **Long Ltd – Corporation tax computation for the year ended 31 March 2018**

	£
Operating profit	817,820
Add depreciation	10,170
	827,990
Less capital allowances (W)	(47,690)
Trading profit	780,300
Less group relief from Road Ltd	(34,900)
Taxable total profits	745,400
Corporation tax	
£745,400 × 19%	141,626

Tutorial note

Group relief is not restricted as the amount claimed is clearly less than 3/12ths of Long Ltd's taxable total profits.

Working: Capital allowances

	AIA	Main pool	Allowances
	£	£	£
TWDV b/f		44,800	
Addition qualifying for AIA			
Lorry	36,800		
AIA	(36,800)		36,800
Transfer to pool	0	0	
Addition not qualifying for AIA			
Motor car		15,700	
		60,500	
WDA @ 18%		(10,890)	10,890
TWDV c/f		49,610	
Allowances			47,690

Wind Ltd – Corporation tax computation for the year ended 31 March 2018

	£
Operating profit	59,490
Add depreciation	5,000
	64,490
Less capital allowances: WDA £900 × 100%	(900)
Trading profit	63,590
Chargeable gain £(29,800 – 21,300)	8,500
Taxable total profits	72,090
Corporation tax	
£72,090 × 19%	13,697

Tutorial notes

1   The balance on the main pool is less than £1,000, so a writing down allowance equal to the unrelieved expenditure can be claimed.

2   A joint election can be made to transfer Long Ltd's capital loss since this will give loss relief earlier than if the loss is carried forward against future gains made by Long Ltd.

Road Ltd – Trading loss for the three-month period ended 31 March 2018

	£
Operating loss	(26,100)
Add donations	2,800
	(23,300)
Less capital allowances: FYA £11,600 × 100%	(11,600)
Trading loss (surrendered as group relief)	(34,900)

Tutorial notes

1   Political donations are not allowable. The qualifying charitable donations are not allowable in the calculation of the trading loss but will be deducted from total profits (see below).

2   The motor car purchased on 3 October 2017 is pre-trading expenditure and is treated as incurred on 1 January 2018. The motor car has CO_2 emissions up to 75 grams per kilometre and therefore qualifies for the 100% first year allowance.

3   Road Ltd's loss can be surrendered under group relief to either Long Ltd or Wind Ltd but if surrendered to Wind Ltd group relief would be restricted as 3/12ths of Wind Ltd's taxable total profits is less than Road Ltd's loss.

Road Ltd – Corporation tax computation for the three-month period ended 31 March 2018

	£
Interest income/Total profits	4,300
Less qualifying charitable donations	(2,400)
Taxable total profits	1,900
Corporation tax	
£1,900 × 19%	361

Tutorial notes

1   The qualifying charitable donations cannot be surrendered as group relief as they are fully relieved against Road Ltd's interest income: only **excess** qualifying charitable donations can be group relieved.

2   A current year claim in Road Ltd would have wasted the qualifying charitable donations, therefore group relief is the most beneficial use of Road Ltd's loss.

(b)   A large company is one whose profits exceed the profit threshold. Profits are the taxable total profits of the company plus the dividends received from other companies, other than those from 51% subsidiaries (group dividends). The threshold must also be divided by the number of related 51% group companies.

For Long Ltd for the year ended 31 March 2018, it is necessary to look at the situation at 31 March 2017 in respect of related 51% group companies. Wind Ltd was a related 51% group company at that date but Road Ltd was not since it only started trading on 1 January 2018.

The profit threshold is therefore £1,500,000/2 = £750,000.

Long Ltd's profits for the year ended 31 March 2018 are:

	£
Taxable total profits	745,400
Add dividends from non-group companies	32,000
Profits	777,400

Long Ltd is therefore a large company in the year ended 31 March 2018. Long Ltd would have to pay instalments for the year ended 31 March 2018 if it had also been large in the year ended 31 March 2017.

235 Retro Ltd

Text references. The computation of taxable total profits is covered in Chapter 19. Losses are dealt with in Chapter 21.

Top tips. For part (a) you might want to start this question by computing the capital allowances. You can then just slot this into the adjustment of profit proforma at the appropriate place.

Easy marks. There were some easy marks for standard adjustments to profit in part (a).

Examining team's comments. Most candidates had little difficulty with part (a). One poor practice was the use of notes and explanations. It was a simple matter, as per the model answer, to just list all the items of expenditure (and show whether or not an adjustment was required), so the use of notes (such as for the gifts and donations) was completely unnecessary and against the guidance given in the note to the requirement. Since the requirement was for a calculation, explanations are not required, and result in wasted time. As regards the capital allowances, many candidates did not appreciate that the delivery van qualified for the 100% annual investment allowance – instead including it in the special rate pool.

There were many perfect answers to part (b), although disappointingly a few candidates tried to time-apportion profits using the opening year rules.

Part (c) caused few problems, although many candidates did not mention that the carry forward would be against the first available profits.

Marking scheme

		Marks
(a)	*Adjustment to profit*	
	Depreciation	½
	Gifts to employees	½
	Gifts to customers	½
	Political donations	½
	Qualifying charitable donations	½
	Impairment loss	½
	Lease of motor car	1
	Health and safety fine	½
	Legal fees	½
	Interest payable	½
	Capital allowances	
	WDV b/f	½
	Delivery van	½
	AIA	½
	Motor car [1]	½
	WDA	½
	Motor car [2]	½
	FYA	½
		9
(b)	Trading profit	½
	Bank interest	½
	Carry back loss relief p/e 31 March 2017	1
	Carry back loss relief in y/e 31 August 2016	1
	Qualifying charitable donations	1
		4
(c)	Unrelieved trading loss amount	1
	Carry forward loss relief	1
		2
		15

(a) **Trading loss for the year ended 31 March 2018**

	£
Loss before taxation	(120,000)
Depreciation	27,240
Gifts to employees	0
Gifts to customers	0
Political donations	420
Qualifying charitable donations	680
Impairment loss	0
Lease of motor car (4,400 × 15%)	660
Health and safety fine	5,100
Legal fees – internet domain name	0
Interest payable	0
Capital allowances (working)	(50,420)
Trading loss	(136,320)

Tutorial notes

1 Gifts to customers are an allowable deduction if they cost less than £50 per recipient per year, are not of food, drink, tobacco or vouchers for exchangeable goods and carry a conspicuous advertisement for the company making the gift. Gifts to employees are an allowable deduction because the gifts will potentially be assessed on the employees as benefits.

2 Interest on a loan used for trading purposes is deductible on an accruals basis.

Working: Capital allowances

	£	Main pool £	Allowances £
WDV brought forward		39,300	
Additions qualifying for AIA			
Delivery van	28,300		
AIA – 100%	(28,300)		28,300
		0	
Addition – Motor car [1]		14,700	
		54,000	
WDA – 18%		(9,720)	9,720
Addition qualifying for FYA			
Motor car [2]	12,400		
FYA – 100%	(12,400)		12,400
		0	
WDV carried forward		44,280	
Total allowances			50,420

Tutorial notes

1 Motor car [1] has CO_2 emissions between 76 and 130 grams per kilometre, and therefore qualifies for writing down allowances at the rate of 18%.

2 Motor car [2] has CO_2 emissions up to 75 grams per kilometre and is new, and therefore qualifies for the 100% first year allowance.

(b)

	Year ended 31 August 2016 £	Period ended 31 March 2017 £
Trading profit	56,600	47,900
Bank interest	1,300	0
	57,900	47,900
Loss against total profits (working)	(24,125)	(47,900)
	33,775	0
Qualifying charitable donations	(540)	
Taxable total profits	33,235	0

Working: Trading loss

For the year ended 31 August 2016, loss relief is restricted to £24,125 (57,900 × 5/12).

(c)   The amount of unrelieved trading loss at 31 March 2018 is £64,295 (136,320 – 47,900 – 24,125).

The unrelieved trading loss can be carried forward and will be relieved against the first available trading profits of the same trade.

236 Lucky Ltd

Text references. The computation of taxable total profits and the computation of the corporation tax liability are covered in Chapter 19. The adjustment to trading profits is dealt with in Chapter 7 and capital allowances in Chapter 8. National insurance contributions are covered in Chapter 12.

Top tips. Administrative aspects of corporation tax are very likely to be examined so don't omit them from your revision.

Easy marks. There were some easy marks for the adjustment to trading profit and computation of corporation tax in part (b).

Examining team's comments. In part (a), most candidates appreciated that an accounting period starts when a company commences to trade, but many could not provide any other circumstances. For example, an accounting period will also start when a company otherwise becomes liable to corporation tax.

In part (b), the aspect of this question which appeared to cause candidates the most difficulties was the lease premium deduction and the difficulties were largely due to a failure to read the question carefully. Candidates were given the amount of the premium assessed on the landlord as income. However, a lot of candidates misread this figure as being the total premium paid.

Part (c) of the question was reasonably well answered.

(**BPP note.** Part (d) has been added to this question and there are no relevant examining team's comments.)

Marking scheme

			Marks
(a)	After end of previous period	1	
	Other situations	1	
			2
(b)	Trading profit		
	Advertising	½	
	Depreciation	½	
	Amortisation	½	
	Lease premium deduction	1½	
	Capital allowances		
	Integral feature addition	½	
	Annual investment allowance	½	
	Computer addition	½	
	Office equipment addition	½	
	Annual investment allowance	1	
	WDA	1	
	Car addition	½	
	FYA	½	
	Interest income	½	
	Corporation tax	½	
			9

		Marks
(c)	Date for retention	1
	Penalty	1
		2
(d)	Capital allowances	1
	National insurance contributions	1
		2
		15

(a) An accounting period will normally start immediately after the end of the preceding accounting period.

An accounting period will also start when a company commences to trade, or otherwise becomes liable to corporation tax.

(b) **Lucky Ltd – Corporation tax computation for the four-month period ended 31 March 2018**

	£
Operating profit	432,600
Advertising	0
Depreciation	14,700
Amortisation	9,000
Deduction for lease premium £46,800/12 × 4/12	(1,300)
Capital allowances (W1)	(80,291)
Trading profit	374,709
Interest income	700
Taxable total profits	375,409
Corporation tax £375,409 @ 19%	71,328

Tutorial note

The advertising expenditure incurred during September 2017 is pre-trading, and is treated as incurred on 1 December 2017. It is therefore deductible and no adjustment is required.

Workings

1 *Capital allowances*

	£	Main pool £	Special rate pool £	Allowances £
Additions qualifying for AIA				
Integral features	41,200			
AIA	(41,200)			41,200
Transfer balance to special rate pool			0	
Computer	6,300			
Office equipment	32,900			
	39,200			
AIA (W2)	(25,467)			25,467
Transfer balance to main pool		13,733		
WDA 18% × 4/12		(824)		824
Addition qualifying for FYA				
Motor car	12,800			
FYA 100%	(12,800)			12,800
Transfer balance to main pool		0		
WDV carried forward		12,909	0	
Total allowances				80,291

2 *Annual investment allowances*

The annual investment allowance is reduced to £66,667 (£200,000 × 4/12) because Lucky Ltd's accounting period is four months long.

Tutorial notes

1 The expenditure which is integral to the building is included in the special rate pool.

2 It is beneficial to claim the annual investment allowance of £66,667 initially against this integral features expenditure, as it would otherwise only qualify for writing down allowance at the rate of 8%.

3 The computer purchased on 19 August 2017 is pre-trading and is treated as incurred on 1 December 2017.

4 The motor car has CO_2 emissions up to 75 grams per kilometre and therefore qualifies for the 100% first year allowance.

(c) Lucky Ltd must retain the records used in preparing its self-assessment corporation tax return until six years after the end of the accounting period, which is 31 March 2024.

A failure to retain records could result in a penalty of up to £3,000 per accounting period. However, the maximum penalty will only be charged in serious cases.

(d) The cost of the car will be included in Lucky Ltd's capital allowance computation and written down at the appropriate rate each year depending on the car's CO_2 emissions.

Lucky Ltd will also have to pay Class 1A national insurance contributions on the company car. Class 1A is deductible from taxable trading profits.

237 Jump Ltd

Text references. The computation of taxable total profits and the corporation tax liability are covered in Chapter 19. Groups of companies are covered in Chapter 22.

Top tips. In part (a), remember to include a zero when an item needs no adjustment; otherwise, you will not be credited for this knowledge.

Easy marks. Most of the adjustments to profit appear regularly in corporation tax questions.

Marking scheme

		Marks
(a)	*Trading loss*	
	Depreciation	½
	Employee training courses	½
	Employee pension contributions	½
	Staff party	½
	Car lease	1
	Accountancy	½
	Legal fees – share capital	½
	Legal fees – renewal of short lease	½
	Entertaining UK customers	½
	Entertaining overseas customers	½
	Political donations	½
	Balancing charge adjustment	½

Capital allowances

Tax written down values b/f	½
Motor car 1	1
Motor car 2	½
Balancing charge	½
Writing down allowance	1
	10

(b)	(i)	Choice of relief	1
	(ii)	Maximum relief claim – 7 m/e 31.12.17	½
		Maximum relief claim – y/e 31.5.17	1½
			2
	(iii)	Maximum surrender	1½
		Skip Ltd	½
			2
			15

(a) **Jump Ltd – Trading loss for the three-month period ended 31 March 2018**

	£
Operating loss	(144,700)
Depreciation	8,100
Employee training courses	0
Employee pension contributions	0
Staff party	0
Lease of motor car £1,200 × 15%	180
Accountancy	0
Legal fees – Issue of share capital	3,800
– Renewal of short lease	0
Entertaining UK customers	1,700
Entertaining overseas customers	790
Political donations	800
Balancing charge (W)	3,330
Trading loss	(126,000)

Working: Capital allowances

	Main pool £	Special rate pool £	Allowances £
WDV brought forward	12,100	5,700	
Proceeds – Motor car [1]		(9,300)	
– Motor car [2]	(6,100)		
Balancing charge		3,600	(3,600)
	6,000		
WDA – 18% × 3/12	(270)		270
WDV carried forward	5,730		
Net balancing charge			(3,330)

Tutorial note

The proceeds for motor car [1] are restricted to the original cost figure of £9,300.

(b) (i) The main factor which will influence Jump Ltd's choice of loss relief or group relief claims is the timing of the relief obtained, with an earlier claim generally being preferable: both in terms of tax rate (the rate of corporation tax for financial year 2016 was 20% whereas for financial year 2017 it is 19%) and cash flow (saving tax sooner is beneficial for cash flow).

Tutorial note

The other possible factor is the extent to which relief for qualifying charitable donations will be lost. However, this is not relevant given that Jump Ltd has not made any charitable donations.

(ii) The maximum loss relief claim for the seven-month period to 31 December 2017 is £42,400, being the total profits for this period.

The loss relief claim for the year ended 31 May 2017 is restricted to £33,250 ((78,600 + 1,200) × 5/12).

(iii) The maximum amount of trading loss which can be surrendered to Hop Ltd is £23,625, being the lower of £23,625 (63,000 × 3/8) and £126,000.

Skip Ltd is not a 75% subsidiary of Jump Ltd, so no group relief claim is possible.

238 Online Ltd (Mar/Jun 17)

Text references. Computing taxable total profits is covered in Chapter 19. Chargeable gains for companies is the subject of Chapter 20. The use of losses is dealt with in Chapter 21. Payment of tax by companies is covered in Chapter 22.

Top tips. Don't forget to answer both parts of the question. In part (b) you only needed to make a couple of points in order to gain the marks.

Easy marks. There should have been easy marks for well-known adjustments such as depreciation and amortisation. The capital allowances computation was quite straightforward.

Examining team's comments. Part (a) was well answered. Surprisingly, the one aspect which consistently caused difficulty was the qualifying charitable donation. Many candidates added this back prior to deducting it, with others grossing up the deduction. Also, it is important that candidates know basic tax rules. Even though all of the items included in the capital allowances special rate pool had been sold, there was no balancing allowance because Online Ltd's trade did not cease. This was another computation where candidates needed to think carefully about where to show workings. In this case, the deduction for the lease premium, capital allowances and the chargeable gain warranted separate workings. It was not a good idea for candidates to attempt a short-cut approach to any of these workings. As regards the chargeable gain, quite a few candidates included the gain from the disposal made three years previously. This shows just how much care needs to be taken over dates.

In part (b) many candidates appreciated that acquiring a 51% group company would mean that the profit threshold for establishing whether Online Ltd is a large company would be reduced to £750,000. It would therefore be likely that the company's corporation tax would in future be payable by quarterly instalments. Having established this point, there was no need to then go on and explain quarterly instalments in detail. If such detail was needed, then this would have been made clear in the requirement. For some candidates, this was another example of where they wanted to answer the question that would have preferred had been set – in this case, explaining why the reliefs available with a 75% group relationship were not available with just a 60% shareholding. Few candidates correctly stated that the dividends received from Offline Ltd, being group dividends, would not form part of Online Ltd's profits when establishing its large company status.

		Marks
(a)	Depreciation	½
	Amortisation	½
	Property loss brought forward	1
	Qualifying charitable donations	½
	Lease premium	
	Amount assessed on landlord	1
	Deduction	1
	Capital allowances	
	Tax written down values b/f	½
	Addition – car	1
	Disposal – car	1
	Disposal –pool	½
	WDA @ 18%	½
	WDA @ 8%	1
	Chargeable gain	
	Disposal proceeds	½
	Share pool – original cost	½
	Share pool – indexation to October 2013	½
	Share pool – disposal October 2013	1
	Share pool – indexation to March 2018	½
	Share pool – disposal March 2018	½
	Capital loss brought forward	½
		13
(b)	Profit threshold reduced	1½
	Group dividends	½
		2
		15

(a) Online Ltd – Corporation tax computation for the year ended 31 March 2018

	£
Operating profit	896,700
Depreciation	21,660
Amortisation	9,000
Deduction for lease premium (W1)	(7,380)
Capital allowances (W2)	(9,824)
Trading profit	910,156
Chargeable gain (W3)	59,967
	970,123
Property business loss brought forward	(12,500)
Qualifying charitable donations	(6,800)
Taxable total profits	950,823

Workings

1 *Deduction for lease premium*

	£
Premium paid	90,000
Less: $90,000 \times 2\% \times (10 - 1)$	(16,200)
Amount assessed on the landlord	73,800
Deduction (73,800/10)	7,380

BPP
LEARNING MEDIA

2   Capital allowances

	Main pool £	Special rate pool £	Allowances £
WDV brought forward	56,700	12,400	
Addition – Motor car	13,700		
Disposals – Motor car	(17,200)		
– Pool		(9,300)	
	53,200	3,100	
WDA – 18%	(9,576)		9,576
WDA – 8%		(248)	248
WDV carried forward	43,624	2,852	
Total allowances			9,824

Tutorial notes

1   The motor car purchased has CO_2 emissions between 76 and 130 grams per kilometre, and therefore qualifies for writing down allowances at the rate of 18%.

2   The proceeds for the motor car which was sold are restricted to the original cost figure of £17,200.

3   Although all of the items included in the special rate pool have been sold, there is no balancing allowance because the business has not ceased.

3   Chargeable gain

	£
Disposal proceeds	90,600
Less: Indexed cost (W4)	(27,355)
	63,245
Less: Capital loss brought forward	(3,278)
Chargeable gain	59,967

4   Share pool

	Number	Indexed cost £
Purchase June 2010	40,000	49,300
Indexation to October 2013		
(49,300 × 0.124)		6,113
		55,413
Disposal October 2013		
(55,413 × 22,000/40,000)	(22,000)	(30,477)
	18,000	24,936
Indexation to March 2018		
(24,936 × 0.097)		2,419
		27,355
Disposal March 2018	(18,000)	(27,355)

(b)   The profit threshold for establishing whether Online Ltd is a large company will be reduced to £750,000 (1,500,000/2), so it is likely that the company's corporation tax will have to be paid by quarterly instalments.

The dividends received from Offline Ltd, being group dividends, will not form part of Online Ltd's profits.

MCQ bank – Value added tax 1

239   Deposit 18 August 2017, Balancing payment 2 September 2017

The basic tax point is the date the goods were supplied (26 August 2017). Where payment is received before the basic tax point, then this date becomes the actual tax point. The tax point for the 10% deposit is therefore the date that it is received (18 August 2017). The actual tax point for the balancing payment is the date the invoice was issued (2 September 2017) as this was within 14 days of the basic tax point.

240   Barry and Chris

Input tax related to zero rated (children's clothing) and standard rated (adult clothing) supplies is recoverable but input tax related to exempt supplies (financial services) is not.

241   £65

	£
Output VAT: £361 × 1/6	60
Less input VAT: £625 × 20%	(125)
VAT due	(65)

Input VAT on the motor car is not recoverable because there is private use. The answer £1,905 allows business use input tax recovery for car. The answer £3,132 allows full input tax recovery on the car. The answer £44 treats petrol as inclusive, instead of exclusive, of VAT.

242   Return 7 July 2017, payment 7 July 2017

The time limit for submission of the return and payment is one month plus seven days after the end of the VAT period.

243   VAT quarter ended 30 June 2018

The value added tax (VAT) on an impaired debt may only be reclaimed once the debt has been outstanding for six months from the due date. The due date in this instance is 10 October 2017; therefore the VAT can be reclaimed in the quarter ended 30 June 2018.

CBE style OTQ bank – Value added tax 2

244   £1,600

The VAT will be calculated on the actual amount received so is £8,000 × 20% = £1,600.

245   £333

Input tax on the motor car is not recoverable because there is private use. However, since there is some use of the car for business purposes, then any VAT charged on repairs and maintenance costs can be treated as input tax without apportionment for private use. The input VAT recoverable is therefore £2,000 × 1/6 = £333.

246   £2,320

	£
New car for salesman	0
New motor van £10,320 × 1/6	1,720
Entertaining UK customers	0
Entertaining overseas customers £3,600 × 1/6	600
Total input tax recoverable	2,320

The answer £5,360 allows full input tax recovery. The answer £4,192 allows business use recovery of input tax on the car. The answer £3,020 allows recovery of input tax on the entertaining of UK customers.

247 £270

The following rules apply to pre-registration input tax:

Goods: if acquired within four years prior to registration and still held on registration date (so the VAT on the inventory of spare parts is recoverable).

Services: if supplied within six months prior to registration (so the VAT on the accountancy fees is recoverable but not that on the legal fees).

248 1 August 2017

Scott is required to notify HMRC within 30 days of exceeding the £85,000 registration threshold ie 30 July 2017 (30 days after the year to 30 June 2017). He will then be registered from 1 August 2017.

249 £4,925

	£
Output VAT: £35,250 × 1/6	5,875
Less input VAT: £5,700 × 1/6	
(UK customer entertaining not recoverable)	(950)
VAT due	4,925

250 0%

Charlie will charge VAT at zero rate because this is an EU transaction to a customer who is VAT registered.

251 Date of payment or receipt determines the VAT period in which the transaction is dealt with. Gives automatic impairment loss relief (bad debt relief).

252 £11,400

£120,000 × 9.5% = £11,400. The flat rate percentage is applied to the full tax inclusive turnover including all standard, zero and exempt supplies.

The answer £10,450 uses only the standard and zero rated supplies. The answer £8,075 uses only standard rated supplies. The answer £9,025 uses only the standard rated and exempt supplies.

253

Join scheme	Tax exclusive annual taxable turnover up to £150,000

Leave scheme	Tax inclusive annual turnover up to £230,000

CBE style OT case – Anne

Text references. Value added tax liability is covered in Chapter 24. Special schemes are dealt with in Chapter 25.

Top tips. Make sure that you read all the information given in the question – you are given this information by the examining team for a reason so you must make use of it when answering the question.

Easy marks. The output tax on cash sales in question 254 should have been easy to deal with.

254 £5,600

Cash sales £28,000 (adult clothes standard rated) × 20%	£5,600

255 £2,292

	£
Credit sales with discount £12,000 × 95% × 90% × 20%	2,052
Credit sales without discount £12,000 × 10% × 20%	240
	2,292

The calculation of output VAT on the credit sales only takes into account the discount for prompt payment for the 90% of customers that took it.

The answer £2,052 is just the output VAT on the discounted sales. The answer £2,280 is the output tax if all sales are treated as discounted. The answer £2,400 is the answer if no sales are treated as discounted.

256 £2,400

	£
Purchases and expenses £11,200 × 20%	2,240
Impairment loss £800 × 20%	160
	2,400

Relief for an impairment loss is not given until six months from the time that payment is due. Therefore relief can only be claimed in respect of the invoice due for payment on 10 April 2017. Obviously the customer did not take up the discount for prompt payment.

257 Anne will be permitted to join the scheme if her expected taxable turnover for the next 12 months does not exceed £1,350,000.

If the value of Anne's taxable supplies exceeds £1,600,000 in the 12 months to the end of a VAT period she must leave the scheme immediately.

Anne will be permitted to join the scheme if she is up to date with both her VAT payments and her VAT returns. Payment in nine monthly instalments is a feature of the annual accounting scheme.

258

Reduced amount of output VAT payable		NOT ADVANTAGE
Automatic impairment loss relief (bad debt relief)	ADVANTAGE	
Only one VAT return each year		NOT ADVANTAGE
Output VAT on 10% of credit sales will be accounted for up to 1 month later than at present	ADVANTAGE	

The output VAT payable will remain the same and accounting for VAT will also remain the same.

Auy and Bim

Text references. The tax point and VAT liability are covered in Chapter 24. Special schemes are dealt with in Chapter 25.

Top tips. Learn the rules about the tax point – they are often examined! For the basic tax point you need to distinguish between supplies of goods (date goods are removed or made available to the customer) and services (date on which services are completed).

Easy marks. There were easy marks in questions 260 and 263 for the computation of the VAT paid or payable by the partnership.

259 2 and 3

If the VAT invoice is issued within 14 days after the basic tax point and payment has not been received before the basic tax point, the invoice date becomes the tax point. The tax point determines the VAT period in which output tax must be accounted for and credit for input tax will be allowed.

The basic tax point for services is the date that services are completed. If the VAT invoice is issued and payment is received before the basic tax point, the actual tax point is the earlier of those two dates.

260 £25,280

The partnership's output VAT for the year ended 5 April 2018 is £25,600 and its total input VAT for the year is £(180 + 140) = £320.

Therefore VAT of £25,280 (25,600 – 320) will have been paid to HM Revenue & Customs for the year ended 5 April 2018.

261 1 and 3

Businesses using the scheme must still issue VAT invoices to their VAT registered customers. Businesses using the scheme cannot reclaim any input tax suffered.

Under the scheme, businesses calculate VAT by applying a fixed percentage to all their income (ie including reduced rate, zero rated and exempt income). A 1% reduction off the flat rate percentage can be made by businesses in the first year that they use the flat rate scheme only if it is also the first year of registration.

262 Join: expected taxable turnover (excluding VAT) for the next 12 months does not exceed £150,000, Continue to use: until its total turnover (including VAT) for the previous year exceeds £230,000

263 £23,291

If the partnership had used the flat rate scheme throughout the year ended 5 April 2018 then it would have paid VAT of £(140,762 + 25,600) = £166,362 @ 14% = £23,291.

Aston

Text references. Registration for value added tax is covered in Chapter 24. VAT invoices, penalties and overseas aspects are dealt with in Chapter 25.

Top tips. Remember that the common penalty regime for errors applies to a number of taxes, including VAT.

Easy marks. There were easy marks for dealing with the registration of Aston in question 264.

264 Liable for registration: 31 January 2018, Date of registration: 1 March 2018

Aston would have been liable to compulsory value added tax (VAT) registration when his taxable supplies during any 12-month period (or the period from commencement of trade, if less) exceeded £85,000.

This happened on 31 January 2018 when taxable supplies amounted to £85,200 (6,300 + 6,400 + 21,900 + 4,800 + 11,700 + 17,100 + 14,800 + 2,200).

Registration is required from the end of the month following the month in which the limit is exceeded, so Aston will have been registered from 1 March 2018 or from an agreed earlier date.

265 Submission: one month and seven days after the end of the VAT period. Payment: one month and seven days after the end of the VAT period.

266 2 and 4

The additional information required is Aston's VAT registration number and an identifying number (invoice number).

267 1 and 4

The transaction is entered on Aston's VAT return as an output and an input. The service is treated as being supplied in the UK since this is where Aston is situated.

The tax point for a supply of such services is the earlier of the time the service is completed and the time the service is paid for. Supplies of services from VAT registered businesses situated elsewhere within the European Union are categorised in the same way as UK supplies and so are not necessarily zero rated.

268 Maximum penalty 30% of the VAT underpaid, Minimum penalty 0% of the VAT underpaid

HM Revenue & Customs (HMRC) will not charge a penalty if Aston has taken reasonable care, provided he informs them of any errors upon subsequent discovery.

However, applying the incorrect rate of VAT is more likely to be treated as careless, since Aston would be expected to check the VAT classification of his supplies.

The maximum amount of penalty will therefore be 30% of the VAT underpaid, but this penalty could be reduced to 0% as a result of a subsequent unprompted disclosure to HMRC.

Starfish Ltd (B)

Text references. Calculation of value added tax (VAT) and transfer of a business as a going concern are covered in Chapter 24. Default interest is dealt with in Chapter 25.

Top tips. In question 273 you need to identify the supplies which will not be subject to VAT as a result of the transfer of going concern rules.

Easy marks. There were some easy marks available in the computation of VAT in question 270.

269   £390

	£
Credit sales revenue discount taken up	
£2,000 × (100 − 4)% × 60% × 20%	230
Credit sales revenue discount not taken up	
£2,000 × 40% × 20%	160
	390

270   £16,420

	£
Cash sales revenue £38,520 × 20/120	6,420
Sale of inventory on cessation £28,800 × 20/120	4,800
Sale of non-current assets £31,200 × 20/120	5,200
	16,420

There is no VAT charged on the sale of the car, as none was recovered on purchase (owing to private usage).

271   £11,324

	£
Expenses £([69,960 − 4,320] = £65,640) × 20/120	10,940
Impairment loss	384
	11,324

Input VAT on business entertainment for UK customers is not recoverable.

Relief for the impairment loss is available because the claim is made more than six months from the time that payment was due, and the debt has been written off in the company's books.

272   7 May 2018

Default interest will be payable from the reckonable date (7 May 2018) to the date of payment.

273   No output VAT would have been due on the sale of the inventory or the sale of the non-current assets.

A sale of a business as a going concern is outside the scope of VAT, and therefore output VAT would not have been due on either the sale of the inventory or the sale of the non-current assets.

CBE style OT case – Greenzone Ltd (B)

274 £42,540

	£
Output VAT	
Sales	38,210
Group sales	4,330
Output VAT	42,540

The tax point for the deposit is the date of payment, so no adjustment is required to the output VAT figure of £38,210.

The answer £38,210 does not include group sales. The answer £42,140 does not include the deposit. The answer £37,810 does not include either group sales or the deposit.

275 £30 recoverable

	£
Output VAT	
Fuel scale charge £320 × 20/120	53
Input VAT	
Fuel purchased £500 × 20/120	(83)
VAT recoverable	(30)

The answer £20 payable adjusts the input tax for private mileage so the input VAT is £500 × 40% × 20/120 = £33. The answer £36 recoverable treats the amounts as VAT exclusive. The answer £53 payable is just the fuel scale charge.

276 £12,560

	£
Total input VAT	12,770
Entertaining UK customers	(210)
Entertaining overseas customers	0
Repainting office building	0
New reception area	0
	12,560

Input VAT on business entertaining is not recoverable unless it relates to the cost of entertaining overseas customers. There is no distinction between capital and revenue expenditure for VAT so input tax is recoverable on both the repainting of the office building (revenue) and the building of the new reception area (capital).

277

ARE LTD		

Are Ltd can register with Greenzone Ltd as a group for VAT purposes as it is UK resident and controlled by Greenzone Ltd. Be Ltd is not controlled by Greenzone Ltd and Doer Inc is not UK resident and does not have a fixed establishment in the UK.

278 Each VAT group must appoint a representative member which must account for the group's output tax and input tax.

Any supply of goods or services by a member of the group to another member of the group is disregarded for VAT purposes.

All members of the group are jointly and severally liable for any VAT due from the representative member. It is not necessary for each company, which is eligible for group registration, to join a particular VAT group.

CBE style OT case – Long Ltd group (B)

279 £53,780

	£
Sales £(52,640 – 1,760)	50,880
Group sales £(1,940 + 960)	2,900
	53,780

The tax point for the deposit is the date of payment, so this will have been included in output VAT for the quarter ended 31 December 2017.

280 £15,638

	£
Expenses	14,720
Hire of photocopier	
£18 × [(4 years × 12 = 48 months) + 3 months]	918
	15,638

Refunds of VAT are subject to a four-year time limit so, in addition to the input VAT for the hire of the photocopier incurred during the quarter ended 31 March 2018, Long Ltd can also claim for the input VAT incurred during the period 1 January 2014 to 31 December 2017.

The answer £14,720 does not include the hire of the photocopies. The answer £14,774 includes only three months of the hire of the photocopier. The answer £14,882 includes an additional six months of hire of the photocopier giving nine months in total – this is a confusion between the rules for recovery of goods and of services.

281 £0

Wind Ltd's sales are exempt from VAT, so the company cannot be registered for VAT and thus cannot recover input tax.

282 £3,500

	£
Expenses	3,120
Advertising	380
	3,500

Input VAT on services incurred prior to registration is subject to a 6-month time limit, so the input VAT of £640 in respect of the advertising expenditure incurred during April 2017 cannot be recovered.

The answer £3,120 does not include the advertising at all. The answer £4,140 includes all the advertising. The answer £3,540 includes only the £640 of advertising expenditure.

283 Supplies of goods or services to Road Ltd from outside the group will be treated as a supply to Long Ltd.

The supplies by Long Ltd to Wind Ltd and Road Ltd would be disregarded for VAT purposes.

Two or more companies are eligible to be treated as members of a group if one of them controls each of the others, or one person (which could be an individual or a holding company) controls all of them, or two or more persons carrying on a business in partnership control all of them. The controlling entity therefore does not need to be a company. It is not necessary for each company, which meets the requirements, to join a particular VAT group.

CBE style OT case – Zim

Text references. Value added tax is dealt with in Chapters 24 and 25.

Top tips. You must make sure you know the thresholds for entering and leaving the flat rate scheme as they are not given in the rates and allowances available in the examination.

Easy marks. Question 284 provided easy marks for working out the net VAT payable.

284 £12,000

		£	£
Sales	– Standard rated £115,200 × 20/120		19,200
	– Zero rated		0
Purchases	– Standard rated £43,200 × 20/120	7,200	
	– Zero rated	0	
			(7,200)
Net VAT payable			12,000

285 £240

Impairment losses £(780 + 660) = 1,440 × 20/120 = £240

Relief for impairment losses is given once six months have expired from the time when payment was due, so relief can be claimed in respect of both impairment losses.

The answer £0 assumes no relief for impairment losses is available. The answer £130 gives relief only on the loss of £780. The answer £110 gives relief only on the loss of £660.

286 Mobile phone £260, Customers £40

Mobile phone £2,600 × 60% (100% – 40%) × 20/120 = £260

An apportionment is made where a service such as the use of a telephone is partly for business purposes and partly for private purposes.

Customers entertainment £240 × 20/120 = £40

Input VAT on business entertainment is not recoverable unless it relates to the cost of entertaining overseas customers.

287

Join	Taxable turnover excluding VAT not more than £150,000 in next 12 months

Leave	Total turnover including VAT more than £230,000 in previous 12 months

288 £15,120

Using the flat rate scheme to calculate his VAT liability, Zim would have paid VAT of £126,000 × 12% = £15,120 for the year ended 31 March 2018.

The answer £13,860 assumes that the 1% reduction is available – be careful of this rule as it only applies in the first year of VAT registration. The answer £13,824 only charges standard rated sales. The answer £9,216 charges the flat rate on sales less expenses.

BPP
LEARNING MEDIA

CBE style OT case – Smart Ltd

289

Register	1 November 2017

Notification	30 November 2017

Smart Ltd was liable to register for VAT from 1 November 2017 because this is the date when it signed the contract valued at £86,000. The company would therefore have known that its taxable supplies for the following 30-day period would have exceeded £85,000. Registration is required from the start of the 30-day period.

Smart Ltd would have had to notify HM Revenue & Customs by 30 November 2017, being the end of the 30-day period.

290

	TRUE	FALSE
Smart Ltd must file its VAT returns online and pay the VAT which is due electronically.	TRUE	
Smart Ltd can choose whether to pay the VAT which is due electronically or by cheque.		FALSE
The deadline for paying any VAT which is due is one month after the end of each quarter.		FALSE
The deadline for filing the VAT return is one month and seven days after the end of each quarter.	TRUE	

Smart Ltd must pay the VAT which is due electronically. The deadline for paying any VAT which is due is one month and seven days after the end of each quarter.

291 The basic tax point is the date on which services are completed.

If a customer pays for services before the basic tax point, the payment date will be the tax point.

292 1 and 4

The scheme will provide automatic relief for an impairment loss should a customer default on the payment of a debt. Output VAT will be accounted for 60 days later than at present, because the scheme will result in the tax point becoming the date when payment is received from customers.

293 Maximum penalty: 30% of the VAT underpaid. Minimum penalty for prompted disclosure: 15% of the VAT underpaid.

294 Jogger Ltd (B)

Marking scheme

			Marks
(a)	Quarter ended 30 September 2016	2	
	Quarter ended 31 March 2017	2	
	Quarter ended 31 March 2018	2	
			6
(b)	One VAT return	1	
	Payments on account	1	
	Limit	1	
	VAT payments up to date	1	
			4
			10

(a) The late submission of the VAT return for the quarter ended 30 September 2016 will have resulted in HM Revenue & Customs (HMRC) issuing a surcharge liability notice specifying a surcharge period running to 30 September 2017.

The late payment of VAT for the quarter ended 31 March 2017 will have resulted in a surcharge of £778 (£38,900 × 2%) because this is the first default in the surcharge period. The surcharge period will also have been extended to 31 March 2018.

The late payment of VAT for the quarter ended 31 March 2018 will therefore have resulted in a surcharge of £4,455 (£89,100 × 5%) because this is the second default in the surcharge period. The surcharge period will also have been extended to 31 March 2019.

(b) The reduced administration from only having to submit one VAT return each year should mean that default surcharges are avoided in respect of the late submission of VAT returns.

In addition, making payments on account based on the previous year's VAT liability will improve both budgeting and possibly cash flow if Jogger Ltd's business is expanding.

Jogger Ltd can apply to use the annual accounting scheme if its expected taxable turnover for the next 12 months does not exceed £1,350,000 exclusive of VAT.

However, the company must be up to date with its VAT payments before it is allowed to use the scheme.

295 Flick (B)

Marking scheme

		Marks	
(a)	Flat rate scheme	1	
	Normal basis	1	
	Conclusion	1	
			3
(b)	No recovery of VAT by customers	1	
	Possible need to absorb VAT	1	
	Conclusion	1	
			3
(c)	VAT period	1	
	Basic tax point	1	
	Deposit	1	
	Balance	1	
			4
			10

(a) Using the flat rate scheme to calculate its VAT liability the partnership will have paid VAT of £(59,700 × 12%) = £7,164 for the quarter ended 31 March 2018.

If the partnership had used the normal basis it would have paid VAT of £(59,700 − 27,300 = 32,400 × 20/120) = £5,400.

It was therefore not beneficial to use the flat rate scheme as the additional cost of £(7,164 − 5,400) = £1,764 for the quarter would appear to outweigh the advantage of simplified VAT administration.

(b) The partnership's sales are all to members of the general public, who cannot recover the input VAT.

It may not therefore be possible to pass the output VAT on to customers in the prices charged. To the extent this is not possible the partnership would have had to absorb all or some of this amount itself as a cost.

It was therefore not beneficial for the partnership to have voluntarily registered for VAT from 1 January 2018. For the quarter ended 31 March 2018 voluntary registration reduced the partnership's profits by a maximum of £7,164 (£5,400 if the normal basis had been used).

(c) Output VAT must be accounted for according to the VAT period in which the supply is treated as being made. This is determined by the tax point.

The basic tax point is the date when the service is completed, which will be the date that a film is screened.

Where payment is received before the basic tax point, then this date becomes the actual tax point. The tax point for each 25% deposit is therefore the date that it is received.

Invoices are issued on the same day as the basic tax point, so this is the tax point for the balance of 75%.

296 Richard (B)

Marking scheme

			Marks
(a)	Compulsory registration limit	½	
	Date registration required	1½	
	Date registration effective	1	
	Consequences of non-registration	1	
			4
(b)	Honesty and integrity	½	
	Cease to act and inform HMRC	1	
	Money laundering notification	½	
			2
(c)	Simplified invoice	1	
	Request for invoice	½	
	Details on invoice: ½ mark per item to maximum	2½	
			4
			10

(a) Richard would have been liable to compulsory VAT registration when his taxable supplies during any 12-month period (or from the commencement of trade, if less) exceeded £85,000.

This happened on 31 October 2017 when taxable supplies were £([10,500 × 4] + [15,000 × 3]) = £87,000.

Registration is required from the end of the month following the month in which the limit is exceeded, so Richard should have been registered from 1 December 2017.

If Richard continued to trade after 1 December 2017 without registering for VAT, he would still have to pay the VAT due from the time he should have been registered.

(b) The matter is one of professional judgement and a trainee Chartered Certified Accountant would be expected to act honestly and with integrity.

If Richard refuses to register for VAT, you should cease to act for him. You must notify HM Revenue & Customs (HMRC) that you no longer act for Richard although you should not provide any reason for this.

You would also be obliged to make a report under the money laundering regulations.

(c) A simplified (or less detailed) VAT invoice can be issued by a trader where the VAT inclusive total of the invoice is less than £250.

Such an invoice should be issued when a customer requests a VAT invoice.

A simplified VAT invoice must show the following information:

- The supplier's name and address
- The supplier's registration number
- The date of the supply
- A description of the goods or services supplied
- The rate of VAT chargeable
- The total amount chargeable including VAT

297 Clueless Ltd (A)

Text references. Special schemes for VAT and overseas aspects of VAT are in Chapter 25.

Top tips. The question stated that the company incurred considerable overtime costs due to its employees working late in order to meet tax return filing deadlines which should have alerted you to one of the advantages of the annual accounting scheme.

Easy marks. There were some easy marks in part (a) for the conditions for the cash accounting and annual accounting schemes.

Marking scheme

			Marks	
(a)		Eligible for both schemes on turnover	1½	
		Up to date with payments for both schemes	1	
		Up to date with returns for cash accounting scheme	½	
		Output tax under cash accounting scheme	1	
		Input tax under cash accounting scheme	1	
		Annual accounting scheme – one return	1	
				6
(b)	(i)	Payment on importation	1	
		Input tax recovery	1	
	(ii)	Output tax on date of acquisition	1	
		Input tax recovery	1	
				4
				10

(a) Clueless Ltd can use both schemes because its expected taxable turnover for the next 12 months does not exceed £1,350,000 exclusive of VAT.

In addition, for both schemes the company is up to date with its VAT payments, and for the cash accounting scheme it is up to date with its VAT returns.

With the cash accounting scheme, output VAT will be accounted for two months later than at present as the date of the cash receipt determines the return in which the transaction is dealt with rather than the invoice date.

The recovery of input VAT on expenses will not be affected as these are dealt with on a cash basis.

With the annual accounting scheme, the reduced administration in only having to file one VAT return each year should save on overtime costs.

(b) (i) **Supplier situated outside the European Union**

Clueless Ltd will have to pay VAT of £22,000 @ 20% = £4,400 to HM Revenue & Customs at the time of importation.

This will then be reclaimed as input VAT on the VAT return for the period during which the machinery is imported.

(ii) **Supplier situated elsewhere within the European Union**

VAT will have to be accounted for according to the date of acquisition. This will be the earlier of the date that a VAT invoice is issued or the 15th day of the month following the month in which the machinery comes into the UK.

The VAT charged of £4,400 will be declared on Clueless Ltd's VAT return as output VAT, but will then be reclaimed as input VAT on the same VAT return.

298 Garfield

Marking scheme

		Marks
(a)	*Output VAT*	
	Discounted sale	1
	Equipment	1
	Input VAT	
	Equipment	½
	Impairment losses	1
	Entertaining	1
	Motor expenses	1½
	VAT payable (including figures provided in question)	1
		7
(b)	Possible schemes	1
	Identify cash accounting scheme as beneficial	½
	Benefits of cash accounting scheme (½ mark each)	1½
		3
		10

(a) **Garfield – Value added tax (VAT) return for the quarter ended 31 March 2018**

	£
Output VAT	
Sales	22,500*
Discounted sale £4,300 × 90% × 20%	774
Equipment £12,400 × 20%	2,480
Fuel scale charge	60*
Input VAT	
Purchases	(11,200)*
Motor car	0*
Equipment	(2,480)
Impairment losses £1,400 × 20%	(280)
Entertaining – UK customers	0*
– Overseas customers £960 × 20/120	(160)
Motor expenses £1,668 (1,008 + 660) × 20/120	(278)
VAT payable	11,416

*Figures provided in question

Tutorial notes

1   Relief for an impairment loss is only available if the claim is made more than six months from the time when payment was due. Therefore, relief can only be claimed in respect of the invoice due for payment on 29 August 2017.

2   Input VAT on business entertainment is recoverable if it relates to the cost of entertaining overseas customers.

(b)   Given Garfield's current annual turnover of £450,000, he can use the cash accounting scheme and the annual accounting scheme, but not the flat rate scheme.

The cash accounting scheme would appear to be the most beneficial scheme for Garfield to use.

The scheme will provide automatic VAT relief for the impairment losses which he is incurring.

Where credit is given to customers, output VAT could be accounted for later than at present.

The recovery of input VAT on most purchases and expenses will not be affected as Garfield pays for these on a cash basis.

Tutorial notes

1   The annual turnover limit for both the annual accounting scheme and the cash accounting scheme is £1,350,000, but for the flat rate scheme it is £150,000.

2   Although the annual accounting scheme would mean only having to submit one VAT return each year (reducing the risk of late return penalties), payments on account are based on the VAT payable for the previous year. From a cash flow viewpoint, this is not beneficial where turnover is decreasing.

299 Zhi

Text references. Self assessment and payment of tax by individuals is covered in Chapter 17. Capital gains tax business reliefs are the subject of Chapter 15. The VAT tax point is dealt with in Chapter 24. Computation of income tax is covered in Chapter 2 and national insurance contributions in Chapter 12. The PAYE system is dealt with in Chapter 4.

Top tips. If you are asked to calculate a reduction in tax, don't waste time setting out a full tax computation. Just work out the reduction using the marginal rate of tax. This is a similar process to working out additional tax covered in Chapter 2 of the Text.

Easy marks. There were some easy marks in part (c) for applying the rules on the tax point.

Examining team's comments. This 10-mark question had a focus on higher skills.

Part (a) was not very well answered and was not attempted by some candidates. Essentially, all that candidates had to do was select the two relevant tax years (out of the three provided), deduct one set of figures from the other, and divide by two.

Part (b) was the only part of the question which was consistently well answered. One particular issue, however, was that some candidates worked out the current capital gains tax liability (prior to the rollover relief claim) despite this being provided. Carefully noting which information has been provided in the question will avoid time being wasted in this manner.

Whether or not candidates did well in part (c) depended on them realising that 1 February 2018 was more than 14 days after 12 December 2017. This being the case, postponing the sales invoice would not affect the basic tax point. Candidates should appreciate that a suggested tax planning strategy might not necessarily be effective, and they need to have the courage to base their answer on this conclusion if led there following the application of basic principles. However, some candidates either did not read the question carefully or chose to answer a question they would have preferred to have been asked, and based their answer on the amount of VAT which could be postponed.

There were some good answers to part (d). However, only a few candidates appreciated that by far the quickest and easiest way to calculate the tax reductions was to work at the margin – rather than producing full before and after tax computations. Of course it was also important to realise that the first employee was a basic rate taxpayer, subject to employee national insurance contributions at 12%, whereas the second employee was a higher rate taxpayer and only subject to employee national insurance contributions at 2%.

			Marks
(a)	No reduction in balancing payment	1	
	Reduction in payment on account	1½	
			3
(b)	Current CGT liability	½	
	Proceeds not reinvested	1	
	Annual exempt amount	1	
	CGT computation	½	
			3
(c)	Basic tax point	½	
	Invoice does not displace	1	
	Cannot reduce VAT payable	½	
			2
(d)	*First employee*		
	PAYE	½	
	NIC – employee	½	
	NIC – employer	½	
	Second employee		
	PAYE	½	
	NIC – employee	½	
	NIC – employer	½	
	Payment date	½	
	Max		3
			10

(a) The balancing payment for 2016/17 due on 31 January 2018 cannot be reduced.

A claim can be made to reduce the payment on account for 2016/17 due on 31 January 2018 by £5,040:

	£
Current POA (27,600 + 4,204) × 50%	15,902
Revised POA (18,000 + 3,724) × 50%	(10,862)
Reduction	5,040

(b)

	£	£
Current CGT liability		12,940
Revised CGT liability		
Proceeds not reinvested (210,000 – 164,000)	46,000	
Annual exempt amount	(11,300)	
	34,700	
CGT: 34,700 at 20%		(6,940)
Reduction		6,000

Tutorial note: Equivalent marks will be awarded if the reduction is alternatively calculated as 30,000 (76,000 – (210,000 – 164,000)) at 20% = £6,000.

(c) The basic tax point for goods is the date when they are made available to the customer, which in the case of Zhi's sale is 12 December 2017.

An invoice date of 1 February 2018 will not affect this because the invoice will not have been issued within 14 days of the basic tax point.

Zhi therefore cannot reduce the amount of VAT payable on 7 February 2018.

(d)

	£
First employee	
PAYE (1,500 at 20%)	300
NIC – Employee (1,500 at 12%)	180
– Employer (1,500 at 13.8%)	207
Second employee	
PAYE (5,000 at 40%)	2,000
NIC – Employee (5,000 at 2%)	100
– Employer (5,000 at 13.8%)	690
Reduction	3,477

The postponed PAYE and NICs of £3,477 will be payable one month later on 22 February 2018.

Mock exams

ACCA Applied Skills

Taxation (TX – UK)

Mock Exam 1
(September 2016 CBE updated to FA 2017)

Question Paper	
Time allowed	**3 hours**
This paper is divided into three sections: Section A – ALL 15 questions are compulsory and MUST be attempted. Section B – ALL 15 questions are compulsory and MUST be attempted. Section C – ALL THREE questions are compulsory and MUST be attempted.	

DO NOT OPEN THIS PAPER UNTIL YOU ARE READY TO START UNDER EXAMINATION CONDITIONS

SECTION A: ALL 15 questions are compulsory and MUST be attempted

1 On 1 July 2016, Sameer made a cash gift of £2,500 to his sister.

On 1 May 2017, he made a cash gift of £2,000 to a friend.

On 1 June 2017, he made a cash gift of £50,000 to a trust.

Sameer has not made any other lifetime gifts.

In respect of Sameer's cash gift of £50,000 to the trust, what is the lifetime transfer of value for inheritance tax purposes after taking account of all available exemptions?

- ○ £48,500
- ○ £44,000
- ○ £46,000
- ○ £46,500 **(2 marks)**

2 On 31 March 2018, Angus sold a house, which he had bought on 31 March 2004.

Angus occupied the house as his main residence until 31 March 2009, when he left for employment abroad.

Angus returned to the UK on 1 April 2011 and lived in the house until 31 March 2012, when he bought a flat in a neighbouring town and made that his principal private residence.

What is Angus' total number of qualifying months of occupation for principal private residence relief on the sale of the house?

- ○ 72 months
- ○ 54 months
- ○ 114 months
- ○ 96 months **(2 marks)**

3 Abena has made the following gross contributions to her personal pension scheme over the past three tax years:

Tax year	£
2014/15	42,000
2015/16	27,000
2016/17	28,000

Abena is entitled to an annual allowance of £40,000 in all tax years from 2014/15 to 2017/18.

What is the maximum gross contribution which Abena can make to her personal pension scheme for the tax year 2017/18 without giving rise to an annual allowance charge?

- ○ £63,000
- ○ £40,000
- ○ £65,000
- ○ £35,000 **(2 marks)**

4   Triangle Ltd is registered for value added tax (VAT) and uses the annual accounting scheme.

For the year ended 31 December 2017, the net VAT payable by Triangle Ltd was £73,500.

For the year ended 31 December 2016, the net VAT payable by Triangle Ltd was £47,700.

Indicate, by clicking on the relevant boxes in the table below, the number and amount of the monthly payments on account of VAT which Triangle Ltd must make in respect of the year ended 31 December 2017 prior to submitting its VAT return for that year.

Number of monthly payments	NINE	TEN
Monthly payment amount	£4,770	£7,350

(2 marks)

5   Lili Ltd commenced trading on 1 January 2017. The company incurred the following expenditure prior to 1 January 2017:

		£
30 November 2009	Initial market research	15,000
6 June 2012	Research into competitors	12,000
31 July 2016	Entertaining potential customers and suppliers	8,000
15 December 2016	Donation to local school fair in exchange for advertising	2,000

What is the amount of Lili Ltd's deductible pre-trading expenditure in respect of the year ended 31 December 2017?

£ [   ]

(2 marks)

6   Paloma has been trading for a number of years. Her tax adjusted trading profit for the year ended 31 May 2017 was £48,000 and for the year ended 31 May 2018 was £43,200.

What is the amount of class 4 national insurance contributions (NIC) payable by Paloma for the tax year 2017/18?

○   £3,225
○   £3,585
○   £3,315
○   £3,375

(2 marks)

7   Identify, by clicking on the relevant boxes in the table below, whether the following statements are true or false.

Corporation tax is a direct tax on the turnover of companies.	TRUE	FALSE
National insurance is a direct tax suffered by employees, employers and the self-employed on earnings.	TRUE	FALSE
Inheritance tax is a direct tax on transfers of income by individuals.	TRUE	FALSE
Value added tax is a direct tax on the supply of goods and services by businesses.	TRUE	FALSE

(2 marks)

8   Which of the following statements concerning self-assessment tax returns for individuals is true?

○   Individuals with tax payable of less than £1,000 for a tax year are not required to file a tax return.

○   Individuals are only required to file a tax return for a tax year if they receive a notice to deliver from HM Revenue & Customs (HMRC).

○   All individuals who submit a tax return on time are able to have their tax payable calculated by HMRC.

○   The tax return for an individual covers income tax, class 1, class 2 and class 4 national insurance contributions and capital gains tax liabilities.   **(2 marks)**

9   In certain circumstances, an individual is automatically not resident in the UK.

Indicate, by clicking on the relevant boxes in the table below, whether the following two individuals satisfy or do not satisfy the tests to be treated as automatically not resident in the UK for the tax year 2017/18.

Eric, who has never previously been resident in the UK. In the tax year 2017/18, he was in the UK for 40 days.

Fran, who was resident in the UK for the two tax years prior to the tax year 2017/18. In the tax year 2017/18, she was in the UK for 18 days.

Eric	SATISFIES	DOES NOT SATISFY
Fran	SATISFIES	DOES NOT SATISFY

(2 marks)

10   Max is employed by Star Ltd. On 6 April 2016, Star Ltd provided Max with a camera for his personal use. The camera had a market value of £2,000 on 6 April 2016.

On 6 April 2017, Star Ltd gave the camera to Max for free. The camera had a market value of £1,400 on 6 April 2017.

What is Max's taxable benefit in respect of the camera for the tax year 2017/18?

Select...   ▼
£1,000
£1,400
£2,000
£1,600

(2 marks)

11   Cora made a cash gift of £300,000 to her niece on 30 April 2012.

She then made a cash gift of £500,000 to her nephew on 31 May 2013.

Both of these amounts are stated after deducting available exemptions.

Cora subsequently died on 31 October 2017.

What amount of inheritance tax was payable as a result of Cora's death in respect of the cash gift of £500,000 to her nephew?

○   £190,000
○   £110,000
○   £114,000
○   £105,000   **(2 marks)**

12 Rajesh is a sole trader. He correctly calculated his self-assessment payments on account for the tax year 2017/18 and paid these on the due dates.

Rajesh paid the correct balancing payment of £1,200 for the tax year 2017/18 on 30 June 2019.

Indicate, by clicking on the relevant boxes in the table below, what penalties and interest Rajesh may be charged as a result of his late balancing payment for the tax year 2017/18.

Penalty	£0	£60
Interest	£14	£33

(2 marks)

13 Oblong Ltd has had the following results:

	Year ended 31 March 2017 £	Year ended 31 March 2018 £
Trading profit/(loss)	79,400	(102,800)
Property business income	6,800	10,100
Qualifying charitable donations	(1,600)	(1,300)

If Oblong Ltd makes a claim to relieve its trading loss of £102,800 for the year ended 31 March 2018 against total profits for the year ended 31 March 2017, how much of this loss will remain unrelieved?

- ○ £6,500
- ○ £16,600
- ○ £9,400
- ○ £23,400

(2 marks)

14 Putting an asset into joint names with a spouse (or a partner in a registered civil partnership) prior to the asset's disposal can be sensible capital gains tax (CGT) planning.

Which of the following **CANNOT** be achieved as a direct result of using this type of tax planning?

Select... ▼
Making the best use of annual exempt amounts
Deferring the CGT due date
Reducing the amount of CGT payable
Making the best use of capital losses

(2 marks)

15 Eva's income tax liability and class 4 national insurance contributions (NIC) for the tax year 2017/18 are £4,840. Her income tax liability and class 4 NICs for the tax year 2016/17 were £6,360.

What is the lowest amount to which Eva could make a claim to reduce each of her payments on account for the tax year 2017/18 without being charged interest?

£ [   ]

(2 marks)

(Total = 30 marks)

SECTION B – ALL 15 questions are compulsory and MUST be attempted

Adana

The following scenario relates to Questions 16 to 20.

Adana died on 17 March 2018, and inheritance tax (IHT) of £566,000 is payable in respect of her chargeable estate. Under the terms of her will, Adana left her entire estate to her children.

At the date of her death, Adana did not own a main residence. She had the following debts and liabilities:

(1)   An outstanding interest-only mortgage of £220,000
(2)   Income tax of £43,700 payable in respect of the tax year 2017/18
(3)   Legal fees of £4,600 incurred by Adana's sister which Adana had verbally promised to pay

Adana's husband had died on 28 May 2006, and only 20% of his inheritance tax nil rate band was used on his death. The nil rate band for the tax year 2006/07 was £285,000.

On 22 April 2006, Adana had made a chargeable lifetime transfer of shares valued at £500,000 to a trust. Adana paid the lifetime IHT of £52,250 arising from this gift. If Adana had not made this gift, her chargeable estate at the time of her death would have been £650,000 higher than it otherwise was. This was because of the subsequent increase in the value of the gifted shares.

16   What is the maximum nil rate band which will have been available when calculating the IHT of £566,000 payable in respect of Adana's chargeable estate?

Select...   ▼
£325,000
£553,000
£390,000
£585,000

(2 marks)

17   What is the total amount of deductions which would have been permitted in calculating Adana's chargeable estate for IHT purposes?

£ [   ]

(2 marks)

18   Indicate, by clicking on the relevant boxes in the table below, who will be responsible for paying the IHT of £566,000 in respect of Adana's chargeable estate, and what is the due date for the payment of this liability.

Responsible persons	BENEFICIARIES OF ADANA'S ESTATE (HER CHILDREN)	PERSONNAL RESPRESENTATIVES OF ADANA'S ESTATE
Due date for payment	17 SEPTEMBER 2018	30 SEPTEMBER 2018

(2 marks)

19   How much of the IHT payable in respect of Adana's estate would have been saved if, under the terms of her will, Adana had made specific gifts of £400,000 to a trust and £200,000 to her grandchildren, instead of leaving her entire estate to her children?

    ○   £240,000
    ○   £160,000
    ○   £0
    ○   £80,000   **(2 marks)**

20   How much IHT did Adana save by making the chargeable lifetime transfer of £500,000 to a trust on 22 April 2006, rather than retaining the gifted investments until her death?

    ○   £260,000
    ○   £207,750
    ○   £147,750
    ○   £200,000   **(2 marks)**

(Total = 10 marks)

Kat Ltd and Kitten

The following scenario relates to Questions 21 to 25.

Kitten is the controlling shareholder in Kat Ltd, an unquoted trading company.

Kat Ltd

Kat Ltd sold a freehold factory on 31 May 2017 for £364,000, which resulted in a chargeable gain of £120,700. The factory was purchased on 1 October 2004 for £138,600, and further capital improvements were immediately made at a cost of £23,400 during the month of purchase. Further improvements to the factory were made during the month of disposal. The relevant retail prices indexes (RPIs) are as follows:

October 2004   188.6
May 2017   270.2

Kat Ltd is unsure how to reinvest the proceeds from the sale of the factory. The company is considering either purchasing a freehold warehouse for £272,000, or acquiring a leasehold office building on a 40-year lease for a premium of £370,000. If either reinvestment is made, it will take place on 30 September 2018.

All of the above buildings have been, or will be, used for the purposes of Kat Ltd's trade.

Kitten

Kitten sold 20,000 £1 ordinary shares in Kat Ltd on 5 October 2017, which resulted in a chargeable gain of £142,200. This disposal qualified for entrepreneurs' relief.

Kitten had originally subscribed for 90,000 shares in Kat Ltd on 7 July 2009 at their par value. On 22 September 2012, Kat Ltd made a 2 for 3 rights issue. Kitten took up her allocation under the rights issue in full, paying £6.40 for each new share issued.

Kitten also sold an antique vase on 16 January 2018, which resulted in a chargeable gain of £27,900.

For the tax year 2017/18, Kitten had taxable income of £12,000.

21   What amount of indexation allowance will have been deducted in calculating the chargeable gain of £120,700 on the disposal of Kat Ltd's factory?

    ○   £47,304
    ○   £40,471
    ○   £70,146
    ○   £60,014   **(2 marks)**

22   If Kat Ltd decides to purchase the freehold warehouse and makes a claim to roll over the chargeable gain on the factory under the rollover relief rules, what will be the base cost of the warehouse for chargeable gains purposes?

    O   £243,300
    O   £272,000
    O   £180,000
    O   £151,300   **(2 marks)**

23   If Kat Ltd decides to acquire the leasehold office building and makes a claim to hold over the chargeable gain on the factory under the rollover relief rules, what is the latest date by which the held-over gain will crystallise?

    O   10 years from 31 May 2017
    O   The date when the office building is sold
    O   40 years from 30 September 2018
    O   10 years from 30 September 2018   **(2 marks)**

24   What cost figure will have been used in calculating the chargeable gain on Kitten's disposal of 20,000 ordinary shares in Kat Ltd?

    O   £12,000
    O   £63,200
    O   £84,800
    O   £20,000   **(2 marks)**

25   What is Kitten's capital gains tax (CGT) liability for the tax year 2017/18?

    O   £15,880
    O   £19,800
    O   £18,670
    O   £17,540   **(2 marks)**

          (Total = 10 marks)

Alisa

The following scenario relates to Questions 26 to 30.

Alisa commenced trading on 1 January 2017. Her sales since commencement have been as follows:

January to April 2017	£7,500 per month
May to August 2017	£10,000 per month
September to December 2017	£15,500 per month

The above figures are stated exclusive of value added tax (VAT). Alisa only supplies services, and these are all standard rated for VAT purposes. Alisa notified her liability to compulsorily register for VAT by the appropriate deadline.

For each of the eight months prior to the date on which she registered for VAT, Alisa paid £240 per month (inclusive of VAT) for website design services and £180 per month (exclusive of VAT) for advertising. Both of these supplies are standard rated for VAT purposes and relate to Alisa's business activity after the date from when she registered for VAT.

After registering for VAT, Alisa purchased a motor car on 1 January 2018. The motor car is used 60% for business mileage. During the quarter ended 31 March 2018, Alisa spent £456 on repairs to the motor car and £624 on fuel for both her business and private mileage. The relevant quarterly scale charge is £291. All of these figures are inclusive of VAT.

All of Alisa's customers are registered for VAT, so she appreciates that she has to issue VAT invoices when services are supplied.

26   From what date would Alisa have been required to be compulsorily registered for VAT and therefore have had to charge output VAT on her supplies of services?

Select...   ▼
30 September 2017
1 November 2017
1 October 2017
30 October 2017

(2 marks)

27   What amount of pre-registration input VAT would Alisa have been able to recover in respect of inputs incurred prior to the date on which she registered for VAT?

- ○ £468
- ○ £608
- ○ £536
- ○ £456

(2 marks)

28   What is the maximum amount of input VAT which Alisa can reclaim in respect of her motor expenses for the quarter ended 31 March 2018?

- ○ £108
- ○ £138
- ○ £180
- ○ £125

(2 marks)

29   Complete the following sentence by matching the correct due date and payment method into the relevant target area.

Alisa has to pay any VAT liability for the quarter ended 31 March 2018

by [   ] using [   ] method.

Due date	Payment method
30 April 2018	an electronic payment
7 May 2018	any payment

(2 marks)

30   Identify, by clicking on the relevant box in the table below, which of the following items of information is **NOT** required to be included by Alisa on a valid VAT invoice.

THE CUSTOMER'S VAT REGISTRATION NUMBER	THE CUSTOMER'S ADDRESS
AN INVOICE NUMBER	A DESCRIPTION OF THE SERVICES SUPPLIED

(2 marks)

(Total = 10 marks)

SECTION C – ALL three questions are compulsory and MUST be attempted

31 Joe

Joe is the managing director and 100% shareholder of OK-Joe Ltd. He has always withdrawn the entire profits of the company as director's remuneration, but given a recent increase in profitability he wants to know whether this basis of extracting the profits is beneficial.

For the year ended 5 April 2018, OK-Joe Ltd's taxable total profits, before taking account of director's remuneration, are £65,000. After allowing for employer's class 1 national insurance contributions (NIC) of £6,892, Joe's gross director's remuneration is £58,108.

The figure for employer's NIC of £6,892 does not deduct the £3,000 employment allowance as this is not available since Joe is the only employee of OK-Joe Ltd.

Required

Calculate the overall saving of tax and NIC for the year ended 5 April 2018 if Joe had instead paid himself gross director's remuneration of £8,000 and dividends of £46,170. **(10 marks)**

Notes

1   You are expected to calculate the income tax payable by Joe, the class 1 NIC payable by both Joe and OK-Joe Ltd, and the corporation tax liability of OK-Joe Ltd for the year ended 5 April 2018.

2   You should assume that the rate of corporation tax remains unchanged.

(Total = 10 marks)

32 Ashura

Ashura has been employed by Rift plc since 1 January 2015. She has also been self-employed since 1 July 2017, preparing her first accounts for the nine-month period ended 5 April 2018. The following information is available for the tax year 2017/18:

Employment

(1)   During the tax year 2017/18, Ashura was paid a gross annual salary of £56,600.

(2)   On 1 January 2018, Ashura personally paid two subscriptions. The first was a professional subscription of £320 paid to an HM Revenue & Customs' (HMRC) approved professional body. The second was a subscription of £680 to a health club which Ashura regularly uses to meet Rift plc's clients. Ashura was not reimbursed for the costs of either of these subscriptions by Rift plc.

(3)   During the tax year 2017/18, Ashura used her private motor car for business purposes. She drove 3,400 miles in the performance of her duties for Rift plc, for which the company paid her an allowance of 55 pence per mile.

(4)   During the tax year 2017/18, Ashura contributed £2,800 into Rift plc's HMRC registered occupational pension scheme and £3,400 (gross) into a personal pension scheme.

Self-employment

(1)   Ashura's tax adjusted trading loss based on her draft accounts for the nine-month period ended 5 April 2018 is £3,300. This figure is before making any adjustments required for:

(i)   Advertising expenditure of £800 incurred during January 2017. This expenditure has not been deducted in calculating the loss of £3,300.

(ii)   The cost of Ashura's office (see note (2) below).

(iii)   Capital allowances.

(2)   Ashura runs her business using one of the five rooms in her private house as an office. The total running costs of the house for the nine-month period ended 5 April 2018 were £4,350. No deduction has been made for the cost of the office in calculating the loss of £3,300.

(3)   On 10 June 2017, Ashura purchased a laptop computer for £2,600.

On 1 July 2017, Ashura purchased a motor car for £19,200. The motor car has a CO_2 emission rate of 137 grams per kilometre. During the nine-month period ended 5 April 2018, Ashura drove a total of 8,000 miles, of which 2,500 were for self-employed business journeys.

Other information

Ashura's total income for the previous four tax years is as follows:

Tax year	Total income £
2013/14	11,100
2014/15	10,800
2015/16	48,800
2016/17	54,300

Required

(a)   State **TWO** advantages for Ashura of choosing 5 April as her accounting date rather than a date early in the tax year such as 30 April. **(2 marks)**

(b)   Calculate Ashura's revised tax adjusted trading loss for the nine-month period ended 5 April 2018. **(6 marks)**

(c)   Explain why it would not be beneficial for Ashura to claim loss relief under the provisions giving relief to a loss incurred in the early years of trade.

Note. You should assume that the tax rates and allowances for the tax year 2017/18 also applied in all previous tax years. **(2 marks)**

(d)   Assuming that Ashura claims loss relief against her total income for the tax year 2017/18, calculate her taxable income for this tax year. **(5 marks)**

(Total = 15 marks)

33 Mable

Mable is a serial entrepreneur, regularly starting and disposing of businesses. On 31 July 2017, Tenth Ltd, a company owned by Mable, ceased trading. On 1 October 2017, Eleventh Ltd, another company owned by Mable, commenced trading. The following information is available:

Tenth Ltd

(1)   For the final four-month period of trading ended 31 July 2017, Tenth Ltd had a tax adjusted trading profit of £52,400. This figure is **before** taking account of capital allowances.

(2)   On 1 April 2017, the tax written down value of the company's main pool was £12,400. On 3 June 2017, Tenth Ltd purchased a laptop computer for £1,800.

   On 31 July 2017, the company sold all of the items included in the main pool at the start of the period for £28,200 and the laptop computer for £1,300. None of the items included in the main pool was sold for more than its original cost.

(3)   On 31 July 2017, Tenth Ltd sold the company's freehold office building for £180,300. The building was purchased on 3 May 2013 for £152,456, and its indexed cost on 31 July 2017 was £164,500.

(4)   During the four-month period ended 31 July 2017, Tenth Ltd let out one floor of its freehold office building which was always surplus to requirements. The floor was rented at £1,200 per month, but the tenant left owing the rent for July 2017 which Tenth Ltd was unable to recover. The total running costs of the office building for the four-month period ended 31 July 2017 were £6,300, of which one-third related to the let floor. The other two-thirds of the running costs have been deducted in calculating Tenth Ltd's tax-adjusted trading profit of £52,400.

(5)   During the four-month period ended 31 July 2017, Tenth Ltd made qualifying charitable donations of £800.

Eleventh Ltd

(1)   Eleventh Ltd's operating profit for the six-month period ended 31 March 2018 is £122,900. Depreciation of £2,580 and amortisation of leasehold property of £2,000 (see note (2) below) have been deducted in arriving at this figure.

(2)   On 1 October 2017, Eleventh Ltd acquired a leasehold office building, paying a premium of £60,000 for the grant of a 15-year lease. The office building was used for business purposes by Eleventh Ltd throughout the six-month period ended 31 March 2018.

(3)   On 1 October 2017, Eleventh Ltd purchased two new motor cars. The first motor car cost £12,600, and has a CO_2 emission rate of 110 grams per kilometre. This motor car is used as a pool car by the company's employees. The second motor car cost £13,200, and has a CO_2 emission rate of 60 grams per kilometre. This motor car is used by Mable, and 45% of the mileage is for private journeys.

(4)   On 1 October 2017, Mable made a loan of £100,000 to Eleventh Ltd at an annual interest rate of 5%. This is a commercial rate of interest, and no loan repayments were made during the period ended 31 March 2018. The loan was used to finance the company's trading activities.

Required

(a)   Calculate Tenth Ltd's taxable total profits for the four-month period ended 31 July 2017.   **(7 marks)**

(b)   Calculate Eleventh Ltd's tax adjusted trading profit for the six-month period ended 31 March 2018.
                                                                                    (8 marks)

                                                                        (Total = 15 marks)

Answers

DO NOT TURN THIS PAGE UNTIL YOU HAVE
COMPLETED THE MOCK EXAM

A plan of attack

If this were the real Taxation (TX – UK) exam and you had been told to turn over and begin, what would be going through your mind?

Perhaps you're having a panic. You've spent most of your study time on income tax and corporation tax computations (because that's what your tutor/BPP Study Text told you to do), plus a selection of other topics, and you're really not sure that you know enough. So calm down. Spend the first few moments or so **looking at the paper**, and develop a **plan of attack**.

Looking through the paper:

Section A contains **15 Objective Test (OT) questions** each worth **2 marks**. These will cover all sections of the syllabus. Some you may find easy and some more difficult. In Question 8, where you are asked to identify the true statement about self-assessment tax returns for individuals, read the possible answers at least twice before you decide which one to select. Don't spend a lot of time on anything you really don't know. For multiple choice questions you are not penalised for wrong answers, so you should answer all of them. If all else fails – guess!

Section B contains **three OT Case** scenarios. These each have **five questions** each worth **2 marks**. Make sure you read the scenario carefully before you start to answer the OTQs.

- **Questions 16 to 20** test your knowledge of inheritance tax (IHT). Question 18 is a quick question as you only need to select two answers, one is the persons responsible for payment of tax and the other is the date for payment.

- **Questions 21 to 25** concern chargeable gains for a company and for an individual. Make sure to double check your calculations to avoid losing marks for simple mistakes. This is particularly applicable to Question 25.

- **Questions 26 to 30** are about value added tax (VAT). Read the questions carefully to make sure you answer the question set. For example, in Question 26 you need to identify the date from which Alisa would have been required to be compulsorily registered, not the date on which the registration limit was exceeded.

In **Section C** you have **three constructed response (long) questions**:

- **Question 31** for **10 marks** is about whether there is an overall tax saving by taking a mixture of dividends and remuneration from a company rather than just remuneration. You need to work out the individual's income tax, the national insurance contributions for an employee and corporation tax.

- **Question 32** for **15 marks** is an income tax computation and also deals with choice of accounting date.

- **Question 33** for **15 marks** is a corporation tax question dealing with a company ceasing to trade and one commencing to trade.

Allocating your time

BPP's advice is always allocate your time **according to the marks for the question** in total and for the parts of the question. But **use common sense**. If you're confronted by an OTQ on a topic of which you know nothing, pick an answer and move on. Use the time to pick up marks elsewhere.

After the exam…**Forget about it!**

And don't worry if you found the exam difficult. More than likely other candidates will too. If this were the real thing you would need to **forget** the exam the minute you left the exam hall and **think about the next one**. Or, if it's the last one, **celebrate**!

Section A

1   £48,500

	£
Gift 1 June 2017	50,000
Less: AE 2017/18 £(3,000 – 2,000 PET 1 May 2017)	(1,000)
AE 2016/17 b/f £(3,000 – 2,500 PET 1 July 2016)	(500)
Chargeable lifetime transfer	48,500

Note that the current tax year annual exemption is used first (against the PET on 1 May 2017 and then against the CLT on 1 June 2017) and then the balance brought forward from the previous tax year.

2   114 months

Qualifying period		Months
31.3.04 – 31.3.09	Actual occupation	60
1.4.09 – 31.3.11	Employed abroad (any length with reoccupation)	24
1.4.11 – 31.3.12	Actual occupation	12
1.10.16 – 31.3.18	Last 18 months ownership	18
Qualifying months		114

Check: non-qualifying months 1.4.12 – 30.9.16 = 54 months, total period of ownership 31.3.04 – 31.3.18 = 168 months = (114 + 54) months.

3   £65,000

	£
2017/18	40,000
2014/15 £(40,000 – 42,000) = £(2,000) excess	0
2015/16 £(40,000 – 27,000)	13,000
2016/17 £(40,000 – 28,000)	12,000
Available annual allowance	65,000

Use the current tax year allowance first and then starting working forwards from the earliest available tax year (maximum three tax years before current year).

4

Number of monthly payments	**NINE**	
Monthly payment amount	**£4,770**	

$$\frac{90\% \times £47,700 \text{ (previous year VAT payable)}}{9} \qquad £4,770$$

5   £14,000

		£
30.11.09	More than seven years before commencement	0
6.6.12	Research deductible	12,000
31.7.16	Entertaining not deductible under general rules	0
15.12.16	Donation for trade purposes deductible	2,000
Deductible pre-trading expenditure		14,000

6   £3,375

	£
£(48,000 – 45,000) = 3,000 @ 2%	60
£(45,000 – 8,164) = 36,836 @ 9%	3,315
Class 1 employee's NIC payable	3,375

The answer £3,225 uses the accruals basis rather than the profits for the year ended 31 May 2017. The answer £3,585 uses a rate of 9% throughout. The answer £3,315 is just the amount chargeable at 9%.

7

Corporation tax is a direct tax on the turnover of companies.		FALSE
National insurance is a direct tax suffered by employees, employers and the self-employed on earnings.	TRUE	
Inheritance tax is a direct tax on transfers of income by individuals.		FALSE
Value added tax is a direct tax on the supply of goods and services by businesses.		FALSE

Corporation tax is a direct tax on profits (not turnover).

National insurance is a direct tax (collected directly from taxpayer either through PAYE or by self-assessment) suffered by employees (Class 1 employee's), employers (Class 1 employer's) and the self-employed (Classes 2 and 4).

Inheritance tax is a direct tax on transfers of capital (not income) by individuals.

Value added tax is an indirect tax (collected by businesses not customers) on the supply of goods and services by businesses.

8   All individuals who submit a tax return on time are able to have their tax payable calculated by HM Revenue and Customs.

> **Examining team's comments.** This question tested candidates' knowledge of various aspects of the income tax self-assessment system. The majority of candidates appreciated that there can be a requirement to file a tax return despite not receiving a notice to do so from HMRC. However, a significant number of candidates chose the last option, despite class 1 national insurance contributions (NIC) not being part of the self-assessment system. Many candidates chose the first option, not remembering that the de minimis limit of £1,000 instead relates to payments on account. All individuals who submit a tax return on time (either a paper return or electronically) are able to have the tax payable calculated by HMRC therefore the third option was the correct answer.
>
> This should have been a fairly straightforward question and it demonstrates the need to carefully read and consider each alternative – not just quickly jump to the first one that seems to fit.

9

Eric	SATISFIES	
Fran		DOES NOT SATISFY

Eric was not previously UK resident and was present in the UK for between 16 and 45 days (see table in Tax Rates and Allowances). He is therefore automatically not UK resident in the tax year 2017/18.

Fran was previously UK resident and was present in the UK for between 16 and 45 days (again, see table in Tax Rates and Allowances). Her residence status is therefore determined by the number of her UK ties so she is not automatically not UK resident in the tax year 2017/18.

10 £1,600

		£	£
2016/17	Use benefit £2,000 × 20%	400	
2017/18	Gift		
	Greater of:		
	(1) Market value at gift	1,400	
	(2) Original cost	2,000	
	Less: use benefit	(400)	
		1,600	
			1,600

11 £114,000

	£	£
31.5.13 PET now chargeable		500,000
Nil rate band at death	325,000	
Less: 30.4.12 PET now chargeable	(300,000)	
		(25,000)
Transfer chargeable to IHT @ 40%		475,000
£475,000 @ 40%		190,000
Less: taper relief (4 to 5 years) @ 40%		(76,000)
IHT payable as a result of Cora's death		114,000

12

Penalty		£60
Interest	£14	

The due date for payment of the balancing payment was 31 January 2019.

Interest is due for the period February 2019 to June 2019 (working in whole months) so is £1,200 × 2.75% × 5/12 = £14.

The penalty date was 30 days after the due date and so payment was less than five months after the penalty date. The penalty due is £1,200 × 5% = £60.

13 £6,500

	Y/e 31.3.17	Y/e 31.3.18
	£	£
Trading income	79,400	0
Property business income	6,800	10,100
Total profits	86,200	10,100
Less: loss against total profits	(86,200)	(10,100)
Taxable trading profits	0	0

Loss memorandum

	£
Trading loss incurred in y/e 31.3.18	102,800
Less: used in y/e 31.3.18	(10,100)
used in y/e 31.3.17	(86,200)
Loss unrelieved	6,500

The qualifying charitable donations are unrelieved.

14   Deferring the CGT due date

The CGT due date will be 31 January following the end of the tax year of the disposal for both spouses/civil partners.

Note the three ways in which tax planning for spouses can be used: making the best use of annual exempt amounts; reducing the amount of CGT payable (eg if one spouse has unused basic rate band); and making best use of capital losses.

15   £2,420

2016/17 Relevant amount $\dfrac{£4,840}{2}$ £2,420

Section B

Adana

16   £585,000

	£
Adana: own nil rate band (lifetime transfer more than 7 years before death)	325,000
Adana's husband: 80% × £325,000 (use 2017/18 nil rate band)	260,000
Maximum nil rate band available	585,000

17   £263,700

	£
Mortgage (debt incurred for consideration)	220,000
Income tax (statutory debt)	43,700
Total deductions	263,700

The legal fees are not deductible as the agreement to pay them is not legally enforceable because no consideration is received.

18

Responsible persons		PERSONNAL RESPRESENTATIVES OF ADANA'S ESTATE
Due date for payment		30 SEPTEMBER 2018

The beneficiaries of Adana's estate will bear the IHT, as it will reduce the amount due to them from the estate, but it is her personal representatives (the executors of her will) who are responsible for making the payment. The IHT on a death estate is due by the end of six months from the end of the month of death.

19   £0

There would be no IHT saving by making either of these gifts as both are chargeable in the same way as gifting the entire estate to Adana's children. The only exempt transfer in relation to the death estate for Taxation (TX – UK) purposes is a gift to a spouse/civil partner.

20   £207,750

	£
Extra IHT on death estate: £650,000 × 40%	260,000
Less: lifetime IHT paid	(52,250)
IHT saving	207,750

Kat Ltd and Kitten

Text references. Chargeable gains for companies is dealt with in Chapter 20. Computation of CGT is covered in Chapter 13 and business reliefs in Chapter 15.

Top tips. Double check your computations! Just because your answer is one of those given, it does not necessarily mean that it is correct.

Easy marks. The indexation allowance in Question 21 was made easier by both the cost and the enhancement expenditure being incurred in the same month.

Examining team's report. Questions involving the indexation allowance, the crystallisation date for a heldover gain and the base cost of shares following a rights issue were well answered.

One of the questions asked for the base cost of an asset against which a rollover relief claim had been made. Although the correct answer was the most popular (with candidates appreciating that the amount of proceeds not reinvested could not be rolled over), a significant number of candidates ignored the amount of proceeds not reinvested and rolled over the full amount of gain.

Another question asked for the taxpayer's CGT liability. Again, the correct answer (the disposal qualifying for entrepreneurs' relief utilised the available basic rate tax band, with the other gain therefore taxed at [20]%) was marginally the most popular. However, many candidates ignored the impact of entrepreneurs' relief on the basic rate band or did not deduct the annual exempt amount.

These two less well answered questions demonstrate the need to be very careful with all aspects of a calculation. One simple mistake means the loss of the two marks available.

21   £70,146

	£
$\dfrac{(270.2 - 188.6)}{188.6} = 0.433 \times £162,000 \; (138,600 + 23,400)$	70,146

22   £243,300

	£
Gain	120,700
Immediately chargeable = amount not reinvested £(364,000 – 272,000)	(92,000)
Deduction from base cost of new warehouse	28,700

The base cost of the new warehouse is £(272,000 –28,700) = £243,300.

23   10 years from 30 September 2018

The gain will become chargeable on the latest of: the date of disposal of the replacement asset; the date it ceases to be used in the trade; and 10 years from its acquisition.

24 £63,200

Date	Transaction	No. of shares	Cost £
7 July 2009	Acquisition at par £1 cost for each £1 share bought	90,000	90,000
22 September 2012	Rights issue 2 new shares for every 3 original shares held @ £6.40	60,000	384,000
		150,000	474,000
5 October 2017	Sale	(20,000)	(63,200)
c/f		130,000	410,800

25 £17,540

	ER gain £	Non-ER gain £
Gains	142,200	27,900
Less: annual exempt amount (best use)		(11,300)
Taxable gains	142,200	16,600
Tax @ 10%/20%	14,220	3,320
Total CGT payable		£17,540

The basic rate band is treated as being used first by the gain qualifying for entrepreneurs' relief. This means that the band is entirely used up and so the tax on the gain not qualifying for entrepreneurs' relief is taxable at 20%.

The answer £15,880 uses the basic rate of 10% on the gain not qualifying for entrepreneurs' relief. The answer £19,800 does not deduct the annual exempt amount. The answer £18,670 sets the annual exempt amount against the gain qualifying for entrepreneurs' relief.

Alisa

Text references. Value added tax is covered in Chapters 24 and 25.

Top tips. For Question 28 note that the fuel scale charge is the basis for **output** tax charged in relation to private use fuel. You were asked to identify the **input** tax which could be reclaimed.

Easy marks. There were easy marks in Question 26 for identifying the date from which the trader would have been required to be compulsorily registered for VAT. However, it was important to read the question carefully to see exactly what was being asked – it was **not** the date on which the registration threshold was reached.

Examining team's comments. Generally, this case question was not as well answered as the previous two. However, candidates made reasonable attempts at questions on the recovery of pre-registration input VAT, how and by when the VAT liability would be paid, and the information included on a valid VAT invoice.

A further question asked for the date of compulsory VAT registration. Although the correct answer was the most popular, many candidates opted for the end of the month in which the registration limit was exceeded.

One of the questions asked for the maximum amount of input VAT which could be reclaimed in respect of motor expenses. The correct answer (ignoring private use) was by a long way the most popular, but a significant number of candidates either adjusted for private use or used the fuel scale charge instead of the actual fuel figure.

26   1 November 2017

	£
January to April 2017 4 × £7,500	30,000
May to August 2017 4 × £10,000	40,000
September 2017	15,500
	85,500

The registration threshold of £85,000 is met by 30 September 2017. Alisa should therefore have notified HMRC by 30 October 2017, with registration effective from 1 November 2017.

27   £456

	£
Website design service: £240 × 6 × 1/6	240
Advertising: £180 × 6 × 20%	216
Input tax reclaimable	456

Pre-registration input tax is recoverable on services which are supplied within six months prior to registration. Note the different calculations for VAT-inclusive and VAT-exclusive amounts.

28   £180

	£
Repairs	456
Fuel	624
	1,080

Input tax reclaimable £1,080 × 1/6	180

Full input tax can be reclaimed on the repairs to the car - the private use of the car is not relevant.

All the input tax will be reclaimed on fuel and the adjustment to private use will be made by charging output tax based on the fuel scale charge.

29   Alisa has to pay any VAT liability for the quarter ended 31 March 2018

by   **7 May 2018**   using   **an electronic payment**   method.

30

THE CUSTOMER'S VAT REGISTRATION NUMBER	

Section C

31 Joe

Marking scheme

	Marks
Profits withdrawn as director's remuneration	
Income tax	1½
Class 1 employee's NIC	1½
Corporation tax	½
Profits withdrawn as a mix of director's remuneration and dividends	
Income tax	3
Class 1 NIC	1
Corporation tax	1½
Overall tax saving	1
	10

Joe – Income tax liability 2017/18 if just remuneration

	Non-savings income £
Director's remuneration/Net income	58,108
Less personal allowance	(11,500)
Taxable income	46,608
Tax	
£33,500 @ 20%	6,700
£(46,608 – 33,500) = 13,108 @ 40%	5,243
Income tax payable	11,943

Joe – National insurance contributions 2017/18 if just remuneration

	£
£(58,108 – 45,000) = 13,108 @ 2%	262
£(45,000 – 8,164) = 36,836 @ 12%	4,420
Class 1 employee's NIC payable	4,682

There will be no corporation tax payable since the profits are entirely withdrawn as director's remuneration (including Class 1 employer's NIC).

Joe – Income tax liability 2017/18 if mix of remuneration and dividends

	Non-savings income £	Dividend income £	Total income £
Director's remuneration	8,000		
Dividends		46,170	
Net income	8,000	46,170	54,170
Less personal allowance	(8,000)	(3,500)	
Taxable income	0	42,670	42,670

Tax	
£5,000 @ 0% (dividend nil rate band)	0
£(33,500 – 5,000) = 28,500 @ 7.5%	2,137
£(42,670 – 33,500) = 9,170 @ 38.1%	3,494
Income tax payable	5,631

There will be no Class 1 NIC for either OK-Joe Ltd or Joe as the earnings are below the NIC employee's and employer's thresholds.

Corporation tax liability of OK-Joe Ltd for the year ended 5 April 2018 if mix of remuneration and divide

	£
Trading profit	65,000
Less director's remuneration	(8,000)
Taxable trading profit	57,000
Corporation tax £57,000 @ 19%	10,830

Summary of tax and NIC liabilities

	Remuneration only £	Mix of remuneration and dividends £
Income tax	11,943	5,631
Class 1 NIC employee's	4,682	0
Class 1 NIC employer's	6,892	0
Corporation tax	0	10,830
Total tax and NIC	23,517	16,461

Therefore the overall tax and NIC saving if Joe extracts profits using a mix of director's remuneration and dividends is £(23,517 – 16,461) = £7,056.

32 Ashura

Text references. Assessable trading income is dealt with in Chapter 9, capital allowances in Chapter 8 and losses in Chapter 10. Employment income is dealt with in Chapters 3 and 4. Taxable income is covered in Chapter 2.

Top tips. In part (d), note the difference between the tax treatment of occupational pension contributions (paid gross and deducted in the income computation giving tax relief at all rates) and personal pension contributions (basic rate relief given by being paid net and further tax relief being given by increasing the basic rate limit so not relevant to this question which only required a calculation of taxable income).

Easy marks. There were some easy marks in part (b) for straightforward adjustments to profit. Part (d) had some easy marks for dealing with the mileage allowance and subscriptions.

Examining team's comments. For part (a), the requirement was to state two advantages of the taxpayer choosing 5 April as an accounting date rather than a date early in the tax year such as 30 April. There were three obvious advantages, and many candidates correctly explained that the application of the basis period rules is more straightforward and that there will be no overlap profits. Less well prepared candidates instead covered the advantages of a 30 April accounting date, so not surprisingly did not achieve high marks.

Part (b) required a calculation of the taxpayer's revised tax adjusted trading loss for the first period of account. This meant adjusting for pre-trading expenditure, use of one of the five rooms in the taxpayer's private house as an office, and capital allowances. There were many good answers to this section, although a common mistake was to not appreciate that each of the three adjustments increased (not decreased) the trading loss.

For part (c), candidates had to explain why it was not beneficial for the taxpayer to claim loss relief under the provisions giving relief to a loss incurred in the early years of trade. It should have been fairly obvious that such a claim would have wasted the personal allowance and not resulted in any tax saving. This section was not as well answered, with many candidates not appreciating that the loss could only be carried back for three years. Some candidates actually explained why a claim would be beneficial.

Part (d) required a calculation of the taxpayer's taxable income (on the basis that loss relief was claimed against total income). This meant taking account of two subscriptions (only one of which was deductible), a mileage allowance deduction for the use of a private motor car for business purposes, and pension contributions (both to an occupational scheme and a personal pension scheme). This section was generally well answered, although many candidates wasted time by calculating the tax liability. The occupational pension scheme contribution was often grossed up (such contributions are not paid net of tax). Many candidates made things more difficult than they needed to be by attempting this section before section (b).

Marking scheme

			Marks
(a)	Two advantages of basis period ending on 5 April (one mark for each)		2
(b)	Trading loss	2½	
	Capital allowances	3½	
			6
(c)	Early years loss relief		2
(d)	Salary	½	
	Mileage	1	
	Pension	1	
	Subscriptions	1	
	Loss	1	
	Personal allowance	½	
			5
			15

(a) **Advantages of choosing 5 April as accounting date rather than earlier date in tax year**

Any **two** of:

The basis period rules are more straightforward.

On commencement, there will be no overlap profits.

On cessation, the final basis period will be a maximum of 12 months. If a date earlier in the tax year is chosen, the final basis period will be longer, up to 23 months with a 30 April year end.

(b) **Ashura – Trading loss for the nine-month period ended 5 April 2018**

	£
Trading loss	(3,300)
Less: pre-trading expenditure	(800)
use of office £4,350 × 1/5	(870)
capital allowance (W)	(2,960)
Adjusted trading loss	(7,930)

Working – Capital allowances

	AIA £	Main pool £	Motor car £	Allowances £
9 months to 5 April 2018				
Additions				
Laptop	2,600			
AIA	(2,600)			2,600
Transfer to pool	0	0		
Motor car			19,200	
WDA @ 8% × 9/12			(1,152) × 2,500/8,000	360
WDA c/f		0	18,048	
Allowances				2,960

Tutorial notes

1   The advertising expenditure incurred in January 2017 is pre-trading expenditure which is treated as incurred on the first day of trading, 1 July 2017. An adjustment is therefore required.

2   Ashura's motor car has CO_2 emissions over 130g/km and therefore only qualifies for writing down allowance at the rate of 8%.

3   The laptop computer purchased on 10 June 2017 is pre-trading capital expenditure and is therefore treated as incurred on 1 July 2017.

(c) **Early years trading loss relief**

Under early years trading loss relief, the loss of £7,930 in 2017/18 would be relieved against her total income of £10,800 in 2014/15 since this is the earliest of the three years 2014/15, 2015/16 and 2016/17.

However, since Ashura's total income for 2014/15 is covered by her personal allowance of £11,500 (assumed), there would be no tax saving by making an early years loss relief claim.

(d)   **Ashura – Taxable income 2017/18**

		£
Salary		56,600
Mileage allowance 3,400 × 10p (55p – 45p)		340
Pension contributions	Occupational	(2,800)
	Personal	(0)
Subscriptions	Professional	(320)
	Health club	(0)
Total income		53,820
Less: loss relief against total income		(7,930)
Net income		45,890
Less: personal allowance		(11,500)
Taxable income		34,390

Tutorial notes

1   The personal pension scheme contribution does not affect the calculation of taxable income, but will instead increase Ashura's basic rate limit by the gross contribution of £3,400.

2   The health club subscription is not an allowable deduction because membership is not a necessary expense for Ashura to carry out the duties of her employment.

3   The loss relief cap does not apply because Ashura's trading loss is less than the greater of £50,000 and 25% of her total income.

33 Mable

Text references. The computation of taxable total profits is covered in Chapter 19. The adjustment to trading profits is dealt with in Chapter 7 and capital allowances in Chapter 8. Property business income is covered in Chapter 5.

Top tips. Be careful when working with short accounting periods. For example, in part (b) you needed to adjust the writing down allowance so that only six months of allowances were given.

Easy marks. There were some easy marks in part (b) for adjustments to profits which should have been well-known.

Examining team's comments. Part (a) was generally very well answered, requiring a calculation of the first company's taxable total profits for the final period of trading. This involved calculating the balancing charge on cessation (all of the items included in the company's main pool being sold), the chargeable gain on the sale of the company's freehold office building and the property business income in respect of one floor of the office building which had been let out. The company has also made qualifying charitable donations. The only consistent problem here was the capital allowances, with many candidates not appreciating that neither the annual investment allowance (a laptop computer had been purchased during the period) nor writing down allowances are given in the period of cessation. A few candidates ignored the cessation altogether and therefore did not calculate a balancing charge.

Part (b) was also well answered on the whole, requiring a calculation of the second company's tax adjusted trading profit for the initial period of trading. This involved adjusting for depreciation and amortisation, calculating the deduction in respect of a lease premium, calculating capital allowances for two motor cars (one car was used as a pool car by the company's employees, with the other having private use by a director) and deducting loan interest in respect of a loan made to the company by a director/owner. Some candidates attempted to calculate benefits in respect of the motor cars and loan which, although correct as regards the motor cars, had no relevance to the requirement. Perhaps not surprisingly, the deduction for the lease premium caused quite a few problems.

		Marks
(a)	Taxable total profits	2½
	Balancing charge	3
	Property business income	1½
		7
(b)	Profit and add-backs	1½
	Interest payable	1
	Lease premium	2½
	Capital allowances	3
		8
		15

(a) **Tenth Ltd – Taxable total profits for the four-month period ended 31 July 2017**

	£
Trading profits	52,400
Balancing charge (W1)	15,300
Adjusted trading profits	67,700
Property business income (W2)	1,500
Chargeable gain £(180,300 – 164,500)	15,800
Total profits	85,000
Less qualifying charitable donations	(800)
Taxable total profits	84,200

Workings

1   *Capital allowances*

	Main pool £	Allowances £
TWDV brought forward	12,400	
Addition		
Laptop computer	1,800	
Disposal		
Main pool items £(28,200 + 1,300)	(29,500)	
Balancing charge	15,300	(15,300)

2   *Property business income*

	£
Rent receivable £1,200 × 4	4,800
Less: Impairment loss	(1,200)
Running costs £6,300 × 1/3	(2,100)
Property business income	1,500

(b) **Eleventh Ltd – Tax adjusted trading profit for the six-month period ended 31 March 2018**

	£
Operating profit	122,900
Add: depreciation	2,580
amortisation	2,000
Less: deduction for lease premium (W1)	(1,440)
interest payable £100,000 × 5% × 6/12	(2,500)
capital allowances (W2)	(14,334)
Tax adjusted trading profit	109,206

Workings

1   *Deduction for lease premium*

	£
Premium paid	60,000
Less: £60,000 × 2% × (15 −1)	(16,800)
Amount taxable on landlord as property business income	43,200

Deduction $\dfrac{£43,200}{15} \times 6/12$ 1,440

2   *Capital allowances*

	FYA £	Main pool £	Allowances £
Addition not qualifying for FYA			
Motor car [1]		12,600	
WDA @ 18% × 6/12		(1,134)	1,134
Addition qualifying for FYA			
Motor car [2]	13,200		
FYA @ 100%	(13,200)		13,200
Transfer to pool	0	0	
TWDV carried forward		11,466	
Allowances			14,334

Tutorial notes

1   Motor car [1] has CO_2 emissions of between 76 and 130g/km. It therefore goes into the main pool and has writing down allowances at 18% scaled down for the short accounting period.

2   Motor car [2] is new and has CO_2 emissions up to 75g/km so therefore qualifies for the 100% first year allowance. This is not scaled down for the short accounting period. The private use of the motor car is not relevant for the company.

ACCA Applied Skills

Taxation (TX – UK)

Mock Exam 2
(Specimen exam CBE updated to FA 2017)

Question Paper	
Time allowed	**3 hours**
This paper is divided into three sections:	
Section A – ALL 15 questions are compulsory and MUST be attempted.	
Section B – ALL 15 questions are compulsory and MUST be attempted.	
Section C – ALL THREE questions are compulsory and MUST be attempted.	

DO NOT OPEN THIS PAPER UNTIL YOU ARE READY TO START UNDER EXAMINATION CONDITIONS

SECTION A: ALL 15 questions are compulsory and MUST be attempted

1   William is self-employed, and his tax adjusted trading profit for the year ended 5 April 2018 was £82,700. During the tax year 2017/18, William contributed £5,400 (gross) into a personal pension scheme.

What amount of Class 4 national insurance contributions (NIC) will William pay for the tax year 2017/18?

O   £4,217
O   £6,708
O   £4,069
O   £3,315   **(2 marks)**

---

2   You are a trainee Chartered Certified Accountant and your firm has a client who has refused to disclose a chargeable gain to HM Revenue & Customs (HMRC).

From an ethical viewpoint, which **TWO** of the following actions could be expected of your firm?

☐   Reporting under the money laundering regulations
☐   Advising the client to make disclosure
☐   Informing HMRC of the non-disclosure
☐   Warning the client that your firm will be reporting the non-disclosure   **(2 marks)**

---

3   Martin is self-employed and for the year ended 5 April 2018 his trading profit was £109,400. During the tax year 2017/18, Martin made a gift aid donation of £800 (gross) to a national charity.

What amount of personal allowance will Martin be entitled to for the tax year 2017/18?

£ ☐   **(2 marks)**

---

4   For the year ended 31 March 2018, Halo Ltd made a trading loss of £180,000.

Halo Ltd has owned 100% of the ordinary share capital of Shallow Ltd since it began trading on 1 July 2017. For the year ended 30 June 2018, Shallow Ltd will make a trading profit of £224,000.

Neither company has any other taxable profits or allowable losses.

What is the maximum amount of group relief which Shallow Ltd can claim from Halo Ltd in respect of the trading loss of £180,000 for the year ended 31 March 2018?

O   £180,000
O   £168,000
O   £45,000
O   £135,000   **(2 marks)**

---

5   For the year ended 31 March 2017, Sizeable Ltd had taxable total profits of £820,000, and for the year ended 31 March 2018 had taxable total profits of £970,000. The profits accrue evenly throughout the year.

Sizeable Ltd has had one 51% group company for many years.

How will Sizeable Ltd pay its corporation tax liability for the year ended 31 March 2018?

O   Nine instalments of £16,400 and a balancing payment of £36,700
O   Four instalments of £46,075
O   Four instalments of £41,000 and a balancing payment of £20,300
O   One payment of £184,300   **(2 marks)**

6   For the year ended 31 December 2017, Lateness Ltd had a corporation tax liability of £60,000, which it did not pay until 31 March 2019. Lateness Ltd is not a large company.

How much interest will Lateness Ltd be charged by HM Revenue & Customs (HMRC) in respect of the late payment of its corporation tax liability for the year ended 31 December 2017?

Select...   ▼
£825
£2,062
£275
£412

(2 marks)

---

7   On 26 November 2017 Alice sold an antique table for £8,700. The antique table had been purchased on 16 May 2013 for £3,800.

What is Alice's chargeable gain in respect of the disposal of the antique table?

○   £4,500
○   £1,620
○   £4,900
○   £0

(2 marks)

---

8   On 14 November 2017, Jane made a cash gift to a trust of £800,000 (after deducting all available exemptions). Jane paid the inheritance tax arising from this gift. Jane has not made any other lifetime gifts.

What amount of lifetime inheritance tax would have been payable in respect of Jane's gift to the trust?

£	

(2 marks)

---

9   During the tax year 2017/18, Mildred made four cash gifts to her grandchildren.

For each of the gifts listed below, click in the box to indicate whether the gift will be exempt or not exempt from inheritance tax under the small gifts exemption.

£400 to Alfred	EXEMPT	NOT EXEMPT
£140 to Minnie	EXEMPT	NOT EXEMPT
A further £280 to Minnie	EXEMPT	NOT EXEMPT
£175 to Winifred	EXEMPT	NOT EXEMPT

(2 marks)

---

10   For the quarter ended 31 March 2018, Faro had standard rated sales of £49,750 and standard rated expenses of £22,750. Both figures are exclusive of value added tax (VAT).

Faro uses the flat rate scheme to calculate the amount of VAT payable, with the relevant scheme percentage for her trade being 12%. The percentage reduction for the first year of VAT registration is not available.

How much VAT will Faro have to pay to HM Revenue & Customs (HMRC) for the quarter ended 31 March 2018?

○   £5,970
○   £3,888
○   £5,400
○   £7,164

(2 marks)

11   Which **TWO** of the following assets will **ALWAYS** be exempt from capital gains tax?

☐ A motor car suitable for private use

☐ A chattel

☐ A UK government security (gilt)

☐ A house   **(2 marks)**

12   Winston invested £8,000 into a cash individual savings account (ISA) during the tax year 2017/18. He now wants to invest into a stocks and shares ISA.

What is the maximum possible amount which Winston can invest into a stocks and shares ISA for the tax year 2017/18?

○ £20,000

○ £12,000

○ £0

○ £10,000   **(2 marks)**

13   Ming is self-employed.

For each of the types of records listed below, click in the box to indicate the date until which Ming must retain the records used in preparing her self-assessment tax return for the tax year 2017/18.

Business records	31 JANUARY 2020	31 JANUARY 2024
Non-business records	31 JANUARY 2020	31 JANUARY 2024

(2 marks)

14   Moon Ltd has had the following results:

Period	Profit/(loss)
	£
Year ended 31 December 2017	(105,000)
Four-month period ended 31 December 2016	43,000
Year ended 31 August 2016	96,000

The company does not have any other income.

How much of Moon Ltd's trading loss for the year ended 31 December 2017 can be relieved against its total profits of £96,000 for the year ended 31 August 2016?

○ £64,000

○ £96,000

○ £70,000

○ £62,000   **(2 marks)**

15   Nigel has not previously been resident in the UK, being in the UK for less than 20 days each tax year. For the tax year 2017/18, he has three ties with the UK.

What is the maximum number of days which Nigel could spend in the UK during the tax year 2017/18 without being treated as resident in the UK for that year?

○ 90 days

○ 182 days

○ 45 days

○ 120 days   **(2 marks)**

(Total = 30 marks)

SECTION B – ALL 15 questions are compulsory and MUST be attempted

Delroy and Marlon

The following scenario relates to Questions 16 to 20.

Delroy and Grant

On 10 January 2018, Delroy made a gift of 25,000 £1 ordinary shares in Dub Ltd, an unquoted trading company, to his son, Grant. The market value of the shares on that date was £240,000. Delroy had subscribed for the 25,000 shares in Dub Ltd at par on 1 July 2007. Delroy and Grant have elected to hold over the gain as a gift of a business asset.

Grant sold the 25,000 shares in Dub Ltd on 18 March 2018 for £240,000.

Dub Ltd has a share capital of 100,000 £1 ordinary shares. Delroy was the sales director of the company from its incorporation on 1 July 2007 until 10 January 2018. Grant has never been an employee or a director of Dub Ltd.

For the tax year 2017/18 Delroy and Grant are both higher rate taxpayers. They have each made other disposals of assets during the tax year 2017/18, and therefore they have both already utilised their annual exempt amount for this year.

Marlon and Alvita

On 28 March 2018, Marlon sold a residential property for £497,000, which he had owned individually. The property had been purchased on 22 October 2002 for £152,600.

Throughout the period of ownership the property was occupied by Marlon and his wife, Alvita, as their main residence. One-third of the property was always used exclusively for business purposes by the couple. Entrepreneurs' relief is not available in respect of this disposal.

For the tax year 2017/18, Marlon is a higher rate taxpayer, but Alvita did not have any taxable income. This will remain the case for the tax year 2018/19. Neither of them has made any other disposals of assets during the year.

16 What is Grant's capital gains tax (CGT) liability for the tax year 2017/18 in respect of the disposal of the shares in Dub Ltd?

    ○   £43,000
    ○   £21,500
    ○   £0
    ○   £40,740   **(2 marks)**

---

17 Which **TWO** of the following statements would have been true in relation to the CGT implications if Delroy had instead sold the 25,000 shares in Dub Ltd himself for £240,000 on 10 January 2018, and then gifted the cash proceeds to Grant?

    ☐   Entrepreneurs' relief would have been available.
    ☐   The CGT liability would have been paid later.
    ☐   The cash gift would not have been a chargeable disposal.
    ☐   The cash gift would have qualified for holdover relief.   **(2 marks)**

---

18 What is Marlon's chargeable gain for the tax year 2017/18?

    ○   £229,600
    ○   £0
    ○   £114,800
    ○   £344,400   **(2 marks)**

19   What is the amount of CGT which could have been saved if Marlon had transferred 50% ownership of the residential property to Alvita prior to its disposal?

    ○   £3,164
    ○   £6,514
    ○   £3,350
    ○   £12,544   **(2 marks)**

20   Why would it have been beneficial if Marlon had delayed the sale of the residential property until 6 April 2018?

Select...   ▼
A lower rate of CGT would have been applicable.
Two annual exempt amounts would have been available.
Principal private residence relief would have been greater.
The CGT liability would have been paid later.

(2 marks)

(Total = 10 marks)

Opal

The following scenario relates to Questions 21 to 25.

You should assume that today's date is 15 March 2018.

Opal is aged 71 and has a chargeable estate for inheritance tax (IHT) purposes valued at £950,000.

She owns two investment properties respectively valued at £374,000 and £442,000. The first property has an outstanding repayment mortgage of £160,000, and the second property has an outstanding endowment mortgage of £92,000.

Opal owes £22,400 in respect of a personal loan from a bank, and she has also verbally promised to pay legal fees of £4,600 incurred by her nephew. Opal expects the cost of her funeral to be £5,200, and this cost will be covered by the £6,000 she has invested in an individual savings account (ISA).

Under the terms of her will, Opal has left all of her estate to her children. Opal's husband is still alive.

On 14 August 2008, Opal had made a gift of £100,000 to her daughter, and on 7 November 2017, she made a gift of £220,000 to her son. Both these figures are after deducting all available exemptions.

The nil rate band for the tax year 2008/09 is £312,000.

You should assume that both the value of Opal's estate and the nil rate band will remain unchanged for future years.

21   What is the net value for the two properties, and related mortgages, which will have been included in the calculation of Opal's chargeable estate of £950,000?

    ○   £816,000
    ○   £564,000
    ○   £656,000
    ○   £724,000   **(2 marks)**

22 Which **TWO** of the following amounts will have been deducted in calculating Opal's chargeable estate of £950,000?

☐ Personal loan from a bank of £22,400

☐ Promise to pay legal fees of £4,600

☐ Funeral cost of £5,200

☐ ISA investment of £6,000   **(2 marks)**

23 What amount of IHT will be payable in respect of Opal's chargeable estate valued at £950,000 were she to die on 20 March 2018?

○ £250,000

○ £338,000

○ £378,000

○ £335,600   **(2 marks)**

24 By how much would the IHT payable on Opal's death be reduced if she were to live for another seven years until 20 March 2025, compared to if she were to die on 20 March 2018?

Select...   ▼
£88,000
£40,000
£128,000
£0

(2 marks)

25 Which **TWO** of the following conditions must be met if Opal wants to make gifts out of her income, so that these gifts are exempt from IHT?

☐ The gifts cannot exceed 10% of income.

☐ The gifts must be habitual.

☐ Opal must have enough remaining income to maintain her normal standard of living.

☐ Opal must make the gifts monthly or quarterly.   **(2 marks)**

(Total = 10 marks)

Glacier Ltd

The following scenario relates to Questions 26 to 30.

The following information is available in respect of Glacier Ltd's value added tax (VAT) for the quarter ended 31 March 2018:

(1) Invoices were issued for sales of £44,600 to VAT registered customers. Of this figure, £35,200 was in respect of exempt sales and the balance in respect of standard rated sales. The standard rated sales figure is exclusive of VAT.

(2) In addition to the above, on 1 March 2018 Glacier Ltd issued a VAT invoice for £8,000 plus VAT of £1,600 to a VAT registered customer in respect of a contract which will be completed on 15 April 2018. The customer paid for the contract in two instalments of £4,800 on 31 March 2018 and 30 April 2018.

(3) The managing director of Glacier Ltd is provided with free fuel for private mileage driven in her company motor car. During the quarter ended 31 March 2018, the total cost of fuel for business and private mileage was £720, of which £270 was for private mileage. The relevant quarterly scale charge is £408. All of these figures are inclusive of VAT.

For the quarters ended 30 September 2016 and 30 June 2017, Glacier Ltd was one month late in submitting its VAT returns and in paying the related VAT liabilities. All of the company's other VAT returns have been submitted on time.

26   What is the amount of output VAT payable by Glacier Ltd in respect of its sales for the quarter ended 31 March 2018?

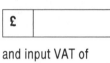

Select... ▼
£2,680
£3,480
£10,520
£1,880

(2 marks)

27   Calculate the amounts required to complete the following sentence:

Glacier Ltd will include output VAT of

£ [ ]

and input VAT of

£ [ ]

on its VAT return for the quarter ended 31 March 2018 in respect of the managing director's company motor car.   **(2 marks)**

28   What surcharge penalty could Glacier Ltd be charged if the company is one month late in paying its VAT liability for the quarter ended 31 March 2018?

○   5% of the VAT liability
○   2% of the VAT liability
○   There will be no penalty
○   10% of the VAT liability   **(2 marks)**

29   What is the minimum requirement which Glacier Ltd needs to meet in order to revert to a clean default surcharge record?

○   Submit four consecutive VAT returns on time
○   Submit any four VAT returns on time and also pay the related VAT liabilities on time
○   Pay four consecutive VAT liabilities on time
○   Submit four consecutive VAT returns on time and also pay the related VAT liabilities on time
       (2 marks)

30   Complete the following sentence by matching one of the 'types of supply' and one of the 'types of customer' into each target area.

Glacier Ltd will be required to issue a VAT invoice when [   ]

is made to [   ] .

Types of supply	Types of customer
a standard rated supply	a VAT registered customer
any type of supply	any customer

(2 marks)

(Total = 10 marks)

SECTION C – ALL three questions are compulsory and MUST be attempted

31 Sarah

You should assume that today's date is 1 March 2017.

Sarah is currently self-employed. If she continues to trade on a self-employed basis, her total income tax liability and national insurance contributions (NIC) for the tax year 2017/18 will be £12,263.

However, Sarah is considering incorporating her business on 6 April 2017. The forecast taxable total profits of the new limited company for the year ended 5 April 2018 will be £50,000 (before taking account of any director's remuneration). Sarah will pay herself gross director's remuneration of £30,000 and dividends of £10,000. The balance of the profits will remain undrawn within the new company.

Required

(a) Determine whether or not there will be an overall saving of tax and national insurance contributions (NIC) for the year ended 5 April 2018 if Sarah incorporates her business on 6 April 2017.

   Notes

   1   You are expected to calculate the income tax payable by Sarah, the Class 1 NIC payable by Sarah and the new limited company, and the corporation tax liability of the new limited company for the year ended 5 April 2018.

   2   The new limited company will not be entitled to the NIC annual employment allowance.

   3   You should assume that the rates of corporation tax remain unchanged.   **(8 marks)**

(b) Advise Sarah as to why her proposed basis of extracting profits from the new limited company is not optimum for tax purposes, and suggest how the mix of director's remuneration and dividends could therefore be improved.

   Note. You are not expected to calculate any revised tax or NIC figures.   **(2 marks)**

(Total = 10 marks)

32 Simon

On 6 April 2017, Simon commenced employment with Echo Ltd. On 1 January 2018, he commenced in partnership with Art, preparing accounts to 30 April. The following information is available for the tax year 2017/18:

Employment

(1)   During the tax year 2017/18, Simon was paid a gross annual salary of £23,700.

(2)   Throughout the tax year 2017/18, Echo Ltd provided Simon with living accommodation. The company had purchased the property in 2007 for £89,000, and it was valued at £143,000 on 6 April 2017. The annual value of the property is £4,600. The property was furnished by Echo Ltd during March 2017 at a cost of £9,400. The living accommodation is not job related.

(3)   On 1 December 2017, Echo Ltd provided Simon with an interest-free loan of £84,000, which he used to purchase a holiday cottage.

Partnership

(1)   The partnership's tax adjusted trading profit for the four-month period ended 30 April 2018 is £29,700. This figure is before taking account of capital allowances.

(2)   The only item of plant and machinery owned by the partnership is a motor car which cost £18,750 on 1 February 2018. The motor car has a CO_2 emission rate of 155 grams per kilometre. It is used by Art, and 40% of the mileage is for private journeys.

(3)   Profits are shared 40% to Simon and 60% to Art. This is after paying an annual salary of £6,000 to Art.

Property income

(1) Simon owns a freehold house which is let out furnished. The property was let throughout the tax year 2017/18 at a monthly rent of £660.

(2) During the tax year 2017/18, Simon paid council tax and water rates totalling £1,320 in respect of the property. He also replaced the property's washing machine during March 2018. The old washing machine was sold for £70, being replaced by a washer-dryer costing £970. The cost of a similar washing machine would have been £730.

Required

(a) Calculate Simon's taxable income for the tax year 2017/18. **(13 marks)**

(b) State **TWO** advantages for the partnership of choosing 30 April as its accounting date rather than 5 April.

(2 marks)

(Total = 15 marks)

33 Naive Ltd

(a) You are a trainee accountant and your manager has asked you to correct a corporation tax computation which has been prepared by the managing director of Naive Ltd. The corporation tax computation is for the year ended 31 March 2018 and contains a significant number of errors:

Naive Ltd – Corporation tax computation for the year ended 31 March 2018

	£
Trading profit (working 1)	372,900
Loan interest received (working 2)	32,100
	405,000
Corporation tax (405,000 at 19%)	76,950

Workings

1 *Trading profit*

	£
Operating profit before interest and taxation	274,530
Depreciation	15,740
Donations to political parties	400
Qualifying charitable donations	900
Accountancy	2,300
Legal fees in connection with the issue of loan notes (the loan was used to finance the company's trading activities)	5,700
Entertaining suppliers	3,600
Entertaining employees	1,700
Gifts to customers (pens costing £40 each and displaying Naive Ltd's name)	920
Gifts to customers (food hampers costing £45 each and displaying Naive Ltd's name)	1,650
Capital allowances (working 3)	65,460
Trading profit	372,900

2 *Loan interest received*

	£
Loan interest receivable	32,800
Accrued at 1 April 2017	10,600
Accrued at 31 March 2018	(11,300)
Loan interest received	32,100

The loan was made for non-trading purposes.

3 *Capital allowances*

	Main pool £	Motor car £	Special rate pool £	Allowances £
Written down value (WDV) brought forward	12,400		13,600	
Additions				
Machinery	42,300			
Motor car [1]	13,800			
Motor car [2]		14,000		
	68,500			
Annual investment allowance (AIA)	(68,500)			68,500
Disposal proceeds			(9,300)	
			4,300	
Balancing allowance			(4,300)	(4,300)
Writing down allowance (WDA) – 18%		(2,520) ×50%		1,260
WDV carried forward	0	11,480		
Total allowances				65,460

(1)   Motor car [1] has a CO_2 emission rate of 110 grams per kilometre.

(2)   Motor car [2] has a CO_2 emission rate of 155 grams per kilometre. This motor car is used by the sales manager and 50% of the mileage is for private journeys.

(3)   All of the items included in the special rate pool at 1 April 2017 were sold for £9,300 during the year ended 31 March 2018. The original cost of these items was £16,200.

Required

Prepare a corrected version of Naive Ltd's corporation tax computation for the year ended 31 March 2018.

Note. Your calculations should commence with the operating profit before interest and taxation figure of £274,530, and you should indicate by the use of zero (0) any items in the computation of the trading profit for which no adjustment is required.   **(12 marks)**

(b)   The managing director of Naive Ltd understands that the company will have to file its self-assessment corporation tax returns online, and that the supporting accounts and tax computations will have to be filed using the inline eXtensible Business Reporting Language (iXBRL). The managing director is concerned with how the company will be able to produce the documents in this format.

Required

Explain the options available to Naive Ltd regarding the production of accounts and tax computations in the iXBRL format.   **(3 marks)**

(Total = 15 marks)

Answers

DO NOT TURN THIS PAGE UNTIL YOU HAVE
COMPLETED THE MOCK EXAM

A plan of attack

If this were the real Taxation (TX – UK) exam and you had been told to turn over and begin, what would be going through your mind?

Perhaps you're having a panic. You've spent most of your study time on income tax and corporation tax computations (because that's what your tutor/BPP Study Text told you to do), plus a selection of other topics, and you're really not sure that you know enough. So calm down. Spend the first few moments or so **looking at the paper**, and develop a **plan of attack**.

Looking through the paper:

Section A contains **15 Objective Test (OT) questions** each worth **2 marks**. These will cover all sections of the syllabus. Some you may find easy and some more difficult. For example, Question 13 on keeping records for tax should be easy marks and you just need to pick the right answers from the table. Don't spend a lot of time on anything you really don't know. For multiple choice questions you are not penalised for wrong answers, so you should answer all of them. If all else fails – guess!

Section B contains **three OT Case** scenarios. These each have **five questions** each worth **2 marks**. Make sure you read the scenario carefully before you start to answer the OTQs.

- **Questions 16 to 20** are about chargeable gains for individuals. In Question 19, note that you are asked for the amount of CGT which could have been **saved** if Marlon had transferred 50% ownership of the residential property to Alvita prior to its disposal so you need to think about how CGT is computed for Alvita bearing in mind that she has no taxable income or other disposals in the year.

- **Questions 21 to 25** concern inheritance tax (IHT). In Question 24, you need to consider how the seven year accumulation period works.

- **Questions 26 to 30** test topics in value added tax (VAT). For Question 26, you need to think about the tax point for the contract in part (2).

In **Section C** you have **three constructed response (long) questions**:

- **Question 31** for **10 marks** is about the potential tax saving by incorporating a sole trader business. You need to work out the individual's income tax, the national insurance contributions for an employee and corporation tax.

- **Question 32** for **15 marks** is an income tax computation and also deals with choice of accounting date.

- **Question 33** for **15 marks** is a corporation tax question and includes capital allowances. Part (b) is about how a company files its corporation tax return and supporting accounts.

Allocating your time

BPP's advice is always allocate your time **according to the marks for the question** in total and for the parts of the question. But **use common sense**. If you're confronted by an OTQ on a topic of which you know nothing, pick an answer and move on. Use the time to pick up marks elsewhere.

After the exam...**Forget about it!**

And don't worry if you found the exam difficult. More than likely other candidates will too. If this were the real thing you would need to **forget** the exam the minute you left the exam hall and **think about the next one**. Or, if it's the last one, **celebrate**!

Section A

1   £4,069

	£
£(45,000 – 8,164) = £36,836 × 9%	3,315
£(82,700 – 45,000) = £37,700 × 2%	754
Class 4 NICs	4,069

The answer £4,217 includes Class 2 NIC. The answer £6,708 uses 9% throughout. The answer £3,315 is just the 9% band liability.

2   Reporting under the money laundering regulations

Advising the client to make disclosure

Your firm should advise the client to make disclosure. Your firm should make a report under the money laundering regulations.

You should not inform HMRC of the non-disclosure. Your firm also should not warn the client that it will be reporting the non-disclosure as this might constitute the criminal offence of 'tipping-off'.

3   £7,200

	£
Personal allowance	11,500
Less restriction £(109,400 – 800 – 100,000) = £8,600/2	(4,300)
Restricted personal allowance	7,200

4   £135,000

	£
The lower of:	
Taxable total profits of Shallow Ltd for the corresponding accounting period (1.7.17–31.3.18) £224,000 × 9/12	168,000
Losses of Halo Ltd for the corresponding accounting period £180,000 × 9/12	135,000

5   Four instalments of £46,075

Profits threshold £1,500,000/2 (related 51% company)   £750,000

Sizeable Ltd was therefore a large company in both years.

Each instalment for the year to 31 March 2018 is
£(970,000 @ 19%) = 184,300/4   £46,075

The answer nine instalments of £16,400 and a balancing payment of £36,700 is based on the previous accounting period's profits using a rate of 20% with each of the instalments being 10% of the liability. This is the VAT annual accounting schedule of payments. The answer instalments of £41,000 and a balancing payment of £20,300 again uses the 20% rate based on the previous year's profits, similar to self assessment for individuals. The answer £184,300 is the full amount of corporation tax which would be payable if Sizeable Ltd was not a large company.

6   £825

Interest runs from due date (1 October 2018) to the date of payment (31 March 2019) which is six months.

£60,000 × 2.75% × 6/12   £825

The answer £2,062 is for a 15 month period from 31 January 2018 to 31 March 2019. The answer £275 is for a two month period from 31 January 2019 to 31 March 2019. The answer £412 is for a three-month period from the filing date of 1 January 2019 to 31 March 2019.

7   £4,500

	£
Proceeds	8,700
Less cost	(3,800)
Gain	4,900

The maximum gain is $5/3 \times £(8,700 - 6,000) = £4,500$.

The chargeable gain is the lower of £4,900 and £4,500, so it is £4,500.

The answer £0 assumes that this is an exempt chattel.

8   £118,750

	£
Net chargeable transfer	800,000
Less nil rate band	(325,000)
	475,000

IHT £475,000 × 20/80 (donor paid tax)	118,750

9

£400 to Alfred		**NOT EXEMPT**
£140 to Minnie		**NOT EXEMPT**
A further £280 to Minnie		**NOT EXEMPT**
£175 to Winifred	**EXEMPT**	

Outright gifts to individuals totalling £250 or less per donee in any one tax year are exempt under the small gifts exemption. The £400 gift to Alfred is therefore not exempt under the small gifts exemption. If gifts total more than £250 the whole amount is chargeable. Therefore neither of the gifts to Minnie which total £(140 + 280) = £420 are exempt under the small gifts exemption. The gift of £175 to Winifred is exempt under the small gifts exemption.

10   £7,164

£(49,750 × 120/100) = 59,700 × 12%   £7,164

Under the flat rate scheme, a business calculates VAT by applying a fixed percentage to its tax inclusive turnover. However, the business cannot reclaim any input tax suffered.

11   A motor car suitable for private use

A UK government security (gilt)

A wasting chattel is exempt, as is a chattel sold for gross proceeds of £6,000 or less. Other chattels are chargeable assets. A house may be exempt if principal private residence relief applies, but is otherwise a chargeable asset.

12   £12,000

£(20,000 − 8,000)   £12,000

The answer £20,000 is the full ISA allowance. The answer £0 assumes that only one ISA can be opened in a tax year and so Winston cannot invest into a stocks and shares ISA having invested in a cash ISA. The answer £10,000 assumes that the ISA limit is divided equally between the two accounts.

13

Business records		31 JANUARY 2024
Non-business records		31 JANUARY 2024

Records must be retained until five years after the 31 January following the tax year where the taxpayer is in business. This applies to all of the records, not only the business records.

14 £62,000

	£
Loss incurred in y/e 31.12.17	105,000
p/e 31.12.16	(43,000)
	62,000
y/e 31.8.16	
Lower of £96,000 × 8/12 = £64,000 and unused loss	(62,000)
C/f	0

Loss relief by deduction from total profits may be given by deduction from current period profits and from the previous 12 months. Therefore relief can be given in the four-month period ended 31 December 2016 and for eight months of the year ended 31 August 2016.

The answer £64,000 is the time apportioned amount of profits. The answer £96,000 assumes that the earlier accounting period profits can be relieved first.

15 90 days

Nigel was not previously resident in the UK. He will be UK resident for 2017/18 with three UK ties if he spends at least 91 days in the UK during that tax year. Therefore the maximum number of days that Nigel could spend in the UK during the tax year 2017/18 without being treated as UK resident for that year is 90 days.

Section B

Delroy and Marlon

> **Text references.** Computing chargeable gains and computation of the CGT liability are covered in Chapter 13. Principal private residence relief is dealt with in Chapter 14. Business reliefs are the subject of Chapter 15.
>
> **Top tips.** Be careful to read all the information given in the scenario. In this case you were told that Grant had used his annual exempt amount but that Alvita had not made any other disposals of assets during the year and so must still have her annual exempt amount available.
>
> **Easy marks.** There were easy marks in Question 16 for a basic gain computation leading to the calculation of CGT. Question 20 should have been quick and easy marks for identification of the correct statement.

16 £43,000

	£
Ordinary shares in Dub Ltd	
Proceeds	240,000
Less cost	(25,000)
Gain	215,000
Less annual exempt amount (already used as stated in question)	(0)
Taxable gain	215,000
CGT: £215,000 × 20%	43,000

Tutorial notes

1   The effect of the gift relief election is that Grant effectively took over Delroy's original cost of £25,000.

2   The disposal does not qualify for entrepreneurs' relief as Grant was neither an officer nor an employee of Dub Ltd and, in any case, had only owned the shares for just over two months (the minimum period for the conditions for the relief to be satisfied is one year).

The answer £21,500 assumes that entrepreneurs' relief applies to the disposal so the rate of tax is 10%. The answer £0 assumes this is an exempt disposal. The answer £40,740 deducts the annual exempt amount – read the question carefully!

17   Entrepreneurs' relief would have been available.

The cash gift would not have been a chargeable disposal.

Delroy's disposal would have qualified for entrepreneurs' relief because for at least one year prior to the disposal:

- Dub Ltd was Delroy's personal company as he owned at least 5% of the ordinary share capital
- Dub Ltd was a trading company
- Delroy was an officer or employee of Dub Ltd

There are no capital gains tax implications of a gift of cash.

18   £114,800

	£
Residential property	
Proceeds	497,000
Less cost	(152,600)
Gain before PPR relief	344,400
Less PPR relief (W)	(229,600)
Gain after PPR relief	114,800

Working

One-third of the residential property was always used exclusively for business purposes, so the principal private residence relief exemption is restricted to £(344,400 × 2/3) = £229,600.

The answer £229,600 is the PPR relief. The answer £0 assumes this is an exempt disposal. The answer £344,400 is the gain before PPR relief.

19   £6,514

		£
Annual exempt amount	£11,300 × 28%	3,164
Basic rate band	£33,500 × (28 – 18)%	3,350
Total tax saving		6,514

The 50% ownership of the house would have been transferred from Marlon to Alvita on a no gain, no loss basis. The effect of this is that 50% of the gain on disposal would accrue to Marlon and 50% to Alvita.

Transferring 50% ownership of the house to Alvita prior to its disposal would have enabled her annual exempt amount and basic rate tax band for 2017/18 to be utilised.

The answer £3,164 is just the annual exempt amount saving. The answer £3,350 is just the basic rate band saving. The answer £12,544 is the annual exempt amount and the basic rate band, all at 28%.

20   The CGT liability would have been paid later.

The disposal on 6 April 2018 would fall into tax year 2018/19 and so the payment date for capital gains tax would be 31 January 2020, rather than 31 January 2019 if the disposal had been made on 28 March 2018 in 2017/18.

Opal

> **Text references.** Inheritance tax is covered in Chapter 18.
>
> **Top tips.** Try drawing a timeline and mark on it the date of Opal's death and the lifetime transfers. Then mark the date which is seven years before Opal's death. It will be clear that the lifetime transfer in 2008 falls more than seven years before Opal's death and is therefore exempt.
>
> **Easy marks.** There were some easy marks for working out the IHT on the death estate in Question 23.

21   £656,000

	£	£
Property one	374,000	
Less repayment mortgage	(160,000)	
		214,000
Property two	442,000	
Less endowment mortgage	0	442,000
Net value of two properties		656,000

There is no deduction in respect of the endowment mortgage as this will be repaid upon death by the life assurance element of the mortgage.

The answer £816,000 does not deduct the repayment mortgage. The answer £564,000 deducts the endowment mortgage. The answer £724,000 deducts the endowment mortgage but not the repayment mortgage.

22   Personal loan from a bank of £22,400

Funeral cost of £5,200

The promise to pay the nephew's legal fees is not deductible as it is not legally enforceable.

23   £338,000

	£
Chargeable estate	950,000

	£
105,000 (W) × 0%	0
845,000 × 40%	338,000
950,000	
IHT on death estate	338,000

Working

	£
Nil rate band at death	325,000
Less: PET 14 August 2008	(0)
PET 7 November 2017	(220,000)
Available nil rate band	105,000

The potentially exempt transfer on 14 August 2008 is exempt from inheritance tax as it was made more than seven years before 20 March 2018.

The answer £250,000 has an unrestricted nil rate band. The answer £378,000 assumes that the PET in 2008 becomes chargeable on Opal's death. The answer £335,600 deducts two annual exemptions from the gift in 2017.

24   £88,000

If Opal were to live for another seven years, then the potentially exempt transfer on 7 November 2017 would become exempt.

The inheritance tax payable in respect of her estate would therefore decrease by £(220,000 × 40%) = £88,000.

25   The gifts must be habitual

Opal must have enough remaining income to maintain her usual standard of living

Glacier Ltd

Text references. Value added tax is covered in Chapters 24 and 25.

Top tips. The tax point is frequently examined and is relevant in Question 26. The basic tax point for a supply of services is the date when they are completed, but if a VAT invoice is issued or payment received before the basic tax point, then this becomes the actual tax point.

Easy marks. There were easy marks in Questions 28 and 29 concerning the default surcharge penalty.

26   £3,480

	£
Sales	
VAT registered customers £(44,600 − 35,200) = £9,400 × 20%	1,880
Additional contract (1 March 2018)	1,600
Output VAT	3,480

The tax point for the contract is when the VAT invoice was issued on 1 March 2018.

27   Glacier Ltd will include output VAT of **£68** and input VAT of **£120** on its VAT return for the quarter ended 31 March 2018 in respect of the managing director's company motor car.

Output VAT £408 × 20/120	£68

Input VAT £720 × 20/120	£120

28   5% of the VAT liability

Glacier Ltd was late in submitting VAT returns and paying the related VAT liability for two previous quarters. The late payment of VAT for the quarter ended 31 March 2018 will therefore result in a surcharge of 5% of the VAT liability for that period since this is the second default during the surcharge period.

29   Submit four consecutive VAT returns on time and also pay the related VAT liabilities on time

30   Glacier Ltd will be required to issue a VAT invoice when | a standard rated supply | is made to | a VAT registered customer | .

Section C

31 Sarah

> **Text references.** Employment income is covered in Chapter 3. The income tax computation is the subject of Chapter 2. National insurance contributions are dealt with in Chapter 12. Corporation tax is covered in Chapter 19.
>
> **Top tips.** Note 1 outlines the steps that you need to take to complete the question.
>
> **Easy marks.** There were some easy marks for basic income tax and corporation tax computations.

(a) Sarah – Income tax liability 2017/18

	Non-savings income £	Dividend income £	Total income £
Director's remuneration	30,000		
Dividends		10,000	
Net income	30,000	10,000	40,000
Less personal allowance	(11,500)		
Taxable income	18,500	10,000	28,500

Tax	
Non-savings income	
£18,500 @ 20%	3,700
Dividend income	
£5,000 @ 0%	0
£5,000 (10,000 – 5,000) @ 7.5%	375
Income tax liability	4,075

Sarah – National insurance contributions 2017/18

	£
Employee Class 1 £(30,000 – 8,164) = 21,836 @ 12%	2,620
Employer Class 1 £(30,000 – 8,164) = 21,836 @ 13.8%	3,013

Corporation tax liability of the new limited company for the year ended 5 April 2018

	£
Trading profit	50,000
Less: director's remuneration	(30,000)
employer's Class 1 NIC	(3,013)
Taxable trading profit	16,987
Corporation tax £16,987 @ 19%	3,228

The total tax and NIC cost if Sarah incorporates her business is £12,936 (4,075 + 2,620 + 3,013 + 3,228).

Therefore, if Sarah incorporated her business there would be additional tax and NIC payable as there would be an increase of £673 (12,936 – 12,263) compared to continuing on a self-employed basis.

(b) The relatively high tax cost of Sarah incorporating her business arises because of her salary attracting both employee and employer NICs.

Restricting the salary to around £8,000 and taxing a correspondingly higher amount of dividends, would significantly reduce her overall tax cost.

32 Simon

Marking scheme

			Marks	
(a)	Employment income			
	Salary		½	
	Living accommodation	annual value	½	
		additional benefit – market value	1	
		additional benefit – limit	½	
		additional benefit – benefit	½	
		furniture	1	
	Loan benefit		1	
	Trading income			
	Accounts profit		½	
	Capital allowances – addition		½	
	Capital allowances – WDA		1½	
	Salary paid to Art		1	
	Profit share		½	
	Trading income 2017/18		1	
	Property business income			
	Rent receivable		½	
	Council tax		½	
	Furniture		1½	
	Personal allowance		½	
				13
(b)	Payment of tax delayed		1	
	Calculation of profits in advance of end of tax year		1	
				2
				15

(a) **Simon – Taxable income 2017/18**

	£
Employment income	
Salary	23,700
Living accommodation – annual value	4,600
Living accommodation – additional benefit (W1)	1,700
Living accommodation – furniture £9,400 × 20%	1,880
Loan benefit £84,000 × 2.5% × 4/12	700
	32,580
Trading income (W2)	8,220
Property business income (W4)	5,940
Net income	46,740
Less personal allowance	(11,500)
Taxable income	35,240

Workings

1   *Living accommodation – additional benefit*

	£
Market value when first provided to Simon	143,000
Less limit	(75,000)
	68,000
Additional benefit £68,000 × 2.5%	1,700

Tutorial note

Where the property was acquired by the employer more than six years before first being provided to the employee, the market value when first so provided is used as the cost of providing the living accommodation.

2   *Trading income*

Simon's share of the partnership's trading profit for the period ended 30 April 2018 is £10,960 calculated as follows:

	£
Trading profit	29,700
Less capital allowances (W3)	(300)
	29,400
Less salary paid to Art £6,000 × 4/12	(2,000)
	27,400
Profit share £27,400 × 40%	10,960
Simon's trading income 2017/18 £10,960 × 3/4	8,220

Tutorial note

Simon's trading income for 2017/18 is for the period 1 January 2018 to 5 April 2018 as this is his first year of trading and the actual basis applies.

3   *Capital allowances*

	Motor car		Allowances
4-month period to 30 April 2018	£		£
Addition	18,750		
WDA @ 8% × 4/12	(500)	× 60%	300
WDA c/f	18,250		

Tutorial note

The partnership's motor car has CO_2 emissions over 130 grams per kilometre and therefore qualifies for writing down allowances at the rate of 8%.

4   *Property business income*

	£	£
Rent receivable £660 × 12		7,920
Council tax and water rates	1,320	
Replacement furniture relief		
Washing machine £(730 – 70)	660	
		(1,980)
Property business income		5,940

Tutorial note

No relief is given for that part of the cost of the washer-dryer which represents an improvement over the original washing machine. Relief is therefore restricted to the cost of a similar washing machine. This figure is then reduced by the proceeds from the sale of the original washing machine.

(b)   The interval between earning profits and paying the related tax liability will be 11 months longer. This can be particularly beneficial where profits are rising.

It will be possible to calculate taxable profits well in advance of the end of the tax year, making it much easier to implement tax planning and make pension contributions.

33 Naive Ltd

Marking scheme

		Marks
(a)	Trading profit	
	Depreciation	½
	Donations to political parties	½
	Qualifying charitable donations	½
	Accountancy	½
	Legal fees	½
	Entertaining suppliers	½
	Entertaining employees	½
	Gift to customers – pens	½
	Gift to customers – food hampers	½
	Capital allowances brought from working	½
	Capital allowances	
	WDV brought forward	1
	Annual investment allowance	1
	Addition – motor car [1]	½
	Addition – motor car [2]	½
	Disposal	½
	WDA @ 18%	½
	WDA @ 8%	1
	Loan interest	1
	Qualifying charitable donations	½
	Corporation tax	½
		12
(b)	HMRC software automatically to produce in iXBRL	1
	Other software automatically to produce in iXBRL	1
	Tagging services and software used by Naive Ltd to tag	1
		3
		15

(a) **Naive Ltd – Corporation tax computation for the year ended 31 March 2018**

	£
Trading profit (W1)	248,340
Loan interest	32,800
Total profits	281,140
Less qualifying charitable donations	(900)
Taxable total profits	280,240
Corporation tax	
£280,240 × 19%	53,246

Workings

1   *Trading profit for the year ended 31 March 2018*

		£
Operating profit before interest and taxation		274,530
Add:	depreciation	15,740
	donations to political parties	400
	qualifying charitable donations	900
	accountancy	0
	legal fees	0
	entertaining suppliers	3,600
	entertaining employees	0
	gifts to customers – pens	0
	gifts to customers – food hampers	1,650
		296,820
Less capital allowances (W2)		(48,480)
Adjusted trading profit		248,340

2   *Capital allowances*

	AIA £	Main pool £	Special rate pool £	Allowances £
WDV brought forward		12,400	13,600	
AIA additions				
Machinery	42,300			
AIA	(42,300)			42,300
Transfer to pool	0	0		
Non-AIA additions				
Motor car [1]		13,800		
Motor car [2]			14,000	
Disposal				
Special rate pool items			(9,300)	
		26,200	18,300	
WDA @ 18%		(4,716)		4,716
WDA @ 8%			(1,464)	1,464
WDV carried forward		21,484	16,836	
Allowances				48,480

Tutorial notes

1   Motor car [1] has CO_2 emissions between 76 and 130 grams per kilometre and therefore qualifies for writing down allowances at the rate of 18%. Cars do not qualify for the AIA.

2   Motor car [2] has CO_2 emissions over 130 grams per kilometre and therefore qualifies for writing down allowances at the rate of 8%. The private use of the motor car is irrelevant, since such usage will be assessed on the employee as a benefit.

(b)   If Naive Ltd has straightforward accounts, it could use the software provided by HM Revenue & Customs. This automatically produces accounts and tax computations in the iXBRL format.

Alternatively, other software which automatically produces iXBRL accounts and computations could be used.

A tagging service could be used to apply the appropriate tags to the accounts and tax computations, or Naive Ltd could use software to tag documents itself.

ACCA Applied Skills

Taxation (TX – UK)

Mock Exam 3
(December 2016 exam PBE updated to FA 2017)

Question Paper	
Time allowed	**3 hours 15 minutes**
This paper is divided into three sections:	
Section A – ALL 15 questions are compulsory and MUST be attempted.	
Section B – ALL 15 questions are compulsory and MUST be attempted.	
Section C – ALL THREE questions are compulsory and MUST be attempted.	

DO NOT OPEN THIS PAPER UNTIL YOU ARE READY TO START UNDER EXAMINATION CONDITIONS

CANDIDATE ANSWER BOOKLET

SAMPLE PAGE ONLY

USE THIS PAGE TO RECORD ANSWERS TO MULTIPLE CHOICE QUESTIONS

- If your question paper has less than 60 questions, fill in the relevant answers only.

- Each multiple choice question has only one correct answer. Fill in one bubble only (A, B, C, or D) to indicate your choice of answer.

- The mark available for each question is indicated on your question paper. There is no penalty for incorrect answers or unanswered questions.

- No marks are awarded if you do not clearly indicate your final choice or if more than one bubble per question is filled in.

- To void a selected answer, place a cross (X) over the bubble.

HOW TO SHADE THE BUBBLES

EXAMPLE

Right mark   Wrong mark

To amend your selection place a cross over unwanted bubble

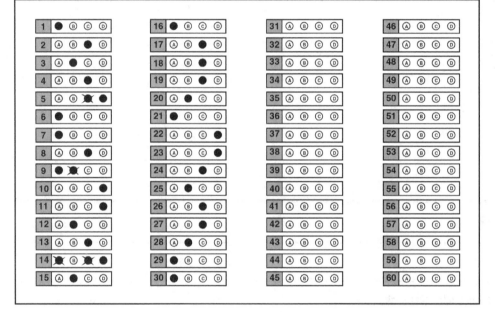

SECTION A: ALL 15 questions are compulsory and MUST be attempted

1   Emil is registered for value added tax (VAT). For the quarter ended 31 March 2018, the input VAT incurred on his purchases and expenses included the following:

	£
Entertaining overseas customers	320
Purchase of new office equipment	1,250
Purchase of a new motor car for business and private use by one of Emil's employees	3,000

What is the amount of input VAT recoverable by Emil in the quarter ended 31 March 2018 in respect of the entertaining, office equipment and motor car?

- ○ £1,250
- ○ £320
- ○ £1,570
- ○ £4,570   **(2 marks)**

2   Acasta Ltd owns 75% of the ordinary share capital of Barge Ltd and 100% of the ordinary share capital of Coracle Ltd. Barge Ltd owns 75% of the ordinary share capital of Dhow Ltd. Coracle Ltd owns 51% of the ordinary share capital of Eight Ltd.

Which companies, along with Coracle Ltd, are within Acasta Ltd's chargeable gains group?

- ○ Barge Ltd, Dhow Ltd and Eight Ltd
- ○ Barge Ltd only
- ○ Barge Ltd and Dhow Ltd only
- ○ None of the other companies   **(2 marks)**

3   Nadia died on 13 February 2004, leaving an estate valued at £275,400 for inheritance tax purposes. Nadia left 50% of her estate to her son and 50% to her husband, Tareq.

Tareq subsequently died on 17 January 2018. Tareq did not own a main residence at the date of his death.

Neither Nadia nor Tareq made any lifetime gifts.

The inheritance nil rate band for the tax year 2003/04 was £255,000.

What is the maximum available nil rate band which can be used when calculating the inheritance tax payable in respect of Tareq's estate?

- ○ £500,500
- ○ £474,500
- ○ £442,300
- ○ £462,700   **(2 marks)**

4   Habib purchased a copyright on 30 April 2001 for £31,320. The remaining life of the copyright at the date of purchase was 30 years. On 30 April 2017, Habib sold the copyright for £27,900.

What is Habib's chargeable gain or allowable loss for the tax year 2017/18 in respect of the disposal of the copyright?

- ○ (£3,420)
- ○ £11,196
- ○ £0
- ○ £13,284   **(2 marks)**

5   Which of the following is the correct definition of an extra-statutory concession?

○   A provision for the relaxation of the strict application of the law where it would lead to anomalies or cause hardship

○   Supplementary information providing additional detail in relation to the general principles set out in legislation

○   HM Revenue & Customs' interpretation of tax legislation

○   Guidance provided to HM Revenue & Customs' staff in interpreting and applying tax legislation

                                                                                                    (2 marks)

6   For what length of time after the end of the tax year for which a self-assessment tax return has been completed is a sole trader required to keep their accounting records?

○   12 months after the 31 January which follows the end of the tax year
○   12 months after the end of the tax year
○   60 months after the end of the tax year
○   60 months after the 31 January which follows the end of the tax year   **(2 marks)**

7   Sanjay commenced trading on 1 January 2017 and prepared his first set of accounts for the six-month period ended 30 June 2017. His second set of accounts were prepared for the year ended 30 June 2018.

Sanjay's tax-adjusted trading profits were:

Six-month period ended 30 June 2017   £8,800
Year ended 30 June 2018   £24,400

What are the class 4 national insurance contributions (NICs) which Sanjay should pay in respect of the tax year 2017/18?

○   £57
○   £0
○   £1,155
○   £1,461   **(2 marks)**

8   Modal Ltd lets out an unfurnished investment property.

During the year ended 31 December 2017, the company received rental income of £3,000 per month and paid electricity (relating to the rental property) of £200 per month. The electricity payment for December 2017 was not paid until 30 January 2018.

Modal Ltd also paid interest of £1,200 per month on a loan taken out to finance the purchase of the rental property.

What amount of property business income will be included in Modal Ltd's corporation tax computation for the year ended 31 December 2017?

○   £33,600
○   £19,200
○   £33,800
○   £19,400   **(2 marks)**

9   Which of the following will **NOT** cause Harper to be treated as automatically UK resident for the tax year 2017/18?

○   Harper spending 192 days in the UK during the tax year 2017/18

○   Harper renting a house in the UK to live in and then occupying it (as her only home) throughout the tax year 2017/18

○   Harper accepting a 15-month contract for a full-time job in the UK on 6 April 2017

○   Harper's husband living in the UK throughout the tax year 2017/18 and Harper staying with him when she visits the UK   **(2 marks)**

10 Somily Ltd filed its self-assessment corporation tax return for the year ended 31 December 2017 on 15 March 2019.

What is the deadline for HM Revenue & Customs (HMRC) to start a compliance check enquiry into Somily Ltd's corporation tax return for the year ended 31 December 2017?

- ○ 30 April 2020
- ○ 31 December 2019
- ○ 15 March 2020
- ○ 31 January 2020 **(2 marks)**

---

11 On 6 April 2017, Melinda rented out a furnished room in her house to Jenny at a rent of £720 a month. Jenny continued to rent the room on the same terms until 5 July 2018.

Melinda continued to live in the house and paid for all of the living expenses, of which £175 a month related to the room rented out to Jenny.

What is Melinda's property income for the tax year 2017/18, assuming that any beneficial elections are made?

- ○ £1,140
- ○ £0
- ○ £6,540
- ○ £2,760 **(2 marks)**

---

12 Three unconnected companies have the following results for corporation tax purposes:

Company	Current accounting period	Number of 51% group companies	Taxable total profits (TTP) £	TTP for previous 12-month period £
Asher Ltd	Year ended 31 March 2018	3	700,000	600,000
Barton Ltd	Four-month period ended 31 December 2017	0	600,000	1,600,000
Chelfry Ltd	Year ended 30 November 2017	0	1,600,000	1,400,000

All the companies have had the same number of 51% group companies for many years. None of the companies have received any dividends.

Which of the three companies will **NOT** have to pay corporation tax by quarterly instalments for the current accounting period?

- ○ Asher Ltd only
- ○ Barton Ltd only
- ○ Chelfry Ltd only
- ○ Barton Ltd and Chelfry Ltd only **(2 marks)**

---

13 David had the following taxable income (after deduction of his personal allowance) for the tax year 2017/18:

Non-savings income	£8,500
Savings income	£2,400
Dividend income	£7,250

What is David's total income tax liability for the tax year 2017/18?

- ○ £2,149
- ○ £2,724
- ○ £2,249
- ○ £2,524 **(2 marks)**

14   Gita died on 17 May 2017. At the date of her death she owned the following assets:

	£
Investment property	390,000
Chattels and cash	70,000
Shares held in an individual savings account (ISA)	60,000

At the date of her death, Gita owed income tax of £25,000 in respect of the tax year 2017/18.

Gita left £100,000 of her estate to her husband, with the remainder of the estate left to her daughter.

What is Gita's chargeable estate for inheritance tax purposes?

O   £335,000
O   £395,000
O   £495,000
O   £420,000   **(2 marks)**

15   Anika sold her entire holding of 3,000 £1 ordinary shares in Distribo Ltd, a trading company, to her son, Hemi, for £53,000 on 14 July 2017. The market value of the shares on that date was £98,000. Anika had purchased the 3,000 shares on 28 October 2004 for £41,500. She has never worked for Distribo Ltd.

What is the amount of gift (holdover) relief (if any) which could be claimed in respect of the disposal of these shares, and Anika's chargeable gain for the tax year 2017/18 after taking account of any available relief?

	Gift relief	Gain
O	£0	£11,500
O	£11,500	£0
O	£45,000	£11,500
O	£56,500	£0

                                                                    (2 marks)

                                                                    (Total = 30 marks)

SECTION B – ALL 15 questions are compulsory and MUST be attempted

Zoyla

The following scenario relates to Questions 16 to 20.

Zoyla's capital gains tax (CGT) liability for the tax year 2017/18 is calculated as follows:

	Gain £
Ordinary shares in Minor Ltd	98,400
Ordinary shares in Major plc	44,100
Annual exempt amount	(11,300)
	131,200
CGT: 10,600 at 10%	1,060
120,600 at 20%	24,120
	25,180

Minor Ltd is an unquoted trading company with an issued share capital of 200,000 £1 ordinary shares. Zoyla has been a director of this company since 1 April 2012. On 20 June 2017, Zoyla sold 20,000 of her holding of 45,000 ordinary shares in Minor Ltd. She had originally purchased 22,500 shares on 15 August 2016 for £117,000. On 12 December 2016, Minor Ltd made a 1 for 1 rights issue. Zoyla took up her allocation under the rights issue in full, paying £7.40 for each new share issued.

Major plc is a quoted trading company with an issued share capital of 2,000,000 £1 ordinary shares. Zoyla has been an employee of Major plc since 1 November 2016 when she acquired 16,000 ordinary shares in the company. On 6 March 2018, Zoyla sold her entire holding of ordinary shares in Major plc to her son for £152,000. On that date, shares in Major plc were quoted on the stock exchange at £9.62–£9.74.

Zoyla will not make any other disposals in the foreseeable future, and her taxable income will remain unchanged.

16   Why did neither of Zoyla's share disposals during the tax year 2017/18 qualify for entrepreneurs' relief?

	Minor Ltd	*Major Ltd*	
O	Size of shareholding	Size of shareholding	
O	Holding period	Holding period	
O	Holding period	Size of shareholding	
O	Size of shareholding	Holding period	**(2 marks)**

17   What cost figure will have been used in calculating the chargeable gain on Zoyla's disposal of 20,000 ordinary shares in Minor Ltd?

- O   £126,000
- O   £104,000
- O   £148,000
- O   £252,000   **(2 marks)**

18   What proceeds figure will have been used in calculating the chargeable gain on Zoyla's disposal of 16,000 ordinary shares in Major plc?

- O   £152,000
- O   £154,400
- O   £153,920
- O   £154,880   **(2 marks)**

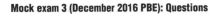

19   If Zoyla had delayed the sale of her 16,000 ordinary shares in Major plc until 6 April 2018, by how long
     would the related CGT liability have been deferred?

     O   11 months
     O   12 months
     O   1 month
     O   6 months   **(2 marks)**

20   Assuming that the tax rates and allowances for the tax year 2017/18 continue to apply, how much CGT
     would Zoyla have saved if she had delayed the sale of her 16,000 ordinary shares in Major plc until the
     following tax year?

     O   £1,060
     O   £4,380
     O   £3,320
     O   £2,260   **(2 marks)**

                                                                                          (Total = 10 marks)

Roman and Paris

The following scenario relates to Questions 21 to 25.

Roman died on 7 August 2017, and his wife Paris died on 18 February 2018.

The couple had attempted to mitigate their inheritance tax (IHT) liabilities when they both made substantial gifts
during 2015. These gifts made full use of their respective nil rate bands of £325,000, but unfortunately neither
Roman nor Paris then survived long enough for any of the gifts to benefit from taper relief. Neither Roman nor Paris
had made any previous lifetime gifts.

Roman

On 4 March 2015, Roman made a cash gift of £210,000 to his daughter. On 26 August 2015, he made a cash gift of
£190,000 to a trust. No lifetime IHT arose in respect of the gift to the trust.

Roman's estate for IHT purposes was valued at £560,000. He did not own a main residence at the date of his death.
Under the terms of his will, Roman left £300,000 to Paris (his wife) and the residue of his estate to his daughter.

Paris

On 12 December 2015, Paris made a gift of 75,000 £1 ordinary shares in Capital Ltd, an unquoted investment
company, to her son. Before the transfer, Paris owned 100,000 of Capital Ltd's 250,000 ordinary shares. The
market value of Capital Ltd's ordinary shares on 12 December 2015 was as follows:

Holding	Market value per share
10%	£5
30%	£6
40%	£8

Paris also made cash gifts of £80, £210, £195 and £460 to various friends during February 2016. The gifts of £80
and £195 were to the same friend.

Paris's estate for IHT purposes was valued at £840,000, including the inheritance from Roman (her husband). She
did not own a main residence at the date of her death. Under the terms of her will, Paris left a specific legacy of
£20,000 to a friend and the residue of her estate to her grandchildren.

21 How much IHT will be payable in respect of the gift made to the trust by Roman as a result of his death?

  ○   £26,400
  ○   £30,000
  ○   £27,600
  ○   £13,200   **(2 marks)**

22 Who will be responsible for paying the IHT arising from Roman's gift to the trust as a result of his death, and when will the tax be due?

  ○   The personal representatives of Roman's estate on 30 April 2018
  ○   The personal representatives of Roman's estate on 28 February 2018
  ○   The trustees of the trust on 30 April 2018
  ○   The trustees of the trust on 28 February 2018   **(2 marks)**

23 For IHT purposes, what was the amount of the transfer of value as a result of Paris's gift of 75,000 ordinary shares in Capital Ltd?

  ○   £450,000
  ○   £600,000
  ○   £675,000
  ○   £425,000   **(2 marks)**

24 What is the amount of the cash gifts made by Paris to her friends during February 2016 **NOT** covered by the small gifts exemption?

  ○   £735
  ○   £460
  ○   £670
  ○   £0   **(2 marks)**

25 What is the amount of IHT payable in respect of Roman's and Paris's estates on death?

	Roman's estate	Paris's estate
○	£224,000	£336,000
○	£104,000	£336,000
○	£104,000	£328,000
○	£224,000	£328,000

                                                   (2 marks)

                                                   (Total = 10 marks)

Ardent Ltd

The following scenario relates to Questions 26 to 30.

Ardent Ltd was incorporated on 1 April 2017 and commenced trading on 1 January 2018. The company voluntarily registered for valued added tax (VAT) on 1 January 2018, preparing its first VAT return for the quarter ended 31 March 2018. Ardent Ltd's sales have been as follows:

2018		Standard rated £	Zero-rated £
	January	24,800	30,100
	February	42,600	28,700
	March	58,300	22,700
		125,700	81,500

Where applicable, the above figures are stated exclusive of VAT.

During the period 1 April to 31 December 2017, Ardent Ltd incurred input VAT of £120 each month in respect of payments made for advertising services. The company also incurred input VAT totalling £400 (£200 each) in respect of the purchase of two laptop computers on 10 July 2017. One of the laptop computers was scrapped on 30 November 2017 at a nil value, and the other laptop was not used until Ardent Ltd commenced trading on 1 January 2018.

During the quarter ended 31 March 2018, Ardent Ltd received standard rated invoices totalling £56,400 (inclusive of VAT) in respect of purchases and expenses. As at 31 March 2018, £11,400 (inclusive of VAT) of the purchases were unsold and therefore included in inventory.

Ardent Ltd was late in submitting its VAT return for the quarter ended 31 March 2018, and in paying the related VAT liability. The company currently does not use either the VAT cash accounting scheme or the annual accounting scheme.

26   From what date would Ardent Ltd have been required to be compulsorily registered for VAT?

      O   1 February 2018
      O   1 March 2018
      O   1 April 2018
      O   1 May 2018   **(2 marks)**

27   What amount of pre-registration input VAT was Ardent Ltd able to recover in respect of the inputs incurred prior to it registering for VAT on 1 January 2018?

      O   £920
      O   £1,120
      O   £1,480
      O   £1,280   **(2 marks)**

28   Ignoring pre-registration input VAT, what amount of VAT should Ardent Ltd have paid to HM Revenue and Customs in respect of the quarter ended 31 March 2018?

      O   £17,640
      O   £32,040
      O   £13,860
      O   £15,740   **(2 marks)**

29   How and by when should Ardent Ltd have filed its VAT return for the quarter ended 31 March 2018?

      O   Either by paper or electronically by 30 April 2018
      O   Electronically by 7 May 2018
      O   Electronically by 30 April 2018
      O   Either by paper or electronically by 7 May 2018   **(2 marks)**

30   For what period after 31 March 2018 will Ardent Ltd need to avoid further defaults in order to revert to a clean default surcharge record, and which VAT scheme may help in avoiding such further defaults?

	Period	VAT scheme
O	12 months	Cash accounting scheme
O	6 months	Cash accounting scheme
O	12 months	Annual accounting scheme
O	6 months	Annual accounting scheme

      (2 marks)

(Total = 10 marks)

SECTION C – ALL three questions are compulsory and MUST be attempted

31 Jack

You should assume that today's date is 15 March 2018 and that the tax rates and allowances for the tax year 2017/18 continue to apply.

Jack, aged 44, is a widower following the recent death of his wife. He has just cashed in a substantial share portfolio and is now considering what to do with the proceeds.

Gift to a trust

The value of Jack's estate is in excess of £1,000,000, and he is worried about the amount of inheritance tax which will be payable should he die. His wife's nil rate band was fully used when she died.

Jack is therefore planning to make an immediate lifetime cash gift of £300,000 to a trust with the funds then being held for the benefit of his two children aged 10 and 12. Jack has not made any previous lifetime gifts.

Personal pension contribution

The only pension contributions which Jack has made previously is the gross amount of £500 per month which he saves into a personal pension scheme. Jack has continued to make these contributions throughout the tax year 2017/18. Although Jack has been saving into this scheme for the previous 15 years, he is concerned that he is not saving enough for his retirement. Jack therefore wants to make the maximum possible amount of additional gross personal pension contribution for the tax year 2017/18, but only to the extent that the contribution will attract tax relief at the higher rate of income tax.

Jack is self-employed, and his trading profit for the tax year 2017/18 is £100,000. He does not have any other income and expects to make the same level of profit in future years.

Individual savings account (ISA)

Jack has never invested any amounts in ISAs. During the next 30 days he would like to invest the maximum possible amounts into stocks and shares ISAs.

Required

(a) Explain, with supporting calculations where necessary, why it is good inheritance tax planning for Jack to make the immediate lifetime cash gift of £300,000 to a trust.

Note. You are not expected to consider taper relief. **(3 marks)**

(b) (i) Advise Jack of the amount of additional gross personal pension contribution he can make for the tax year 2017/18 which will benefit from tax relief at the higher rate of income tax, and explain why this is a tax efficient approach to pension saving. **(4 marks)**

(ii) Calculate the amount of unused pension annual allowances which Jack will be able to carry forward to the tax year 2018/19 if the contribution in (i) above is made. **(1 mark)**

(c) Advise Jack as to the maximum possible amount which he can invest into stocks and shares ISAs during the next 30 days. **(2 marks)**

(Total = 10 marks)

32 Array Ltd

Array Ltd provides its employees with various benefits. It does not payroll benefits.

The benefits were all provided throughout the tax year 2017/18 unless otherwise stated.

Alice

Alice was provided with a petrol-powered motor car which has a list price of £24,600. The motor car has an official CO_2 emissions rate of 118 grams per kilometre. Alice made a capital contribution of £5,600 towards the cost of the motor car when it was first provided to her by Array Ltd.

Alice was also provided with fuel for her private journeys. The total cost to Array Ltd of fuel for the motor car during the tax year 2017/18 was £1,500.

During the tax year 2017/18, Alice drove a total of 12,000 miles, of which 8,000 were for business journeys.

Buma

Buma was provided with a loan of £48,000 on 1 October 2015, which she used to renovate her main residence. Buma repays £1,000 of the capital of the loan to Array Ltd each month, and by 6 April 2017 the amount of the loan outstanding had been reduced to £30,000. In addition, Buma paid loan interest of £240 to Array Ltd during the tax year 2017/18.

The taxable benefit in respect of this loan is calculated using the average method.

Claude

On 6 July 2017, Claude was provided with a mobile telephone. The telephone is a smartphone which is mainly used by Claude for personal internet access. It was purchased by Array Ltd on 6 July 2017 for £600.

On 6 January 2018, Claude was provided with a home entertainment system for his personal use. This was purchased by Array Ltd on 6 January 2018 for £3,200. The market value of the home entertainment system on 5 April 2018 was £2,400.

Denise

During May 2017, Array Ltd paid £10,400 towards the cost of Denise's removal expenses when she permanently moved to take up her new employment with Array Ltd, as she did not live within a reasonable commuting distance. The £10,400 covered both her removal expenses and the legal costs of acquiring a new main residence.

During February 2018, Array Ltd paid for £340 of Denise's medical costs. She had been away from work for three months due to an injury, and the medical treatment (as recommended by a doctor) was to assist her return to work.

Required

(a) State how employers are required to report details of employees' taxable benefits to HM Revenue and Customs following the end of the tax year, and the deadline for submitting this information for the tax year 2017/18. **(2 marks)**

(b) Calculate the taxable benefits which Array Ltd will have to report to HM Revenue and Customs in respect of each of its employees for the tax year 2017/18.

Note. Your answer should include an explanation for any benefits which are exempt or partially exempt. **(11 marks)**

(c) Calculate the class 1A national insurance contributions which Array Ltd would have had to pay in respect of its employees' taxable benefits for the tax year 2017/18, and state when this would have been due if paid electronically. **(2 marks)**

(Total = 15 marks)

33 Wretched Ltd

Wretched Ltd commenced trading on 1 August 2017, preparing its first accounts for the eight-month period ended 31 March 2018.

Wretched Ltd is incorporated in the United Kingdom, but its three directors are all non-resident in the United Kingdom. Board meetings are always held overseas.

The following information is available:

Trading loss

The trading loss based on the draft accounts for the eight-month period ended 31 March 2018 is £141,200. This figure is **before** making any adjustments required for:

(1)   Advertising expenditure of £7,990 incurred during April 2017. This expenditure has not been deducted in arriving at the trading loss for the eight-month period ended 31 March 2018 of £141,200.

(2)   The premium which was paid to acquire a leasehold office building on a 10-year lease.

(3)   Capital allowances.

Premium paid to acquire a leasehold office building

On 1 August 2017, Wretched Ltd paid a premium to acquire a leasehold office building on a 10-year lease. The amount of premium assessed on the landlord as income was £34,440. The office building was used for business purposes by Wretched Ltd throughout the eight-month period ended 31 March 2018.

Plant and machinery

On 1 August 2017, Wretched Ltd purchased three laptop computers at a discounted cost of £400 per laptop. The original price of each laptop was £850, but they were sold at the discounted price because they were ex-display.

Wretched Ltd also purchased three second-hand motor cars on 1 August 2017. Details are:

	Cost £	CO_2 emissions rate
Motor car [1]	8,300	64 grams per kilometre
Motor car [2]	12,300	110 grams per kilometre
Motor car [3]	14,100	145 grams per kilometre

Property business income

Wretched Ltd lets out a warehouse which is surplus to requirements. The warehouse was let out from 1 August to 31 October 2017 at a rent of £1,400 per month. The tenant left on 31 October 2017, and the warehouse was not re-let before 31 March 2018.

During the eight-month period ended 31 March 2018, Wretched Ltd spent £2,100 on advertising for tenants.

Due to a serious flood, Wretched Ltd spent £5,900 on repairs during January 2018. The damage was not covered by insurance.

Loss on the disposal of shares

On 20 March 2018, Wretched Ltd sold its entire 1% shareholding of £1 ordinary shares in Worthless plc for £21,400. Wretched Ltd had purchased these shares on 5 August 2017 for £26,200.

The indexation factor from August 2017 to March 2018 is 0.017.

Other information

Wretched Ltd does not have any 51% group companies.

Wretched Ltd will continue to trade for the foreseeable future.

Required

(a) State, giving reasons, whether Wretched Ltd is resident or not resident in the United Kingdom for corporation tax purposes. **(1 mark)**

(b) Assuming that Wretched Ltd is resident in the United Kingdom, calculate the company's trading loss, property business loss and capital loss for the eight-month period ended 31 March 2018.

Note. You should assume that the company claims the maximum available capital allowances. **(11 marks)**

(c) Explain how Wretched Ltd will be able to relieve its trading loss, property business loss and capital loss for the eight-month period ended 31 March 2018. **(3 marks)**

(Total = 15 marks)

Answers

**DO NOT TURN THIS PAGE UNTIL YOU HAVE
COMPLETED THE MOCK EXAM**

A plan of attack

If this were the real Taxation (TX – UK) exam and you had been told to turn over and begin, what would be going through your mind?

Perhaps you're having a panic. You've spent most of your study time on income tax and corporation tax computations (because that's what your tutor/BPP Study Text told you to do), plus a selection of other topics, and you're really not sure that you know enough. So calm down. Spend the first few moments or so **looking at the paper**, and develop a **plan of attack**.

Looking through the paper:

Section A contains **15 Objective Test (OT) questions** each worth **2 marks**. These will cover all sections of the syllabus. Some you may find easy and some more difficult. For Question 5, make sure you carefully consider each statement about extra-statutory concessions before making your choice. Don't spend a lot of time on anything you really don't know. For multiple choice questions you are not penalised for wrong answers, so you should answer all of them. If all else fails – guess!

Section B contains **three OT Case** scenarios. These each have **five questions** each worth **2 marks**. Make sure you read the scenario carefully before you start to answer the OTQs.

- **Questions 16 to 20** are about chargeable gains for an individual. In Question 18, do you know how quoted shares are valued if there is an element of a gift?

- **Questions 21 to 25** tests your knowledge of inheritance tax (IHT). Don't forget to double check your calculations especially in Question 21.

- **Questions 26 to 30** concerns value added tax (VAT). Question 29 should be easy marks about payment of VAT.

In **Section C** you have **three constructed response (long) questions**:

- **Question 31** for **10 marks** covers a number of areas of tax planning. These are inheritance tax lifetime gifts, pensions and individual savings accounts.

- **Question 32** for **15 marks** is an income tax computation which also tests national insurance contributions. The scenario involves the provision of employment benefits.

- **Question 33** for **15 marks** is a corporation tax question. The test for UK residence is examined, the calculation of losses for companies and the use of those losses.

All of these questions are compulsory.

This means that you do not have to waste time wondering which questions to answer.

Allocating your time

BPP's advice is always allocate your time **according to the marks for the question** in total and for the parts of the question. But **use common sense**. If you're confronted by an OTQ on a topic of which you know nothing, pick an answer and move on. Use the time to pick up marks elsewhere.

After the exam…**Forget about it!**

And don't worry if you found the exam difficult. More than likely other candidates will too. If this were the real thing you would need to **forget** the exam the minute you left the exam hall and **think about the next one**. Or, if it's the last one, **celebrate**!

Section A

1   £1,570

	£
Entertaining overseas customers	320
Purchase of new office equipment	1,250
Input tax recoverable	1,570

Note the difference between entertaining overseas customers (input tax recoverable) and UK customers (input tax not recoverable). Input tax is not usually recoverable on cars with any private use – this could be by the owner of the business or an employee.

2   Barge Ltd and Dhow Ltd only

Companies are in a chargeable gains group if at each level there is a 75% holding and the top company has an effective interest of over 50% in the group companies.

There is a 75% holding of Barge Ltd by the top company Acasta Ltd so this is in Acasta Ltd's chargeable gains group.

There is a 75% holding of Dhow Ltd by Barge Ltd and an effective interest of over 50% (75% × 75% = 56.25%) by Acasta Ltd in Dhow Ltd so Dhow Ltd is also in Acasta Ltd's chargeable gains group.

Coracle Ltd is in Acasta Ltd's chargeable gains group (given in question). However, there is no 75% holding between Coracle Ltd and Eight Ltd so Eight Ltd cannot be in Acasta Ltd's chargeable gains group.

> **Examining team's comments.** This question tested candidates' knowledge of the group relationship which is necessary for chargeable gains purposes. The most popular answer was the second option, with candidates appreciating that Barge Ltd was included because of the 75% group relationship with Acasta Ltd (and that Eight Ltd was correspondingly excluded). However, Dhow Ltd is also included in the chargeable gains group because the 75% group relationship need only be met at each level, subject to Acasta Ltd having an effective interest of over 50% (and 75% of 75% is 56.25%). So the correct answer was the third option.
>
> This demonstrates the need to carefully consider each alternative – not just quickly jumping to the most obvious one.

3   £474,500

	£
Nil rate band (NRB) at Nadia's death in 2003/04	255,000
NRB used at Nadia's death	(137,700)
Unused NRB available for transfer	117,300
Tareq's NRB 2017/18	325,000
Nadia's transferred NRB adjusted for 2017/18 rate	
£117,300 × $\dfrac{325,000}{255,000}$	149,500
Total NRB available for Tareq's estate	474,500

4   £13,284

	£
Proceeds	27,900
Less cost £31,320 × $\dfrac{14}{30}$	(14,616)
Gain	13,284

5   A provision for the relaxation of the strict application of the law where it would lead to anomalies or cause hardship

6   60 months after the 31 January which follows the end of the tax year

7 £1,155

	£
2017/18	
Second year: basis period first 12 months of trading	
1.1.17 to 30.6.17	8,800
1.7.17 to 31.12.17 6/12 × £24,400	12,200
Taxable profit	21,000
Class 4 NICs £(21,000 − 8,164) = 12,836 @ 9%	1,155

The answer £57 uses £8,800 as the taxable profit. The answer £1,461 uses £24,400 as the taxable profit.

8 £33,600

	£
Rent receivable £3,000 × 12	36,000
Less electricity payable £200 × 12	(2,400)
Property business income	33,600

The electricity expense is deductible on an accruals basis so the late payment for December 2017 does not affect the deduction. Finance costs for a company are a loan relationship and so not deducted in computing the property business income. They are also not subject to the finance cost restriction which only applies to individuals.

9 Harper's husband living in the UK throughout the tax year 2017/18 and Harper staying with him when she visits the UK

The first three answers are automatic UK residency tests. The last answer is a combination of two of the sufficient ties tests and so is not an automatic UK residency test.

10 30 April 2020

The corporation tax return should have been filed by 31 December 2018. It was therefore filed late. The deadline for HM Revenue and Customs (HMRC) to start a compliance check enquiry is therefore the quarter day following the first anniversary of the actual filing date of 15 March 2019 so is 30 April 2020.

11 £1,140

	£
Rent receivable £720 × 12	8,640
Less rent a room limit	(7,500)
Property business income	1,140

This is less than the normal basis of assessment which would be £8,640 − (175 × 12) = £6,540.

12 Chelfry Ltd only

Asher Ltd was a large company in the current period and the previous period as its TTP exceeded the limit of £1,500,000/(3 + 1) = £375,000 in both periods and so will have to pay corporation tax by quarterly instalments for the current period.

Barton Ltd was a large company in the current period and the previous period as its TTP exceeded the limit of £1,500,000 in the previous period and £1,500,000 × 4/12 = £500,000 in the current period and so will have to pay corporation tax by quarterly instalments for the current period.

Chelfry Ltd was a large company in the current period as its TTP exceeded the limit of £1,500,000, but was not a large company in the previous period as its TTP did not exceed the limit. It is therefore not required to pay corporation tax by quarterly instalments for the current period.

13 £2,149

	£
Non-savings income	
£8,500 @ 20%	1,700
Savings income	
£1,000 @ 0%	0
£1,400 (2,400 – 1,000) @ 20%	280
Dividend income	
£5,000 @ 0%	0
£2,250 (7,250 – 5,000) @ 7.5%	169
Income tax liability	2,149

14 £395,000

	£
Investment property	390,000
Chattels and cash	70,000
Shares in an ISA	60,000
Income tax owed	(25,000)
Total estate	495,000
Less spouse exemption	(100,000)
Chargeable estate	395,000

Remember that the ISA exemptions only apply for income tax and capital gains tax.

15 Gift relief £45,000, Gain £11,500

	£
Proceeds (MV)	98,000
Less cost	(41,500)
Gain before relief	56,500
Gift relief (balancing figure)	(45,000)
Gain = actual proceeds minus original cost	
£(53,000 – 41,500)	11,500

Section B

Zoyla

16 Minor Ltd Holding period, Major Ltd Size of shareholding

A disposal of shares in a company qualifies for entrepreneurs' relief if the company is the individual's personal company, which is one where the shareholder owns at least 5% of the ordinary share capital of the company, the company is a trading company and the shareholder is an officer or employee of the company. These conditions must be satisfied for at least one year prior to the disposal of the shares.

The shares in Minor Ltd were acquired on 15 August 2016 and disposed of on 20 June 2017 and so the conditions were not satisfied for at least one year.

The shares in Major Ltd were a shareholding of (16,000/2,000,000 × 100) = 0.8% and so Major Ltd was not Zoyla's personal company due to the size of the shareholding.

17 £126,000

Date	Transaction	No. of shares	Cost £
15 August 2016	Acquisition	22,500	117,000
12 December 2016	Rights issue 1 new share for every 1 original share held @ £7.40	22,500	166,500
		45,000	283,500
20 June 2017	Sale	(20,000)	(126,000)
c/f		25,000	157,500

18 £154,880

The actual proceeds are £152,000 but this must be compared with the market value of the shares to see if this is a sale at an undervalue. The market value per share is £9.62 + 1/2(9.74 − 9.62) = £9.68. The total market value is therefore £9.68 × 16,000 = £154,880 which is used as the proceeds for capital gains tax purposes.

19 12 months

The date of the CGT liability on the sale of Major Ltd shares on 6 March 2018 (tax year 2017/18) was 31 January 2019. If Zoyla had delayed the sale until 6 April 2018 the disposal would have been in the tax year 2018/19 and so the CGT liability would have been due on 31 January 2020 thus deferring the payment by 12 months.

20 £3,320

	£
Tax saved due to availability of another annual exempt amount: £11,300 × 20%	2,260
Tax saved due to part of the gain being taxed at basic rate instead of higher rate:	
£10,600 × (20% − 10%)	1,060
Total CGT saving	3,320

The answer £1,060 is just the higher rate tax saving. The answer £4,380 uses 20% for both calculations. The answer £2,260 is just the annual exempt amount saving.

Roman and Paris

Text references. Inheritance tax is the subject of Chapter 18.

Top tips. A gift of shares in an unquoted company will usually involve a computation of the amount by which the donor's estate decreases as in Question 23. You need to compare the value of the shareholding before the gift and after the gift.

Easy marks. There were easy marks in Question 22 for identifying the persons responsible for paying the inheritance tax on death on the chargeable lifetime transfer and the date of payment.

21   £26,400

		£	£
4 March 2015	Gift	210,000	
	Less: annual exemption 2014/15	(3,000)	
	annual exemption 2013/14 b/f	(3,000)	
	Potentially exempt transfer		204,000
26 August 2015	Gift	190,000	
	Less: annual exemption 2015/16	(3,000)	
	annual exemption 2013/14 b/f	(0)	
	Chargeable lifetime transfer		187,000
7 August 2017	Nil rate band at death	325,000	
	Less PET now chargeable and within seven years of CLT	(204,000)	
	Available nil rate band for CLT	121,000	
	IHT on CLT:		
	£121,000 @ 0%		0
	£66,000 @ 40%		26,400
	£187,000		26,400

The calculation above is for teaching purposes to show in detail how the computation works. In the exam you could simplify it to:

$£((190,000 - 3,000) - (325,000 - (210,000 - 3,000 - 3,000)))$ @ 40% = £26,400

Examining team's comments. This question caused particular problems. The requirement was to establish how much inheritance tax was payable in respect of a chargeable lifetime transfer as a result of the donor's death. The chargeable lifetime transfer had been preceded by a potentially exempt transfer. In selecting the most popular alternative, candidates failed to take account of the £3,000 annual exemptions which were available. In selecting the second most popular alternative, candidates did not appreciate that the two gifts were made in consecutive tax years, meaning that three annual exemptions were available rather than the two used in this option.

This demonstrates just how careful candidates need to be in using each piece of information given, be it a date, number or fact.

22   The trustees of the trust on 28 February 2018

23   £675,000

	£
Before: 100,000 @ £8	800,000
After: 25,000 @ £5	(125,000)
Transfer of value	675,000

Before the transfer, Paris owned a 100,000/250,000 × 100 = 40% shareholding and after the transfer she owned a 25,000/250,000 × 100 = 10% shareholding.

24   £735

	£
Gifts to same friend exceeding £250 in tax year £(80 + 195)	275
Gift exceeding £250	460
Gifts not covered by small gifts exemption	735

25   Roman's estate £104,000, Paris's estate £336,000

Roman's estate

	£
Death estate	560,000
Less spouse exemption	(300,000)
Chargeable death estate	260,000
Nil rate band used by lifetime transfers	
£260,000 @ 40%	104,000

Paris's estate

	£
Chargeable death estate	840,000
Nil rate band used by lifetime transfer	
£840,000 @ 40%	336,000

There is no exemption for legacies on death to another person other than a spouse or civil partner.

Ardent Ltd

Text references. Value added tax is covered in Chapters 24 and 25.

Top tips. In Question 27, note the different time limits for pre-registration input tax to be recovered. The time limit for services is six months before registration but for goods it is four years before registration.

Easy marks. There were easy marks in Question 29 for the filing requirement and date.

26   1 April 2018

	£
January 2018 £(24,800 + 30,100)	54,900
February 2018 £(42,600 + 28,700)	71,300
	126,200

Note that all taxable supplies (here standard rated and zero rated) are taken into account when working out whether the registration threshold has been exceeded.

The registration threshold of £85,000 is met by 28 February 2018. Ardent Ltd should therefore have notified HMRC by 30 March 2018, with registration effective from 1 April 2018.

27   £920

	£
Advertising: £120 × 6 months (max) before registration	720
Computer acquired in four years before registration and still held at registration	200
Input tax reclaimable	920

28   £15,740

	£
Output tax £125,700 @ 20%	25,140
Less input tax £56,400 × 1/6	(9,400)
VAT payable to HMRC	15,740

It is not relevant whether the purchases are still held in inventory.

29   Electronically by 7 May 2018

30   Period: 12 months, Scheme: Annual accounting scheme

A trader must submit one year's returns on time and pay the VAT shown on them on time in order to break out of the surcharge liability period and the escalation of surcharge percentages.

The annual accounting scheme may help because only one VAT return is required each year so there are fewer occasions to trigger a default surcharge.

Section C

31 Jack

Marking scheme

			Marks	
(a)		Chargeable lifetime transfer	1	
		No inheritance tax	1	
		Inheritance tax saving	1	
				3
(b)	(i)	Higher rate income	1	
		Available annual allowances	2	
		Minimising cost of pension saving	1	
				4
	(ii)	Unused annual allowances		1
(c)		ISA limits	1	
		Maximum investments	1	
				2
				10

(a) The gift will be a chargeable lifetime transfer of £294,000 (£300,000 less annual exemptions of £3,000 for 2017/18 and 2016/17).

No lifetime inheritance tax will be payable because this is less than the nil rate band, and if Jack survives for seven years, there will be no additional inheritance tax liability either.

The value of Jack's estate will therefore be reduced by £300,000, which will mean an eventual inheritance tax saving of £120,000 (£300,000 at 40%).

Tutorial note

Although it might itself be fully exempt, the chargeable lifetime transfer will have to be taken into account when calculating any inheritance tax liability arising on any further lifetime transfers which may be made within the following seven years. After seven years, a further gift can be made to a trust.

(b) (i) For 2017/18, £(100,000 − 11,500 − (33,500 + (500 × 12))) = £49,000 of Jack's income is currently taxable at the higher rate of income tax.

This is less than the available annual allowances of £(40,000 × 4 − ((500 × 12) × 4)) = £136,000 for 2017/18.

Restricting the amount of personal pension contributions to the amount qualifying for tax relief at the higher rate will minimise the cost of pension saving because each £100 saved will effectively only cost £60 (£100 less 40% tax relief).

Tutorial notes

1   Unused annual allowances can be carried forward for up to three years.

2   Although Jack's approach to pension saving will maximise the available tax relief, it will mean that some carried forward annual allowances are wasted.

(ii) Jack will have unused allowances of £68,000 being £(40,000 − 6,000) = £34,000 from 2015/16 and the same amount for 2016/17 to carry forward to 2018/19.

(c) Jack can invest in an ISA for 2017/18 by 5 April 2018, and another ISA for 2018/19 between 6 April 2018 and 5 April 2019.

The maximum possible amount which he can invest into stocks and shares ISAs during the next 30 days is therefore £20,000 × 2 = £40,000.

32 Array Ltd

Text references. Employment income is dealt with in Chapter 3 and 4.

Top tips. Make sure you know the filing dates for the main forms that need to be submitted to HMRC and the payment dates for payments that need to be made to HMRC.

Easy marks. There were easy marks in part (b) for standard benefit computations. However, you must be very accurate in your computations to obtain all the marks available.

Examining team's comments. This was the income tax question. It was well answered.

In part (a), many candidates appreciated that reporting is done using form P11D, but the submission deadline was often not known. Less well prepared candidates often discussed (at length) submission details for self-assessment tax-returns.

There were many exceptional answers to part (b). Common mistakes included:

- For the car and fuel benefits, not ignoring the fuel cost and the mileage figures – both of which were irrelevant to the benefit calculations.

- For the beneficial loan, not commencing calculations with the amount of the loan outstanding at the start of the tax year – this figure was given – but instead trying to work from the original loan amount.

- For the home entertainment system, using the value at the start of tax year rather than the original purchase price.

Part (c) was reasonably well answered, although a few candidates included employee salaries when calculating the class 1A national insurance contributions.

			Marks
(a)	Form P11D	1	
	Submission deadline	1	
			2
(b)	*Alice*		
	Car benefit percentage	1	
	Car use taxable benefit	2	
	Fuel taxable benefit	1	
	Buma		
	Interest benefit	2	
	Deduction for interest paid by employee	½	
	Claude		
	Mobile phone	1	
	Home entertainment system	1½	
	Denise		
	Relocation costs	1	
	Medical costs	1	
			11
(c)	Class 1A NIC	1	
	Payment date	1	
			2
			15

(a) Details of employees' taxable benefits are reported to HM Revenue & Customs (HMRC) using a form P11D for each employee.

The P11D submission deadline for 2017/18 is 6 July 2018.

(b) **Alice**

The relevant percentage for the car benefit is 18% + 4% ((115 – 95)/5) = 22%.

The motor car was available throughout 2017/18, so the taxable benefit is £(24,600 – 5,000) × 22% = £4,312.

The fuel benefit is £(22,600 × 22%) = $\underline{£4,972}$.

Tutorial notes

1   The amount of capital contribution which can be used to reduce the list price when calculating a car benefit is restricted to £5,000.

2   The proportion of business mileage is not relevant to the calculation of the car benefit.

Buma

	£
$\dfrac{30,000 + (30,000 - (1,000 \times 12))}{2} \times 2.5\%$	600
Less interest paid	(240)
Taxable benefit	360

Claude

The provision of one mobile telephone does not give rise to a taxable benefit even if the telephone is a smartphone.

The taxable benefit for the use of the home entertainment system is £(3,200 × 20% × 3/12) = £160.

Tutorial note

The home entertainment system has not been given to Claude, so the market value on 5 April 2018 is irrelevant.

Denise

Only £8,000 of the relocation costs is exempt, so the taxable benefit is £(10,400 – 8,000) = £2,400.

The payment of medical costs of up to £500 does not result in a taxable benefit provided the medical treatment is recommended in writing by a medical professional to assist an employee to return to work following a period of absence due to ill-health or injury lasting at least 28 days.

(c)   The employer's Class 1A NIC payable by Array Ltd for 2017/18 is £(4,312 + 4,972 + 360 + 160 + 2,400) = 12,204 @ 13.8%) = £1,684.

If paid electronically, this would have been payable by 22 July 2018.

33 Wretched Ltd

Marking scheme

			Marks
(a)	Company residence		1
(b)	*Trading loss*		
	Pre-trading expenditure	1	
	Deduction for lease premium	1½	
	Capital allowances		
	Additions qualifying for AIA	1	
	AIA	½	
	Motor car [1]	1	
	Motor car [2]	½	
	Motor car [3]	½	
	WDA main pool	1	
	WDA special rate pool	1	
	Property business loss		
	Rent receivable	½	
	Advertising	½	
	Repairs	½	
	Capital loss		
	Proceeds	½	
	Cost	½	
	Indexation allowance	½	
			11
(c)	Trading loss relief	1	
	Property business loss relief	1	
	Capital loss relief	1	
			3
			15

(a) Companies which are incorporated in the UK such as Wretched Ltd are resident in the UK regardless of where their central management and control is exercised.

(b) **Wretched Ltd – period ended 31 March 2018**

Trading loss

	£
Trading loss	(141,200)
Advertising expenditure	(7,990)
Deduction for lease premium £(34,440/10) × 8/12	(2,296)
Capital allowances (W)	(4,424)
Revised trading loss	(155,910)

Tutorial note

The advertising expenditure incurred during April 2017 is pre-trading and is treated as incurred on 1 August 2017. It is therefore deductible, and an adjustment is required.

Working

Capital allowances

	AIA £	Main pool £	Special rate pool £	Allowances £
Additions qualifying for AIA				
Laptops £400 × 3	1,200			
AIA	(1,200)			1,200
Transfer to pool	0	0		
Additions not qualifying for AIA				
Motor car [1]		8,300		
Motor car [2]		12,300		
Motor car [3]			14,100	
		20,600		
WDA @ 18% × 8/12		(2,472)		2,472
WDA @ 8% × 8/12			(752)	752
TWDVs carried forward		18,128	13,348	
Allowances				4,424

Tutorial notes

1   The original cost of the laptops is irrelevant.

2   Although motor car [1] has CO_2 emissions up to 75 grams per kilometre, it is second hand and therefore does not qualify for the 100% first year allowance. It instead qualifies for writing down allowances at the rate of 18%.

3   Motor car [2] has CO_2 emissions between 76 and 130 grams per kilometre and therefore qualifies for writing down allowances at the rate of 18%.

4   Motor car [3] has CO_2 emissions over 130 grams per kilometre and therefore qualifies for writing down allowances at the rate of 8%.

Property business loss

	£
Rent receivable £1,400 × 3	4,200
Less: advertising	(2,100)
repairs	(5,900)
Property business loss	(3,800)

Capital loss

	£
Disposal proceeds	21,400
Less: cost	(26,200)
indexation allowance	(0)
Property business loss	(4,800)

Tutorial note

Where a company makes a capital loss, then no indexation allowance is available because it cannot be used to increase a loss.

(c)   The trading loss of £155,910 will be carried forward and relieved against the first available trading profits of the same trade.

The property business loss of £3,800 will be carried forward and relieved against the first available total profits.

The capital loss of £4,800 will be carried forward and relieved against the first available chargeable gains.

Tax tables

SUPPLEMENTARY INFORMATION

1.   Calculations and workings need only be made to the nearest £.
2.   All apportionments may be made to the nearest month.
3.   All workings should be shown in Section C.

TAX RATES AND ALLOWANCES

The following tax rates and allowances are to be used in answering the questions.

Income tax

		Normal rates	Dividend rates
Basic rate	£1 – £33,500	20%	7.5%
Higher rate	£33,501 – £150,000	40%	32.5%
Additional rate	£150,001 and over	45%	38.1%

Savings income rate nil band	– Basic rate taxpayers	£1,000
	– Higher rate taxpayers	£500
Dividend nil rate band		£5,000

A starting rate of 0% applies to savings income where it falls within the first £5,000 of taxable income.

Personal allowance

	£
Personal allowance	11,500
Transferable amount	1,150
Income limit	100,000

Residence status

Days in UK	Previously resident	Not previously resident
Less than 16	Automatically not resident	Automatically not resident
16 to 45	Resident if 4 UK ties (or more)	Automatically not resident
46 to 90	Resident if 3 UK ties (or more)	Resident if 4 UK ties
91 to 120	Resident if 2 UK ties (or more)	Resident if 3 UK ties (or more)
121 to 182	Resident if 1 UK tie (or more)	Resident if 2 UK ties (or more)
183 or more	Automatically resident	Automatically resident

Child benefit income tax charge

Where income is between £50,000 and £60,000, the charge is 1% of the amount of child benefit received for every £100 of income over £50,000.

Car benefit percentage

The base level of CO_2 emissions is 95 grams per kilometre.

The percentage rates applying to petrol cars with CO_2 emissions up to this level are:

50 grams per kilometre or less	9%
51 grams to 75 grams per kilometre	13%
76 grams to 94 grams per kilometre	17%
95 grams per kilometre	18%

Car fuel benefit

The base figure for calculating the car fuel benefit is £22,600.

Individual savings accounts (ISAs)

The overall investment limit is £20,000.

Property income

Basic rate restriction applies to 25% of finance costs.

Pension scheme limits

Annual allowance	£40,000
Minimum allowance	£10,000
Income limit	£150,000

The maximum contribution that can qualify for tax relief without any earnings is £3,600.

Authorised mileage allowances: cars

Up to 10,000 miles	45p
Over 10,000 miles	25p

Capital allowances: rates of allowance

Plant and machinery

Main pool	18%
Special rate pool	8%

Motor cars

New cars with CO_2 emissions up to 75 grams per kilometre	100%
CO_2 emissions between 76 and 130 grams per kilometre	18%
CO_2 emissions over 130 grams per kilometre	8%

Annual investment allowance

Rate of allowance	100%
Expenditure limit	£200,000

Cash basis

Revenue limit	£150,000

Cap on income tax reliefs

Unless otherwise restricted, reliefs are capped at the higher of £50,000 or 25% of income.

Corporation tax

Rate of tax – Financial year 2017	19%
– Financial year 2016	20%
– Financial year 2015	20%
Profit threshold	£1,500,000

Value added tax (VAT)

Standard rate	20%
Registration limit	£85,000
Deregistration limit	£83,000

Inheritance tax: tax rates

Nil rate band	£325,000
Residence nil rate band	£100,000
Excess – Lifetime rate	20%
– Death rate	40%

Inheritance tax: taper relief

Years before death	Percentage reduction
Over 3 but less than 4 years	20%
Over 4 but less than 5 years	40%
Over 5 but less than 6 years	60%
Over 6 but less than 7 years	80%

Capital gains tax

	Normal rates	Residential property
Rates of tax — Lower rate	10%	18%
— Higher rate	20%	28%
Annual exempt amount		£11,300
Entrepreneurs' relief — Lifetime limit		£10,000,000
— Rate of tax		10%

National insurance contributions
(Not contracted-out rates)

Class 1 Employee	£1–£8,164 per year	Nil
	£8,165–£45,000 per year	12%
	£45,001 and above per year	2%
Class 1 Employer	£1–£8,164 per year	Nil
	£8,165 and above per year	13.8%
	Employment allowance	£3,000
Class 1A		13.8%
Class 2	£2.85 per week	
	Small profits threshold	£6,025
Class 4	£1–£8,164 per year	Nil
	£8,165–£45,000 per year	9%
	£45,001 and above per year	2%

Rates of interest (assumed)

Official rate of interest	2.50%
Rate of interest on underpaid tax	2.75%
Rate of interest on overpaid tax	0.50%

BPP
LEARNING MEDIA

Review Form – Taxation (TX – UK) (10/17)

Name: _____   Address: _____

_____

_____

How have you used this Kit?
(Tick one box only)

☐ On its own (book only)

☐ On a BPP in-centre course_____

☐ On a BPP online course

☐ On a course with another college

☐ Other _____

Why did you decide to purchase this Kit?
(Tick one box only)

☐ Have used the complimentary Study Text

☐ Have used other BPP products in the past

☐ Recommendation by friend/colleague

☐ Recommendation by a lecturer at college

☐ Saw advertising

☐ Other _____

During the past six months do you recall seeing/receiving any of the following?
(Tick as many boxes as are relevant)

☐ Our advertisement in *Student Accountant*

☐ Our advertisement in *Pass*

☐ Our advertisement in *PQ*

☐ Our brochure with a letter through the post

☐ Our website www.bpp.com

Which (if any) aspects of our advertising do you find useful?
(Tick as many boxes as are relevant)

☐ Prices and publication dates of new editions

☐ Information on product content

☐ Facility to order books

☐ None of the above

Which BPP products have you used?

Study Text	☐	*Passcards*	☐	*Other*	☐
Practice & Revision Kit	☑	*i-Pass*	☐		

Your ratings, comments and suggestions would be appreciated on the following areas.

	Very useful	Useful	Not useful
Passing Taxation (TX – UK)	☐	☐	☐
Questions	☐	☐	☐
Top Tips etc in answers	☐	☐	☐
Content and structure of answers	☐	☐	☐
Mock exam answers	☐	☐	☐

Overall opinion of this Practice & Revision Kit	Excellent ☐	Good ☐	Adequate ☐	Poor ☐

Do you intend to continue using BPP products?   Yes ☐   No ☐

The BPP author of this edition can be emailed at: accaqueries@bpp.com

Review Form (continued)

TELL US WHAT YOU THINK

Please note any further comments and suggestions/errors below.